Competition Law, Regulation & SMEs in the Asia-Pacific

Competition Law, Regulation & SMEs in the Asia-Pacific

Understanding the Small Business Perspective

Edited by
Michael T. Schaper
and Cassey Lee

ISEAS YUSOF ISHAK
INSTITUTE

First published in Singapore in 2016 by
ISEAS Publishing
30 Heng Mui Keng Terrace
Singapore 119614

E-mail: publish@iseas.edu.sg • Website: bookshop.iseas.edu.sg

The responsibility for facts and opinions in this publication rests exclusively with the authors and their interpretation do not necessarily reflect the views or the policy of the publisher or its supporters.

ISEAS Library Cataloguing-in-Publication Data

Competition Law, Regulation and SMEs in the Asia-Pacific : Understanding the Small Business Perspective / editors, Michael T. Schaper and Cassey Lee.
   1. Competition, Unfair—Asia.
   2. Competition, Unfair—Pacific Area.
   3. Small business—Asia.
   4. Small business—Pacific Area.
   I. Schaper, Michael T.
   II. Lee, Cassey.
K1575 A8C73   2016

ISBN 978-981-4695-80-0 (soft cover)
ISBN 978-981-4695-81-7 (E-book PDF)

Typeset by International Typesetters Pte Ltd

CONTENTS

SECTION 2: SMEs AND COMPETITION LAW

SECTION 3: COUNTRY STUDIES

FOREWORD

In many Asia-Pacific economies, competition law and regulation has been in operation for decades, setting the rules of the game for business. Typically the law covers the behaviours of dominant firms (i.e. vertical arrangements) and anti-competitive practices in markets (i.e. horizontal arrangements). But while such regulation is designed as a general framework for firm behaviour, those frameworks have not always kept pace with modern developments.

Competition law was traditionally seen as something to guide the behaviour of large or dominant firms. But the role of Asia-Pacific Economic Cooperation (APEC) small and medium-sized enterprises (SMEs) is changing as they become more connected to the international economy. Electronic commerce and global supply chains are encouraging them to become more globalized. New technologies are acting as disruptive forces to existing markets, and international supply chains are altering the traditional nature of vertical arrangements.

These changing realities have implications for modern competition law and regulation. Regulatory authorities need to understand the new roles of SMEs, and communicate their legal obligations.

Policymakers need to design systems that encourage harmonized or similar commercial standards across borders, and there needs to be common views about how to enforce behaviours across borders with appropriate cross-border judicial resolutions. Public and private dispute resolution systems need to be accessible to SMEs.

My own experience in competition law in the 1990s was that competition laws were not particularly well designed for SMEs, and that SMEs were not particularly well informed about them. It is very pleasing to see so much progress since then, as this book spells out.

Congratulations to the ISEAS – Yusof Ishak Institute and the authors for drawing our attention to these issues. This book and the seminar that it is based on are important steps in remedying the gaps in knowledge and policy in the Asia-Pacific.

Dr Alan E. Bollard
Executive Director, APEC Secretariat
Chairman, New Zealand Commerce Commission (1992–97)

ABOUT THE CONTRIBUTORS

Based at Murdoch University's Singapore campus, **Azad Singh Bali** is currently working on a project that studies productivity in the Singapore economy as it restructures to cope with the economic and sociopolitical challenges of an affluent but rapidly ageing economy. His academic training is in economics and public policy (specializing in public sector economics). Bali's research explores aspects of policy theory (particularly issues related to coordination, capacity, design, governance, and learning) in social policy in Asia. Email: a.bali@murdoch.edu.au

Jenny Buchan (LLB, LLM, PhD) is an Associate Professor in the Business School at UNSW Australia (University of New South Wales), where she teaches franchise law and contract law. Prior to this she worked for nineteen years as a commercial lawyer. Buchan is the author of *Franchisees as Consumers: Benchmarks, Perspectives and Consequences* (2013), the book review editor of the *Journal of Marketing Channels*, and a member of the editorial advisory board of the *International Journal of Franchising Law*. Buchan is a member of the Australian Competition and Consumer Commission's Small Business & Franchising Consultative Committee, the Law Society of NSW, the International Society of Franchising, and Australian Restructuring, Insolvency and Turnaround Association (ARITA). She researches franchise law and policy, focusing on the intersection of franchising, consumer protection, and insolvency law. Email: jm.buchan@unsw.edu.au

Rachel Burgess is an independent consultant and researcher offering specialist competition law advice and training. She has specialized in competition law in Australia, the United Kingdom and Asia for fifteen years, working in both private practice and the government, and advised a wide spectrum of clients, from government ministers, senior civil servants, and military personnel, through to senior company lawyers and board directors, commercial managers and their staff. In recent years, Burgess has worked closely with the Malaysia Competition Commission and provided advice to other ASEAN member states. She has authored a number of book chapters and papers on competition law and spoken at numerous national and international conferences. Email: rbcompetitionlaw@gmail.com

Leela Cejnar is a Senior Lecturer at UNSW's (University of New South Wales) Business School, where her area of research and teaching is competition law. She has previously worked for the Australian Competition and Consumer Commission (ACCC); more recently, she has assisted the ACCC with the development of its tertiary online education programme, which was trialled in UNSW's introductory business law course in 2013. Email: L.cejnar@unsw.edu.au

Paul Davidson has completed a Bachelor of Economics (Hons) and Bachelor of Laws from the University of New England. From 2011–15 he was a research economist at the Productivity Commission of Australia and worked on a number of projects with specific focuses on competition, consumer protection, and small business. He is currently a research economist at the Australian Parliamentary Library where he is responsible for providing research to Members and Senators on competition policy. Email: Paul.Davidson@aph.gov.au

A Sydney-based competition lawyer, **Brent Fisse** has acted for clients in a wide range of industries, including information technology, health, telecommunications, energy, transport, motor vehicles, music, metals, retail grocery, financial services, sports, tourism, recruitment, and publishing and broadcasting. His clients have included regulatory agencies and the New Zealand Ministry of Economic Development. He is a consultant to the Asian Development Bank on competition law and policy, and the co-author (with Caron Beaton-Wells) of *Australian Cartel*

Regulation (2011), as well as numerous papers on competition law and policy. Fisse is also an adjunct professor of law at the University of Sydney, a member of the Law Council of Australia's Competition and Consumer Committee, and the managing director of an SME (small and medium-sized enterprise), Lexpert Publications Pty Ltd. Email: brentfisse@gmail.com

Knut Fournier is currently the Chairman of the Hong Kong Competition Association and a member of the Hong Kong competition team at Linklaters. He was, until recently, teaching law at the City University of Hong Kong. Prior to moving to Hong Kong, he worked as a monitoring trustee for competition authorities in Europe, the United States, Brazil, and China. He has published extensively on competition law, including recently on Hong Kong telecom merger remedies, and on competition policy and the Hong Kong broadcasting sector. He holds law degrees from the University of Paris and from Kings College London, and is currently finishing a PhD on Hong Kong competition law at the University of Leiden in The Netherlands. Email: knut.fournier@gmail.com

Yoshifumi Fukunaga is a Consulting Fellow at the Research Institute for Economy, Trade and Industry in Tokyo, and was formerly a Senior Policy Coordinator of the Economic Research Institute for ASEAN and East Asia in Jakarta. He researches a variety of issues regarding the ASEAN Economic Community, including competition policy, and has published in the *Journal of Asian Economics*, amongst others. He received his Master of Laws degree from Harvard Law School, and holds an M.A. in International Relations from the Fletcher School of Law and Diplomacy at Tufts University. He is also a registered attorney-at-law in the state of New York. Email: fukunaga-yoshifumi@rieti.go.jp

An associate professor in the Faculty of Business at the University of Wollongong in Australia, **Charles Harvie** has published extensively on the economies of China, Korea, and Southeast Asia. His long-term research focus has been on the role and contribution of entrepreneurship and SMEs to the region, and he is currently examining economic development and regional integration issues amongst the various ASEAN economies, with a particular focus on Cambodia, Laos, Myanmar, and Vietnam. Harvie is also the author or editor of sixteen books on these and related topics. Email: charvie@uow.edu.au

Shuya Hayashi's main research area is competition law in the European Union, United States, and Japan, and his current research projects are focused on merger regulations, competition and regulation in the telecommunications sector, and intellectual property law. He has also been actively engaged in developing policy recommendations for the Japanese government in relation to competition law and policy, and is a member of the American Antitrust Institute, acting as an international advisor for Japanese issues. Email: shuya.hayashi@law.nagoya-u.ac.jp

Sun Hyung Sonya Kim is currently a Professor of Clinical Law at Korea University's School of Law, and Chief Operations Officer for the university's Innovation, Competition & Regulation Law Centre. She has undertaken several studies on competition law and intellectual property law in Korea, China and the Asian region. She holds a Juris Doctor (JD) degree from New York University School of Law. Email: sonyakim23@korea.ac.kr

Yong Jung Kim is presently a Research Fellow in the Construction and Economic Research Institute of Korea. He was previously a Research Professor of the Innovation, Competition & Regulation Law Centre at Korea University, and has participated in SME-related research projects concerning large scale retailers, subcontracting arrangements, and unfair practices. His main research interests are currently subcontracting, bidding systems, unfair practices in the Korean construction industry, and competition law. Email: kimyongjung@gmail.com

Viet Le is a Lecturer in Entrepreneurship in the Faculty of Business and Law at Swinburne University in Australia. He has researched and published in the fields of entrepreneurship, SME development, and enterprise performance, and has a particular interest in efficiency and productivity issues, exports, and innovation. He lectures on new venture development and management, business innovation, and the economics of SMEs. Email: clle@swin.edu.au

Cassey Lee is currently Senior Fellow at the ISEAS – Yusof Ishak Institute, Singapore. His previous appointments have included positions at the University of Wollongong in Australia, the Nottingham University Business School in Kuala Lumpur, and the University of Malaya. Lee received his PhD in economics from the University of California, Irvine. His current research focuses on competition policy, regulatory reforms, and firm-level studies related to innovation, productivity, and trade. He has published in numerous peer-reviewed journals, including the *Journal of Economic Dynamics and Control, Kyklos, Journal of Economic Surveys, Journal of Asian Economics,* and *Economic Modelling.* Email: cassey_lee@iseas.edu.sg

R. Ian McEwin holds the Khazanah Nasional Chair of Regulatory Studies at the University of Malaya, specializing in ASEAN competition law and economics. In 2002, he was recruited by the Singapore Ministry of Trade and Industry to help draft its competition law and set up the Singapore Competition Commission, before becoming its inaugural chief economist. Since then, he has been a Visiting Professor at the National University of Singapore and at Chulalongkorn University in Bangkok. He was recently appointed to the Foundation Board of Advisors of the Global Antitrust Institute at the George Mason University School of Law in Washington. McEwin has a law degree with first class honours and a PhD in economics, both from the Australian National University. Email: mcewin@me.com

Peter McKiernan is Dean of the School of Management and Governance at Murdoch University in Western Australia. He is an active researcher engaged in the analysis of changing political, economic, and social trends, their impact on strategic formulation and implementation for businesses. He has authored or edited several books, including *Sharpbenders* and two volumes on the *Historical Evolution of Strategic Management,* published widely in peer-reviewed journals in Europe and the United States, and was a co-founder of the *European Management Review.* McKiernan has served as President of the British Academy of Management and President of the European Academy of Management and is a Fellow of the Royal Society for the Arts. Email: peter.mckiernan@murdoch.edu.au

Alexandra Merrett is an independent competition lawyer and a Senior Fellow at the University of Melbourne. Between 2006 and 2012, she was a senior enforcement lawyer for the Australian Competition and Consumer Commission (ACCC), frequently involved in complex litigation. Prior to joining the ACCC, Merrett worked at a number of national law firms, principally in the areas of competition, commercial, and corporate law. Email: alexandramerrett@bigpond.com

A commissioner at the Productivity Commission of Australia from 2010–15, **Warren Mundy** holds a PhD from Kings College, Cambridge in economics. He has presided over the Commission's inquiries into local governments as a regulator, regulator engagement with small business, and business entries and exits in Australia. He has also served as the commissioner responsible for the Australian Competitive Neutrality Complaints Office, and is an adjunct professor with the University of NSW. Email: warren@bluestoneconsulting.com.au

Lip-Hang Poh is Assistant Director in the Policy and Markets Division of the Competition Commission of Singapore, with a special focus on abuse of dominance investigations and mergers. He was attached to the South African Competition Commission in 2012 on an international staff exchange, previously interned at RBB Economics (a London-based competition consultancy practice), and holds degrees in economics from both the Singapore Management University and the University College London. His research interests are on how competition law enforcement affects productivity growth, industries, and small firms. Email: liphang@gmail.com

Shila Dorai Raj was the founding Chief Executive Officer of the Malaysia Competition Commission from June 2011, retiring in December 2014. She was responsible for setting up the agency and laying the foundations for the implementation of national competition law. She was named as the top 100 women who have excelled in the field of anti-trust in the world by the *Global Competition Review* in 2014. Email: shila_tra@hotmail.com

Michael T. Schaper is currently Deputy Chairman of the Australian Competition and Consumer Commission (ACCC). He is also a previous president of the Small Enterprise Association of Australia and New Zealand, has served as Small Business Commissioner for the Australian Capital Territory, and in 2009 was named "national small business champion" by the Council of Small Business Organisations of Australia. Schaper has previously managed a community small business centre; been an adviser to both state and federal governments; and held lecturing, professorial, and dean roles at a number of Australian universities. He is an Adjunct Professor with Curtin University and Senior Honorary Research Fellow at the University of Western Australia. Email: michael.schaper@accc.gov.au or Michael.schaper@gmail.com

Vince See Eng Teong is the first Malaysian to have completed his doctorate study in competition law and policy, obtaining a PhD from Nagoya University. He also holds a law degree from King's College, London, and was a keynote speaker at the launch of the *ASEAN Handbook on Competition Policy and Law* in 2010. His publications include the *Journal of the Japanese Institute of International Business Law*, the *European Journal of Law and Economics*, the *Competition & Consumer Law Journal*, and the *Journal of World Intellectual Property*. Email: set2contacts@gmail.com

Andrew F. Simpson is a lawyer with more than twenty years of experience in competition law and economic regulation throughout the Asia-Pacific region. He previously practised law with Gilbert+Tobin in Sydney and Hong Kong, and was Assistant General Counsel with the New Zealand Commerce Commission. In 2009, Simpson founded Certari Consulting Ltd., which advises governments on competition and regulatory policy, supports regulators in enforcement, and assists businesses with compliance. He is a consultant to the Asian Development Bank on competition law and policy. Email: ASimpson@ CertariConsulting.com

Rhonda L. Smith is a Senior Lecturer in the Economics Department at the University of Melbourne. Smith is regularly engaged by private parties to provide economic input, particularly in relation to mergers and competition litigation. She has acted both as an expert and strategic witness in many significant Australian cases. She is a former commissioner at the Australian Competition and Consumer Commission (ACCC), was a member of the Copyright Law Reform Committee, and is presently a member of the Australian Copyright Tribunal. Smith sits on the Commonwealth Consumer Advisory Committee. Email: rhondals@unimelb.edu.au

David Storey, OBE, is a Professor in the Department of Business Management and Economics at University of Sussex, United Kingdom. His book, *Understanding the Small Business Sector*, is, according to Google Scholar, currently the most highly cited work on small business. He was a member of the UK government's Small Business Council, has worked with the Organization for Economic Cooperation and Development (OECD) on projects such as their country reviews of Mexico in 2006 and 2011, their *Handbook on SME Policy Evaluation*, and new enterprise development in North Africa and the Middle East. He has also worked with the Inter-American Development Bank and the International Finance Corporation, including the development of an enterprise plan for Malaysia. Email: d.j.storey@sussex.ac.uk

Iwakazu Takahashi originally graduated from Waseda University's Faculty of Law in 1970, and then obtained both a master's degree in 1973 and a PhD in 1998 from the same institution. He started his academic career as a Lecturer in Law at Kanagawa University, Yokohama, in 1979, and has been Professor of Law at Meiji University, Tokyo since 2001. His special focus is on competition law, international economic law, and consumer law. Email: t.iwakaz@gmail.com

A lecturer in the Faculty of Economics at the University of Trisakti in Jakarta, **Tulus T.H. Tambunan** is also the head and main researcher at the Center for Industry, Small and Medium Enterprises, and Business Competition Studies in the same university. He holds a PhD in Economics from Erasmus University in The Netherlands, and since

1995, he has been the Indonesia country researcher for the Geneva-based World Economic Forum, which publishes the annual *Global Competitiveness Report*. He has conducted numerous studies into various issues related to micro, small, and medium enterprises. Email: sjahrir@rad.net.id

Wee-Liang Tan is Associate Professor of Strategic Management at the Singapore Management University. His current research interests are in entrepreneurship, family business, international cooperation and corporate governance. He has published in *Entrepreneurship Theory and Practice, Family Business Review, Journal of High Technology Management Research*, and *Journal of Business Research*. Tan has served as an expert consultant for the Asia-Pacific Economic Cooperation (APEC), the Asian Productivity Organisation, the Colombo Plan Secretariat, and the Commonwealth Secretariat. On the professional front, he was International President of the Institute of Chartered Secretaries and Administrators (ICSA) in 2004. He is a Wilford White Fellow of the International Council for Small Business. Email: wltan@smu.edu.sg

Rachel Trindade is an independent competition lawyer who has advised on a wide range of business structures and transactions in the private and public sectors. Prior to starting her own practice in 2002, she was a partner with a national Australian law firm. Trindade has handled competition, merger, and access issues across a range of industries that include energy, infrastructure, transport and logistics, manufacturing, distribution, and retailing. Along with Alexandra Merrett and Rhonda Smith, she is the co-publisher of *The State of Competition*, providing regular analysis of Australian competition issues. Email: trindade@bigpond.net.au

Christopher Vas is Academic Director of the Executive Education Centre at Murdoch University in Western Australia. He is the co-author of the books *Tackling Challenges of Productive Growth in Resource Dependent Countries: The Experience of Ghana and Indonesia* and *Demystifying Productivity for Better-Informed Policy*, and has also published papers in leading journals, such as the *Journal of Comparative Policy Analysis: Research and Practice*. Email: c.vas@murdoch.edu.au

Peter Waring is the Dean of Murdoch University's Singapore campus. He has previously held academic positions at the University of Newcastle, Australia and at the UNSW (Asia), including periods as the Acting Pro Vice Chancellor (International) for the University of Newcastle. A qualified lawyer, Waring also holds degrees in commerce and management. He is the co-author of four books on employment relations and has published more than sixty book chapters and articles in leading international and national journals. His research and teaching interests include employment relations, human resource management, corporate governance, and labour law. He has lived in Malaysia and Singapore for the past fourteen years. Email: p.waring@murdoch.edu.au

Mark Williams is currently a Professor of Law at the University of Melbourne. He has lived and taught in Hong Kong for over twenty years, specializing in competition law in China, Hong Kong, and other Asian jurisdictions. He is also the executive director of the Asian Competition Forum, established in 2005 to encourage discussion about competition-related issues in the region. He has worked with several national governments and international organizations (such as APEC and ASEAN) on competition projects. He holds a PhD from King's College, London and is admitted as a solicitor in England and Hong Kong. Email: mwilliams@asiancompetitionforum.org

Kunlin Wu is a LLD candidate at Nagoya University in Japan. Before joining the LLD programme, he obtained his bachelor and master's degrees in law from the National Taiwan University. His research interests include competition law, telecommunications law, and intellectual property law. Email: trooper0919@gmail.com

Bernadine Zhang Yuhua was previously an analyst with the APEC Policy Support Unit, providing policy analysis and evaluations of various region-wide initiatives. Prior to APEC, Zhang previously worked as a teaching and research assistant at universities in Singapore and China, and as a consultant for the World Bank in the lead up to the inaugural World Cities Summit in 2008. She holds a master's degree in public policy from the National University of Singapore and a bachelor's degree in economics from Shanghai Jiao Tong University, China. Email: Bernadine_zhang@yahoo.com

1

INTRODUCTION
Making the Invisible SME More Visible in Competition Policy and Law

Michael T. Schaper and Cassey Lee

Introduction

Small and medium-sized enterprises (SMEs) are the biggest single group of businesses to be found globally, and represent the overwhelming majority of trading enterprises in almost every regulatory jurisdiction around the world.[1] The importance of SMEs is reflected in the presence of industrial policies supporting SME development in many countries. Curiously, however, SMEs are almost invisible when competition policy and law issues are discussed or analysed. This is all the more surprising given the lack of consensus amongst countries with competition law on whether SMEs merit a differential treatment in competition law implementation and enforcement.

This book seeks to rectify the relative neglect in research and policy discussions on the role of the SME sector in competition policy and law. A number of issues are addressed in this book. What are the unique features of small firms? In what ways can competition regulators effectively engage with the SME sector? Finally, should we construct our competition laws to take into account the differences between large and small firms? These are some of the issues which this book examines.

Competition Law in the Asia-Pacific

The Asia-Pacific region contains one of the richest and most diverse mixtures of competition law regimes to be found globally. On the one hand, these include some of the oldest, best known, and deeply embedded legal frameworks, some of them more than a century old. There is also a separate cohort of jurisdictions whose systems are now several decades old; and yet there are also many which are either relatively new, or are still coming to fruition.

Canada, for example, introduced one of the earliest modern competition laws to be adopted by a nation state, having enacted its Act for the Prevention and Suppression of Combinations Formed in Restraint of Trade in 1889. Its neighbour, the United States, enacted the Sherman Anti-Trust Act federally just a year later and, in doing so, also gave rise to an alternative descriptor for this entire body of law.

Several decades later, a number of other countries in the Asia-Pacific region also adopted their own laws. Japan was one of the earliest leaders, legislating an Act on Prohibition of Private Monopolization and Maintenance of Fair Trade in 1947. Australia passed the Trade Practices Act in 1974 (which was subsequently renamed the Competition & Consumer Act 2010), whilst South Korea enacted its Monopoly Regulation and Fair Trade Act in 1980, New Zealand its Commerce Act in 1986, and Taiwan the Fair Trade Act in 1991.

The start of the twenty-first century then saw a fresh wave of laws introduced into jurisdictions which did not previously have a regulatory framework for competition, including Papua New Guinea (the Independent Consumer and Competition Act 2002), India (the Competition Act 2003), Singapore (the Competition Act 2004), China (Anti-Monopoly Law 2007), Hong Kong (Competition Ordinance 2010), and Malaysia (the Competition Act 2010).

Ostensibly, such laws have usually been framed to cover all businesses operating within a particular jurisdiction. The elements of what is to be found within these statutes and implementation guidelines can vary enormously. Some regulatory frameworks are quite limited in scope, covering only a limited number of activities, such as mergers and cartels. Others can be far more extensive, branching out into many other different realms of business behaviour, such as resale price maintenance, unconscionable conduct, and unfair trading terms. In some nations, both consumer and competition law regulation are to be found in the one Act and enforced by the same agency; in other regions, this has never been the case.

In general, though, most legal frameworks are intended to cover all businesses trading in the relevant jurisdiction. Yet there are also times when special rules are made for one or another type of business. Sometimes this may be an exemption for a particular industry sector.

Some countries, however, have gone so far as to specifically set the development of SMEs as one of the guiding objectives in their competition laws. Section 1.1 of the current Canadian Competition Act (1985), for example, explicitly states that one of its objectives is to "... ensure that small and medium-sized enterprises have an equitable opportunity to participate in the Canadian economy". Another more extreme example is Indonesia's competition law which excludes all small businesses (Article 50h). What is it about the SME sector that warrants such special consideration?

Small and Medium-sized Enterprises

Businesses, like people, are not all the same. Enterprises can differ in many varied ways: the industry (or industries) they operate in, the legal structure they adopt, the number of employees they have, and so on. Perhaps the most obvious one to the outside observer is that of size.

Almost every country in the world uses a somewhat different definition of what constitutes micro, small, medium, and large scale firms. For some, it is based solely on the headcount (number of workers) they have; for others it may be a combination of assets, turnover, and/or employees. Definitions of an SME may vary from one place to another, but in general it is recognized that these are all independent enterprises who are not part of a larger corporation; instead they are usually owned and managed by its owners, who usually also contribute most, if not all, of its capital (Australian Bureau of Statistics 2007).

Regardless of how firm size is defined, one striking feature emerges time and time again: SMEs are the largest single group of businesses in almost every country around the world. This figure averages out at around 95 per cent of all actively trading firms in most economies, including those in the Asia-Pacific region.

In fact, the biggest single group of business ventures to be found around the world — the unincorporated, sole person microbusiness operating from the owner's home —- often does not show up in many official statistics, since they are so small that it is often hard to register or count such enterprises.

Size, of course, is not in itself the only determinant of how every business will react in every possible situation. SMEs are incredibly diverse. They are to be found in every sector of the economy, and range from the very smallest and simplest (such as the sole trader working on a venture part-time) to very complex organizations (perhaps listed on a national stock exchange, with a diverse spread of products, and/or with hundreds of employees). And yet all of them, for the purposes of competition regulation, are generally expected to comply with the law as well as any billion-dollar multinational corporation.

Once an overlooked area of academic research, in the last forty years studies into the SME sector have burgeoned. Qualitative and quantitative examinations of almost all aspects of business operations, the environment in which firms trade, and of the policy context in which they are regulated, have helped identify a number of distinctive features about most SMEs.

Despite this growing body of research, competition law and its impact on the small business sector has rarely been examined in any detail, either by competition agencies, policy development bodies or academia. It is a curious anomaly, for whilst there is a large body of work (in disciplines such as economics and political economy) which argues that open, free competition can facilitate the growth of new products, markets, and business opportunities — which in turn should foster enterprising new business ventures — there has been little effort to examine the application of these laws to the SME community.

TABLE 1.1
**Competitive Dynamics: Some Typical Differences Between
Small and Large Firms**

	SMEs	Large Firms
Number of business establishments	Single	Multiple
Geographical distribution	Limited	Limited or wide
Product/service range	Limited	Limited or wide
Market share	Limited	Significant
Customer base	Small	Numerous
Likelihood of business failure/exit	High	Low
Compliance cost burden	Proportionately high	Proportionately low
Knowledge of, and access to, regulatory information	Limited; ad-hoc	Sophisticated; extensive
Knowledge of, and access to, marketplace information	Limited; ad-hoc	Sophisticated; extensive
Ability to access established supply sources	Difficult	Easy
Level of financial resources	Typically small and limited	Substantial
Use of external legal and economic advisers	Limited; ad-hoc	Systematic; structured

Source: Adapted from Schaper (2010).

What is broadly recognized, however, is that small firms face different competitive dynamics and challenges than their larger counterparts (see Table 1.1). When compared to the biggest commercial organizations (Schaper 2010), they:

- *Have only a limited service or product offering* — most SMEs only sell a small range of goods, which may in fact be as few as just one or two different products;

- *Face a greater range of competitors* — most commonly the majority of these will, in fact, be other SMEs;
- *Possess only a small market share* — apart from successful niche specialists, most businesses have only a minor part of any market that they operate in;
- *May be heavily dependent on just one or two key customers* — especially in the manufacturing or wholesale trade sector, these clients can often account for most of the business's entire earnings;
- *Geographically restricted* — small-scale enterprises usually only have one (or, perhaps occasionally, two) premises. Even in an online age, many of them find that the majority of their customers and sales still come from a relatively limited geographic region;
- *Are usually operated by the owner/founder* — the manager of the business is also the original entrepreneur. Their personal goals and ambitions, skill sets, knowledge, and world view often spell out the way the firm will operate, which is in marked contrast to the more strategic, rational, and pre-planned approach adopted by most large corporations;
- *Have a much higher failure rate* — the newer or smaller a firm is, the greater the likelihood that it will cease trading, close, or be taken over by another enterprise. Less than half of all enterprises survive for more than five years;
- *Experience a proportionately greater regulatory compliance cost* — the relative expenditure of resources (time, effort, staff, and money) required to be fully compliant with the law is far greater for micro-ventures and small-scale firms than it is for a large corporation;
- *Suffer from regulatory information asymmetry* — because there are so many of them, individual small enterprises are less likely to be approached or assisted by government agencies, or to receive information about legal compliance issues;
- *Rarely have access to all available market information* — because there is a resource, time, and effort cost in collecting such data, many micro- and small-sized business operators have only limited knowledge of competitor and supplier prices, consumer wants, and changing market conditions;

- *Find it harder to access existing suppliers and wholesalers* — new ventures, especially in the retail sector, are often a risky proposition for established firms to deal with, as their likelihood of failure is so much higher;
- *Have far fewer resources* — most SMEs operate on limited financial capacity. They have low turnover, small profit margins, tight cash flow, and possess limited financial reserves. Similarly, they have fewer human resources and — because the operator is required to do so many different tasks — are less able to devote time and effort to any one particular task;
- *Are less likely to be a member of the relevant industry association* — membership of formal business groups is often quite low; and
- *Use professional advice sparingly* — because of the cost and time involved, firms tend to ignore or bypass legal counsel, unless there is a pressing issue which cannot be avoided.

Each of these factors will, of course, be different for each individual enterprise. But when examined collectively, it is very clear that SMEs are quite different to large firms and usually operate at a comparative disadvantage to bigger enterprises.

The challenge for competition lawmakers and agencies, then, is a simple one: if small businesses are different from large ones, should this difference be taken into account? And if so, exactly how?

Contributions in this Book

This book comprises twenty-one essays that assess a number of different issues in this new field of academic and practical enquiry. They provide a wide array of perspectives by authors with diverse backgrounds such as lawyers practising in the region, academics, competition law agency staff, representatives of multilateral agencies and independent think-tanks, consultants and advisers to the SME sector, and even the former CEO of one competition agency and the deputy chair of another.

The contributions are organized into three major sections. Section 1 — Theories and Basic Concepts — examines some of the big picture and practical issues involved in this topic. In Chapter 2, Lee and Zhang explore the link between competition policy and growth, whilst Tan and Poh (Chapter 3) suggest that there is sometimes a major disconnect and tension between policies designed to support the SME sector, and the level playing field approach required when competition law is applied. Storey (Chapter 4) outlines one of the earliest quantitative examinations of small business operators, the competitive issues they face on a daily basis, and their attitudes to competition regulators. A more recent assessment of competition law regulators and their dealings with Australian SMEs is provided by Mundy and Davidson in Chapter 5. The section concludes with a contemporary issue — the use of electronic resources by competition agencies to reach out to the small firm sector, written by Schaper and Cejnar (Chapter 6).

In Section 2 — SMEs and Competition Law — the issue of how SMEs are treated in competition laws is examined in detail. Merrett, Smith, and Trindade (Chapter 7) suggest that the use of *per se* provisions can be a two-edged sword — sometimes helping small businesses comply more easily, yet at other times creating a degree of inflexibility that works against them. See and Fukunaga (Chapter 8) assess the arguments as to why SMEs should occasionally be excluded from the application (in whole or part) of competition law, whilst Buchan (Chapter 9) examines the impact of competition law on franchising, a particular segment of the small business sector that is already regulated in many Asia-Pacific jurisdictions. The implications of the nature of the Chinese family business structure and practices for competition law enforcement is examined by McEwin (Chapter 10). Burgess (Chapter 11) discusses the anti-competition behaviour of trade associations in new competition jurisdictions and the potentially positive role such organizations can play in assisting compliance to competition law.

The final Section 3 — Country Studies — provides a detailed look at these issues within particular nations and self-governing territories. It provides a fascinating series of snapshots as to how particular legal frameworks and competition agencies deal with the SME issue. Bali, McKiernan, Vas, and Waring (Chapter 12) explore the nexus between competition and productivity in the context of SMEs in Singapore's manufacturing sector. Hayashi and Wu (Chapter 13) examine Japan, whilst Kim and Kim (Chapter 14) deal with neighbouring South Korea. Both are countries with long-standing competition laws. The experience of countries with more recent legal frameworks are examined by Tan and Poh (Chapter 15), who look at the case of Singapore; Tambunan (Chapter 16), who assesses contemporary issues in Indonesia; and Raj and Burgess (Chapter 17), who assess the work of the Malaysian Competition Commission. Le and Harvie (Chapter 18) discuss developments in Vietnam since the opening up of its economy, whilst Williams (Chapter 19) looks at the largest Asian economy, China. Fournier (Chapter 20) critiques the work of the Hong Kong competition regulator. Takahashi (Chapter 21) discusses the manner in which Japan's Subcontract Act complements its competition law in regulating the relationship between TV stations and their SME sub-contractors in the country's broadcasting industry. Finally, the emergent patchwork of competition laws in Pacific Island states are discussed by Simpson and Fisse (Chapter 22).

Key Themes

So, what are the key findings and observations from these various chapters? Each of the authors makes his/her own unique insights and arguments, but there are some common themes.

Small businesses are an integral part of the competition law framework in every country. Although their numbers and economic impact differs from one country to the next, SMEs are the biggest constituency in every jurisdiction — and that produces significant issues for the construction and administration of competition law.

SME-specific provisions in competition law can help address other legal shortcomings. Numerous jurisdictions have attempted to make particular provisions to help small firms. These have included *per se* provisions, arbitrary thresholds above or below which the law will apply, the capacity to seek exemptions from a law, or mechanisms to continue working collectively in certain circumstances. However, such laws need to be carefully constructed and administered — after all, sometimes the tools designed to help small firms (such as *per se* provisions) have occasionally also hurt small firms.

Competition law is often opposed by SMEs. Competition law is often viewed as a two-edged sword for most small enterprises. Whilst there is a recognition that small firms are sometimes the potential victims of anti-competitive practices by other (usually larger) enterprises, there is also some scepticism about the ability of regulators to protect them from such breaches. At other times, SMEs are also common contraveners of the law, especially when there is a long prior history of group price-setting and collective market behaviour. Their business practices are often closely scrutinized by newly established competition agencies.

SME policy and competition policy can often conflict. Government and public policy often simultaneously have differing (and somewhat opposing) approaches to SMEs. Competition law regimes may require all firms to be treated dispassionately and equally, and to assume that all parties are equal before the law. However, most nations are also keen to implement industrial policies that are aimed at fostering greater levels of entrepreneurship and enterprise development via various programmes including selective assistance, encouraging clusters to foster innovation, leveraging cross-firm learning, and benchmarking to various SMEs.

Competition agencies need to recognize and actively engage with the small business sector. Regulators and enforcers of competition law should be aware of the unique characteristics of the SME sector. It is not sufficient to simply presume that SMEs will automatically make an effort to learn and comply with the competition laws; there has to be an active and ongoing effort to engage with and educate the sector.

Industry bodies have a significant role to play. Small firms do not act individually; often their collective voice is even more important. Professional bodies, chambers of commerce and industry, and industry associations can sometimes act as a supporter of competition law enforcement and education. At other times, though, they have been some of the fiercest opponents of the introduction of such laws. Occasionally, they help facilitate breaches of the law through cartel-like joint actions.

Cultural, historical, and social differences matter. The nations of the Asia-Pacific region vary enormously not only in their economic and political systems, but also in many other dimensions. In many Asian nations, there are significant linguistic, ethnic, and cultural differences between different communities, which means that regulators need to reach out and promote in many languages, not just English. Collective business activities by small businesses (sometimes historically carried out on the basis of family, kin, ethnicity, or language) are often deeply-embedded, long-standing ways of doing business, but may work at cross-purposes to the objectives of competition law.

Much more remains to be learnt about small businesses. There is still a lack of specific information about SMEs in the region, in many different ways. Their knowledge, attitude, and behaviours towards competition laws have only been briefly sketched to date. Likewise, the actual measurable impact of competition policy and law on them is not known. There is also a lack of empirical data on the causal link between competition law and productivity within the small firm sector.

A Possible Future Research Agenda

The contributions in the book are more than just a set of observations and commentaries about the current state of affairs. A number of the chapters also identify areas where more research and greater practical knowledge is needed. In doing so, they help lay out a prospective research agenda, covering (but not necessarily limited to) issues such as:

The nature of competition faced by SMEs. What anti-competitive practices do small firms face in practice? To what extent are cartels, price fixing, the misuse of market power, and other illegal forms of market behaviour actually experienced by SMEs in the marketplace? Does this vary from one jurisdiction to another?

Knowing, believing, and learning. How much do managers/owners actually know about competition laws? What do business owners think about competition law? How can education and information outreach programmes be designed to best reach SMEs? What factors encourage or inhibit compliance with competition law within the SME sector?

Participation in anti-competitive business practices. How frequently do micro-, small-, and medium-sized businesses engage in illicit business behaviour, and what form does it take? How successful are such illegal practices, who facilitates them, and what are the chances of being detected and punished?

What are the macro-level impacts of competition law on SMEs? Does competition law lead to changes in entry and exit rates in the industry? In countries with newly introduced competition frameworks, there is scope to determine both the pre- and post-regulatory changes of such measures.

The impact of non-legal variables. Competition law is not just driven by the structuring and enforcement of regulations; it is also very much impacted by other factors, such as community attitudes, culture, family and kin associations, history, and third parties (such as industry association). How do these issues affect the operation of competition law in the Asia-Pacific?

These fields of enquiry can be addressed in a number of different ways. Legal scholarship has always been used in examining competition law, but other disciplines (such as management and sociology) can also have much to contribute. Likewise, different tools and research methodologies can also be employed, both qualitative and quantitative.

No doubt there are many more questions that could also be examined, and which could add considerably to the body of knowledge. Now is the time to begin such work. This is a brand new field for competition law, and one in which the results have great potential to affect its future evolution. Few individual agencies have examined such issues; nor have the various international competition forums, such as the International Competition Network. There are significant opportunities for proactive researchers and commentators to make a lasting contribution to this new and emerging topic.

Conclusion

The small business sector is many things — diverse, large, enterprising, difficult to pin down, entrepreneurial, and sometimes just plain confusing to those unfamiliar with its foibles. None of these, however, justify ignoring or overlooking the importance of such firms in the development and enforcement of competition law regimes. Indeed, the fact that they are so different and challenging is a particular reason why we need to know more, not less, about such businesses.

We hope that this book begins that process, by providing some ideas and perspectives which will assist lawmakers, competition agencies, the legal profession, and the small business sector itself. And we look forward to seeing debate and discussion on this topic grow in the years to come, as it surely must.

We appreciate the thought and effort put in by our many authors, and thank them for their time and dedication in working alongside us to produce this volume. Finally, our thanks also go to the ISEAS – Yusof Ishak Institute, especially the Director, Mr Tan Chin Tiong, and to our ever-capable research assistant, Ms Reema Bhagwan Jagtiani. The former has generously supported this project since its inception, with the Institute funding a symposium on the topic in May 2015, and, finally, publishing the volume now in front of you. And Reema has played an invaluable role in helping prepare both the symposium and in managing the production of this book.

NOTE

1. The term "small firm" is used interchangeably with "small and medium-sized enterprise" (SME) in this book.

REFERENCES

Australian Bureau of Statistics, *Counts of Australian Businesses, Including Entries And Exits*. Cat. no. 8165.0. Canberra: Australian Bureau of Statistics, 2007.

Schaper, Michael T. "Competition Law, Enforcement and the Australian Small Business Sector". *Small Enterprise Research* 17, no. 1 (2010): 7–18.

SECTION 1

Theories and Basic Concepts

2

SMEs, COMPETITION LAW, AND ECONOMIC GROWTH

Cassey Lee and Bernadine Zhang Yuhua

SMEs (small and medium-sized enterprises) account for over 95 per cent of enterprises in APEC (Asia-Pacific Economic Cooperation) economies. There are differences in the concentration of SMEs between developed and developing economies. The role of SMEs in economic growth is best understood within a theoretical framework focusing on firm dynamics and firm size distribution. The entry and exit of small firms is a critical aspect of economic growth. There is some empirical evidence indicating that economic growth is associated with competition law. Micro-level evidence is likely to be needed to investigate how competition law affects SME's role in economic growth.

Introduction

The concept of "competition" has a near mythical status in economics. Economists have often used Adam Smith's "invisible hand" to illustrate the point that competition amongst buyers and sellers seeking to maximize their gains also benefits society. Less attention has been paid to Smith's cognizance that sellers can collude to the detriment of consumers. Likewise, Joseph Schumpeter has argued that the prospects of market power is also a key driver of innovation. Such contradictory perspectives on the role of competition have continued to perpetuate themselves in modern post-war theories of economic growth as well as the attendant empirical studies. Thus, the role of competition in economic growth is far from clear. To add to the predicament of policymakers and regulators seeking more direct answers, the nature and role of SMEs in economic growth is likely to be inconclusive and possibly even elusive as well.

Despite the existing knowledge gap, competition laws — legislation promoting market competition — have been implemented in many countries. To date, more than 130 jurisdictions around the world have implemented competition statutes in one form or another. It is thus useful to reassess what we know about SMEs, competition law, and how both are related to economic growth.

The purpose of this chapter is to provide a brief synthesis of what is known in the research literature, by examining the theoretical and empirical relationships between SMEs, competition law, and economic growth. The chapter will attempt to critically reflect on a few key questions. First, what is the nature and role of SMEs in the economy? Second, what role do SMEs play in economic growth? Finally, how does competition law affect this role?

To examine the above issues, this chapter begins with a discussion of the nature and role of SMEs in national economies. It is followed by an examination of the role of SMEs in economic growth, and then examines whether competition law has an effect on the SME role in economic growth.

The Nature and Role of SMEs in Selected Economies

A key characteristic of all economies is the diverse or heterogeneous nature of firms engaged in business activities. Dimensions of firm heterogeneity include ownership type (such as the number of owners, private versus state-owned, incorporated or unincorporated entities, listed or not listed on the stock exchange), size (including variables such as the number of employees, total revenues, total fixed assets, or market value) and performance (total revenues, total profits). Amongst these dimensions, firm size has been a focal point for policymaking, and increasingly attention has been focused on those that fall into the SME category.

But what is an SME? There is currently no global consensus on how to define such an entity. Several dimensions are used by international bodies such as the International Finance Corporation (IFC) and the European Commission (EC). For example, according to the IFC (2012), an SME is a registered firm qualifying under either two of the three criteria: no more than 300 staff, less than US$15 million of total assets, or less than US$15 million of total annual sales. According to the EC, however, an SME is a firm with less than 250 employees, and an annual turnover of less than €50 million, or with an annual balance sheet of less than €43 million (EC 2005).

In the Asia-Pacific region, there is also no single definition of an SME that is universally accepted across all economies. Different criteria or combinations of criteria have been adopted to characterize SMEs in various jurisdictions (see Table 2.1). Four of the most often-used criteria are number of employees, annual sales (or revenue, or turnover, or average receipts), assets, and capital (or investment).[1] Even amongst these dimensions there is considerable variation from one country to another. In certain nations, for example, criteria are specified at a sector level, whilst other countries apply them uniformly. Furthermore, the definitions of SMEs are not static, as some countries tend to revise their definitions every few years to take into account changing macroeconomic situations.

SMEs in the Asia-Pacific region generally account for over 95 per cent of enterprises in selected economies in the region (see Table 2.2). Depending on the size and structure of the economy, the number of SMEs varies substantially, ranging from just 5,427 in Brunei Darussalam in 2010 to 57,895,721 in Indonesia in 2013. SMEs make up 99 per cent of enterprises among half of the selected economies. This includes both developed economies (such as Australia, Canada, Japan, and the United States), and developing economies (Indonesia, Korea, Mexico, Papua New Guinea, Peru, the Philippines, and Singapore). Only in Chile and Papua New Guinea is the share of SMEs in total enterprises below 95 per cent, at 84 per cent and 92 per cent respectively.

SMEs play an important role in employment creation, as they tend to be more labour-intensive than large enterprises (see Table 2.3). Based on the latest available data, SMEs employ a majority of the workforce in many economies. Particularly in Canada, Indonesia, Korea, Papua New Guinea, and Thailand, SMEs account for over 80 per cent of total employment. It is noteworthy that SME employment in

TABLE 2.1
SME Definitions in Selected Economies

		Employees	Sales/Revenue	Assets	Capital/Investment	Sector
Australia	Micro	<5				
	Small	5–19				
	Medium	20–199				
Brunei Darussalam	Micro	1–5				
	Small	6–50				
	Medium	51–100				
Canada	Small	1–99				
	Medium	100–499				
Chile	Micro		<UF 2,400			
	Small		UF 2,400–25,000			
	Medium		UF 25,001–100,000			
China	SME		≤RMB 20 million			Agriculture, forestry, animal husbandry and fishery
		<1,000	≤RMB 400 million			Manufacturing
			≤RMB 800 million			Construction
		<200	≤RMB 400 million			Wholesale businesses
		<300	≤RMB 200 million			Retail

Economy	Category	Employees			Sector
		<1,000	≤RMB 300 million		Transportation
		<200	≤RMB 300 million		Warehousing
		<1,000	≤RMB 300 million		Postal
		<300	≤RMB 100 million		Hotel service, catering
		<2,000	≤RMB 1 billion		information transmission
		<300	≤RMB 100 million		Software and information service
			≤RMB 2 billion		Real estate
		<1,000	≤RMB 50 million		Estate management
		<300	≤RMB 1.2 billion		Leasing and business service
Hong Kong, China	SME	<50			Non-manufacturing
		<100			Manufacturing
Indonesia	Micro	1–4	<IDR 300 million	<IDR 50 million	
	Small	5–19	<IDR 2.5 billion	<IDR 500 million	
	Medium	20–99	<IDR 50 billion	<IDR 10 billion	
Japan	Micro	≤20			Manufacturing and others
		≤5			Wholesale trade
		≤5			Service industry
		≤5			Retail trade

TABLE 2.1 (*continued*)

	Employees	Sales/ Revenue	Assets	Capital/ Investment	Sector
SME	≤300			≤JPY 300 million	Manufacturing and others
	≤100			≤JPY 100 million	Wholesale trade
	≤100			≤JPY 50 million	Service industry
	≤50			≤JPY 50 million	Retail trade
Korea					
SME		≤USD 150 million			Manufacturing (six sectors): electrical equipment, clothing, bag/shoes, wood pulp/ paper, primary metal, furniture
		≤USD 100 million			Manufacturing (twelve sectors): cigarette, automobile, chemical, metal processing, food, textile, lumber, oil refinery, rubber/ plastic, electronic/ computer/video/ communication, machine/equipment, other transportation equipment

Agriculture/forestry/ fishing, wholesale and retail, electrical/gas/ water works	Mining, construction	Manufacturing (six sectors): beverage, printing machine/duplicator, medicine/medical products, non-metallic mineral, medical service/precision, other product manufacturing	Transportation	Waste water treatment, environmental conservation	Publication/information service
	≤USD 80 million				

TABLE 2.1 (continued)

	Employees	Sales/Revenue	Assets	Capital/Investment	Sector
		≤USD 60 million			Repair and other personal service
					Business support service
					Science and technology service
					Health care/social welfare
					Arts/sports service
		≤USD 40 million			Lodging/restaurant
					Finance/insurance
					Education service
					Real estate/lease
Malaysia	Micro <5	<MYR 300,000			Manufacturing
	<5	<MYR 300,000			Services and other sectors

Country	Size	Employees			Sector
	Small	5–75	<MYR 15 million		Manufacturing
	Small	5–30	<MYR 3 million		Services and other sectors
	Medium	75–200	<MYR 50 million		Manufacturing
	Medium	30–75	<MYR 20 million		Services and other sectors
Mexico	Micro	0–10	≤MXN 4 million		Industry, trade, services
	Small	11–50	≤MXN 100 million		Industry, services
	Small	11–30	≤MXN 100 million		Trade
	Medium	51–100	≤MXN 250 million		Industry
	Medium	31–100	≤MXN 250 million		Trade
	Medium	51–100	≤MXN 250 million		Services
New Zealand	SME	≤19			
		≤50			
Papua New Guinea	Micro	<5	<PGK 200,000	<PGK 200,000	
	Small	<20	<PGK 5,000,000	<PGK 10,000,000	Manufacturing, construction and engineering
	Medium	<100	<PGK 20,000,000	<PGK 20,000,000	
	Micro	<5	<PGK 200,000	<PGK 200,000	
	Small	<40	<PGK 5,000,000	<PGK 5,000,000	Agriculture, tourism, forestry, fisheries, service and other sectors
	Medium	<100	<PGK 10,000,000	<PGK 10,000,000	

TABLE 2.1 (*continued*)

	Employees	Sales/Revenue	Assets	Capital/Investment	Sector
Peru					
Micro		≤150 UIT			
Small		≤1,700 UIT			
Medium		≤2,300 UIT			
Philippines					
Micro	1–9			≤PHP 3 million	
Small	10–99			>PHP 3 million to <PHP 15 million	
Medium	100–199			>PHP 15 million to <PHP 100 million	
Russia					
Micro	1–15	≤RUB 60 million			
Small	16–100	≤RUB 400 million			
Medium	101–250	≤RUB 1 billion			
Singapore					
Micro		<SGD 1 million			
Small		≥SGD 1 million to <SGD 10 million			
Medium		≥SGD 10 million to <SGD 100 million			
SME	<200	<SGD 100 million			

Country	Category	Number of employees	Financial threshold	Sector
Chinese Taipei	Micro	<5		
	SME	<200	≤TWD 80 million	Manufacturing, construction, mining, quarrying
		<100	≤TWD 100 million	other sectors
Thailand	Small	≤50	≤THB 50 million	Manufacturing
		≤50	≤THB 50 million	Services
		≤25	≤THB 50 million	Wholesale
		≤15	≤THB 30 million	Retail
	Medium	51–200	>THB 50 million to 200 million	Manufacturing
		51–200	>THB 50 million to 200 million	Services
		26–50	>THB 50 million to 100 million	Wholesale
		16–30	>THB 30 million to 60 million	Retail
United States	Small	<500		Most manufacturing and mining industries
			<USD 7.5 million	Non-manufacturing

TABLE 2.1 (continued)

	Employees	Sales/Revenue	Assets	Capital/Investment	Sector
Vietnam					
Micro	≤10				Agriculture, forestry and fishery; industry and construction; commerce and services
Small	11–200			≤VND 20 billion	Agriculture, forestry and fishery
	11–200			≤VND 20 billion	Industry and construction
	11–50			≤VND 10 billion	Commerce and services
Medium	201–300			>VND 20 billion to ≤VND 100 billion	Agriculture, forestry and fishery
	201–300			>VND 20 billion to ≤VND 100 billion	Industry and construction
	51–100			>VND 10 billion to ≤VND 50 billion	Commerce and services

TABLE 2.2
Number of SMEs and SMEs as a Share of Total Enterprises

APEC Economy	No. of SMEs	% of Total Enterprises	Year
Australia	2,096,548	99.83	2014
Brunei Darussalam	5,427	97.50	2010
Canada	1,105,972	99.86	2012
Chile	854,539	84.23	2013
China	≈18,000,000		2014
Hong Kong, China	321,113	98.27	2014
Indonesia	57,895,721	99.99	2013
Japan	3,852,934	99.73	2012
Korea	3,351,404	99.90	2012
Malaysia	645,136	97.30	2011
Mexico	4,193,501	99.80	2013
New Zealand	459,035	97.13	2013
Papua New Guinea	44,285	92.03	2013
Peru	1,513,006	99.45	2013
Philippines	937,327	99.59	2013
Russia	5,588,600	95.50	2013
Singapore	187,719	99.34	2014
Chinese Taipei	1,331,182	97.64	2013
Thailand	2,763,997	97.16	2013
United States	5,707,941	99.68	2012
Vietnam	324,808	97.64	2012

Notes:
1. For Australia, data shown are of mid-year.
2. For Canada, data do not include businesses without a Canada Revenue Agency payroll deduction account.
3. For Hong Kong, China, there is no official definition of a microenterprise. Data do not cover the entire business units due to incomplete coverage of the Quarterly Survey of Employment and Vacancies. Establishments in the Central Register of Establishments with the same main business registration number (BRN) and engaged inactivities of the same industry section are grouped into one business unit for the purpose of calculating the number of SMEs.
4. For New Zealand, data are of February.
5. For Papua New Guinea, data include 32,692 formal SMEs and 11,593 formalized enterprises.
6. For the Philippines, data include only the formal sector of the economy.
7. For the United States, data include only employer firms.
Source: See Appendix 2.1.

TABLE 2.3
Number of SMEs Employees and SMEs' Share of Total Employment

APEC Economy	No. of SMEs Employees	% of Total Employment	Year
Australia	7,241,000	68.27	2013
Brunei Darussalam	59,179	59.41	2010
Canada	9,993,484	89.90	2012
Chile	3,663,029	42.06	2013
Hong Kong, China	1,313,680	47.10	2014
Indonesia	114,144,082	96.99	2013
Japan	32,167,484	69.72	2012
Korea	13,059,372	87.70	2012
Malaysia	5,135,605	57.50	2013
Mexico	15,297,783	71.40	2013
New Zealand	583,600	30.07	2013
Papua New Guinea	468,502	98.00	2013
Peru	9,530,850	60.77	2013
Philippines	4,770,445	63.69	2013
Russia		25.00	2013
Singapore	2,229,000	65.83	2014
Chinese Taipei	8,588,000	43.85	2013
Thailand	11,414,702	80.96	2013
United States	56,062,893	48.36	2012
Vietnam	6,740,000	61.55	2012

Notes:
1. For Australia, the SME employment and total employment do not cover the financial and insurance sectors, and the general government component of public administration and safety, education and training, and health care and social assistance. Data are of mid-year.
2. For Hong Kong, China, there is no official definition of a microenterprise.
3. For New Zealand, data are of February.
4. For Papua New Guinea, SMEs' share in total employment includes 85 per cent labour force that is engaged in the informal sector.
5. For Peru, employment data include the public sector, private sector, self-employed, and housekeeper.
6. For the Philippines, data include only the formal sector of the economy.
7. For Singapore, data consist of only SMEs in the services and manufacturing sectors, and exclude public administration activities and own account workers (e.g. freelancers, taxi drivers, hawkers). The 2013 data is preliminary, while the 2014 data is an estimate.
8. For the United States, data include only employer firms.
9. For Vietnam, employment with private enterprises is used as a proxy of SME employment.
Source: See Appendix 2.1.

Russia is quite low, at 25 per cent in 2013. This might be explained by the large informal sector in Russia, as employment in this domain is not covered by official statistics. In New Zealand, the share of SME employment is also relatively low, at 30 per cent in 2013 but this may be because the definition for small enterprises is capped at nineteen employees.

SMEs' contribution to the economy (in terms of GDP — gross domestic product — or value added) is relatively less substantial than employment creation (see Table 2.4). Only Australia, China, Indonesia, and Japan have their SMEs producing more than 50 per cent of its GDP. In eleven other nations, SMEs account for 30 to 50 per cent of economic output. An outlier is Papua New Guinea, where SMEs only account for 13 per cent of GDP in 2013.

A breakdown of SMEs by size categories shows that micro and small enterprises are the overwhelming majority in each economy (see Table 2.5). This is especially true with microenterprises, who usually make up over 70 per cent of SMEs. Among fourteen selected economies, micro- and small enterprises represent over 95 per cent of SMEs. The only two economies that have a larger share of medium enterprises are Brunei Darussalam and Japan, at 33 per cent and 13 per cent correspondingly.

Within any economy, there are a few sectors that have a large proportion of SMEs, such as wholesale and retail trade; professional, scientific, and technical services; and manufacturing (see Table 2.6). Depending on the structure of the economy, the concentration of SMEs also differs. Wholesale and retail trade have the largest number of SMEs in eleven selected economies, accounting for 18 to 48 per cent of total SMEs. In other economies, sectors with the largest number of SMEs are: construction in Australia (16 per cent); agriculture in Indonesia (49 per cent); rental, hiring, and real estate services in New Zealand (22 per cent); and professional, scientific, and technical services in the United States (13 per cent). A distinction of concentration of SMEs exists between developed economies and developing economies. In developed economies, the top three sectors with the largest number of SMEs constitute less than 50 per cent of total SMEs, while in developing economies, the top three sectors represent over 50 per cent (and in fact, often over 70 per cent) of all SMEs.

There are also sectors that have a relatively low number of SMEs (see Table 2.7). These include electricity, gas, water, and waste

TABLE 2.4
Economic Contribution of SMEs

APEC Economy	Measure	SMEs' Share	Year
Australia	Industry value added	55.72	2013
Brunei Darussalam	Gross value added	17.30	2010
Canada	GDP	27.00	2011
Chile	GDP	18.90	2011
China	GDP	60.00	2014
Hong Kong, China	Value added	41.00	2013
Indonesia	GDP	60.34	2013
Japan	GDP	54.55	2011
Korea	GDP	47.70	2012
Malaysia	GDP	33.10	2013
Mexico	GDP	34.70	2008
New Zealand	GDP	28.43	2011
Papua New Guinea	GDP	13.30	2013
Peru	GDP	41.20	2007
Philippines	Value added	35.67	2006
Russia	GDP	21.00	2013
Singapore	GDP	45.80	2014
Chinese Taipei	GDP	45.12	2011
Thailand	GDP	37.40	2013
United States	GDP	44.60	2010
Vietnam	GDP	46.00	2013

Notes:
1. For Australia, industry value added, instead of GDP, is used to measure SMEs' contribution to economy. The industry value added does not include the financial and insurance sectors and the general government component of public administration and safety, education and training, and health care and social assistance. Data are of mid-year.
2. For Brunei Darussalam, gross value added is used to measure SMEs' contribution to economy.
3. For Hong Kong, China, there is no official definition of a microenterprise. Value added is used to estimate SMEs' contribution to economy. Value added is equal to the gross value of output minus the value of the goods and services used in production, which excludes community, social, and personal services.
4. For Malaysia, 2013 data is preliminary.
5. For New Zealand, data is of March 2011.

6. For Papua New Guinea, SMEs' contribution to GDP does not include the large informal sector.
7. For the Philippines, value added is used to estimate SMEs' contribution to economy.
8. For Singapore, 2014 data is an estimate.

Source: See Appendix 2.1.

TABLE 2.5
Distribution of SMEs by Size

APEC Economy	Medium	Small	Micro	Year
Australia	2.47	9.54	88.00	2014
Brunei Darussalam	33.24	66.76	—	2010
Canada	1.64	98.36	—	2012
Chile	3.15	21.05	75.08	2013
Indonesia	0.09	1.13	98.78	2013
Japan	13.24	—	86.76	2012
Korea	2.77	10.14	87.01	2012
Malaysia	3.08	19.96	76.95	2011
Mexico	0.80	3.65	95.55	2013
Peru	0.20	4.70	95.20	2013
Philippines	0.40	9.26	90.34	2013
Russia	0.25	4.20	95.56	2013
Singapore	4.68	15.66	79.66	2013
Thailand	0.48	99.52	—	2013
United States	1.70	22.20	75.70	2009
Vietnam	2.50	30.00	67.50	2011

Notes:
1. For Australia, data shown are of mid-year.
2. For Canada, data do not include businesses without a Canada Revenue Agency payroll deduction account.
3. For Singapore, data consist of only SMEs in the services and manufacturing sectors, and exclude public administration activities and own account workers (e.g. freelancers, taxi drivers, hawkers).
4. For the Philippines, data include only the formal sector of the economy.
5. For the United States, data include only employer firms.
6. For the Philippines, data include only the formal sector of the economy.
7. For the United States, data include only employer firms.

Source: See Appendix 2.1.

TABLE 2.6
Concentration of SMEs in Selected Economies

Share of SMEs	Highest 1		Highest 2		Highest 3		Sum %
	Sector	%	Sector	%	Sector	%	
Australia (2014)	Construction	16.1	Professional, Scientific and Technical Services	11.9	Rental, Hiring and Real Estate Services	10.8	38.9
Brunei Darussalam (2010)	Wholesale and Retail Trade	34.7	Other Service Activities	13.3	Manufacturing	12.6	60.7
Canada (2012)	Wholesale and Retail Trade	18.8	Construction	11.6	Professional, Scientific and Technical Services	11.5	41.9
Chile (2013)	Wholesale and Retail Trade; Repair of Motor Vehicles, Motorcycles and Personal and Household Goods	37.6	Real Estate, Renting and Business Activities	10.2	Transport, Storage and Communications	9.9	57.7
Hong Kong, China (2014)	Import/Export Trade and Wholesale	35.5	Retail	14.3	Professional and Business Services	13.4	63.2
Indonesia (2012)	Agriculture	49.0	Trade, Hotel, and Restaurant	27.0	Transportation and Communication	6.9	82.9
Japan (2012)	Retail Trade	18.0	Accommodations and Food Services	14.1	Construction	12.1	44.2
Korea (2012)	Wholesale and Retail Trade	27.9	Transportation	20.1	Accommodation and Food Service Activities	10.8	58.7
Malaysia (2011)	Services	90.1	Manufacturing	5.9	Construction	3.0	98.9
Mexico (2013)	Trade	48.3	Private Services not Financial	38.1	Manufacturing	11.5	97.9
New Zealand (2013)	Rental, Hiring and Real Estate Services	21.8	Agriculture, Forestry and Fishing	14.6	Professional, Scientific and Technical Services	10.9	47.3
Peru (2013)	Trade	45.9	Services	39.0	Manufacturing	9.6	94.4

Economy	Sector 1	Share	Sector 2	Share	Sector 3	Share	Total
Philippines (2013)	Wholesale and Retail Trade; Repair of Motor Vehicles and Motorcycles	46.4	Accommodation and Food Service Activities	13.6	Manufacturing	12.5	72.5
Russia (2013)	Trade	39.6	Real Estate, Rent Services	20.2	Construction	11.6	71.4
Chinese Taipei (2013)	Services	79.9	Industrial	19.2	—	—	99.1
Thailand (2012)	Wholesale, Retail Trade, Repair of Motor Vehicles	43.6	Manufacturing	17.7	Hotel and Restaurants	11.1	72.4
United States (2012)	Professional, Scientific, and Technical Services	13.4	Other Services (except Public Administration)	11.6	Retail Trade	11.3	36.2
Vietnam (2011)	Services	66.5	Industry and Construction	30.1	—	—	96.6

Notes:
1. For Australia, data shown are of mid-year.
2. For Canada, data do not include businesses without a Canada Revenue Agency payroll deduction account.
3. For New Zealand, data shown are of February.
4. For Singapore, data consist of only SMEs in the services and manufacturing sectors, and exclude public administration activities and own account workers (e.g. freelancers, taxi drivers, hawkers).
5. For the United States, data include only employer firms.
Source: See Appendix 2.1.

TABLE 2.7
Sectors with Lowest Share of SMEs in Selected Economies

Share of SMEs	Lowest 1		Lowest 2		Lowest 3		
	Sector	%	Sector	%	Sector	%	Sum %
Australia (2014)	Electricity, Gas, Water and Waste Services	0.27	Public Administration and Safety	0.35	Mining	0.39	1.02
Brunei Darussalam (2010)	Mining and Quarrying	0.63	Human Health and Social Work Activities	0.72	Information and Communication	1.73	3.08
Canada (2012)	Mining, Quarrying and Oil and Gas Extraction	0.88	Forestry, Fishing and Hunting	1.21	Information, Culture and Recreation	2.93	5.01
Chile (2013)	Extraterritorial Organizations and Bodies	0.00	Public Administration and Defence; Compulsory Social Security	0.02	Private Households with Employed Persons	0.04	0.06
Hong Kong, China (2014)	Mining and Quarrying; Electricity and Gas Supply, and Waste Management; and Construction Sites	0.40	Transportation, Storage, Postal and Courier Services	2.53	Manufacturing	3.17	6.10
Indonesia (2012)	Electricity	0.03	Mining	0.58	Construction	2.23	2.84
Japan (2012)	Electricity, Gas, Heat Supply, and Water	0.02	Mining and Quarrying of Stone and Gravel	0.04	Compound Services	0.09	0.15
Korea (2012)	Manufacturing	0.01	Agriculture and Forestry	0.02	Fishing	0.05	0.09
Malaysia (2011)	Mining and Quarrying	0.05	Agriculture	1.04	—	—	1.09
Mexico (2013)	Other activities	2.13					2.13
New Zealand (2013)	Mining	0.13	Electricity, Gas, Water and Waste Services	0.21	Public Administration and Safety	0.21	0.56
Peru (2013)	Fishing	0.24	Mining	0.64	Agricultural	1.59	2.47

Country	Sector		Sector		Sector		Total
Philippines (2013)	Electricity, Gas Steam, and Air Conditioning Supply	0.10	Mining and Quarrying	0.10	Water Supply, Sewerage Waste Management, and Remediation Activities	0.14	0.34
Russia (2013)	Agriculture	3.20	Transport, Communication	6.70	Others	8.50	18.40
Chinese Taipei (2013)	Agriculture	0.90	—	—	—	—	0.90
Thailand (2012)	International Organizations and Foreign Organizations	0.01	Public Administration and Defence; Compulsory Social Securities	0.01	Fishing	0.05	0.06
United States (2012)	Utilities	0.10	Unclassified	0.12	Management of Companies and Enterprises	0.33	0.56
Vietnam (2011)	Agriculture, Forestry, and Fishery	0.98	Others	2.40	—	—	3.39

Notes:
1. For Australia, data shown are of mid-year.
2. For Canada, data do not include businesses without a Canada Revenue Agency payroll deduction account.
3. For New Zealand, data shown are of February.
4. For Singapore, data consist of only SMEs in the services and manufacturing sectors, and exclude public administration activities and own account workers (e.g. freelancers, taxi drivers, hawkers).
5. For the United States, data include only employer firms.
Source: See Appendix 2.1.

services; mining and quarrying; and agriculture, forestry, and fishery. In half of the selected economies, mining and quarrying and electricity, gas, water, and waste services have less than 1 per cent of total SMEs. Agriculture, forestry, and fishery also has a lower share of SMEs, usually below 3 per cent (although two notable exceptions can be found in Indonesia and New Zealand, which have a higher proportion of SMEs in these fields). In the sectors of public administration and safety (defence), international organizations and foreign organizations, there are also few SMEs, usually no more than 1 per cent.

In summary, SMEs are significant players in the economy, although there is some diversity in the presence and share of contribution across various dimensions such as sectors, level of development, and country size. The next question is: what role do they play in economic growth?

SMEs and Economic Growth

As economic growth is a long-term phenomenon, theories of economic growth and the accompanying empirical work have primarily focused on macro-level factors such as demographic changes, capital accumulation, and technological innovation. Even though micro-level theorizing of economic growth can be seen in some of the early works of the founding fathers of economics, macro-type growth theories became de rigueur with the emergence of Keynesian-based growth theories à la Swan-Solow and Harrod-Domar. However, this macro-micro dichotomy has been eroded in recent years.

Since the 1980s, trade and growth theories have been increasingly fashioned using a heterogeneous firms framework. This approach incorporates micro foundations which assume a population of heterogeneous firms. More recently, growth models with heterogeneous firms have made it possible to dwell on the relationship between firm size and economic growth. The greater availability of micro data (such as at plant level or establishment level) has also brought about more empirical work on micro-level productivity dynamics.

a. Firm Size Distribution

A starting point of analysis is what does a "typical" firm size distribution look like? Whilst many of the recent studies incorporating firm size distribution dates back to 2003/4, the preoccupation with this topic dates back to the 1930s. There is a consensus within the empirical literature that firm size distribution is skewed so that large firms account for a disproportionately higher share of total employment or output (Sutton 1997; Luttmer 2010). However, small firms typically account for more than 90 per cent of total business establishments (Schaper 2006; Schaper et al. 2008).

Over the years, research on firm size distribution has focused on two major aspects. First, scholars have attempted to formally characterize the density function or the heavy tail portion of firm size distributions. A number of candidates have been proposed such as Gibrat, Pareto, and Zipf. Second, attempts have been made to theorize the processes that yield the observed firm size distribution. In many cases, the stochastic process used to model the observed firm distribution has very much depended on the postulated formal characterization of the firm size distribution.

However, despite the need to ensure consistency between firm size distribution and the process that generates it, an economic explanation would require models with additional features that take into account micro-level determinants of firm dynamics. Aspects of such dynamics should include entry, exit, growth, and decline. Generally speaking, firm dynamics are determined by two broad classes of factors: internal and external.

Internal factors include entrepreneurship, managerial talent, human capital, management practices, organizational structure, and ownership structure (Lucas 1978; Bloom et al. 2010). External factors include market competition, access to financing, market/industry regulations, research and development (R&D), exporting, and other factors related to investment climate. In reality, the effects of internal and external factors cannot be isolated from each other — there are interactions between these factors. Such interactions underlie the differences in performance by firm size.

b. *Firm Size Distribution and Economic Growth*

A key point in the earlier section on SMEs in selected economies is that SMEs dominate in terms of the number of establishments but less proportionally in terms of GDP. The latter fact might be construed as supporting a view that SMEs are less important than large firms. This may not entirely be true. This issue can be analysed by examining the sources of growth at the micro-level.

Economic growth is a dynamic process in which more outputs are produced due to factor (capital and labour) accumulation and technological change (innovation). At the micro-level, this can take place through existing firms expanding their production (including introducing new products), and by new firms entering the market and commencing production.

However, the focus on output expansion misses the point of reallocation of resources (such as capital and labour) from less to more efficient firms. This takes place when inefficient firms reduce their output or exit the market. Selection effect — that is, the replacement of inefficient firms by more efficient ones — is thus an important aspect of economic growth. Reallocation and selection effects have been emphasized in much of the recent literature (see, for example, Foster et al. 2001; Bartelsman et al. 2013). Estimates from the U.S. manufacturing sector suggest that around 15–20 per cent of all job creation and destruction can be attributed to the entry and exit of firms. A key determinant and predictor of exit is productivity. Two other facts are important. First, there is also strong evidence of a positive relationship between productivity and firm size (Bartelsman et al. 2013). Second, the firm turnover rate (entry-exit or churning rate) is generally higher amongst smaller firms. These observations suggest that SMEs play a crucial role via selection and reallocation in the economy.

Another issue worth reflecting on is the role that SMEs might play in economic growth through innovation. There is evidence that R&D rises proportionately with firm size, more specifically business unit size (Cohen 2010). In an attempt to find a link between firm size and growth at the sectoral level, Pagano and Schivardi (2003) have suggested that the positive correlation between firm size and productivity growth is strengthened by R&D activities. Taken at face value, this implies that large firms have a bigger role in generating economic growth via innovation. More recent studies paint a more complex picture. First, the work of Li and Rama (2015) has suggested that a more comprehensive firm sample might weaken the correlation between firm size and productivity. Second, Aghion and Griffith

(2005) argue that a firm's distance to the technology frontier could be a more important factor.

c. How Does Competition Law Affect the SMEs' Role in Economic Growth?

When discussing the role of competition law in economic growth, it is worth remembering the difference between competition policy and competition law. Most definitions suggest that competition law is a subset of competition policy. The latter includes government regulations, decision-making by the executive, and policies in other fields (such as trade policy) that affect the degree of competition in domestic markets. In a sense, competition law is more focused and is constrained by provisions within various enacted statutes.

The empirical evidence linking competition law to economic growth is very sparse. This is partly due to methodological difficulties. As Baker (2003) has noted, it is difficult to quantify the deterrence effects of competition law. Thus, most studies have employed a cross-country analysis. However, such studies are constrained by the availability of comparable international data on competition law, especially as it relates to the performance of antitrust regimes in areas such as enforcement. One of the earliest studies to do this was Hylton and Deng (2007), who collected data on the coverage of competition laws in 102 countries. Their study did not look at the relationship between competition law and economic growth *per se*, but instead examined how competition law was related to the degree of competition. The authors found a positive association between the scope of competition law and the intensity of competition.

Voigt (2009) attempted to analyse the correlation between competition and productivity (measured as total-factor productivity or TFP). Competition was represented by four composite variables measuring competition law's position and provisions, the use of economic approach, and the independence of competition agencies. There was some evidence of a positive relationship between competition law and TFP, though it was not very strong. Voigt (2009) also suggested that the quality of institutions might matter. This is related to political rights, civil liberties and government effectiveness — factors that can influence the independence of competition agencies.

These findings are supported by Ma (2011) in a study involving 101 countries. Ma found that the effectiveness of competition law enforcement could be indirectly shaped by institutional factors, such as government effectiveness and rule of law. A more recent study by Petersen (2011) has also reaffirmed the positive links between competition law and economic growth over a ten-year period.

Another potential indirect approach is to investigate the link between competition law and levels of entrepreneurship within one or more nations. This is particularly relevant given that new firms (entrants) are likely to be SMEs. Schaper et al. (2010) undertook an empirical cross-country analysis involving twenty-one countries. Two proxies for competition law were used, namely the range and effectiveness of competition law. Entrepreneurship was measured by the proportion of the adult population that had begun a business. This study found that no discernible correlation between competition law and entrepreneurship could be detected, possibly due to the difficulty in effectively measuring such concepts as entrepreneurship and competition law.

On balance, these studies do provide a limited body of cross-country evidence that there can be a positive relationship between competition law and economic growth. However, none of the existing empirical studies have examined how SME-related provisions or enforcement of competition law is related to economic growth.

Conclusion

SMEs clearly play an important role in the economy. This is evident irrespective of the many ways in which "SME" has been defined by national economies. Within the context of the entire spectrum of firm size distribution, there are clearly differences between SMEs and large firms. Their relative contribution to economic growth is likely to differ across sectors. Within a sector, reallocation and selection effects are important drivers of economic growth. SMEs, in particular, play a crucial role in the entry-exit process. How competition law affects the SMEs' role in economic growth is not entirely clear at this point. Part of this problem is due to the availability of measures and data on competition law and factors such as entrepreneurship and entry-exit dynamics. It is also related to how competition law is framed and enforced, which depends on the guiding economic framework i.e. Schumpeterian (dynamic) competition or neoclassical (static) competition.

Appendix 2.1

Data Sources for SMEs:

- **Australia:** Small Business Policy Unit, The Treasury, Australian Government; Australian Bureau of Statistics, Counts of Australian Businesses (including Entries and Exits, June 2010 to June 2014) and Australian Industry 2012–13.
- **Brunei Darussalam:** Department of Economic Planning and Development, based on Economic Census 2007 and 2011.
- **Canada:** Small Business Branch, Industry Canada, Government of Canada; Statistics Canada, Labor Force Survey.
- **Chile:** Internal Revenue Service; Chile Central Bank.
- **China:** On the Issuance of Classification Standards for SMEs, jointly issued by the Ministry of Industry and Information Technology, the National Bureau of Statistics, the National Development and Reform Commission, and the Ministry of Finance.
- **Hong Kong, China:** Census Register of Establishments, Quarterly Survey of Employment and Vacancies, Quarterly Employment Survey of Construction Sites, conducted by Census and Statistics Department of Hong Kong, China.
- **Indonesia:** State Ministry of Cooperatives & SMEs, Indonesia.
- **Japan:** New Small and Medium Enterprise Basic Law, Small and Medium Enterprise Agency, Ministry of Economy, Trade and Industry.
- **Korea:** Small and Medium Business Administration and Small & Medium Business Corporation, Korea.
- **Malaysia:** SME Annual Report 2011/2012 and 2013/2014 by SME Corporation Malaysia; Census of Establishments and Enterprises 2005 and Economic Census 2011 by Department of Statistic Malaysia.
- **Mexico:** Official Gazette of the Federation; National Institute of Statistics and Geography, INEGI.
- **New Zealand:** Statistics New Zealand Business Demography February 2012 and February 2013, Statistics New Zealand National Accounts 2010 and March 2011, Ministry of Business, Innovation & Employment.
- **Papua New Guinea:** Department of Trade Commerce and Industry; Tebbutt Research, Report for SME Baseline Survey for the Small-Medium Enterprise Access to Finance Project; Small Business Development Corporation Survey; Carolyn Blacklock, PNG SME Definition and Market Snapshot.
- **Peru:** Ministry of Production, DIGECOMTE; Ministry of Labor; SUNAT.
- **Philippines:** National Statistics Office and Small and Medium Enterprise Development Council Resolution.
- **Russia:** Rosstat; Federal Tax Service of Russia.
- **Singapore:** Department of Statistics, Singapore; Economic Development Board, Singapore; SPRING Singapore.
- **Chinese Taipei:** White Paper on SMEs, Chinese Taipei; Industry, Commerce and Service Census; Small and Medium Enterprise Administration, Ministry of Economic Affairs, Chinese Taipei.
- **Thailand:** Ministry of Industry, Thailand; Office of SME Promotion of Thailand; the Office of National Economic and Social Development Board, Thailand.
- **United States:** Small Business Size Standards, Small Business Administration, United States; Country Business Patterns.
- **Vietnam:** Agency for Enterprise Development, Ministry of Planning and Investment.

Appendix 2.1   (*continued*)

Notes:

1. For Australia, a small business is an actively trading business with 0–19 employees. Actively trading businesses are businesses that have an Australia Business Number (ABN) and are actively remitting in respect of a GST (goods and services tax) role. Non-employing businesses are sole proprietorships and partnerships without employees, and are considered as small businesses by the Australian Bureau of Statistics (ABS). The employment size ranges are based on "headcount", rather than a measure of full-time equivalent persons. ABS also recognizes that an employment-based sizing measure may not be applicable to businesses in certain sectors, such as agriculture, and that financial measures, based on turnover or asset holdings for example, may also be used to classify businesses as SMEs. On certain occasions, small businesses could also be defined by annual turnover.

2. For Canada, SMEs do not include the category of "indeterminate", which are businesses without a Canada Revenue Agency payroll deduction account. The workforce in the "indeterminate" category include contract workers, family members, and/or business owners.

3. For Chile, there is no unique definition of an SME. The Ministry of Planning and Cooperation (MIDEPLAN) defines SMEs based on the number of persons employed using data from the National Socio-economic Survey (CASEN), while the Ministry of Economy (MINECON) defines SMEs based on the level of annual sales using data from the Internal Tax Service (SII). Unidades de Fomento (UF) is a unit of account indexed to the Consumer Price Index; the average of the daily values for 31 August 2012 of one UF was CLP 22,549.68. SMEs in Chile are firms with annual sales up to UF 100,000. Financial institutions define SMEs by the loan size.

4. For China, SMEs are defined by the number of employees and operating income. Sector specific definitions for micro, small, and medium enterprises are also available.

5. For Indonesia, the definition of an SME can vary throughout the economy. The State Ministry of Cooperatives and SMEs defines SMEs based on net assets, excluding land and buildings, and annual sales. Statistics Indonesia (BPS) defines SMEs based on employment.

7. For Malaysia, SMEs can be defined based on either total annual sales or revenue or on the number of full-time employees. A business only needs to fulfil one criterion to be qualified in the group size of SMEs.

8. For New Zealand, SMEs are not officially defined. However, enterprises with fewer than twenty employees have traditionally been used and referred to as small enterprises, e.g. in amendments to the Employment Relations Act.

9. For Peru, the value of Applicable Tax Unit for the year 2013 was equal to USD 1369.

10. For the Philippines, SMEs can be defined based on either total assets, or on the number of employees.

11. For Singapore, SMEs are defined as enterprises with operating receipts of not more than SGD 100 million or employment of not more than 200 workers for all sectors. Medium enterprises are defined as enterprises with operating receipts between SGD 10 million and SGD 100 million, or enterprises with operating receipts of more than SGD 100 million and employment of not more than 200 workers.

12. For Chinese Taipei, SMEs are defined based on either sales revenue or paid-in capital depending on the sector. Other agencies may define SMEs based on the number of regular employees. Other sectors include agriculture, forestry, fisheries, animal husbandry; water, electricity, gas; wholesale and retail; transportation; warehousing and communications; hotel and restaurant operations; finance and insurance; real estate and leasing; industrial and commercial services; social and personal services.

13. For Thailand, fixed assets, excluding land and property, are used.

14. For the United States, SMEs are defined based on either the number of employees or average annual receipts or average assets depending on the sector, with specific size standards for all for-profit industries. Size standards based on the number of employees range from 100 to 1,500 employees, size standards based on average annual receipts range from USD 5.5 million to USD 38.5 million, and for depository institutions and credit card issuing companies, a small enterprise is one with less than 500 million in average assets.

15. For Vietnam, SMEs are defined based on the registered capital at business registration agencies and/or on the average number of annual permanent employees.

NOTE

1. In addition, some countries include microenterprises and the self-employed in their SME statistics.

REFERENCES

Acs, Zoltán J., Randall Morck, and Bernard Yeung. "Productivity Growth and Firm Size Distribution". In *Entrepreneurship, Small and Medium-Sized Enterprises and the Macroeconomy*, edited by Zoltán J. Acs, Bo Carisson, and Charlie Karisson. Cambridge: Cambridge University Press, 1999.

Aghion, Philippe, Nick Bloom, Richard Blundell, Rachel Griffith, and Peter Howitt. "Competition and Innovation: An Inverted-U Relationship". *Quarterly Journal of Economics* 120, no. 2 (May 2005): 701–28.

Aghion, Philippe and Rachel Griffith. *Competition and Growth: Reconciling Theory and Evidence*. Cambridge, Mass.: The MIT Press, 2005.

Baker, Jonathan B. "The Case for Antitrust Enforcement". *Journal of Economic Perspectives* 17, no. 4 (2003): 27–50.

Bartelsman, Eric, John Haltiwanger, and Stefano Scarpetta. "Measuring and Analyzing Cross-country Differences in Firm Dynamics". In *Producer Dynamics: New Evidence from Micro Data*, edited by Timothy Dunne, J. Bradford Jensen, and Mark J. Roberts. Chicago: University of Chicago Press, 2009.

———. "Cross-Country Differences in Productivity: The Role of Allocation and Selection". *American Economic Review*, American Economic Association 103, no. 1 (2013): 305–34.

Bloom, Nicholas, Aprajit Mahajan, David Mackenzie, and John Roberts. "Why Do Firms in Developing Countries Have Low Productivity?". *American Economic Review* 100, no. 2 (2010): 619–23.

Bloom, Nicholas and John Van Reenen. "Measuring and Explaining Management Practices Across Firms and Countries". Centre for Economic Performance Discussion Paper 716 (2006).

———. "Measuring and Explaining Management Practices Across Firms and Countries". *Quarterly Journal of Economics* 122, no. 4 (2007): 1341–1408.

Cohen, Wesley. "Fifty Years of Empirical Studies of Innovative Activity and Performance". In *Handbook of the Economics of Innovation*, vol. 1, edited by Bronwyn H. Hall and Nathan Rosenberg. North Holland, 2010.

European Commission (EC). "What is an SME?", 2005. Available at <http:// ec.europa.eu/growth/smes/business-friendly-environment/sme-definition/ index_en.htm>.

Foster, Lucia, John Haltiwanger, and C.J. Krizan. "Aggregate Productivity Growth: Lessons from Microeconomic Evidence". In *New Developments in*

Productivity Analysis, edited by Charles R. Hulten, Edwin R. Dean, and Michael J. Harper. Chicago: University of Chicago Press, 2001.

Foster, Lucia, John Haltiwanger, and Chad Syverson. "Reallocation, Firm Turnover, and Efficiency: Selection on Productivity or Profitability?" *American Economic Review* 98, no. 1 (2008): 394–425.

Holmes, Thomas and James Schmitz. "Competition and Productivity: A Review of Evidence". *Annual Review of Economics* 2 (2010): 619–42.

Hsieh, Chang-Tai and Peter J. Klenow. "Misallocation and Manufacturing TFP in China and India". *Quarterly Journal of Economics* 124, no. 4 (2009): 1403–48.

Hylton, Keith N. and Fei Deng. "Antitrust Around the World: An Empirical Analysis of the Scope of Competition Laws and Their Effects". *Antitrust Law Journal* 74, no. 2 (2007): 271–341.

International Finance Corporation (IFC). "Interpretation Note on Small and Medium Enterprises and Environmental and Social Risk Management", 2012. Available at <http://www.ifc.org/wps/wcm/connect/de7d92804a29ffe9ae04af8969adcc27/InterpretationNote_SME_2012.pdf?MOD=AJPERES>.

Li, Yue and Martin Rama. "Firm Dynamics, Productivity Growth and Job Creation in Developing Countries: The Role of Micro- and Small Enterprises". *World Bank Research Observer* 30, no. 1 (2015): 3–38.

Lucas, Jr., Robert E. "On the Size Distribution of Business Firms". *Bell Journal of Economics* 9, no. 2 (1978): 508–23.

Luttmer, Erzo G.J. "Models of Growth and Firm Heterogeneity". *Annual Review of Economics* 2, no. 1 (2010): 547–76.

Ma, Tay-Cheng. "The Effect of Competition Law Enforcement on Economic Growth". *Journal of Competition Law & Economics* 7, no. 2 (2011): 301–34.

Pagano, Patrizio and Fabiano Schivardi. "Firm Size Distribution and Growth". *The Scandinavian Journal of Economics* 105, no. 2 (2003): 255–74.

Petersen, Niels. "Antitrust Law and the Promotion of Democracy and Economic Growth". *Journal of Competition Law & Economics* 9, no. 3 (2011): 593–636.

Schaper, Michael T. "Distribution Patterns of Small Firms in Developed Economies: Is There An Emergent Global Pattern?" *International Journal of Entrepreneurship and Small Business* 3, no. 2 (2006): 183–89.

Schaper, Michael T., Anne Clear, and Geoff Baker. "Competition Policy and Entrepreneurship Development: Some International Comparisons". *European Competition Law Review* 31, no. 6 (2010): 226–30.

Schaper, Michael T., Leo Paul Dana, Robert B. Anderson, and Peter W. Moroz. "Distribution of Firms by Size: Observations and Evidence from Selected Countries". *International Journal of Entrepreneurship and Innovation Management* 8, no. 6 (2008): 718–26.

Sidak, J. Gregory and David J. Teece. "Dynamic Competition in Antitrust Law". *Journal of Competition Law and Economics* 5, no. 4 (2009): 581–631.

Sutton, John. "Gibrat's Legacy". *Journal of Economic Literature* 35 no. 1 (1997): 40–59.

Syverson, Chad. "Product Substitutability and Productivity Dispersion". *Review of Economics and Statistics* 86, no. 2 (2004): 534–50.

———. "What Determines Productivity?" *Journal of Economic Literature* 49, no. 2 (2011): 326–65.

Voigt, Stefan. "The Effects of Competition Policy on Development — Cross-Country Evidence Using Four New Indicators". *Journal of Development Studies* 45, no. 8 (2009): 1225–48.

3

COMPETITION POLICY AND SME POLICY
Strange Bedfellows?

Wee-Liang Tan and Lip-Hang Poh

"East is east and west is west, never the twain shall meet."

Rudyard Kipling (1889),
The Ballard of East and West

SME (small and medium-sized enterprise) policy seeks to promote small
businesses in ways that encourage the pooling of risks, sharing of resources, and
networking. These activities can, however, sometimes lead to anti-competitive
behaviour that competition law seeks to remove. Are the two sets of policies
in conflict? This question is explored by using the example of Singapore and
the approach taken by the Competition Commission of Singapore.

Policymakers faced with the likelihood of SMEs being unable to adjust
to competition law have nevertheless in the past usually opted to apply the
law uniformly to all firms. Alternatively, though many competition advocates
would frown on it, some policymakers have granted blanket exemptions to
SMEs. However, there is a possible middle ground. Singapore's competition
regulator defines a clear set of activities that it views as anathema and
designates others, the non "hard-core" activities, as deserving different
treatment when SMEs are involved.

Introduction

Public policies often have differing objectives. In an ideal world, these different goals would be compatible and complementary, fitting neatly alongside each other; as the oft-misquoted lines from Kipling's poem above prima facie suggests, they would not meet or conflict. In truth, however, Kipling was highlighting the exact opposite, as becomes evident when one reads the whole poem.

The same applies to public policy. The rules, programmes, laws, and assistance made by government, legislatures, and other arms of the state can and often does overlap, and sometimes even conflicts with each other. In this chapter, we explore the potential conflict between two sets of policy: competition and small to medium-sized enterprise (SME) policies. Are they strange bedfellows? And is there a "middle way" in which the two can successfully work alongside each other?

In theory and intent, they both should benefit SMEs. Competition policy seeks as level a playing field as possible in the economy, through the enforcement of competition law and the opening up of sectors in the economy to competitive dynamics. (We focus on competition law, the major aspect of competition policy, in the discussion that follows, whilst recognizing that a wider definition of "competition policy" can also include topics such as free trade agreements, sectoral deregulation, market liberalization, and many other issues.) Competition authorities seek to eliminate restrictive trade practices (such as market price rigging and unfair market practices), as it is believed that reining in such anti-competitive behaviour enables new entrants to enter and compete in the marketplace.

SME policy, on the other hand, serves different objectives depending on the state of the small business sector in a nation. If there is high level of unemployment, SME policy is often focused on job creation. In other economies, the emphasis may be on SME capacity building via technology transfer. In some regions, the focus is on increasing participation by disadvantaged communities or particular segments of the population, such as young entrepreneurs and female business owners. In other places, it may seek to encourage more small firms to export, to grow larger, to improve their performance by benchmarking, or to increase their market share.

Yet the two policy regimes do have the capacity to work at odds to each other, despite the best of intentions. Overzealous competition officials may restrict businesses from all forms of cooperation, for example, whilst SME agencies may simultaneously advocate active cooperation and information sharing amongst SMEs.

This chapter examines areas of potential conflict between the two sets of policy. If SME development policies encourage potential anti-competitive behaviour, how should this situation be resolved? These questions are explored, using one jurisdiction — that of Singapore — as a case in point.

The Republic of Singapore is a small and open economy. Its nominal gross domestic product (GDP) in 2014 was S$390 billion (Department of Statistics Singapore 2014) and its trade to GDP ratio 351 per cent (World Bank 2016), one of the highest in the world.[1]

The nation's competition policy landscape consists of some sector-specific competition codes (such as that relating to telecommunications) and the Competition Act that covers all other parts of the economy. The prohibitions of the Act came into force in phases between 2006 and 2007. The Competition Commission of Singapore (CCS) was set up to enforce the Act, whilst sectoral regulators (such as the Infocomm Development Authority of Singapore) are responsible for enforcing their particular codes and promoting the development of that sector.

SMEs account for the majority of the island's enterprises. SPRING Singapore, the government agency responsible for small business development and assistance, defines them as either enterprises with annual sales turnovers of S$100 million or less, or firms with less than 200 workers. In 2014, 99 per cent of all Singaporean businesses were SMEs. They provided 50 per cent of Singapore's GDP and employed more than 70 per cent of its workforce (SPRING Singapore May 2014; July 2014).

SME Policy versus Competition Policy

What is the Goal and Purpose of SME Policy?

In many respects, it is to provide a helping hand that small firms cannot otherwise obtain. It is often argued that SMEs frequently lack much-needed financial resources, capabilities, technology, personnel, and ideas. The measures under the rubric "SME policy" have been variously referred to as small business policy, local enterprise policy, entrepreneurship policy, and/or microenterprise policy. In addition to policies explicitly focused on small firms, these businesses may also be targeted by policymakers working in other fields (for example, in many nations rural and regional economic development strategies often touch on SME assistance).

The interest of governments in smaller enterprises is a relatively new one, as has been the development of specific programmes to assist them. Interest in SME policy began with Birch's breakthrough research findings. Birch (1979) reported that over 80 per cent of new jobs were being generated in small rather than large U.S. firms, with new and young firms being the engines of growth in the U.S. economy (Stevenson and Lundström 2001).

As SMEs share a common characteristic — smallness — that is integrally related to their weaknesses and lack of resources, SME policies and programmes often attempt to deal with small firms' access to resources. In 1994, for example, SME Ministers throughout the APEC (Asia-Pacific Economic Cooperation) region collectively:

> ... agreed that APEC's role in support of SMEs should focus first on addressing the areas where SMEs face the greatest handicaps. These include human resource development, access to information, technology and technology sharing, the availability of finance and market access (APEC 1994).

The range of potential measures which can be brought to bear in pursuit of these objectives is wide. It can include grants, subsidies, training, mentoring, advisory services, preferential contracts with government agencies, and many other activities. In practice, it is generally targeted towards either individual firms or industry clusters, and frequently takes one of a limited number of common form. Hu (2007, p. 288) has observed that "most host economies [have] initiated their SME policies based on more than one of the prominent features of SMEs.

They are job generation, competitiveness, resilience, networking, and entrepreneurship."

SME policy measures have also been called support (Gibbs 2000), or enterprise ecosystems (e.g. Moore 1993, 1996); others, the authors included, prefer the term "entrepreneurial infrastructure" (Tan et al. 2000). Entrepreneurial infrastructure represents a subset of the more general industrial infrastructure — the facilities and services present in an economy which encourage the birth of new ventures and the growth and development of SMEs (Tan et al. 2000). It provides SMEs with assistance with tasks, required resources, information, and knowledge. Resources, for example, may take the form of people, equipment, social capital, or finance. SMEs are also often unaware of the body of information that could enable them to better compete, and such knowledge is frequently overlooked by busy business owners.

In Singapore, for example, the elements of entrepreneurial infrastructure include those shown in Table 3.1; the table is only illustrative and is not a comprehensive depiction of all of the entrepreneurial infrastructure available to Singaporean firms.

In contrast to SME policy, competition law policy that relates to SMEs focuses primarily on the development, enforcement, and interpretation of regulations and statutes. In many countries, there are either exemptions for many smaller enterprises (such as in Indonesia), provisions for joint collective action (such as in Australia), or minimum market thresholds below which abuse of dominance provisions do not apply (such as in Malaysia). Some jurisdictions have instituted *per se* provisions, which give small enterprises a clear "black and white" sense of what is permitted behaviour. A number also have provisions dealing specifically with subsets of the broader SME population, such as franchisees (like in South Korea) or subcontractors (like in Japan).

Table 3.2 shows that the two sets of policies serve different purposes, and that they sometimes also overlap. Indeed, arguably there is a common agenda between the two sets of policies. With competition policy, SMEs are not the focus but they are the beneficiaries. SMEs benefit when dominant players that engage in abusive market practices are reined in. When price fixing and mergers are subject to scrutiny, smaller players who do not command or influence the market have a better opportunity to participate in markets.

TABLE 3.1
Selected Elements of an Entrepreneurial Infrastructure

Assistance with Tasks	Resources	Required	
		Information	Knowledge
Management consultants whose fees are reimbursable	Financing for productivity and innovation	Information available at libraries and electronic databases	Training available at various incubators, accelerations, and tertiary institutions
Assistance available through the Enterprise Development Centres established at trade associations	Loans available through local banks	Information available through the first stop centre linking all government agencies	Capacity building for SME employees

TABLE 3.2
Key Features of Competition and SME Policies

Feature	Competition Law	SME Policy
Focus	Industries, markets, and their consequent effects on the macro-economy	Individual SMEs or groups of SMEs
Measures	Usually negative and punitive in nature on firms or groups of firms	Usually positive to develop firms or agents who will be able to help firms
Key idea	Free competition is good for everyone	To address SME development and to provide elements of entrepreneurial infrastructure that will assist them
Frowns or Favours	Frowns upon anti-competitive behaviour which can take on the following forms: • groupings and cooperation amongst firms that lead to cartels; • dominant players abusing their market position; and • creation of dominant position or collusive business environment (through mergers)	Favours harnessing SME characteristics like networking in SME policy execution

SME Policy and Anti-Competitive Behaviour

Despite the best intentions of policymakers to avoid conflicts between
the different portfolio arms of government, sometimes small businesses
respond to SME development or assistance policy measures in
unanticipated ways. This can include potentially anti-competitive
behaviour that may run foul of the law. We begin by examining two
SME policy recommendations and two social trends in Singapore that
have produced such outcomes.

Hu (2007) and others have already noted that small enterprise
owners and entrepreneurs often draw extensively on their business
networks. These networks provide a forum to share information,
cooperate, and overcome the sense of isolation that many entrepreneurs
report facing. Not surprisingly, policymakers have also promoted
networks as a key aspect of SME support; the policy has been
especially popular in Europe and the United Kingdom since the
1990s (Gibbs 2000). In a similar mould, the Singapore government
initiated an Action Community for Entrepreneurship programme in
2003 to bring business operators together; it also launched the Local
Enterprise and Association Development (LEAD) programme in 2005
to initiate "partnerships with industry associations that are willing
to take the lead in industry development and drive initiatives to
improve the overall capabilities of SMEs in their industries" (SPRING
Singapore 2014).

SME policymakers also promoted cooperation between SMEs as
a means to overcome their lack of resources and smallness in size.
One such venture was the Business Fusion Programme, an initiative
launched in conjunction with Singapore's SME21 report in 2001, the
aim of which was to "facilitate the pooling of resources and expertise
among SMEs so that they have greater economies of scale and
stronger capabilities", enabling them to respond quickly to market
demands and to access new markets (MITA 2000). Some national
government agencies, and in particular SPRING, have not stopped
simply at encouraging domestic cooperation; they have extended
such activities to include interregional SME cooperation. Memoranda
of understanding to promote SME cooperation between Singaporean
and Japanese firms, and between local enterprises and Italian ventures,
have also been signed in recent years (Mizuho Corporate Bank 2013;
Intro International 2013).

Singapore policymakers are not alone in recommending that SMEs should actively cooperate with each other. The participating officials at the 19th APEC SME Ministerial Meeting in St. Petersburg, Russia, for instance, issued a joint statement entitled "Promoting SME cooperation for greater innovative growth in the Asia-Pacific region", in which they argued that cooperation would be a useful tool for start-ups (APEC 2012). The Organization for Economic Cooperation and Development (OECD) also lists cooperation as one of the criteria it uses to evaluate the performance of member nation small business support programmes; this framework has since been adopted by the ASEAN (Association of Southeast Asian Nations) SME Agencies Working Group in developing the ASEAN SME Policy Index. In it, ASEAN countries are assessed on, *inter alia*, their success in fostering technology cooperation and the promotion of clusters and business networks (ERIA 2014). Other policy bodies also stress cooperative behaviours, such as the Global Alliance for SMEs. In its Shanghai Manifesto on Global SME Cooperation, a call was made to both governments and private sector bodies to facilitate more SME cooperation (Global Alliance of SMEs 2009).

Broader societal trends have also recently stressed the value of collaboration between individuals and micro- or small-sized firms. Collaborative consumption is one such area, where individuals, families, communities, and even businesses can share resources. Crowdfunding, the pooled use of cars, and subletting of accommodation are all part of the emerging so-called "sharing economy", and have spawned new business models such as Airbnb, Kickstarter, and Uber that bring together many potentially competing service providers under one banner.

Another social norm influencing SME behaviour is the importance attached to relationships in Asia. Many SMEs in Southeast Asia are of Chinese descent and part of the Chinese diaspora. Relationships and network contacts are part and parcel of their business life. *Guanxi* and its relevance to Chinese culture and businesses has been examined in much prior research (see for example, Huang et al. 2013). Close relationships are an integral part of doing business in much of Southeast Asia, and frequently take the form of meetings with other SMEs, the exchange of information, and joint commercial ventures.

The sharing of information and the exploration of ways to collaborate are basic elements of human behaviour when people meet. When encountering people for the first time, the way to overcome silence and shyness is to either ask questions or volunteer information. When business people meet, therefore, there is a high likelihood that information pertaining to business operations, the markets they serve, their common business experiences and problems, and perhaps even their pricing decisions, will be shared.

Through these practices, small firm operators may engage in behaviours that unintentionally contravene competition law, and its prohibitions on collusion and tacit market-sharing provisions. In Singapore, for example, the Competition Act has proscriptions similar to other jurisdictions that prohibit anti-competitive "collaboration": Section 34 of the Act prohibits anti-competitive agreements and conduct that prevent, restrict, and distort competition (CCS 2007a); Section 47 prohibits conduct on the part of two or more firms abusing a collective dominant position (CCS 2007b); and Section 54 prohibits mergers (and joint ventures) that substantially lessen competition (CCS 2012).

However, Section 33(4) of the same law provides a useful mechanism to deal with situations where some state-sanctioned activities contradict the prohibitions of the Act. It states that the prohibitions do not apply to activities carried on by "(a) the Government, (b) any statutory body; or (c) any person acting on behalf of the Government or that statutory body ..." Hence, some obviously anti-competitive collaborations that are "mandated" by policymakers are not caught under the purview of the Act. That being said, CCS also advises the government and other public authorities on policies relating to competition matters. The anti-competitive effects of such policies can therefore be duly considered in their formulation and implementation phases.

A Middle Path? The Singapore Experience

Formal legislative "escape clauses" are one way to deal with some (narrowly defined) situations when the goals of competition law and SME development potentially clash. What else can competition regulators do to accommodate the situation SMEs are in? Is strict enforcement the only way? Should competition authorities always apply the letter of the law?

In Singapore, CCS has explored a middle way between complete laxity rendering the competition law meaningless (exempting SMEs) and strict enforcement. Firstly, CCS has publicly spelt out the non-negotiable elements of anti-competitive behaviour. CCS has made it clear that four types of "hard core" anti-competitive agreements (namely, price-fixing, bid-rigging, market sharing, and output limitation) are strictly prohibited. Next, it has also indicated the areas within which SMEs will be treated differently to larger enterprises. In its guidelines, for example, CCS (2007a, para 2.19) provides that agreements between SMEs are rarely capable of distorting competition appreciably within the Section 34 prohibition.

In paragraph 2.19 of the same published guidelines, CCS has also declared that it will interpret and enforce agreements between smaller undertakings (businesses) differently: these arrangements will rarely be prohibited. Innocent discussions, exchanges of business processes, swapping of knowledge about new products or services, discussions about the means of market entry, and studies of market conditions between SMEs will not draw the bite of the regulator. These guidelines are helpful to SMEs because there is a presumption in their favour, though CCS can still enforce the Section 34 prohibition where the situation warrants it.

So far, the agency appears to have kept true to its statements of intention, even in cases involving hard core anti-competitive agreements. CCS has in fact dealt with many SMEs in collusive or collaborative arrangements with the proverbial light touch. In one case, for example, four SME producers of "fa gao", a Chinese cupcake-like pastry most commonly eaten during Chinese New Year, had agreed to increase their prices uniformly in 2008. This situation was a clear case of price fixing. Upon confirming the existence of an agreement, CCS chose not to prosecute the firms, but instead persuaded them to disband their agreement and henceforth independently set their prices (CCS 2008).

Similarly, when the Singapore School Transport Association (SSTA), representing some 900 school bus operators, decided to announce that it would be raising the fees charged by its members in 2008, CCS did not bring the full force of the law on it. All of the SSTA's members were SMEs. Even though the conduct fell squarely within the prohibition against price fixing agreements, CCS instead met with the SSTA, pointing out that its proposed price guidelines infringed the Act. The SSTA subsequently recanted its proposal (Yeo 2008).

The position taken by CCS with regard to anti-competitive mergers and abuse of dominance situations involving SMEs has been similar. In its merger procedures, CCS has taken the position that mergers (including joint ventures) involving only small companies are unlikely to infringe the Section 54 prohibition. It states that

> ... CCS is unlikely to investigate a merger situation that only involves small companies, namely where the turnover in Singapore in the financial year preceding the transaction of each of the parties is below S\$5 million and the combined worldwide turnover in the financial year preceding the transaction of all of the parties is below S\$50 million (CCS 2012, para 3.5).

Similarly, CCS's guidelines on the abuse of dominance note that SME business conduct is unlikely to be abusive:

> 3.9 An undertaking which is a small or medium enterprise ... is rarely capable of conduct that has an appreciable adverse effect on competition in Singapore. However the CCS reserves the right to investigate alleged anti-competitive conduct of an SME if such appears to be warranted (CCS 2007b).

The stance taken by CCS in treating SME behaviour as prima facie non-offending has also provided small firms with the means to learn from their mistakes. Where they have not committed a substantial breach of the local law, they are able to repent (turn back on their "sins" and move in the opposite direction). This is not simply an exercise of grace. It demonstrates an understanding of the longer term purpose behind the introduction of competition law — changing ongoing business behaviour so that it promotes competition.

To expect all SMEs in Singapore to have an awareness of the law, and to expect their compliance in a short period of time, would be a tall order. A parallel can be drawn from the experience of other economic agencies in Singapore, who also face complaints from SMEs that there is insufficient publicity about SME programmes and incentives. Tan et al. (2000) found that SME owners often did not use such programmes because they were unaware of them; but once made aware, they often started to understand them and then utilized such services.

CCS also operates a notification system, where businesses can formally approach the regulator for guidance or decisions on whether their agreements infringe the Act. The stance taken by CCS to "overlook" collaborative SME conduct that might infringe the abuse of dominance and anti-competitive merger prohibitions prevents situations where beneficial SME cooperation that has an overall benefit might otherwise be stymied by the "black letter" of competition law.

CCS has adopted a tolerant approach towards SMEs, granting leeway to them where they are engaged in activities outside the core anti-competitive activities. This approach strikes a balance between strict enforcement and total exemption for SMEs. This middle way has even been extended to hard core anti-competitive activities where CCS has been able to intervene (such as in the "fa gao" case), before the businesses have acted on their price-fixing agreements. This approach allows for learning by SMEs of competition law compliance and allows the agency to devote its resources to enforcing much more serious breaches of the law that would have a wider impact on the nation's overall economy and its consumers.

Conclusion

Policymakers faced with the likelihood of SMEs being unable to adjust to competition law have, in the past, usually opted to apply the law uniformly to all firms. Alternatively, though many competition advocates would frown on it, some policymakers grant exemptions to SMEs. However, in implementation, there is scope for recommending the middle ground — the path which CCS is treading. CCS defines a clear set of activities that it views as anathema and designates others, the non "hard core" activities, as deserving different treatment when SMEs are involved. By taking a position that SMEs are operating outside of the core prohibited activities unless the contrary is proven, CCS provides a situation where SMEs can operate and policymakers can continue to support firms without them accidentally straying into the forbidden zone.

The philosophy adopted by competition regulators often shapes the stance and approach adopted by its business community. A pro-SME philosophy would see exemptions from competition law being granted to SMEs, whilst a legalistic approach would see strict competition law enforcement being adopted. This chapter has illustrated a middle path where SMEs are not granted universal exemptions, but instead an approach has been consciously adopted that seeks to intervene, correct, educate, and guide in situations where the anti-competitive behaviour can be prevented. This stance has much to offer. Ultimately, the goal remains the same — greater competition in the economy — but there is more than one way to get the small business sector moving towards it.

NOTE

The views expressed in this chapter are personal and do not represent the official position of the Competition Commission of Singapore (CCS). The views shall not in any way restrict or confine the ability of CCS to carry out its duties and functions as set out in the Competition Act (Cap. 50B).

1. At the time of writing, S$1.40 = US$1.

REFERENCES

Asia-Pacific Economic Cooperation (APEC). "Ministerial Statements: 1994 APEC Small and Medium Enterprises Ministerial Meeting", 22–23 October 1994. Available at <http://www.apec.org/Meeting-Papers/Ministerial-Statements/Small-and-Medium Enterprise/1994_sme.aspx> (accessed 23 November 2014).

———. "SME Market Access and Internationalization: Medium-term KPIs for the SMEWG Strategic Plan", June 2010. Available at <http://publications.apec.org/publicationdetail.php?pub_id=1050> (accessed 3 December 2014).

———. "Promoting SME Cooperation for Innovative Growth in the APEC Region". 19th APEC SME Ministerial Meeting Joint Statement, 3 August 2012. Available at <http://www.apec.org/Press/News-Releases/2012/0803_smemm.aspx> (accessed 27 November 2014).

Birch, David G.W. *The Job Generation Process*. Cambridge, Mass.: MIT Program on Neighborhood and Regional Change, 1979.

Buczynski, Beth. *Sharing is Good*. Gabriola Island, B.C., Canada: New Society Publishers, 2013.

Burgess, Rachel Melissa. "Teaching Old Dogs New Tricks: SMEs and Malaysia's New Competition Law". Small Enterprise Association of Australia and New Zealand 27th Annual SEAANZ Conference Proceedings, Sydney, 16–18 July 2014.

Competition Commission of Singapore (CCS). "CCS Guidelines on the Section 34 Prohibition", June 2007a. Available at <https://www.ccs.gov.

sg/legislation/~/media/ custom/ccs/files/legislation/ccs%20guidelines/
s34jul07final.ashx> (accessed 25 March 2015).

———. "CCS Guidelines on the Section 47 Prohibition", June 2007b. Available at
<https://www.ccs.gov.sg/legislation/~/media/custom/ccs/files/legislation/
ccs%20guidelines/s47jul07final.ashx> (accessed 25 March 2015).

———. "CCS Stops Price Increase Agreement Between Four "Fa Gao" (发糕)
Manufacturers", 7 April 2008. Available at <https://www.ccs.gov.sg/media-
and-publications/media-releases/ccs-stopsprice-increase-agreement-between-
four-fa-gao--manufacturers> (accessed 22 December 2015).

———. "CCS Guidelines on Merger Procedures 2012", 1 July 2012. Available at
<https://www.ccs.gov.sg/legislation/~/media/custom/ccs/files/legislation/
ccs%20guidelines/revised20merger20guidelines20procedures202012.ashx>
(accessed 25 March 2015).

Department of Statistics Singapore. "Gross Domestic Product", 2014. Available
at <http://www.singstat.gov.sg/statistics/latest-data#1> (accessed
25 March 2015).

Economic Research Institute for ASEAN and East Asia (ERIA). *ASEAN SME
Policy Index 2014: Towards Competitive And Innovative ASEAN SMEs*. Jakarta:
Economic Research Institute for ASEAN and East Asia, June 2014.

Gibb, A.A. "Academic Research and the Growth of Ignorance. SME Policy:
Mythical Concepts, Myths, Assumptions, Rituals and Confusions".
International Small Business Journal 18, no. 3 (May 2000): 13–35.

Global Alliance of SMEs. "Shanghai Manifesto on Global SME Cooperation",
13 July 2009. Available at <http://www.globalsmes.org/html/
index.php?func=shanghai_manifesto&lan=en> (accessed 27 November
2014).

Hu, Ming-Wen. "Overview of SME Policies in Selective Economies". In *The
Policy Environment for the Development of SMEs*. Chinese Taipei: Chinese
Taipei Pacific Economic Cooperation Committee and the Pacific Economic
Cooperation Council, 2007.

Huang, Kai-Ping, Tsungting Chung, Jane Tung, and Sheng Chung Lo. "Guanxi
Embeddedness and Trust Building in Chinese Business Markets: A
Confucianism Perspective". *Journal of Applied Sciences* 13, no. 3 (2013): 333–40.

Intro International. "Italy, Singapore Sign MOU on Cooperation Between
SMEs", 24 July 2013. Available at <http://www.introinternational.com/
en/component/content/article/25-news/93-italy-singapore-sign-mou-on-
cooperation-between-smes> (accessed 22 December 2015).

Ministry of Information and the Arts (MITA), Singapore. "Opening Address
by Mr Tang Guan Seng, Senior Parliamentary Secretary, Ministry of
Trade and Industry, Launch of Testcal and Business Fusion Programme",
29 November 2000. Available at <http://www.nas.gov.sg/archivesonline/
data/pdfdoc/tgs20001129f.pdf> (accessed 23 November 2014).

Mizuho Corporate Bank. "MOU Between JBIC, Mizuho Corporate Bank, and SPRING Singapore to Promote Business Collaboration Between SMEs in Japan and Singapore", 27 May 2013. Available at <http://www.mizuhobank.com/company/release/cb/pdf/news_20130527.pdf> (accessed 27 November 2014).

Moore, James F. "Predators and Prey: A New Ecology of Competition". *Harvard Business Review* 71, no. 3 (1993): 75–86.

———. *The Death of Competition: Leadership and Strategy in the Age of Business Ecosystems*. New York: HarperBusiness, 1996.

SPRING Singapore. "Enterprise Development Centres Geared Up to Help SMEs Raise Productivity", 8 October 2010. Available at <http://www.news.gov.sg/public/sgpc/en/ media_releases/agencies/spr%20spore/press_release/P-20101008-1> (accessed 22 December 2015).

———. "Local Enterprise and Association Development (LEAD) Programme", 2014. Available at <http://www.spring.gov.sg/Developing-Industries/Industry-Initiatives/LEAD/Pages/Local-Enterprise-and-Association-Development.aspx> (accessed 22 December 2015).

———. "SME Centres are Helping Businesses Seize Opportunities for Growth", May 2014. Available at <http://www.spring.gov.sg/Inspiring-Success/Enterprise-Stories/Pages/Bringing-Assistance-Closer-to-SMEs.aspx> (accessed 25 March 2015).

———. "Welcome Address by Tan Kai Koe at the Executive Development Scholarship Award Ceremony 2014", 18 July 2014. Available at <http://www.spring.gov.sg/NewsEvents/PS/Pages/Welcome-Address-by-Tan-Kai-Hoe-atthe-Executive-Development-Scholarship-Award-Ceremony-2014-20140718.aspx> (accessed 25 March 2015).

Stevenson, Lois and Anders Lundström. *Patterns and Trends in Entrepreneurship/ SME Policy and Practice in Ten Economies. Volume 3 of the Entrepreneurship Policy for the Future Series*. Stockholm: Swedish Foundation for Small Business Research, 2001.

Tan, Teck-Meng, Tan Wee-Liang, and John E. Young. "Entrepreneurial Infrastructure in Singapore: Developing A Model and Mapping Participation". *Journal of Entrepreneurship* 9, no. 1 (2000): 1–33.

World Bank Data. "Trade (% of GDP)", 2016. Available at <http://data.worldbank.org/indicator/NE.TRD.GNFS.ZS> (accessed 25 April 2016).

Yeo, Ghim Lay. "Higher School Bus Fares for Some". *Straits Times*, 14 December 2008. Available at <http://news.asiaone.com/News/Education/Story/A1Story20081212-107364.html> (accessed 2 December 2014).

4

THE COMPETITIVE EXPERIENCE
OF UK SMEs
Fair and Unfair

David Storey

Although there has been a considerable amount of research undertaken on the impact of competition policy upon (large) enterprises and upon consumers, there is almost no empirical work that examines any link between competition policy and small and medium-sized enterprises (SMEs). This chapter addresses this issue. It finds that one third of firms are aware of anti-competitive practices such as price fixing, cartels, and tender agreements and one quarter have actually been a victim of such practices. Its second key finding is that among SME "victims", the most likely response is to "shrug their shoulders and get on with it". The third key finding is that this reaction is considerably less likely amongst male owners of larger SMEs who have a degree-level qualification. This implies the competition authorities have to recognize that many SMEs are the victims of anti-competitive behaviour, but the latter's response to this reflects the diversity that characterizes the SME population.

Introduction

Competition policy, as framed by governments, is directed towards those firms with "market power". Because large firms are more likely than small firms to be able to influence market prices, it is the former that have been the focus of attention of national, and sometimes international, competition authorities.

The prime role of competition policy, certainly in the United Kingdom, has been to seek to benefit consumers, and to have large firms as its key target. In contrast, small and medium-sized enterprises (SMEs) are viewed as more likely to be the victims, rather than the perpetrators, of anti-competitive practices.

So, although there has been considerable research undertaken on the impact of competition policy upon (large) enterprises and upon consumers (see Motta 2004 for a review), there is almost no UK-based work that examines any link between competition policy and SMEs.

Small and Large Firms

Storey and Greene (2010) argue that, other than pure scale, SMEs are different from larger enterprises in several important respects. First, SMEs normally lack any form of market power. In other words, by changing their output, they are unable to influence prices in their marketplace. Second, SMEs are very unlikely to be able to restrict or eliminate the entry of new firms in their markets. So, if they develop a profitable niche, it is very unlikely that they will be able to prevent another firm entering that marketplace to compete against them. Third, SMEs lack individual credibility, especially when dealing with governments. So, although large firms may be consulted when, for example, new legislation is being considered and developed, this is much less likely for the individual SME. Finally, and perhaps most importantly, SMEs are not faceless corporations. They are normally owned and managed by the same individuals, rather than by salaried managers on behalf of shareholders. This means SMEs very clearly reflect the personality of the person or persons who own and manage them. Hence they are as diverse as any other group of human beings — with some seeking rapid growth whilst others are clear "lifestylers".

In short, SMEs are not scaled-down versions of larger firms. Their owners have a multiplicity of different objectives, they lack market power, and sometimes access to resources. But they can be innovative, light on their feet, and flexible; and it is these characteristics that enable them to compete with firms of all sizes, but in a myriad of different ways.

The central point of this distinction between large firms and SMEs is that, if public policymakers wish to create a competitive marketplace in which both consumers and SMEs thrive, they have to take steps that differ from those that they would take in a marketplace dominated by large firms.

Apart from pure scale, SMEs differ from large firms in three ways. The first key difference between firms of different sizes is reflected in risk. The larger firm, because it is likely to be operating in many markets, providing a wide range of goods and services, is more able to absorb losses in one part of its portfolio than a smaller firm with a single product, selling into a single market, possibly even to a single customer. The converse is that a small firm which has a single product, market, or customer where demand is buoyant can exhibit exceptionally rapid growth because all its eggs are in a single basket. Research on SMEs that exhibit rapid growth, however, suggests that after "bursts" of growth, they tend to return to the norm, partly because their growth stimulates entry of new firms (see Parker et al. 2010; Delmar et al. 2003). The response by individual SME owners to this issue is also likely to differ markedly between firms. Some may expand in order to diversify and so spread the risk, whereas others will forgo the opportunity to grow in order to avoid risk. Governments have recognized this issue in policy formulation. In the area of business advice to SMEs, more intensive assistance may be provided to firms which seek to grow. Some governments have also acknowledged that, when business failure has occurred, there may be benefits to society in enabling business owners to more easily discharge their responsibilities and start another enterprise. This reflects a belief that business owners learn from previous experience and that society benefits from them returning to being a business owner.

The second key difference between large firms and SMEs is that, as a group, the latter are likely to exhibit a wide variety of objectives in running their business. Some seek rapid growth whereas others are "lifestylers". This diversity of objectives magnifies the performance variation that is characteristic of SMEs. In an ideal world, governments would have different policies directed towards different groups of SMEs but, in practice, governments find this difficult. Instead, "one size fits all" is viewed as both equitable and administratively convenient. Unfortunately, this approach is never likely to satisfy the heterogeneous SME sector, particularly when the "one size" that is chosen is viewed by SME owners as that appropriate primarily for large firms.

A third key difference is that SMEs differ massively from large firms in terms of their ability to influence public policy formulation. SMEs often view legislation as a disproportionate "burden" upon them because their unit cost of compliance is considerably higher than that of larger firms. The effect of these "burdens" is argued to reduce the rate at which firms are founded, to slow the growth of existing firms, and to raise the closure rate. This seems to induce two very different responses from SME owners — again reflecting the heterogeneity of the sector. Some owners respond by deliberately ignoring the matter, whilst others are simply unaware of changes, finding that the running of their business is sufficiently challenging without the additional complication of responding to new legislation. A third response, by what we will later refer to as "Networkers", is to join an organization which both makes them aware of current and expected future changes and but also helps them respond in a cost-effective manner. Such organizations might be small business lobby organizations or they may be trade associations that deal with all sizes of firm in a specific sector.

The SME Dimension of Competitiveness, Competition, and Competition Policy

The above contextual review suggests that SME owners are keenly aware of the presence of competitors in their marketplace. Even if they do not currently face intense competition, SME owners recognize there is always the risk that a competitor may emerge.

This, of course, is the case for larger firms as well as for SMEs. But where SMEs differ is that the large firm is more likely to have "deep-pockets" enabling them to fight the competition, whereas most SMEs do not have access to such funds. For them, any new competition could easily be terminal.

The issue facing policymakers, however, is that whilst new competition may be the death knell for an individual SME, it may also be a powerful stimulant to competitiveness in an economy. Disney et al. (2003) show that, amongst manufacturing single establishment firms — which are typically SMEs — 100 per cent of all productivity gains came about because the new entrants were more productive than those that exited. There was no productivity gain amongst surviving firms. In contrast, there were productivity gains amongst surviving multi-establishment firms (which are typically larger firms). Finally, the same study also showed that market competition enhances both the level and growth of productivity.

This implies that competition enhances competitiveness, but also that increasing productivity amongst SMEs is more likely to result in firm exits than is the case for larger firms. In short, the price to be paid for higher productivity amongst SMEs is business closure.

Competition, however, must be fair and not be an abuse of market power (Vickers 2005). Given the nature of SMEs, it is much more likely that they will be the abused party — the "victims" — than in the case of larger firms. In this sense, SMEs might seem to be the obvious beneficiary of policies intended to ensure markets are competitive and fair.

In practice, many SME owners are unlikely to be easily persuaded that competition policy is in their best interests for several reasons. First, many recognize that enhancing competition could undermine the viability of their own business. They may also recognize that the objective of policy is to improve benefits for consumers rather than producers, of whatever size. Second, many SME owners are fundamentally suspicious of all aspects of government, and view policy changes as yet another "burden". Third, many SME owners, although affected by unfair competition, will be unaware of their rights of appeal. Even if they are aware, many will not view the "hassle" of appeal as worthwhile. Finally, many SME owners will not be able to distinguish between competition which is fair, but damaging to them, and that which is unfair.

Deriving Hypotheses

The previous discussion suggests that SMEs would be expected to be keenly aware of competitive threats from large firms, from other SMEs, and also from potential new entrants. This distinguishes them from large firms which are more likely to be insulated from competition from SMEs. It also emphasized the diversity amongst SMEs and the expectation that awareness of competition and their response to it would vary between "types" of SMEs.

Our expectation is that SME owners who are well-educated, well-informed, and running growing businesses in "modern" sectors are likely to respond to issues of fair and unfair competition in a different way from those who we will later refer to as "Isolationists". The former are more likely to be competitive, to be able to distinguish between fair and unfair competition, and to be prepared to take action where that competition is thought by them to be unfair. In contrast, the "Isolationists" are more likely to "just get on with it". We hypothesize:

H1: Awareness of, and Response to, Competition Varies Between "Types" of SMEs

A core belief of competition authorities is that more competition is desirable and in the interests of the consumer, subject to such competition being "fair". For this reason we hypothesize that SMEs would view their markets as being highly competitive and hence risky for them.

H2: SMEs Regard Their Marketplace as Risky

Nevertheless, even if SMEs view their marketplace as risky, it may be difficult for them to assess whether this risk stems from their competitors anti-competitive trading practices or because their competitors have a real competitive advantage.

Ideally we would like to assess the reported experience of SMEs, of what they regard as anti-competitive practices and then to reach a judgement upon whether such practices are fair or unfair. However, the first step is to assess the scale and nature of their trading experience. We hypothesize:

H3: SMEs will have Considerable Experience of "Unfair Trading Practices" such as Price Fixing, Cartels, or Collusive Tendering Arrangements

The extent to which the competition authorities are able to respond to the concerns of an individual SME depends heavily on the extent to which instances are reported to them. However, it is widely recognized that SMEs frequently seek to minimize their involvement with organs of government that they view as bureaucratic and slow-moving (Storey and Greene 2010).

The under-reporting of anti-competitive practices amongst small firms is expected to be widespread for several reasons. The first is that many SME owners take the view that "we are too small to be of interest". Second, they might be intimidated by the time and need for documentation of the evidence base. Finally, there may be a concern that the case would take so long to resolve that they could be out of business well beforehand. We hypothesize:

H4: Considerable Under-reporting of Unfair Trading Practices is the Norm for SMEs

Having experienced unfair trading practices and, if H_4 is confirmed, decided against reporting this to the authorities, the SME is faced with a range of options. The first is to ignore it, but the consequences could be disastrous. The second is to address it in a competitive manner. The expectation is that SMEs will be more likely to "fight fire with fire" in the marketplace for the product or service. We hypothesize:

H5: If They Experienced Anti-Competitive Trading Practices, SMEs will Respond to Them in the Marketplace

The Sample: Derivation and Characteristics

To test these hypotheses, 500 UK SMEs were interviewed by telephone between 18 and 31 May 2005. The sample was structured to reflect the sectoral and geographical distribution of UK SMEs, as reflected in official data based on VAT (value added tax) registrations. The survey work was undertaken by NOP World for Citigate Dewe Rogerson.

The broad characteristics of the firms are shown in Table 4.1. The first column shows the sectoral distribution, which broadly parallels official data.

However, since experience of competition, fair or unfair, was likely to increase with business duration, it was decided to weight the sample to focus more heavily on longer established, rather than new, businesses. Reflecting this choice, the age distribution of the firms shown in column 4 of Table 4.1 shows the sample contained a

TABLE 4.1
Characteristics of the Sampled Firms

Sector	%	Age of Business	%	Number of Employees	%
Manufacturing	13	Up to 5 years	18	Less than 10	46
Wholesale/Retail	20	5–10 years	17	10–49	43
Professional business services	29	10–20 years	21	50–249	11
Catering/leisure	7	More than 20 years	43		
Motor trades	8				
Construction	11				
Others	13				
TOTAL	100	TOTAL	100	TOTAL	100

high proportion of mature businesses, with 43 per cent being more than twenty years old. Finally, although 46 per cent of sampled firms had less than ten workers, this is actually an underestimate of the proportion of UK SMEs of this size.

In short, the sample was a sectoral representation of UK SMEs, but weighted disproportionately towards larger and more mature firms.

The personal characteristics of the business owners are shown in Table 4.2. Column 2 shows that 37 per cent of respondents had a degree. This is considerably higher than expected, given that Fraser (2005) had earlier found that only 23 per cent of UK small business owners had a degree qualification, and perhaps is indicative of the sample being weighted more heavily towards longer established, and larger, businesses. The latter is also likely to explain the larger than expected "older" business founders shown in column 6. Finally, column 8 shows that about one third of business owners had previously or currently owned another business. This is also slightly higher than might be expected.

In terms of gender, Fraser (2005) had previously reported that 19 per cent of UK businesses were owned by females, so the current sample had a comparatively higher proportion of female owners. Although Fraser did not report on prior business experience, the results in

TABLE 4.2
Characteristics of Business Respondents

Education	%	Gender	%	Age	%	In Business Before	%
Degree or higher	37	Male	71	16–24	4	Yes	31
Vocational Qualifications	17	Female	29	25–34	14	No	69
'A' Level, 'O' Level or none	34			35–44	26		
				45–54	33		
				55–64	17		
				65+	4		
				Not specified	4		
TOTAL	100	TOTAL	100	TOTAL	100	TOTAL	100

Table 4.2 were broadly in line with those of Greene et al. (2008), who report that about one third of business founders had some prior experience as an owner.

Testing the Hypotheses

H1: Awareness of, and Response to, Competition Varies Between "Types" of SMEs

In examining Hypotheses H_2 to H_5 we also identified where there were marked differences between "types" of SMEs.

H2: SMEs Regard Their Marketplace as Risky

Table 4.3 shows that SMEs reported a more mixed picture than might have been expected of the nature of competition that they face. Broadly, similar proportions of SMEs viewed their marketplace as "very safe" (11 per cent) as those who viewed it as "very risky" (10 per cent). However, on balance, more firms were likely to report their markets to be safer rather than riskier, which may be a surprise given the high risk of closure amongst SMEs. On balance, therefore, support for H_2 was weak.

There was some variations in the replies. Firms that were five to ten years old were the most likely to view their market as risky. Those who thought their market was safe were much more likely to be firm owners who viewed their enterprise as competitive. The

TABLE 4.3
Market Hostility and Business Risk Index

	%	Comments
1. Very safe	11	Owners who thought their firms were highly competitive were much more likely to regard their market as safe.
2. Fairly safe	24	No clear variation by firm type
3 Neither	38	No clear variation by firm type
4. Fairly risky	16	No clear variation by firm type
5. Very risky	10	Owners who were most likely to view their market as risky were those whose firms were between five to ten years old.

latter finding implies that SME owners are less concerned with an "objective" measure of competition, and more concerned with how their firm is able to respond to that competition.

H3: SMEs will have Considerable Experience of "Unfair Trading Practices"

The reported awareness of anti-competitive practices such as price fixing, cartels, or tender agreements is reported in Table 4.4. We also asked business owners how they would score their own business in terms of its interaction with other businesses and their owner, where 1 = "I try to run my business in isolation" and 5 = "I am an avid networker". We then defined an "Isolationist" as someone who scored 1 or 2, and a "Networker" as someone who scored 4 or 5.

Awareness was, overall, not high with significantly more firms being wholly unaware of such practices than those that were strongly aware. Awareness was highest amongst firms in manufacturing and construction, and amongst those owners who viewed themselves as "Networkers" rather than "Isolationists". In contrast, awareness was lowest amongst firms in business and professional services.

TABLE 4.4
Responses to "Are You Aware of Anti-Competitive Practices (Price Fixing, Cartels, Tender Agreements, etc.) in Your Industry?"

	%	Comments
Strongly agree	19	Those most likely to be strongly aware are owners in manufacturing (40%) and construction (40%). Networkers (23%) were more likely to be aware than Isolationists.
Somewhat agree	14	
Neither agree nor disagree	18	
Somewhat disagree	19	
Wholly disagree	28	Those most likely to be wholly unaware were those in professional and business services (41%).
Don't know	3	

Of course awareness may strongly reflect hearsay — perhaps reflected in the result that awareness was high amongst "Networkers" and low amongst "Isolationists". An alternative test is to ask whether the respondents themselves had ever been a victim of such anti-competitive practices.

The results of this are reported in Table 4.5, which shows that 44 per cent of respondents had never themselves been a victim of anti-competitive practices, suggesting much stronger awareness of such practices than personal experience.

Those most likely to report being a victim are low competitiveness, high-risk businesses located in Northern England and Scotland. Victims were also more concentrated in retail and wholesale trades.

TABLE 4.5
Responses to "Have You Been a Victim of Price Fixing or
Other Anti-Competitive Practices?"

	%	Comments
Strongly agree Agree somewhat	12 11	• 19% of high-risk businesses "strongly agreed" they had been a victim. • 36% of low competitiveness firms, to some extent, agreed, compared with 21% of high competitiveness firms. • 27% of Northern England and Scotland firms, to some extent, agreed they had been victims compared with 17% in the south of England. • 32% of wholesale/retail firms agreed to some extent that they had been victims, compared with 17% of business and professional services firms.
Neither agree nor disagree	14	
Disagree somewhat Strongly disagree	16 44	• Only 33% of high risk businesses disagreed strongly that they had been a victim. • 63% of high competitiveness firms, to some extent, disagreed compared with only 40% of low competitiveness firms.
Don't know	3	

Conversely, those least likely to report being a victim are businesses that the owner views as competitive.

A third approach is to seek to assess the severity or impact of anti-competitive practices. SME owners were asked if they felt that anti-competitive behaviour was damaging their business. Their answers are shown in Table 4.6. It shows that about a quarter of firms agreed, to some extent, that anti-competitive behaviour was damaging their business. However, more than twice this proportion disagreed.

Again there were important differences according to firm type. For example, wholesale and construction firms were most likely, and business and professional services the least likely, to report damage. The SME owners viewing their own firm as competitive but risky were most likely to report damage.

Overall, the support for H3 was weaker than might have been expected. Awareness of unfair trading practices was limited to perhaps 40 per cent of SMEs, and strong personal experience was limited to perhaps 12 per cent of firms. This is broadly similar to the 14 per cent who reported personal evidence of anti-competitive behaviour damaging their business.

TABLE 4.6
Responses to "Anti-Competitive Behaviour is Damaging Our Business"

	%	Comments
Strongly agree	14	Firms most likely to strongly agree were those that recognize their own business as risky (25%), those who viewed themselves as highly competitive (29%), and those firms in wholesale and construction.
Agree somewhat	10	
Neither agree nor disagree	22	
Disagree somewhat	22	
Strongly disagree	29	Those firms most likely to strongly disagree were in professional and business services.
Don't know	3	

H4: Considerable Under-reporting of Unfair Trading Practices is the Norm for SMEs

Faced with unfair competition, SME owners can take a number of actions. Table 4.7 reports responses — 43 per cent of SME owners stated that they would use competitive strategies to respond to it; 27 per cent said they would ignore it; and only 22 per cent responded that they would report it. The majority of SME owners would therefore seek to respond, but not by involving the authorities. Instead they said they would "raise their own game". This is broadly in line with the expectations underpinning H4.

TABLE 4.7
Responses to "Faced with Price Fixing, What Would You Do?"

	%	Comments
Report it	22	25% of owners with a degree said they would report it.
		26% of larger SMEs said they would report it.
		26% of firms in the south of England said they would report it.
		27% of wholesale retail firms said they would report it.
		25% of male-owned businesses said they would report it, compared with 15% of female-owned businesses.
Ignore it	27	35% of those owners with Higher National Diplomas (HNDs) or lower would ignore it.
		34% of micro-firms would ignore it.
		35% of manufacturers said they would ignore it.
Use competitive strategies	43	48% of owners with a degree said they would respond competitively.
		48% of larger SMEs said they would respond competitively.
		55% of female-owned businesses said they would use competitive strategies compared with 38% of male-owned businesses.
Don't know	8	

However, there continued to be differences in the emphasis of response between different types of SME owners. Those who said they would report price fixing were SMEs owned by graduates, larger SMEs, those located in the south of England, and those owned by a male. Those most likely to ignore it were micro-firms, those owned by individuals with low or zero educational qualifications, and those in the manufacturing sector. Those most likely to competitively respond to price fixing were owners of larger businesses, those with a degree, and those owned by a female.

What therefore seems clear is that only about one in five SMEs affected by price fixing would report it, implying that perhaps the scale of recorded price fixing in an economy is considerably less than the reality.

The likelihood of reporting again varies according to "types" of SMEs and according to the nature of the unfair practice. Table 4.8 shows, for example, that those most likely to report price fixing were male-owned firms, in the south of England, and in wholesale/ retail, whereas those most likely to report collusion were less competitive businesses, those where the owner had higher educational qualifications, and those in construction. Finally, those most likely to report pressure to postpone billing, predatory pricing, and entry prohibition were located in the wholesale/retail sectors.

TABLE 4.8
SMEs Most Likely to Report Unfair Competitive Practices

	%	Comments
Price fixing	22	Male-owned, larger firms, those in the south of England and those in wholesale/retail
Collusion	31	Less competitive businesses owned by founders with higher educational qualifications, construction businesses
Postpone billing	24	Wholesale/retail businesses
Predatory pricing	9	Wholesale/retail businesses
Entry prohibition	24	Wholesale/retail businesses

H5: If They Experienced Anti-Competitive Trading Practices, SMEs will Respond to Them in the Marketplace

Table 4.9 shows that, faced with all forms of anti-competitive practices, SME owners said they would choose to "take them on" using competitive strategies, rather than report it. The only unfair practice where reporting was almost as likely as "taking them on" was when faced by "collusion between more than one company to set tender prices themselves". Finally, the anti-competitive practice most likely to be ignored was "where a large competitor is trying to push the SME out of the market by cutting their prices in the short

TABLE 4.9
Responses to "What Would You Do When Faced with the Following Anti-Competitive Practices?"

	Report It %	Ignore It %	Use Competitive Strategies %	Don't Know %
Price fixing of products or services by your competitors	22	27	43	8
Collusion between more than one company to set tender prices themselves	31	24	34	11
Being forced to postpone billing for products or services supplied	24	19	37	21
A large competitor tries to push you out of the market by cutting prices in the short term and not covering their costs.	9	37	49	5
A large company using discriminatory pricing to stop new entrants coming into the market.	24	28	40	9

term and not covering their costs". It is interesting that, whilst such predatory pricing is the focus of much competition law, it is the anti-competitive practice that SME owners say they would be most likely to ignore. This could be taken as a further illustration of competition policy reflecting the focus of interest of large, rather than small, firms.

At the opposite end of the spectrum, Table 4.10 shows those SME owners who were most likely to respond to anti-competitive practices by ignoring them. These were newer, microenterprises, firms that view themselves as being less competitive than their rivals, and those owned by "Isolationists". The sectors in which ignoring such practices was most common were construction, manufacturing, and the motor trades.

Finally, Table 4.11 shows those SME owners who said they were most likely to respond to anti-competitive practices by using competitive strategies. Those most likely to respond by "taking them on" were larger SMEs, those owned by owners with a degree, and those in the manufacturing sector.

TABLE 4.10
Responses to "Would You Ignore an Anti-Competitive Practice?"

	%	Comments
Price fixing	27	Business founders with low educational qualifications, microenterprises, manufacturing enterprises
Collusion	24	Microenterprises, businesses run by isolated founders, construction businesses
Postpone billing	19	Businesses in motor trades
Predatory pricing	37	Businesses run by isolated founders, microenterprises, businesses in manufacturing and in motor trades, younger businesses
Entry prohibition	28	Low-risk businesses, less competitive businesses, microenterprises, motor trade businesses, long established businesses

TABLE 4.11
Responses to "When Would You Respond to
Anti-Competitive Practices by Using Competitive Strategies?"

	%	Comments
Price fixing	43	Firms with owners having degree, larger SMEs, female-owned SMEs
Collusion	34	Firms owned by "Networkers", firms owned by those without prior business ownership experience, young businesses, and those in motor trade and manufacturing
Postpone billing	37	Larger SMEs, manufacturing
Predatory pricing	49	Larger SMEs
Entry prohibition	40	Firms with owners having a degree, larger SMEs, firms between five to ten years old

Conclusions and Interpretations

Our key empirical finding is that one third of SMEs are aware of anti-competitive practices and one quarter have actually been a victim of such practices.

In this event, by far the most frequent reaction of SME owners is to retaliate by "taking them on". The second most likely reaction is to ignore it — with this being considerably more likely than the third option of reporting it.

However, what has been stressed continually is that there is no "typical SME". It is clear that reporting attitudes and reactions differs according to a whole variety of factors, such as the size of the SME, the sector in which it operates, and the personal characteristics of the owner.

To illustrate, the SME owner most likely to ignore anti-competitive behaviour is the owner of a micro-firm, with low or zero educational qualifications, in the construction, motor trade, or manufacturing sector, and who recognizes that his or her firm is uncompetitive. This owner frequently regards him- or herself as an "Isolationist".

This type of owner is radically different from one who responds competitively to the threat. Such an individual is more likely to be the owner of a larger SME, a "Networker" rather than an "Isolationist", female, and the owner of a young, rather than a mature, business.

We now turn to interpreting the implications of these findings for those delivering competition policy, but seeking to do so through the lens of an SME, rather than a large firm.

Given that perhaps one quarter of SMEs have some experience of anti-competitive practices, and one third are aware of them in their sector, the topic is worthy of further investigation, if only because these figures imply large numbers of firms are affected. What is less clear is whether this experience is of unfair competitive practice or whether it is merely uncompetitive firms bemoaning the presence of more competitive rivals. We suspect it is both, but have little idea which of the two is the more important. This points towards the need for small-scale case analyses.

Our second key finding is that reporting such practices is not the typical reaction of an SME. Most prefer to either ignore it or to respond to it directly. Policymakers therefore need to know more about whether this is because firms are unaware of their rights or whether, even if they were aware, they would still choose to avoid time-consuming legal involvement. The evidence is that different types of SME owners will respond in very different ways. This implies that a campaign to raise awareness targeted towards those groups most likely to be responsive could be beneficial — although such an approach does not necessarily mean that the most serious cases are always addressed.

Third, whilst SME owners are clearly aware of the benefits of competition to the economy, very few think that enhanced competition would benefit their own firm. This means that a campaign to "sell" the benefits of competition would be very difficult since individual SME owners would not see this as being in their own interest.

Governments, therefore, face a dilemma in enforcing competition policy. They recognize that heightened levels of competition can play a key role in leading to higher productivity. On the other hand, the consequences of such policies are likely to lead to higher levels of exits amongst SMEs than amongst larger firms. The challenge is to ensure that fair competition is promoted and unfair competition is outlawed.

REFERENCES

Delmar, Frederic, Per Davidsson, and William B. Gartner. "Arriving at the High Growth Firm". *Journal of Business Venturing* 18, no. 2 (2003): 189–216.

Disney, Richard, Jonathan Haskel, and Ylva Heden. "Restructuring and Productivity Growth in UK Manufacturing". *Economic Journal* 113, no. 489 (2003): 666–94.

Frankish, J., R. Roberts, and David Storey. "Do Entrepreneurs Really Learn? Or Do They Just Tell Us That They Do?" *Industrial and Corporate Change* 22, no. 1 (2008): 73–106.

Fraser, Stuart. *Finance for Small and Medium-Sized Enterprises: A Report on the 2004 UK Survey of SME Finances*. London: Bank of England, 2005.

Greene, Frances J., Kevin F. Mole, and David Storey. *Three Decades of Enterprise Culture: Entrepreneurship, Economic Regeneration and Public Policy*. Basingstoke: Palgrave MacMillan, 2008.

Hart, P.E. and N. Oulton. "Job Creation and Destruction in the Corporate Sector: The Relative Importance of Births, Deaths and Survivors". National Institute of Social and Economic Research, Discussion Paper, No. 134 (1998).

Hull, L. and R. Arnold. *New Zealand Firm Growth as Change in Turnover*. Wellington: Ministry of Economic Development, 2004.

Motta, Massimo. *Competition Policy: Theory and Practice*. Cambridge: Cambridge University Press, 2004.

Parker, Simon C., David Storey, and Arjen van Witteloostuijn. "What Happens to Gazelles? The Importance of Dynamic Management Strategy". *Small Business Economics* 35, no. 2 (2010): 203–26.

Storey, David. "The Competitive Experience of UK SMEs: Fair and Unfair". *Small Enterprise Research* 17, no. 1 (2009–10): 19–29.

Storey, David and Francis J. Greene. *Small Business and Entrepreneurship*. London: Pearson, 2010.

Vickers, John. "Abuse of Market Power". *Economic Journal* 115, no. 504 (2005): F244–61.

Watson, J. *SME Performance: Separating Myth from Reality*. Cheltenham: Edward Elgar, 2010.

5

COMPETITION REGULATOR ENGAGEMENT WITH THE SMALL BUSINESS SECTOR

Warren Mundy and Paul Davidson

What constitutes "best practice" in terms of the interaction that a competition agency has with its own national small business constituency? This chapter discusses what "engagement" is, provides an overview of the general concepts and issues involved in developing an engagement framework, and examines some of the actual tools used in engagement, with a specific focus on Australian examples.

Small businesses can be both the victims of anti-competitive practices and the perpetrators of offences against consumers. Engagement by competition regulators with small businesses is both about their rights and their responsibilities, but should these be approached separately or holistically?

Research suggests that regulators often wish to act in certain ways to deliver upon their regulator objectives but find that statute law either prohibits or fails to facilitate sound engagement approaches. Discretion, though, must be weighed against predictability, transparency, and accountability. The approaches to the issue of discretion taken by different nations, and how this relates to small businesses are examined.

Introduction

Despite a plethora of inquiries into regulatory burdens, good regulatory design, and the regulatory circumstances in many industries and across a wide range of countries, little attention has been paid to how regulators interact with businesses, especially small ones. Yet this is critical, as the Queensland Chamber of Commerce and Industry of Australia noted:

> "... in many cases it is the approach of regulators — their communication, advice and support, enforcement and reporting requirements — that have the most significant impact on business owner[s]" (PC 2013, p. 37).

The characteristics of small businesses can warrant a different approach to engagement by regulators, including by agencies tasked with promoting competition and consumer protection. As noted by the Council of Small Business Organisations of Australia (COSBOA):

> ... The previous [Australian Competition and Consumer Commission (ACCC)] chairman showed good skills and abilities in communicating with large businesses, but in our view he showed no understanding in how to communicate with the small business community. He did not understand the difference between big and small business, indeed we always felt that he demanded that small business have the same skills and abilities as big business (COSBOA 2013, p. 5).

Although the competition law obligations of businesses vary between countries, the scope of matters that can attract the attention of competition regulators is always narrower for small businesses. However, less attention should not be paid by regulators to the quality of their engagement practices. Indeed, the nature of small businesses, especially in relation to their compliance capacity, behoves all regulators, competition and otherwise, to take particular care in their small business engagement activities.

Since its establishment in 1998, the Australian Government's microeconomic policy and regulatory advisory body, the Productivity Commission, has conducted a range of inquiries into the design, enforcement, and implementation of regulations. Yet despite the importance of regulator engagement, only recently has the Australian Government asked the Productivity Commission to specifically focus on how regulators work, impact, and interact with businesses, a process which has resulted in the report entitled *Regulator Engagement with Small Business* (PC 2013). This chapter applies the findings and insights from that report to the activities of competition and consumer protection regulators — indeed in many countries, including Australia, these activities are undertaken by the same regulatory agency.

In preparing this chapter, the authors have reviewed the competition laws and associated engagement practices of a range of APEC (Asia-Pacific Economic Cooperation) countries. Consistent with the findings of the Productivity Commission for Australian regulators in the broad, the larger, more mature competition regulators generally have better developed engagement practices. That said, the authors have not been able to identify any specific competition regulator that we consider to be best practice or a model for engagement with small businesses for others to replicate.

There is significant variation in the maturity of APEC competition regulators, and in the laws they administer, which influences their actual engagement approach. For instance, if a regulator and the law are relatively new, the principal goal for the regulator will be informing businesses of their rights and obligations and, equally, demonstrating that there will be consequences from breaches of the law. Thus, there may initially be a greater focus on enforcement. As the regime matures and the need to demonstrate the regime's "teeth" ebbs, the regulator's emphasis should be placed on fostering (and maintaining) compliance by businesses and educating businesses.

The following discussion provides a guide to, or at least a way to think about, engagement approaches for regulators and policymakers as their competition law frameworks develop.

What are the Interactions of Competition Regulators with Small Businesses?

Competition law covers a wide range of interactions between businesses as well as between businesses and consumers, but tends to particularly focus on the activities of firms that have, in many cases, "a significant degree of market power". How this is defined varies. For example, in Vietnam, a dominant position for the purpose of merger laws or activities that might lead to the creation of such circumstances constitutes more than 30 per cent market share. In Malaysia, a dominant position "means a situation in which one or more enterprises possess such significant power in a market to adjust prices or outputs or trading terms, without effective constraint from competitors or potential competitors". Small businesses, by their very nature, are unlikely to fall foul of such laws. However, they may be victims of the abuse of market power by larger firms in their capacity as competitors, suppliers to those firms, or consumers of the larger firm's output. Thus, the role of the competition regulator is largely one of educating small businesses about their rights and pursuing breaches by larger firms. In pursuing these ends, competition regulators need to ensure that their data gathering and prosecutorial activities do not impose disproportionate costs or risks on affected small businesses.

Competition laws also deal with arrangements that firms enter into with each other that affect competition. Whilst some of these arrangements *per se* may be illegal, such as the prohibition in the Australian Competition and Consumer Act 2010 (Commonwealth) against resale price maintenance (Section 48), there can be significant uncertainty as to whether other arrangements between two or more businesses would unlawfully impact on competition. From a small business perspective, collusion with competitors is likely to be the principal concern, where, if a breach of the law is established, the consequences for the businesses involved can be profound.

The challenge for the regulator is thus to educate small businesses about what conduct is acceptable, and if this is uncertain, to reduce this uncertainty; and, in the event of a breach, to have in place proportionate, cost effective strategies that remedy the breach and promote future compliance.

An example of one simple way to reduce uncertainty can be found in the system of Canadian "binding options". Section 124.1 of the Canadian Competition Act 1985 permits any person to apply to the Commissioner, with supporting information, for an opinion in relation to proposed conduct or practice that the applicant proposes to engage in, and the Commissioner may provide a written opinion for the applicant's guidance. If all facts provided are accurate, a written opinion is binding on the Commissioner, so long as the facts remain substantially unchanged and the conduct or practice is carried out substantially as proposed.

Competition regulators are also concerned about the behaviour of individual firms in dealing with their customers. In general, obligations are placed upon businesses, large and small, not to act in a false, misleading, or unconscionable way, and to avoid unfair contract terms in their dealing with each other and with final consumers. With regard to consumer protection, the task of the competition regulator is similar to anti-competitive behaviour — education and enforcement.

Specific obligations towards dealings with consumers are often set out in separate legislation and may be enforced by separate consumer protection or fair trading agencies. However, consumer protection often falls within the scope of competition regulators' activities, and there are synergies between the types of engagement with small business.

Competition Law Compliance Challenges of Small Businesses

The Productivity Commission identified a range of compliance challenges for small businesses (PC 2013, pp. 67–78). At the heart of many problems, and most germane to competition law regulators, is the small business operator's lack of capacity to understand and respond to what can be complex laws, often in stressful circumstances of potential enforcement action. Lack of awareness of compliance obligations is more likely if the "official language" is not the operator's first language, if the relevant law has recently changed, or if the business is newly established. Here, the regulator's approach can help resolve or exacerbate the problem:

> These people in small business do not have experts to assist them. They do not have paymasters, OH&S [occupational health and safety] experts, tax experts, health experts etc. These businesses are people who normally have very good skills in one or two areas and then are asked to be experts on a range of other issues. The behaviour of the regulator becomes a key to achieving compliance. If the regulator expects big business behaviour and knowledge from a small business then the regulator fails (COSBOA 2013, p. 3).

A survey by the Productivity Commission suggests many Australian regulators do not treat small businesses differently — 60 per cent of the regulators that responded indicated that they did not treat small businesses differently, 15 per cent indicated that they do so because they were required to by law, and many others because they chose to (PC 2013). Conversely, fair trading, tenancy or consumer protection regulators were more likely to make a distinction: 62 per cent treated them differently even though there was no explicit requirement to do so, whilst nearly 30 per cent treated them differently because they were required to do so. The survey also showed that in both groups, a significant majority of the regulators with a duty to treat small businesses differently did more than was strictly required.

Failure by regulators to differentiate between business size might not be a problem from a small business policy perspective if the processes have been designed with small businesses in mind. In all APEC countries, small businesses are the dominant type of business — for example, at least 95 per cent of businesses are classified as small in Australia, New Zealand, and Malaysia (ABS May 2013; Statistics New Zealand 2014; Department of Statistics Malaysia 2012). Research undertaken by the Productivity Commission (2012a; 2013) and the expressed concerns of small businesses suggest that many regulators, and those developing legislation, do not understand the compliance capacities of the bulk of these businesses.

Where regulators treated small businesses differently, the Productivity Commission survey found that 60 per cent tailored their education and training, while over 40 per cent used tailored forms and simplified requirements. This response was even more prevalent for fair trading, tenancy, and consumer protection regulators that treated small businesses differently — 62 per cent used simplified requirements, 54 per cent tailored forms, and 77 per cent tailored coaching. How regulators engage with small businesses is necessarily in part determined by their operating legislation. However, legislation is typically necessarily broad and is focused on the regulation's objectives, rather than the means by which those objectives are met. This leaves significant discretion to regulators in deciding how to balance their resourcing so as to provide information, education, and assistance. In other words, the regulators that chose to treat small businesses differently tend to do so through the way they engage.

There has been a strong theme in the academic and public policy literature over the last decade or so that giving regulated businesses the greatest possible opportunity to design their own compliance framework to achieve the required outcomes minimizes the associated regulatory costs (see, for example, Gunningham and Grabosky 1998; PC 2012*b*). Whilst it is desirable for small businesses to be consulted in the design and implementation of regulation when it comes to enforcement, the Productivity Commission found that they exhibit a strong preference for being told what they need to do to achieve compliance, as opposed to being left on their own to achieve an optimal regulatory strategy for their business (PC 2013, pp. 14, 71, 88).

Indeed, small businesses have indicated their frustration in not being able to gain clear and direct guidance as to what constitutes compliant behaviour. The regulator response of "we can't give you legal advice, you need to work out for yourself what is required" came in for particular criticism. The Queensland Chamber of Commerce and Industry described the result as small businesses "… either end up being noncompliant or have to seek costly legal/ expert advice from consultants" (PC 2013, p. 88). Whilst assistance *may* be available from other businesses and industry associations, such a legalistic approach is both unnecessary from a legal perspective and unhelpful to the small business.

A Comment on Regulatory Agencies' Culture

The benefits a community extracts from its competition law framework depend primarily upon the quality of the law itself; the risk management approach of the regulator (namely, its targeting of its resources to areas of greatest risk whose mitigation has the potential greatest benefits); and the ways in which the regulator goes about dealing with businesses.

The regulator's culture, which embodies the implicit rules, beliefs, and expectations of behaviour under which regulatory officers operate, largely determines both their approach to risk management and engagement with business. Culture influences the regulator's perceptions of the skills and information required by its staff to do their jobs. Culture is also critical to the way the regulator exercises discretion in assessment of risks, responds to non-compliance, and uses enforcement tools. A regulator that views its role as enforcing regulation is more likely to impose unnecessary costs on business and the economy, than one that seeks to facilitate business activity whilst mitigating the risks posed to the community.

While a regulatory agency's culture ultimately depends on its leaders, governments can influence culture. For example, in its Autumn Statement of December 2012, the UK Government announced its intention to introduce a "growth duty" for some fifty-seven non-economic regulators. Whilst not directed at competition regulators, this obligation aimed to:

> ... incentivise regulators to make improvements to the business experience of regulation and foster a regulatory environment conducive to economic growth. To be clear, compliant growth is what is being sought, not non-compliant or illegal economic activity that undermines markets to the detriment of consumers, the environment and legitimate businesses (DBIS 2013, p. 7).

A regulatory culture that seeks to avoid unnecessary burdens for those regulated is not incompatible with a low tolerance for non-compliant behaviour. For example, regulators that deal with potentially costly or catastrophic outcomes need a culture that has a low tolerance of non-compliance, but can still aim to facilitate compliance through education, rather than purely through punitive action. Governments can also influence culture in a negative way. For example, adverse political reactions associated with an outcome being mitigated, even if compliance with a robust regulatory framework has been achieved, can make a regulator excessively risk averse.

Competition regulators generally do not deal with issues that pose substantial or catastrophic risks to the physical well-being of individuals, the community, or the environment. Furthermore, it is unlikely that the consequences of non-compliance with competition law by individual small businesses on the economy will be significant. Hence, competition regulators can generally take a less risk adverse stance. That said, widespread non-compliance can obstruct proper market development and function and deter consumers, suppressing growth. Yet, while the consequences of a heavy regulatory hand on one business may not be significant, if applied broadly, this too can suppress growth.

To promote growth, regulators need to find the balance that minimizes the cost of compliance for business, with sufficient threat of discovery and redress for non-compliant businesses to provide an incentive to comply. This points to a broad educative approach, including tailored sectoral advice where particular issues may arise on a permanent or temporary basis, coupled with strong enforcement and some approvals where allowed by law.

Towards Best Practice Engagement for Competition Regulators

There is potential for unnecessary regulatory burdens to be created by a regulator's approach through:

- **Ineffective communication:** lack of effective communication with business about regulatory requirements, including proposed changes; lack of guidance or inconsistent advice about what constitutes compliance.
- **Heavy-handed enforcement:** excessive prescriptiveness in interpreting regulations; rigid enforcement actions; an adversarial attitude to business owners; poor communication on why a breach was considered to have occurred, and what must be done to be compliant.
- **Unduly onerous compliance requirements:** excessive number of inspections or audits, given the business's compliance record or risk of an adverse outcome; unnecessary extensive reporting requirements; the supply of similar/same information to a number of government organizations.
- **Excessive licensing and approval processes:** unnecessary evidentiary or establishment requirements; excessive delays in processing licensing applications; unduly frequent re-registration processes (PC 2013, pp. 36–37).

As discussed, communication and enforcement are the most important areas of engagement for competition regulators. Routine inspections and reporting is much less common in relation to competition regulation than is the case, say, for areas of regulation involved with public safety, such as food standards and environmental protection. Competition regulators are also rarely involved in licensing and approvals of business activity for small businesses, although they can be for large businesses in relation to mergers and acquisitions. Given this, these last two issues are not discussed in this chapter.

Communication

Competition law is complicated. Competition regulators need to appreciate that they and other regulators are operating in an environment of a growing number and range of regulations of which small businesses need to be aware. In communicating regulatory requirements to small businesses, regulators should place a premium on simplicity, clarity, brevity, and accessibility — a small business is not just a big business on a smaller scale, but one that operates in a fundamentally different way, and may lack the time, knowledge, and often the motivation to understand complex legal issues (COSBOA 2013).

It is also important that competition regulators understand the consequences of extending their communication efforts too far. As the Harper Review of competition policy noted in relation to Australia's competition regulator, the ACCC:

> ... this important educative role can cross over into advocacy of particular policy positions. An advocacy role can compromise stakeholders' perceptions about the impartiality of the ACCC in its enforcement of the law ... the ACCC would continue to have a role in communicating to the public through the media, including explaining enforcement priorities, educating business about compliance, and publishing enforcement outcomes (Australian Government 2014, pp. 292–93).

Regulators' perceptions of good communication do not always coincide with those of small businesses. Figure 5.1 shows differences between the perceptions of Australian regulators and businesses of the usefulness of various communication approaches. In particular, regulators consider their websites to be one of the most effective means of communicating with small businesses. Small businesses, on the other hand, find regulator websites less useful than advice from third parties (such as accountants and solicitors, although third parties may find websites useful) or from other business owners. Industry associations have reported to the Productivity Commission that the quality of regulator websites varies substantially. Interestingly, Productivity Commission research shows social media was the information channel that small businesses least preferred.

Regulators should ensure that their engagement approach remains effective for small business people who are from non-dominant language backgrounds and/or have cultural perspectives that may impact on

FIGURE 5.1
Communication Approaches — Who Views Them as Effective?

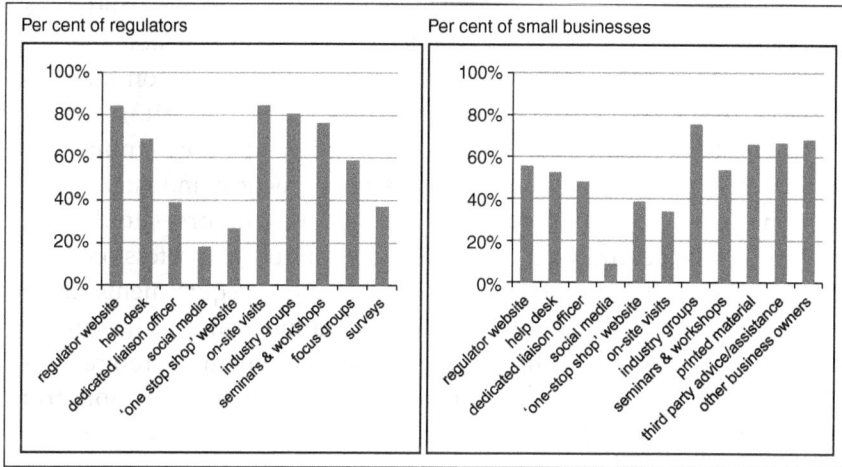

Source: PC (2013).

their response to regulatory activities. A good example is to be found in the approach of the New South Wales Office of Fair Trading in working with non-English speaking community organizations and media outlets to implement changes flowing from the enactment of the Australian Consumer Law in 2011 (PC 2013, p. 10).

Competition regulators can and should produce simple plain language guides such as the ACCC's *Small Business and the Competition and Consumer Act: Your Rights and Responsibilities* (ACCC 2012). Unfortunately, at the time of writing, this guide is not available in languages other than English, although most of Australia's state-based fair trading regulators provide information to businesses relating to consumer protection in a variety of languages.

The use of web-based and other electronic solutions by regulators disseminating information is increasing. Such approaches are particularly important as an after-hours access point for small businesses. Websites should have good information architecture so they are navigable and have clear hyperlinks. They should also use plain language and be visually attractive. Most importantly, they should answer the questions commonly asked by small businesses and provide the relevant information rather than simply provide links to legislation.

While web-based and other electronic solutions have the potential to deliver improved communication, appropriate strategies must be maintained for less computer literate business owners and those without Internet access. For example, recent estimates found around one quarter of Australian businesses in the accommodation and food services sector do not have Internet access (ABS June 2013).

Regulators should be prepared to modify their communication approach to ensure small businesses receive practical, industry-specific information on regulatory requirements. Regulators should also, as far as possible, draw on the networks of industry, professional, and business associations to communicate regulatory requirements and to ensure that advice is specific and readily implementable in different business environments. In addition to exploiting the preference of many small businesses for sourcing regulatory information from other businesses and industry associations, this approach removes any perceived liability associated with regulators providing business-specific (rather than general) advice. It also can provide greater impetus for compliance, as it identifies acceptable standards of behaviour for businesses. However, as many small businesses are not members of industry associations, such an approach should complement rather than substitute for a regulator's own interactions with small businesses.

Regulators can learn how to improve their performance through the use of stakeholder advisory groups, which can also act as a conduit for small businesses. The ACCC uses such a group as a means of identifying better ways to achieve compliance and ensure small businesses are (and consider that they are) adequately consulted on regulatory changes. Regulators should put in place systems to ensure that information collected through consultations with businesses is used to inform ongoing improvements in regulatory processes.

As noted above, competition regulator engagement is about both the rights of small businesses and their obligations. Communication strategies that seek to address these simultaneously should:

- reduce the time involved for the small business in receiving and assimilating the information and the number of regulatory interactions;

- create more cooperative relations between the regulator and the small business by the regulator showing the small business what it can do to protect them; and
- reduce the engagement cost for regulators.

Having a single body regulate both the competition and consumer functions further reduces the communication costs of both regulators and small businesses. These are in addition to more general benefits of combining these regulatory functions, identified most recently by the Australian review of competition policy (Australian Government 2014, p. 60).

Enforcement

A first step for governments concerned with the impact of regulator engagement on small businesses is to ensure that the regulatory frameworks — including the institutional and governance arrangements under which regulators operate — do not inhibit regulator adoption of best enforcement practices. Figure 5.2 shows the

FIGURE 5.2
The Enforcement Pyramid for Competition Regulators when Engaging with Small Businesses

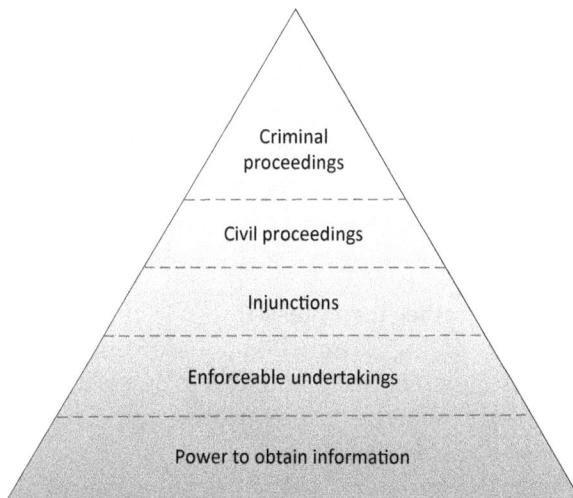

Criminal
proceedings

Civil proceedings

Injunctions

Enforceable undertakings

Power to obtain information

Source: Adapted from Ayers and Braithwaite (1992).

key suite of enforcement options that competition regulators should have available to them.

The tools available to regulators to enforce compliance are established in legislation or government directives and can shape their approach to engagement with businesses. Better outcomes for small businesses and the community are achieved when regulators have a range of tools that enable them to tailor their responses to breaches (or potential breaches) of regulation in a proportionate way, rather than having to rely solely on combative approaches such as initiating legal proceedings.

Table 5.1 suggests that even in more developed APEC economies, competition regulators may not have access to a full range of potential enforcement tools. The consequences of this are either sanctions that are disproportionate so compliance is achieved at excessive costs, or weak enforcement, increasing the likelihood of breaches.

Irrespective of the available tools, a regulator's enforcement approach will reflect the organization's overall posture. A regulator's approach can be:

- **Proactive rather than reactive:** Proactive approaches encourage, persuade, and highlight ways to achieve or require compliance before a breach occurs. They are preventative. In contrast, reactive approaches involve following up on complaints or adverse inspection results. Of course, in some respects, reactive approaches can have proactive effects where action to rectify a breach has a broader educative or deterrent effect.
- **Cooperative rather than combative:** Cooperative approaches focus on education, advice, working together, appealing to self-interest, and mutual interdependence. In contrast, combative approaches often involve the threat of severe penalties as the incentive for compliance. The central idea behind a combative approach is deterrence.
- **Discretionary rather than prescriptive:** While heavily influenced by the type of regulation being enforced, a discretionary approach is more tempered and able to assess alternative means of compliance, whereas a prescriptive approach entails strict enforcement and interpretation.

As noted above, regulator posture changes over time as the regulatory regime matures and as businesses become better aware of their

Table 5.1

Available Enforcement Tools to a Selection of APEC Competition Regulators

Tool	Australia	Malaysia	Mexico	New Zealand	Singapore	US and Canada	Vietnam
Merger control	✓	✓	✓	✓	✓	✓	✓
Power to obtain information	✓	✓	✓	✓	✓	✓	✓
Enforceable undertakings	✓	✓	✗	Limited	✗	✗	✓
Injunctions	✓	✗	✓	✓	✗	✓	Limited
Civil proceedings	✓	✓	✓	✓	✓	✓	Limited
Criminal proceedings	✓	✓	✗	✓	✓	✓	✗
Imposition of fine without court proceedings	✗	✓	✓	✗	✓	✗	✓

Sources: Various competition agency statutes, various competition agency websites; ICN (2008).

compliance obligations. Engagement approaches are also likely to change when major regulatory reforms are introduced.

It is inevitable that despite the best educative efforts of competition law regulators, some small businesses will be prosecuted for failure to comply with their competition law obligations. When it comes to litigation, government (of which competition regulators are a part) should behave in a reasonable fashion. This is because of the inherent power of government, the obligation of government to act in the public interest, and the large resource capacity of government. "Model litigant" rules typically require government agencies to act honestly and fairly, deal promptly with litigation, not seek to take advantage of an impecunious opponent, and not pursue unmeritorious legal points for tactical advantage. These rules are particularly important to allow small businesses to achieve fair outcomes and have been adopted by the New Zealand Commerce Commission (Commerce Commission, New Zealand 2009), as well as applying generally to all Australian government agencies — including the ACCC. The Productivity Commission has recently recommended that these rules be extended to all state, territory, and local government agencies across Australia (PC 2014, pp. 429–42).

Conclusion

The key to effective competition regulation of small businesses is for regulators and policymakers to give careful thought to the ultimate purpose of competition law — to improve the living standards of citizens though fostering competitive innovative markets, whilst deterring the use of market power to the detriment of consumers — and to the capacity of small businesses to comply.

The challenge for policymakers is fairly straightforward — provide clear institutional direction about regulatory directives, equip the regulator with a full set of appropriate tools, and ensure that regulator behaviour is monitored and directives and incentives adjusted over time where necessary.

The challenge to regulatory leaders is trickier. They must develop an effective culture that understands both what the organization is trying to achieve and the challenges that are faced by small businesses in compliance. A regulator must balance its resource use between education and enforcement, bearing in mind that over time, this balance may need adjusting.

Hopefully, this chapter provides some useful ideas to those faced with these challenges.

REFERENCES

Australian Bureau of Statistics (ABS). "Australian Industry, 2011–12". Cat. no. 8155.0. 28 May 2013.

———. "Summary of IT Use and Innovation in Australian Business, 2011–12". Cat. no. 8166.0. 20 June 2013.

Australian Competition and Consumer Commission (ACCC). *Small Business and the Competition and Consumer Act: Your Rights and Responsibilities*. Canberra: Australian Competition and Consumer Commission, 2012.

Australian Government. "Competition Policy Review: Draft Report", 22 September 2014. Available at <http://competitionpolicyreview.gov.au/draft-report/>.

Ayres, Ian and John Braithwaite. *Responsive Regulation: Transcending the Deregulation Debate*. Oxford: Oxford University Press, 1992.

Commerce Commission, New Zealand. "Model Litigant Policy", 2009. Available at <http://www.comcom.govt.nz/the-commission/commission-policies/model-litigantpolicy/> (accessed 15 October 2014).

Council of Small Business Australia (COSBOA). "Study into Regulator Engagement with Small Business: A Response from the Council of Small Business Organisations of Australia", March 2013.

Department for Business Innovation and Skills (DBIS), United Kingdom. *Government Response — Non-economic Regulators: Duty to Have Regard to Growth*, 2013. Available at <https://www.gov.uk/government/uploads/system/uploads/attachment_data/file/263265/13-1018-growth-consultation-response.pdf> (accessed 29 October 2014).

Department of Statistics Malaysia. *Economic Census 2011, Profile of Small and Medium Enterprises*, 2012.

Gunningham, Neil and Peter Grabosky. *Smart Regulation: Designing Environmental Policy*. Oxford: Oxford University Press, 1998.

International Competition Network (ICN). *International Competition Network Cartels Working Group, Subgroup 1 — General Framework: Setting of Fines for Cartels in ICN Jurisdictions*. Report to the 7th ICN Annual Conference, Kyoto, April 2008. Luxembourg: European communities, 2008.

Mundy, Warren. "Regulator Engagement with Small Business". In *Meeting the Globalisation Challenge: Smart and Innovative SMEs in a Globally Competitive*

Environment, edited by B. Kotey et al. Melbourne: Tilde University Press, 2014.

Productivity Commission (PC). *Performance Benchmarking of Australian Business Regulation: Role of Local Government as a Regulator*. Research Report. Canberra: Productivity Commission, 2012*a*.

———. *Regulatory Impact Analysis: Benchmarking*. Research Report. Canberra: Productivity Commission, 2012*b*.

———. *Regulator Engagement with Small Business*. Research Report. Canberra: Productivity Commission, 2013.

———. *Access to Justice Arrangements*. Inquiry Report No. 72. Canberra: Productivity Commission, 2014.

Statistics New Zealand. "New Zealand Business Demography Statistics: At February 2014", 2014. Available at <http://www.stats.govt.nz/browse_for_stats/businesses/business_characteristics/BusinessDemographyStatistics_HOTPFeb14.aspx> (accessed 18 March 2015).

6

DEVELOPING ONLINE COMPETITION LAW EDUCATION TOOLS FOR SMEs

Michael T. Schaper and Leela Cejnar

This chapter discusses some of the ways in which online information and education programmes can be developed to help small and medium-sized enterprises (SMEs) better understand their rights and obligations under competition law. It begins by briefly examining the rationale for doing so; outlines some of the characteristics of SME information-seeking behaviour; discusses some elements needed for a successful online education strategy; and then reviews different approaches today in a selection of countries. Most regulatory agencies provide only a very limited amount of SME-specific material online, largely based on print publications, although some more interactive tools are being developed. A detailed example is provided of the online education programmes developed by the Australian Competition and Consumer Commission. Some common themes in successful education campaigns include providing formal certification; using simple, direct, and relevant material; obtaining third party endorsement from industry associations; using effective evaluation tools; and developing a network of educational users.

Introduction

Is it possible to build a culture of a well-informed and well-educated SME (small and medium-sized enterprise) community that understands the major elements of a national competition law regime, the logic behind its creation, how individual firms should comply with the law, and how they are able to actively also exercise their rights within the law?

For many regulators, policymakers, and enforcement bodies, knowledge of competition law is a given. It is, after all, the key subject that they deal with on a day-to-day basis. However, for the owners, managers and staff of most SMEs, it is only one of many pieces of disparate information that they must understand, process, and comply with.

Competition law is also complex. It can contain many different precepts, involve a sophisticated understanding of both economics and law, and in many jurisdictions, may also contain numerous *per se* provisions and exemptions. It is not necessarily the easiest body of regulations for a layperson to absorb, understand, and apply in practice.

There is often substantial information asymmetry and many wrongful assumptions. Regulators who know the chapter and verse of their laws and regulations expect small businesses to be equally fluent in these requirements. Large firms, who have considerable internal resources and access to specialist advisers and trainers, know much more than their smaller counterparts, thus accentuating the disparities in their relative strengths. And whilst consumers are often the target of state-sponsored education campaigns designed to raise awareness of their rights, few equivalent campaigns focus on business owners/managers.

As a result, there is often a large gap between what SMEs do know about competition law, and what regulators and the law expect them to know (IFF Research 2015). Bridging these two is a concern for the small business sector, and the provision of appropriate information, delivered via the most effective channel, is one tool that can help rectify this gap.

Governments around the world have also been increasingly adopting online channels as their preferred means of communication and information dissemination with the business community. This has been driven by a number of factors: it is a relatively inexpensive communication tool; it has a potentially vast audience reach; and it allows firms to access only the information which they want or need.

What measures, then, have various competition regulators taken online to promote SME awareness and education? This chapter examines that issue. It begins by briefly examining the rationale for doing so; discusses current knowledge of SME information-seeking behaviour and some elements needed for a successful online education strategy; and then discusses different approaches today in a selection of countries. A detailed example is provided of the Australian online SME programme, followed by some suggestions for other agencies contemplating an online education strategy.

Why Bother to Educate SMEs?

There are sound arguments as to why the provision of online information and SME education programmes should be a major priority for most competition regulators.

To begin with, SMEs represent the vast majority of all trading enterprises in most, if not all, countries. As the other chapters in this book have pointed out, micro-, small-, and medium-sized firms represent more than 90 per cent of businesses in most Asia-Pacific jurisdictions, and up to 99 per cent in many cases. It makes sense, then, to focus on small firms as an education priority.

A proactive and wide-ranging education strategy also has the capacity to make a regulator's role much easier. A small business community that understands why a law exists, how it is applied, and what is required to be compliant is far easier to work with than a community which operates in ignorance, half-truths, or misinformation.

And, as most enforcement agencies well know, prevention is far better than cure. An agency which just relies on a detection and prosecution strategy, rather than investing effort to proactively head off future breaches of the law, will have to expend considerably greater resources to perhaps achieve the same level of overall compliance. Wide-ranging, effective information can possibly make the regulator's job easier in future, by spending time now to educate the next generation of business operators.

A good education programme should also focus on ensuring that SMEs know their rights, not just their responsibilities. As is discussed in a number of other chapters in this book, many competition law regimes make special allowances for small firms in particular circumstances, or give them certain rights that are denied to larger corporations — such as the right to collectively bargain, or exemption from abuse of dominance claims. However, most small enterprises are unlikely to be aware of these rights, or to actively exercise them, unless it is brought directly to their attention.

SME Information-seeking Behaviour

Over the last thirty years, a body of research — admittedly still limited — into information-seeking and usage amongst small businesses has begun to emerge, along with improved insights into education tools and approaches for SMEs. In the late 1990s, for example, the Asia-Pacific Economic Cooperation (APEC) SME Planning and Liaison Group commissioned a report into ways to improve the dissemination of government information to SMEs in general (Acuity Consulting 1998). Interestingly, however, very little literature yet exists on the subject of competition law education.

As Burke and Jarratt (2004, p. 126) have noted, most forms of self-education and information-seeking by SME owners, managers, and operators generally "… does not reflect exhaustive strategic analysis, but rather [an] … opportunistic or instinctive approach". For owners/managers of businesses, critical issues include a high degree of easy access, user-friendliness, and a large measure of convenience (Jorosi 2007). Indeed, they "tend to use and consider most important those sources that are convenient and require minimal aggressive effort to employ", according to Franklin and Goodwin (1983, p. 11).

These features have also been noted in a number of different Asia-Pacific countries. Thassanabanjong et al. (2009), for example, have reported that Thai SME managers prefer to use informal, unstructured approaches, while SME operators in New Zealand have generally been reluctant to put formal training programmes in place, although online self-paced training has begun to grow in popularity (Moore 2004).

More recent research has also indicated that business operators tend to focus on quite pragmatic and immediately useful information, rather than more generalized concepts and constructs. The United Kingdom's *Quarterly Survey of Small Business in Britain* (Blundel 2013) has shown that information about government laws and regulations is the most important priority for owners, well ahead of taxation, accounting, operational, or human resource issues. However, they often have difficulty in actually finding useful information from government agencies, and often report that even when accessed, it is often delivered in an overly-vague, generalized or formalistic manner which they cannot immediately or practically apply to their own enterprise (Schaper 2014).

Traditionally, most so-called competition law "education campaigns" have been of limited focus and limited effectiveness. In most cases, there has been one overriding function — to warn small businesses about the dangers of non-compliance with the law, and to highlight the risks (such as prosecution) that they may face if they fail to observe it. A large degree of attention is usually drawn to the outcome of individual prosecutions, such as the issuing of infringement notices, administrative resolutions or court action. Such communication is also often one-way in nature (from the regulator out to the business community) and has employed a relatively limited number of well-established dissemination channels, such as press releases, public speeches, and print publications from the agency (Productivity Commission 2013). There is often an implicit assumption that, once having released such information out into the public sphere, it will somehow be transmitted to and absorbed by the general small business sector.

Such educational campaigns are largely ineffective. They often ignore the existent evidence about the real nature of SME information-gathering, usage, and decision-making. And in an age of burgeoning diffuse communication channels, it blindly assumes that every business operator is keenly scouring the local newspaper for the latest nugget of information put out by the local competition law enforcer.

Developing an Effective Online Education Strategy

Online tools are not a magic panacea to all the learning problems or shortfalls of SMEs, and must be used prudently. Roy (2009) has suggested that they are best employed under certain circumstances, such as when businesses require a high level of flexibility, round-the-clock access, course content that can be personalized and delivered to meet the needs of the learner, and the ability to test user knowledge.

Sambrook (2003) has suggested that SME e-learning is also highly dependent upon the development of user-friendly online materials. Content which is interesting, well-presented, well-written in easy-to-understand language (that is, contains no jargon), and which provides the right amount and level of information, is more likely to be successful.

There are some drawbacks to relying on online learning tools, however. As a number of researchers have indicated (Caskey and Subriana 2007; Bagshaw and Bagshaw 2002), it is an incomplete educative tool: many SMEs also need person-to-person contact to effectively supplement their learning. Electronic contact can lack some of the richness and effectiveness that only comes about when people learn in a face-to-face environment.

Nevertheless, if a decision is made to go online, then there are several other issues that should also be taken into account when devising an education programme for SMEs:

What is your focus? What are you intending to achieve with the education project? Competition and consumer law in many jurisdictions is often complex and broad-ranging. Do you want business operators to emerge with a detailed, highly technical knowledge of all the detailed minutiae of competition law — or do you just want them to have enough broad knowledge so that they will be aware of when they might be breaking the law?

What does the industry think and want? Programmes that are developed in consultation with small business operators, their industry associations, and their professional advisers (such as accountants and lawyers) are more likely to be effective than those that are unilaterally devised by a competition agency. Whilst this may take time and draw on agency resources, it almost invariably produces an educational tool that is more relevant and accessible to business operators.

Who is your target audience? The SME sector is more diverse than most regulators recognize. Small business operators can be found in every industry sector, and the law may apply quite differently in one industry to another. In addition, the size and sophistication of their enterprises can also vary markedly, from the very simple sole trader with a limited market through to entrepreneurs in quickly-growing enterprises with multiple markets. It is often also important to distinguish between the learning needs of the firm owners, the day-to-day managers, and the employees of the firm. Their needs and learning objectives are not always the same.

What commitment is required from SME participants? Some information campaigns are simple, concise, and short; others may require a lengthy investment of time and effort by the intended recipients. An overly-brief message may not cover material in sufficient detail, but a long complex one will usually reduce the willingness of people to participate.

How practical is it? Direct relevance and usefulness is an important criterion for most business operators, especially if they are being asked to invest time and effort in educating themselves on a topic that may not reap immediate rewards.

What is the best delivery channel? There is more than one "online" tool available today. Information can be delivered not just via a more traditional website page, but also social media outlets, email, and apps, amongst others.

What is your time-frame? Some measure of patience is crucial. Most education strategies are, by their nature, long-term projects. They take time to develop and implement, and there may also be a considerable time lag between the point at which a businessperson accesses information to the moment that they apply the learnt material to their business activities.

Varied Approaches to SME Education and Information

Almost all competition regulators utilize a variety of tools to educate businesses and the public about competition and consumer laws. Most regulators use links to online publications such as newsletters, guidelines, procedures, handbooks, and frequently asked questions (FAQs) to generally explain what the law is about, what is required to comply with the law and how to go about doing so. Some also provide links to seminars, workshops, or education tools created by third parties. Approaches and content vary from one jurisdiction to another, as summarized in Table 6.1.

TABLE 6.1
Online SME Education Resources

Australia	Competition & consumer law education programs	<http://www.ccaeducationprograms.org/>
European Commission	Small business portal	<http://ec.europa.eu/small-business/most-of-market/rules/index_en.htm>
Germany	Information leaflet on SME cooperation	<http://www.bundeskartellamt.de/SharedDocs/Publikation/EN/Merkblaetter/Leaflet%20-%20Cooperation%20 for%20SMUs.pdf?__blob=publicationFile&v=3>
International Competition Network	Cartel awareness	<http://www.internationalcompetitionnetwork.org/working-groups/current/cartel/awareness/general.aspx>
Japan	Guidelines to protect against unfair trade practices by large-scale retailers	<http://www.jftc.go.jp/en/legislation_gls/index.html>
Malaysia	FAQs for SMEs	<http://mycc.gov.my/sites/default/files/brochures/FAQ-for-SMEs.pdf>
Singapore	Manga, animation, and videos	<https://www.ccs.gov.sg/education-and-compliance/education-resources>
South Africa	Guide to the Competition Act	<http://www.compcom.co.za/brochures/>
United Kingdom	Competition law compliance: guidance for businesses	<https://www.gov.uk/government/collections/competition-and-consumer-law-compliance-guidance-for-businesses>
United States	FTC Business Centre	<https://www.ftc.gov/tips-advice/business-center>

Source: Compiled by the authors.

In some countries, publicly available advice is generically directed to all businesses; there is no special focus on SMEs as such. An example is the U.S. Federal Trade Commission (FTC), which has a "Business Center" that contains a blog site, legal resources, videos, guidelines, and publications on specific consumer protection issues, whilst other parts of its "tips and advice" section provide fact sheets on a variety of competition topics, case examples, and FAQs. Within each topic there are links to more detailed guidance materials developed by the FTC and the Department of Justice. All of this information is aimed at businesses in general, as well as at consumers, rather than specifically at SMEs.

Some other jurisidictions provide competition material information online via broader small business portals that cover a range of different topics. For example, the European Commission's European Small Business Portal provides readers with links to information on numerous topics, including "competition rules", "rules for dealing wth consumers", and "market rules". Each "rule" links the SME to relevant websites, which in turn provide materials such as reference publications (including legislation, policy documents, and handbooks), brochures and fact sheets, FAQs, and, in relation to consumer issues, some generic video links.

A number of individual jurisdictions have provided some limited information online specifically for SMEs. One example is the South African Competition Commission, whose key legislation, the Competition Act (1998), stipulates that the law should "ensure that small and medium-sized enterprises have an equitable opportunity to participate in the economy". In light of this, it has produced for SMEs (and historically disadvantaged persons), a comprehensive guide to the Competition Act, which explains restrictive practices that are prohibited by the legislation, case examples, exemptions for SMEs, and the impact of mergers on SMEs. Notably, it is also one of the few agencies to explicitly state and clarify what matters the Commission cannot deal with, thus avoiding the issue of inflated expectations or unrealistic requests from small firm operators.

The United Kingdom's Competition and Markets Authority has also published some specific guides to assist and educate SMEs. Its website offers downloadable competition and consumer law compliance guidance for businesses, which includes sixty-second summaries and case studies. It also offers some downloadable specific publications for owners and directors of small businesses on how to comply with competition law (including "four-step processes" to easy compliance).

The German federal government competition agency, the Bundeskartellamt, has a specific information leaflet on the possibilities of cooperation for SMEs, which is available from its website. In addition to discussing when small firms may legally cooperate together, it also defines what consitutes a small or medium-sized firm. In a similar vein, the Malaysian Competition Commission has produced a SME-specific brochure ("FAQs for SMEs") that provides examples as to when and how the Malaysian Competition Act 2010 applies to small businesses, information sharing with competitors, dealing with trade associations and suppliers, and tendering for government contracts.

A more sophisticated approach is taken by Singapore's Competition Commission, which has a dedicated Education and Compliance menu on its website. In addition to information on how to develop a conventional compliance programme, it also includes a one-stop interactive learning tool, which is designed to provide a clear overview of some key dos and don'ts for businesses (including SMEs). A novel approach is the use of stories and animated drawings or comics ("manga"), covering topics such as cartels, mergers, abuse of dominance, and price-fixing. Finally, an animation contest has also been developed in conjunction with a local university. The Singaporean strategy is discussed in more detail in another chapter in this book. Whilst most of this material is more likely to appeal to consumers and small enterprises than large corporations, it has not been designed or promoted as having a specific focus on SMEs.

Japan's Fair Trade Commission has issued guidelines relating to anti-competitive behaviour by "large-scale" retailers, whilst the Japanese Ministry of Economy, Trade and Industry (METI) also has a dedicated office for competition policy. Using a "manga-style" approach similar to that found in Singapore, METI has produced a specific brochure for SMEs, entitled "A Guide to the Antimonopoly Act for SMEs — Is It a Cartel!?".

The global forum for national competition agencies, the International Competition Network, has established a Cartel Awareness and Outreach to Business Working Group. Its work is ongoing and, as such, the development of relevant online SME education and outreach materials between agencies is a work in progress. At the time of writing, the Working Group's materials include some of the SME outreach and education tools developed by the Australian Competition and Consumer Commission (ACCC), the Singapore Competition Commission, South African Competition Commission, the Bundeskartellamt, and Japan's Fair Trade Commission.

All of the above country profiles show that some competition agencies are already beginning to use online tools to help educate SMEs. However, most of them are quite limited in scope and it is rare to find a substantial suite of online educational instruments specifically prepared for SMEs. Indeed, in many cases, online tools amount to not much more than an electronic copy of a brochure. One exception is the recent work of the ACCC.

The ACCC Online Education Project

The ACCC is an omnibus regulatory agency that has responsibility for multiple different SME-related functions under the Australian national Competition and Consumer Act 2010 (previously known as the Trade Practices Act 1974). These include not only general competition law, but also consumer protection, the national product safety regime, a mandatory Franchising Code of Conduct, and the national Scamwatch alert centre, amongst others. There are also a number of specific small business protections embedded within both the competition and consumer law provisions. As such, the range of SME-related material is considerable (Schaper 2010). Whilst the organization has long maintained a small number of SME outreach officers, their reach is necessarily limited, given there are some 2.1 million SMEs trading in Australia.

In 2009, a strategic decision was made to broaden the scope of the agency's educative function by also offering online materials. The first online programme, that relating to franchising, was developed under a contract by Griffith University and launched in July 2010.

The ACCC now has a suite of learning tools funded by the Commission, geared towards a combination of three different audiences — SME operators, prospective franchisees, and tertiary students — all available from the one dedicated, publicly-accessible website operating under its own specific web address, "Competition & Consumer Law Education Programs".

Each of the three different programmes contains a set of modules that outlines the key provisions of the Competition & Consumer Act 2010, and which have been customized to meet the particular needs of the target audience.

The programme for SME operators includes a range of both competition and consumer topics, covering cartels; misuse of market power; setting minimum prices for resale; exclusive dealing; false or misleading advertising; unfair selling practices; unconscionable conduct; consumer guarantees; product safety and scams. Users of the programme can either work through all the modules or can select the ones most relevant to the particular business. At the end of each module, there is a short self-assessment quiz to test the user's understanding of each module.

The franchising programme is specifically geared towards prospective franchisees (that is, intending purchasers of a franchise agreement), and covers six modules. These explain and define the concept of franchising; discuss franchise disclosure rules; explain the basics of operating within a franchise; give an overview of the Franchising Code of Conduct; explain intellectual property issues; and discuss some questions to ask franchisors. It also contains an assessment element, and successful completion of all of these generates a certificate of completion.

The tertiary education programme comprises twelve training modules — six focused on competition law (covering issues such as cartels, misuse of market power, resale price maintenance, and exclusive dealing) and the remainder on consumer-related provisions (such as misleading and deceptive conduct, product safety, consumer guarantees, social media, and scams). It has been expressly developed to encourage educators to include the material within their own curriculum and courses.

As such, a key element of this programme has been the "take and teach" approach to module development — rather than being a whole semester-long course, each module has been created so as to allow individual academics to teach it on a stand-alone basis, without any prior knowledge assumed on the part of either student or academic. Teaching staff are also provided with a corresponding instructor's manual, which contains reading materials, assessment tools, and learning aids. A set of PowerPoint presentations for each topic is made available, and there are additional quiz and discussion questions and answers. Students have direct access online to basic materials, and each module takes approximately twenty minutes to complete. Teaching materials are made available free of charge to all tertiary institutions, and the content is updated regularly by the ACCC to maintain its currency.

Tertiary institutions are encouraged to adapt the programme as they see fit. The content is sufficiently broad that it can be incorporated into either undergraduate or postgraduate units, as well as into both law and non-law courses (such as individual units in small business management, marketing, advertising, economics, media, or communications). This allows universities to use individual modules in any particular class that they chose — for example, the "false and misleading advertising practices" module may be equally inserted into a semester unit offered in journalism, marketing, entrepreneurship, or other related fields.

The programme was pre-tested over a semester within the School of Taxation and Business Law at the University of New South Wales, and formally launched at a presentation to the Australian Business Deans' Council in November 2013.

A database of academics teaching and working in the competition law area, and who have an interest in these teaching tools, has also been created. Now known as the Tertiary Educators Network, it has over one hundred subscribers from more than fifteen different universities, colleges, and other educational institutions. By mid-2015, more than 13,000 users had accessed the programme. Over 1,600 module quizzes had been completed by students, with an average pass rate of 81 per cent. Ten universities, six technical colleges, and two high schools had adopted the material in part or whole, and several more were considering its adoption.

The results to date have also been encouraging for the other online tools. By June 2015, more than 17,000 users had accessed the general small business materials, whilst some 8,100 people had logged on to the franchising pre-entry education programme, with almost 1,200 having earned a certificate of completion by undertaking all six modules.

Evaluation of the three online education programmes has taken place on a periodic basis. An examination of the franchising programme, for example, has revealed that students who complete the course generally report a much better understanding of what a franchise entails, are more likely to actually proceed into a franchise than non-completers, and are more satisfied with franchising as a business model once they actually sign up (Frazer et al. 2013). Educators delivering parts of the tertiary programme were qualitatively surveyed twice in 2014, and their suggestions and feedback on the materials were sought. In addition to seeking a greater number of discussion and tutorial questions, most were also strongly of the view that certificates of completion should be introduced. Similar feedback has also been given with regard to the general small business modules.

Challenges and Suggestions for Improvement

Creating effective online tools, information and education for SMEs is not a particularly easy task. As the early parts of this chapter indicate, most agencies do not have any SME-specific material, relying instead on generic material for all businesses. As a result, there is only a very small so-called "community of practice" amongst competition regulators with an interest in, and experience of, SME online education. If an agency wants to turn to another for advice and support in developing its own small business education programme, there is currently only a limited number of experienced regulators. In many cases, it is often easier and more convenient to draw on the experience of other arms of government working in the online learning arena, although it may be sometimes difficult to directly translate their innovations and pedagogy into a direct application of competition and consumer law.

However, there are already some important lessons that have emerged from the small nucleus of existing tools, and which might also be useful to other agencies contemplating a similar programme in future:

Certification matters. In many cases, small business owners and operators value the chance to "get a piece of paper" to prove they have completed an online course. It can generate a sense of self-achievement amongst owners, and can also be valuable in ensuring their staff are competition-aware. Whilst such forms are not a formal qualification, they matter to entrepreneurs, many of whom do not have the capacity to undertake other, more formal and more expensive education programmes.

Keep most material simple, direct and relevant. For most businesspeople, a basic explanation of the basic elements of competition law, along with some practical advice as to how it might apply in common business contexts, is much more valuable than a detailed legal exposition. As such, it is recommended that regulators avoid giving overly complex terminology, differing judicial interpretations, and the minutiae of the law. SME operators are pragmatists: they want their information in clear, concise form. And case studies of real world firms are especially valued, as entrepreneurs can relate to the experience of other entrepreneurs.

Get third party endorsement. It is strongly advisable to consult with industry associations and SMEs groups when initially developing material. Such bodies can be an invaluable reference source for developing the curriculum, pretesting its effectiveness, and then actively promoting its usage once launched.

Devise an effective evaluation mechanism. If at all possible, build in a relatively simple but effective tool to test the learning of participants. A common example is the use of true-or-false or multiple choice questions, both of which can be processed easily online. In some cases, this can be useful in issuing certificates of completion; but it can also be valuable in measuring which issues or topics are important to your audience, and whether or not the education materials provided to them are genuinely helping them to learn.

Develop a network of educational users. As the ACCC Tertiary Educators Network example shows, an important complement to the overall educational strategy is the need to reach out to educators with an interest in this topic. One common area is universities (where, increasingly, competition law education is a growing area of interest, both for business and law schools). Other organizations may also be interested, such as industry associations and professional institutes, both of whom have an interest in the ongoing education of their members. This can provide regulators with a valuable reference group to help them periodically review and update their materials, advocate, and promote their tools in the broader business community, and suggest other educational strategies.

Conclusion

Clearly, there is a role and opportunity for online programmes to assist both SMEs and competition agencies in their respective tasks. Well-designed and promoted education material can help agencies inculcate a greater understanding amongst small firms in an economical and resource-effective manner, whilst also empowering small firms to become aware of both their rights and responsibilities under competition law.

However, the application of online tools to small firms is still in a comparatively rudimentary stage. As the above discussion shows, many agencies do not have any SME-specific material, relying instead on generic "business" material. Furthermore, the body of research into this topic is passingly small: little is known about what subject areas SMEs really want to understand, what barriers and triggers drive them to use such material (or fail to use it), what instructional method is most appropriate, and so forth. This clearly is an area that would benefit greatly in future from the joint contributions of regulators, educators, and researchers.

REFERENCES

Acuity Consulting. *Strengthening Links: Disseminating Government Information to Small and Medium Enterprises — A Comprehensive Approach*. A Report for the Department of Workplace Relations and Small Business, on behalf of the Asia-Pacific Economic Co-operation (APEC) SME Planning and Liaison Group. Canberra: Commonwealth of Australia, 1998.

Bagshaw, Mike and Caroline Bagshaw. "Radical Self-Development — A Bottom Up Perspective". *Industrial & Commercial Training* 34, no. 5 (2002): 194–99.

Blundel, Richard. *Quarterly Survey of Small Business in Britain*, vol. 29, no. 3. Milton Keynes: The Open University Business School, 2013.

Burke, G. Ian and Denise Jarratt. "The Influence of Information and Advice on Competitive Strategy Definition in Small- and Medium-Sized Enterprises". *Qualitative Market Research: An International Journal* 7, no. 2 (2004): 126–38.

Caskey, Kevin R. and Brian Subriana. "Supporting SME E-commerce Migration Through Blended E-learning". *Journal of Small Business and Enterprise Development* 14, no. 4 (2007): 670–88.

Franklin, Stephen G. and Jack S. Goodwin. "Problems of Small Business and Sources of Assistance: A Survey". *Journal of Small Business Management* 21 (April 1983): 5–12.

Frazer, Lorelle, Debra Grace, Scott Weaven, and Jeff Giddings. *Preparation for Franchising: A Study of Prospective and Current Franchisees*. Brisbane: Griffith University, 2013.

IFF Research. *UK Businesses' Understanding of Competition Law: Report Prepared for the Competition and Markets Authority, United Kingdom*. London: IFF Research, 2015. Available at <https://www.gov.uk/government/publications/uk-businessesunderstanding-of-competition-law> (accessed 2 June 2015).

Jorosi, Boemo Nlayidzi. "The Information Needs and Information Seeking Behaviours of SME Managers in Botswana". *Libri* 56, no. 2 (2007): 97–107.

Moore, Patricia. "Investing in Your People". *New Zealand Business* 18, no. 6 (2004): 29–31.

Productivity Commission, Commonwealth of Australia. *Regulator Engagement with Small Business*. Canberra: Productivity Commission, 2013.

Roy, Andrée. "The Training Process of SMEs: What Motivates SMEs to Use E-Learning". *International Journal of Advanced Corporate Learning* 2, no. 3 (2009): 66–73.

Sambrook, Sally. "E-learning in Small Organizations". *Education and Training* 45, no. 8/9 (2003): 506–16.

Schaper, Michael T. "Competition Law, Enforcement and the Australian Small Business Sector". *Small Enterprise Research* 17, no. 1 (2010): 7–18.

————. "Is Anybody Listening? Improving Government Information and Communication to Small Business". In *Meeting the Globalisation Challenge: Smart and Innovative SMEs in a Globally Competitive Environment*, edited by Bernice Kotey, Time Mazzarol, Delwyn Clark, Dennis Foley, and Tui McKeown. Melbourne: Tilde University Press, 2014.

Thassanabanjong, Kitiya, Peter Miller, and Teresa Marchant. "Training in Thai SMEs". *Journal of Small Business and Enterprise Development* 16, no. 4 (2009): 678–93.

SECTION 2

SMEs and
Competition Law

7

THE APPLICATION OF
*PER SE*s TO SMEs
The Type 1 Error No One Notices?

*Alexandra Merrett, Rhonda L. Smith, and
Rachel Trindade*

In this chapter, we consider the impact of per se *laws on small and medium-sized enterprises (SMEs). Drawing on Australia's unusual adjudication/enforcement model, we assess SMEs' use of legitimate mechanisms designed to avoid overreach of the* per se *prohibitions, as well as the enforcement of those prohibitions against SMEs. These measures provide a basis for comparing compliance and non-compliance by small business and their larger counterparts.*

Our analysis demonstrates that SMEs hardly ever attract regulatory attention for potentially lessening competition. Yet, in Australia, they feature in almost 50 per cent of per se *proceedings, and are responsible for almost 80 per cent of matters resolved via (non-judicial) undertakings. At the same time, SMEs are under-represented as users of Australia's statutory immunity processes. These factors combine to suggest that* per se *prohibitions impose a competitive hindrance which disproportionately affects SMEs as against larger businesses.*

In designing competition laws, therefore, one must be wary of an overzealous approach to per se *prohibitions. If, as the Australian experience suggests, there is little or no prospect that conduct by SMEs will give rise to a "pernicious effect on competition", then the law should be slow to impose conclusive presumptions to the contrary.*

Introduction

> "The true test of legality is whether the restraint imposed is such as
> merely regulates and perhaps promotes competition or whether it is
> such as may suppress or even destroy competition." (Justice Brandeis,
> Chicago Board of Trade vs United States 1918)

Small and medium-sized enterprises (SMEs) are the heartbeat of the
modern economy. Despite increasing corporatization and globalization,
they remain responsible for most economic growth and innovation —
indeed former U.S. President Ronald Reagan observed, "Entrepreneurs
and their small enterprises are responsible for almost all the economic
growth in the United States" (Reagan 1988). For all their economic
significance, however, SMEs tend to be treated as the "exception" rather
than the rule when it comes to competition laws.

In this chapter, the appropriateness of *per se* laws for SMEs is
examined, remembering that:

> The rationale for per se rules is to avoid a burdensome inquiry into actual
> market conditions in situations where the likelihood of anticompetitive
> conduct is so great as to render unjustified the costs of determining
> whether the particular case at bar involves anticompetitive conduct
> (Jefferson Parish Hospital District No. 2 vs Hyde 1984).

Australia's unusual adjudication/enforcement model allows for the
measuring of SMEs' use of legitimate mechanisms designed to avoid
overreach of the *per se* prohibitions, as well as the enforcement of
those prohibitions against SMEs. These factors enable a comparison
of compliance and non-compliance by small business as against large
business, allowing the impact of *per se* prohibitions to be tested.

Designing a Competition Regime

Per se provisions prohibit outright certain types of conduct, regardless
of the impact on competition. Depending on the jurisdiction, they
can arise in different ways. In Australia, *per se* laws are specified
in the Competition and Consumer Act (Commonwealth) 2010 (the
CCA; formerly the Trade Practices Act 1974). For example, the cartel
provisions (discussed in further detail below) prohibit conduct which
meets various statutory definitions: the only questions to be proven in
court are whether the conduct occurred and if the relevant definitions

are satisfied. Conversely, in the United States, *per se* provisions are judge-made rules interpreting legislation which have been drafted in broader terms. *Per se* prohibitions are often contrasted with "competition-tested" prohibitions or "rule of reason" analysis, whereby conduct is only condemned if it adversely affects competition.

Before considering the impact of *per se* prohibitions on SMEs, one must understand the role of these provisions and their different significance for small businesses as compared with larger firms. Competition law prohibits various types of anti-competitive conduct to ensure competitive markets, efficient operation of those markets, and improved social welfare. The implicit assumption is that conduct that might damage the competitive process should be carefully analysed to determine whether it has the purpose and/or the effect of increasing market power or substantially lessening competition. Given this, the use of *per se* provisions is the exception, not the default.

When applying a competition law, there is a risk that conduct will be found incorrectly to be anti-competitive ("Type 1 error"). Type 1 error is contrasted with Type 2 error, which occurs when the law fails to capture anti-competitive conduct. When designing a competition regime, one seeks to balance the two to minimize the risk of *any* error. From a policy perspective, however, Type 1 error is generally considered more harmful to overall welfare and "big business" can be quick to suggest that regulators risk "chilling competition" if they overreach, particularly in relation to mergers and market power issues (see, for example, Business Council of Australia 2014).

The Economic Rationale for *Per Se* Prohibitions

The premise for *per se* prohibitions is that, over time, certain conduct has been found almost invariably to be anti-competitive. Thus, *per se* rules apply to:

> agreements or practices which because of their pernicious effect on competition and lack of any redeeming virtue are conclusively presumed to be unreasonable and therefore illegal without elaborate inquiry as to the precise harm they have caused or the business excuse for their use (Northern Pacific Railway Co. vs United States 1958).

Alternatively, *per se* provisions may arise as a matter of principle, that is, in the absence of empirical evidence of harm. For example, price may be considered so vital to the operation of markets that it should not be manipulated (Krattenmaker 1988), and accordingly, a jurisdiction may institute a *per se* rule against price-fixing.

If conduct can be confidently designated as anti-competitive, then prohibiting it *per se* has significant benefits, for both regulators and businesses. It is often stated that *per se* rules make for efficient enforcement, implying quicker and cheaper outcomes. In terms of establishing a contravention in court, this is likely to be correct. It is only necessary to prove that the conduct occurred, thereby avoiding a forensic examination of its purpose and effect. The length of a trial is also likely to be reduced. These factors generally mean that, wherever possible, *per se* contraventions will be pleaded by competition regulators. Nevertheless, in deciding penalty, courts often consider the benefit that the participants obtained from the conduct, as well as any damage to competition. This represents at least a partial reversion to a "rule of reason" analysis and can reduce the time and cost benefits otherwise obtained.

Hard and fast rules can also benefit businesses. A clear understanding of how to "colour between the lines" avoids expensive advice to determine whether certain competitive strategies are legitimate. So long as all businesses play by the same rules, there is an even playing field and reduced compliance costs.

But *per se* rules also have disadvantages. There are few forms of conduct that are invariably anti-competitive, especially as the conduct itself does not determine this. For example, while market sharing arrangements are generally anti-competitive, sometimes they are not harmful and may even increase welfare, for example by ensuring a service's availability (such as a weekend roster for doctors in a small town). Furthermore, our understanding of the likely economic impact of particular conduct is continually developing. For example, resale price maintenance has typically been regarded as a vertical price fix and so frequently prohibited *per se*. However, in 2007, the U.S. Supreme Court decided that it should be subject to a rule of reason assessment because it may be competitively neutral or even pro-competitive (Leegin Creative Leather Products, Inc. vs PSKS, Inc. 2007).

As *per se* rules focus on the type of conduct rather than its context, they are by definition indiscriminate, occasionally resulting in errors. Thus:

> Per se rules always contain a degree of arbitrariness. They are
> justified on the assumption that the gains from the imposition of the
> rule will far outweigh the losses and that significant administrative
> advantages will result. In other words, the potential competitive
> harm plus the administrative costs of determining in what particular
> situations the practice may be harmful must far outweigh the
> benefits that may result. If the potential benefits in the aggregate are
> outweighed to this degree, then they are simply not worth identifying
> in individual cases (Justice Thurgood Marshall, quoted in Bork 1978,
> p. 18).

The risk of mistakenly finding that particular conduct is anti-competitive
(a Type 1 error) increases when assessments depart from a rule of
reason analysis in favour of *per se* treatment. However, regulatory costs
(for both regulators and businesses) increase when applying rule of
reason analysis. Thus, the choice of decision rules involves a trade-off
between the risk of decision errors and regulatory cost. Christiansen
and Kerber (2006) illustrate this as follows:

The optimal decision minimizes "the sum of welfare losses through
wrong decisions (error costs) and regulation costs" (Christiansen and
Kerber 2006, p. 224). Clearly, this requires accepting a level of error.
Thus,

> The test of a good legal rule is not primarily whether it leads to the
> correct decision in a particular case, but whether it does a good job
> deterring anticompetitive behaviour throughout the economy given all
> relevant costs, benefits and uncertainties associated with diagnosis and
> remedies (Joskow 2002, pp. 99–100).

Yet, if these errors fall on a particular class of business (such as
small firms), rather than across the board, there may be cause for
concern.

The trade-off represented in Figure 7.1 does not incorporate
mechanisms designed to reduce the risk of error. Generally defences
or carve-outs are available, although these reduce the time and cost
benefits from the use of *per se* rules. In Australia, the arbitrariness of
per se rules is managed via various exceptions, anti-overlap provisions
and statutory immunity processes. This approach — adopted (with
modifications) in New Zealand and Papua New Guinea — has
the advantage of flexibility, but can entrench disadvantage if these
management strategies are not equally accessible. The *per se* rules

FIGURE 7.1
Regulatory Cost vs Error Cost

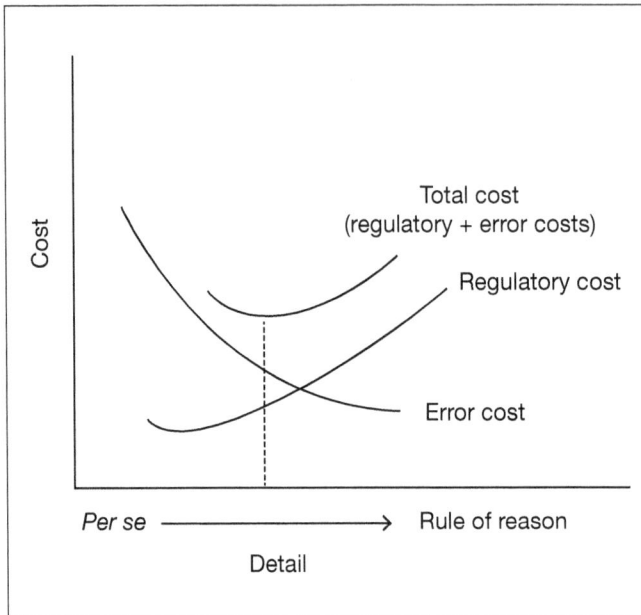

Source: Christiansen and Kerber (2006), p. 232.

clearly apply to all types of businesses, but can all types of businesses equally navigate the exceptions?

The Australian Approach

Australia's principal competition laws are contained in Part IV of the CCA, which also serves as the model for New Zealand's Commerce Act 1986 and Papua New Guinea's Independent Consumer and Competition Commission Act 2002. Part IV contains a complex array of *per se* prohibitions, competition-tested provisions, and a unilateral conduct provision. The competition-tested provisions apply to mergers, particular types of vertical arrangements, and more generally, to bilateral or multilateral arrangements, and are triggered only when the relevant conduct substantially lessens competition (the SLC test). The *per se* prohibitions, conversely, prohibit specified conduct regardless of its impact on competition. Australia has statutory *per se* prohibitions for "cartel" offences (price-fixing, output restriction, market sharing, and bid rigging); exclusionary provisions (effectively another form of market sharing); third line forcing (essentially a supplier inducing a customer to buy from a specified third party); and resale price maintenance (that is, a supplier inducing downstream retailers to sell at or above a specified price).

When legislative reforms have been debated, the Australian system lends itself to a certain laziness: there is little need to consider potential overreach, as the various *per ses* are subject to a multitude of carveouts, anti-overlap provisions, and immunity processes. Nonetheless, as is increasingly apparent, the sheer complexity of Australia's framework means this approach to managing Type 1 error creates an uneven playing field, separating those who can afford expert advice from those who cannot.

There are three basic means of ensuring conduct which does not lessen competition conforms to Australia's *per se* regime: structuring to avoid the application of *per se* prohibitions; structuring to trigger specific exceptions or defences; or making use of the statutory immunity process. The first two strategies — while the least visible — are in fact the principal means of avoiding the *per se* prohibitions. For example, with the assistance of sophisticated legal advice, it is possible to ensure collaborative conduct triggers an anti-overlap mechanism or activates the CCA's joint venture exceptions. In numerous scenarios, expert advice can ensure conduct is subject to an SLC test and falls outside the scope of the *per se* provisions. There is, however, no means to measure the extent to which these strategies are used in the business community.

Nonetheless, the Australian Competition and Consumer Commission (ACCC) in its adjudication capacity is required to publish information concerning the third "avoidance" strategy: statutory immunity. Its immunity registers — together with the ACCC's enforcement activities — can inform our views as to the application of *per se* prohibitions to SMEs.

Statutory Immunity in Australia

The CCA has three statutory immunity processes:

Authorization: this is possible for all conduct falling under Part IV, except misuse of market power (subject to very confined exceptions).

Notification: only possible for exclusive dealing under Section 47 of the CCA. Section 47 is generally competition-tested, but it also contains a *per se* prohibition against third line forcing. Overwhelmingly, notifications are used to protect third line forcing.

Collective bargaining notification: this simulates the procedural benefits of notification but provides the breadth of immunity of authorisation. This regime was specifically implemented for small business (see, for example, ACCC 2011*b*).

Each process has its particular advantages, disadvantages, and intended uses. For present purposes, we have created "data sets" reflecting the recent use of each process to facilitate observations about the parties using them and their relative "success" in doing so. To this end, applicants have been classified in various ways, including as small, medium, or large businesses. This has been an informal categorization, as there generally tends to be limited public information about the size of the firms involved in these applications. Mostly, however, the categorization of particular businesses was a straightforward exercise — the only exception being businesses which were small in Australia but backed by a large overseas parent. These have been categorized as "large", as the objective of the present exercise is to consider the impact of *per se* prohibitions on those businesses less able to access expert advice.

Authorization

Authorization is slow, expensive, and very public. The filing fee is (generally) AUD7,500; the statutory time-frame for resolving applications is six months (capable of a six-month extension); public submissions are actively sought; and public consultations occur regularly. While waiver of the filing fee is possible, the legal fees associated with preparing the application, supporting submission, and managing the process tend to be many times the filing fee itself.

The legal test for obtaining authorization takes two legislative forms, but essentially asks whether the ACCC is satisfied that the proposed conduct provides a public benefit that outweighs the likely detriment (generally measured in terms of a lessening of competition). This is known as the public benefit test.

Considering all 137 finalized authorization applications published on the ACCC's public register for the years 2009–13, 132 were granted (albeit sometimes on conditions) and five were denied. One further application was withdrawn following an adverse draft determination. As Figure 7.2 shows, around 40 per cent of applications were for collective bargaining or for large business transactions, with a further 20 per cent being industry schemes (generally codes of conduct or industry levies). There were just two stand-alone applications by SMEs.

Most collective bargaining authorizations were filed by or on behalf of small businesses (thirty-five in total), of which thirty-three were by industry bodies. There were nine filed by large businesses, six by local government, and four involving intra-practice price setting (e.g. by dentists) — accordingly, these last ones were

FIGURE 7.2
Types of Authorization Application/Applicant, 2009–13

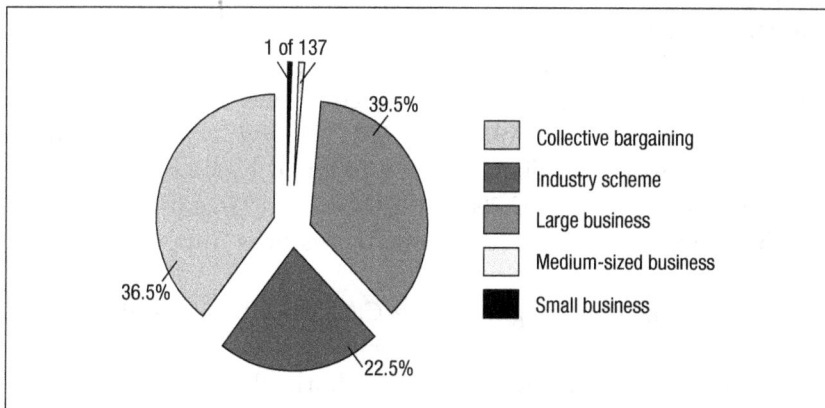

FIGURE 7.3
Breakdown of Collective Bargaining Authorizations, 2009–13

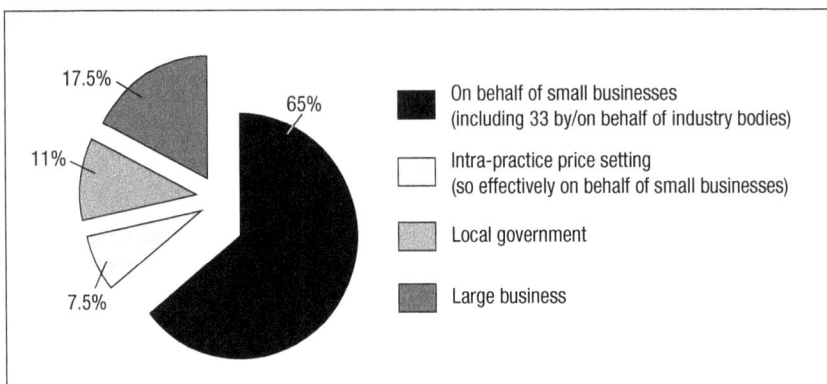

also effectively on behalf of small businesses. This is shown in Figure 7.3.

There appears to be no common link between the matters in which authorization was denied, other than a determination that the public benefit test was not satisfied. The relevant matters involved: common price setting by ophthalmologists (via an industry body which boasted 60 per cent of Australian ophthalmologists as members) (ACCC 2013 A91360); minimum advertising prices by a group of independent retailers, many of which were quite substantial players in the affected markets (ACCC 2013, A91335); an issue of competition for the market, where an exclusive arrangement was considered a disincentive for potential entrants (ACCC 2010, A91235); a co-insurance arrangement involving government-owned electricity generators (ACCC 2010, A91198 & A91199); and a revenue-sharing arrangement between airlines which was found to lessen competition on particular routes (ACCC 2009, A91097 & A91098). No authorization which could be considered a "small business" application was denied.

The authorization sought by the Casuarina Business Precinct in the Northern Territory in 2009 is instructive in the application of the CCA to small businesses. The authorized conduct related to a "Liquor Accord" involving (mostly) small businesses in a local retail precinct — the members of the accord agreed to limit alcohol sales in order to reduce anti-social and criminal behaviour. The proposed conduct (supported by the Territory government) was considered "likely to produce public benefit by reducing anti-social behaviour, including inappropriate, aggressive and occasionally violent behaviour, in the Precinct... [A]ny likely detriments are limited" (ACCC 2011*a*, A91201 & A91202, 4.52). Authorization was sought for just three years. It is hard to imagine circumstances in which competition in an antitrust market could have been substantially lessened by the proposed conduct; nonetheless, the operation of the *per ses* meant it would only be lawful if authorized. No fee waiver for the authorization was sought or offered, and the professional costs of the application process are likely to have been significant.

Notification

While the legal test for notification is effectively the same as for authorization, the process is quite different: the filing fee is low (AUD100) and immunity for third line forcing is, by default, granted after fourteen days. The default mechanism also affects the onus — it is for the ACCC to say that the public benefit test is not satisfied (a process known as "revocation"). This also creates a more private process, whereby third party submissions are rarely sought and ACCC assessments irregularly published. That said, the immunity offered is very confined, applying only to exclusive dealing (including third line forcing). Accordingly, there is no protection against other *per se* prohibitions such as resale price maintenance and the cartel provisions.

The simplicity of the process is also reflected in the supporting documentation required. While most are prepared by competition lawyers, handwritten applications by small businesses are not uncommon. Unsurprisingly, therefore, notification is much more widely used than authorization. In 2013 alone, there were 466 notifications lodged against thirty authorizations. The ACCC has somewhat modified its reporting of notifications over time, but during the last five years, total annual notifications have ranged from

650–750 per year, of which around 400–500 appear to be "separate" notifications (based on its annual reports for those years).

We examined the first one hundred third line forcing notifications listed on the ACCC register for 2013. As Figure 7.4 indicates, thirty-three of those notifications were lodged by small businesses, nine by medium-sized businesses, five by industry bodies, and forty-four by large businesses. There were also nine group notifications — i.e. separate businesses lodging identical notifications which had apparently been prepared concurrently (see, for example, ACCC 2013, N97129, N96882, N96979 and N97050). All up, forty-eight notifications could be said to be by or on behalf of SMEs.

Of the SME notifications, six related to payment systems (referencing particular card users); ten concerned house and land packages; six involved franchises (mostly in the start-up phase) and fourteen were parties dealing with one of Australia's largest businesses, Telstra — these notifications were apparently (and once, expressly — ACCC 2013, N96549) at the behest of Telstra.

FIGURE 7.4
Types of Notification Application/Applicant, 2013

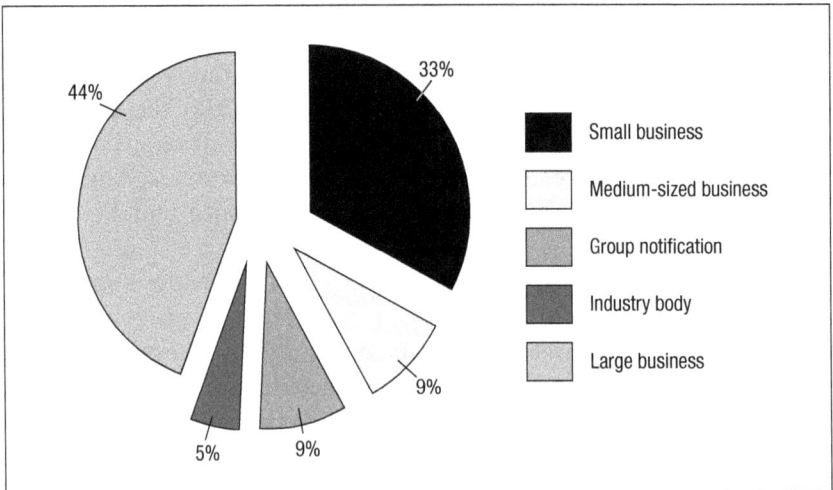

Intriguingly, not one of the one hundred notifications was revoked. Whilst revocation can occur at any time following notification, there have been just two revocations in the last five years (ACCC 2010, N94049 and N94032 & N94034). As noted earlier, it is difficult to determine how many "separate" notifications were filed in this period, but we estimate 2,000–2,500. Both revocations involved sporting bodies limiting access to their facilities/services (the first, for persons participating in non-sanctioned events; the second, for failure to obtain accreditation from a specified licensing body). In both cases, the ACCC considered that the notified conduct would render alternative leagues/licensing bodies less competitive.

Collective Bargaining Notifications

The scope of protection offered by a collective bargaining notification is similar to authorization, but the process is much closer to the general notification procedures. The fee is AUD1,000. A monetary limit applies to the protected conduct, such that each party to the notice must reasonably expect that their transactions with the "target" will not exceed AUD3 million per year (subject to variation by regulation). No ACCC decision has been appealed, so the process has never been reviewed by the Australian Competition Tribunal or the courts.

Given the limited use of the process, we examined all applications lodged between 2007 (when the process was instituted) and 2014. There were thirty-five applications, thirty-two of which were finalized (this includes five repeat notifications following the expiry of an earlier process). While most applications were by or on behalf of small businesses, more than 20 per cent were by large businesses. Two notifications have been revoked, and another three withdrawn following draft objection notices. While collective bargaining notifications have never been high, they notably dropped following two objections by the ACCC (see Figure 7.5). In 2014, just one notification was lodged but it was subsequently withdrawn following the ACCC's initial objection.

FIGURE 7.5
Applications for Collective Bargaining Notifications, 2007–14

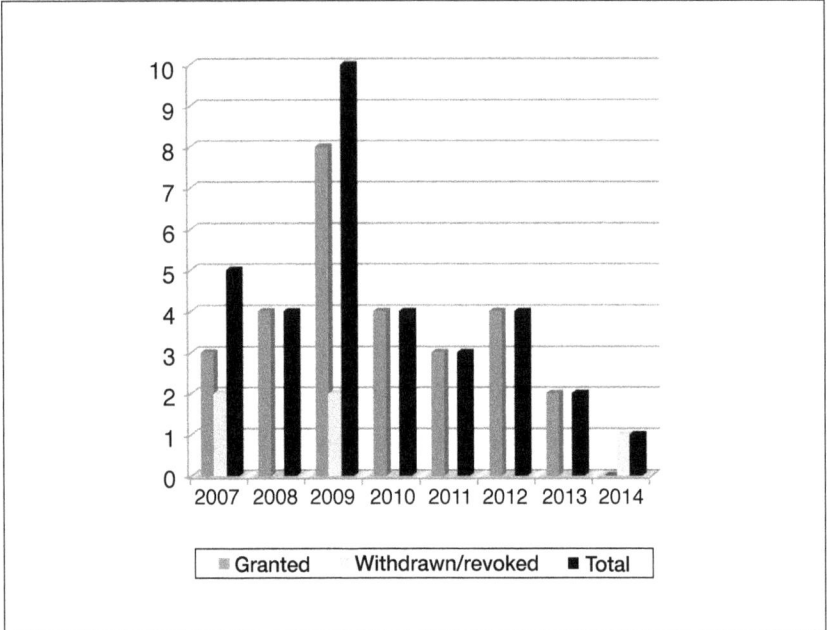

10
9
8
7
6
5
4
3
2
1
0

2007 2008 2009 2010 2011 2012 2013 2014

Granted   Withdrawn/revoked   ■ Total

Observations

Comparing the three immunity processes, the denial/revocation rate for each is very low. Strangely, however, collective bargaining notifications — albeit off a small sample — have the highest rate of unsuccessful applications (authorization 5/137 — 3.65 per cent; notifications 2/2000+ — <0.1 per cent; collective bargaining notifications 2/32 — 6.25 per cent). One also observes that where SMEs lack a champion (principally, an industry body), their use of the statutory immunity processes (particularly authorization) is extremely low. In the relevant period, just three authorizations were lodged by actual SMEs (as distinct from an industry body on their behalf). Even apparently "stand-alone" applications by SMEs (much more common for notification) are frequently at the instigation of a large business with which they deal. Finally, the rate at which small businesses use the general authorization provisions for collective bargaining arrangements, rather than the collective bargaining notification regime, suggests the calibration of the latter is quite wrong. This conclusion is underlined by the ACCC's recent introduction of a streamlined *authorization* process for collective bargaining by small business (ACCC 2011*c*).

Given the frequent use of the notification process by SMEs (48 per cent of those reviewed, as against 30 per cent of authorization applications), the ease and affordability of the process is clearly critical to its use. As hardly anyone uses the collective bargaining notification process, however, this means SMEs are almost invariably unable to lawfully engage in conduct that triggers the cartel provisions (including exclusionary provisions) or the prohibition against resale price maintenance. Thus, they are subject to the arbitrariness of Australia's extensive *per se* regime, but seemingly unable to navigate the various legitimate mechanisms which temper its operation.

Enforcement Action

The other relevant factor to consider is the extent of non-compliance with CCA provisions by SMEs, particularly "prosecution" rates for competition-tested prohibitions as against *per se* prohibitions. In Australia, non-compliance can be measured both by actual proceedings (almost invariably launched by the ACCC), as well as undertakings given to the ACCC.

Between 2009 and 2013, the ACCC filed thirty-four cases under Part IV. Combining separate proceedings for the same cartel, however, there were twenty-two distinct cases. Of these twenty-two cases, only five were competition-tested, and all of these were against large businesses. Of these, only one was a stand-alone SLC case (a merger). The other cases each involved an alleged misuse of market power — in other words, SMEs were never a target. Of the seventeen *per se* proceedings, six involved small businesses. These were all resolved by consent in the ACCC's favour. Another two were against medium-sized businesses: one was resolved by consent (in the ACCC's favour), whilst the other was unsuccessfully contested by the firm. Taking the cases against large businesses, nine of twenty-sven were (or are still) contested. Three of those cases have been finalized, with the target company successfully defending its conduct in each case.

Many less serious matters are resolved via Section 87B of the CCA. This allows the ACCC to accept court-enforceable undertakings in relation to matters arising under the CCA. Section 87B is widely used to address ACCC concerns relating to past conduct as well as to forestall concerns regarding future conduct (e.g. for mergers). ACCC enforcement investigations are frequently resolved by such undertakings (sometimes in conjunction with legal proceedings).

Between 2009 and 2013, the ACCC accepted sixty-three undertakings relating to Part IV conduct. As Figure 7.6 shows, this consisted of twenty-seven *per se* matters; two which were both *per se* and competition-tested; eleven non-merger SLCs; and twenty-three merger SLCs. Only two SLC undertakings were given by SMEs —

FIGURE 7.6
Breakdown by Type of Section 87B Undertakings, 2009–13

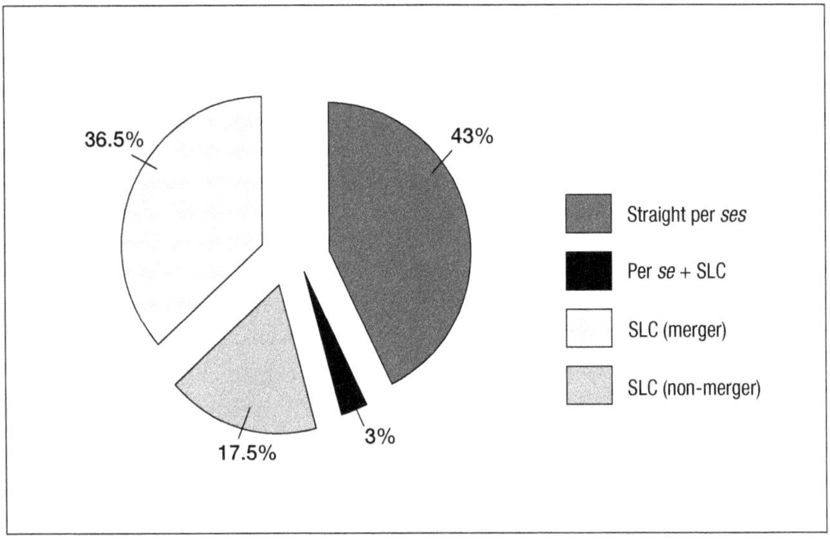

one by a supermarket (an industry sector subject to close scrutiny in Australia), and the other in support of a notification. All other SLC undertakings were given by large businesses. Of the *per se* undertakings, around 80 per cent were given by SMEs. As indicated in Figure 7.7, the actual breakdown was: large business, six; medium-sized business, five; small business, eighteen. For the *per se* undertakings involving SMEs, ten were for resale price maintenance. There were also three separate cartels (giving rise to thirteen undertakings).

Considering both legal proceedings and undertakings, it is clear that SMEs hardly ever prompt SLC concerns. Yet they are the respondents in almost 50 per cent of *per se* proceedings, and are providing 80 per cent of *per se* undertakings. The extent of legal proceedings is particularly concerning (eight of seventeen *per se* cases): lacking the resources to contest the allegations, SMEs almost invariably "cop a plea". But as cases against large business demonstrate, the ACCC can be fallible — frequently, when a matter is contested, the ACCC fails to substantiate its case.

FIGURE 7.7
Breakdown of *Per Se* Undertakings by Business Type, 2009–13

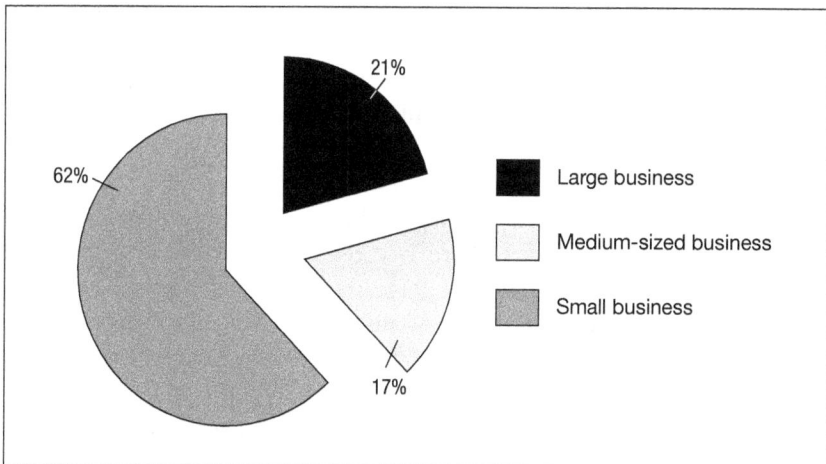

Conclusion

Competition policy is frequently framed in terms of avoiding Type 1 error for fear of chilling competition. As noted by Varney and Clarke (2013), however, there is a strong link between Type 1 error and the extent to which conduct is subject to *per se* prohibitions: "Broad concern with Type 1 error was entirely understandable when antitrust doctrine treated wide swaths of conduct under the *per se* rule ..." (Varney and Clarke 2013, p. 1569). But, at least in Australia, the typical concern is the impact of Type 1 error on large businesses — specifically whether the legislative regime is likely to restrict the ability of large businesses to engage in competitive conduct.

This analysis demonstrates, however, that a significant Type 1 error impacting SMEs is being overlooked: such businesses are disproportionately prosecuted for *per se* conduct while virtually never being considered to damage competition. Although such enterprises are using statutory immunity processes where they are affordable and/or effective, SMEs clearly do not consider the broad protection offered by authorization to be accessible. One can assume that they are similarly stymied from accessing the advice necessary to structure conduct in a manner that avoids the *per se* prohibitions. Thus SMEs are almost invariably unable to arrange their affairs in order to engage lawfully in conduct that falls within Australia's broad *per se* provisions.

In considering these conclusions, recall that *per se* prohibitions reflect a *presumption* of harm. As noted by the Australian Competition Tribunal, a *per se* offence "is an offence which Parliament has assumed will by its very nature have an anti-competitive effect" (Application by Michael Jools [2006] ACompT 5, [22]). But where there is no evidence of harm, we should revisit the presumption. As many Asia-Pacific Economic Cooperation (APEC) nations look to develop their own competition laws, there is a temptation to start with *per se* prohibitions before working up to more sophisticated competition-tested provisions. Nonetheless, one must be wary of an overzealous approach to *per se* prohibitions. If, as the Australian experience suggests, there is little or no prospect that conduct by small to medium enterprises will give rise to a "pernicious effect on competition", then the law should be slow to impose conclusive presumptions to the contrary.

REFERENCES

Australian Competition and Consumer Commission (ACCC). "ACCC & AER Annual Report". FY09/10, 10/11, 11/12, 12/13 and 13/14. Available at <http://www.accc.gov.au/publications/accc-aer-annual-report> (accessed 31 March 2015).

————. "Public Registers". Available at <http://registers.accc.gov.au/content/index.phtml/itemId/3673> (accessed 31 March 2015).

————. "Air New Zealand Limited & Air Canada — Authorisations — A91097 & A91098", 2009.

————. "Australian Ice Hockey Federation Incorporation — Notification — N94049", 2010.

————. "Brisbane International Speedway Pty Ltd & Ors — Notifications — N94032 & N94034", 2010.

————. "Brisbane Marine Pilots Pty Ltd — Authorisation — A91235", 2010.

————. "Guide to Exclusive Dealing Notifications", 2010. Available at <http://www.accc.gov.au/publications/guideto-exclusive-dealing-notifications> (accessed 29 March 2015).

————. "Macquarie Generation & Ors — Authorisations — A91198 & A91199", 2010.

————. "Casuarina Business Precinct Stakeholders Committee — Authorisations — A91201 & A91202", 2011*a*.

————. "Guide to Collective Bargaining Notifications 2011", 2011*b*. Available at <http://www.accc.gov.au/publications/guide-to-collective-bargaining-notifications-2011> (accessed 29 March 2015).

————. "Streamlined Collective Bargaining for Small Business", 2011*c*. Available at <http://www.accc.gov.au/system/files/Streamlined Collective Bargaining.pdf> (accessed 29 March 2015).

————. "A Ace Car Rentals Pty Ltd — Notification — N97129", 2013.

————. "Apex Car Rentals Pty Ltd — Notification — N96882", 2013.

————. "Australian Society of Ophthalmologists Incorporated — A91360", 2013.

————. "Authorisation Guidelines 2013", 2013. Available at <http://www.accc.gov.au/publications/authorisationguidelines-2013> (accessed 29 March 2015).

————. "AVP Solutions Pty Ltd — Notification — N96549", 2013.

————. "Bargain Car Rentals Australia Pty Ltd — Notification — N96979", 2013.

————. "Carljohn Pty Ltd t/a Newcastle Car and Truck Rental — Notification — N97050", 2013.

————. "Narta International Pty Ltd — Authorisation — A91335", 2013.

————. "Tasmanian Farmers & Graziers Association — Revocation and Substitution — A91197", 2015.

Bork, Robert H. *The Antitrust Paradox*. New York: Free Press, 1978.

Business Council of Australia. "Submission to the Competition Policy Review Draft Report", November 2014. Available at <www.competitionpolicyreview. gov.au/files/2014/12/BCA.pdf> (accessed 30 March 2015).

Chicago Board of Trade v. United States 246 U.S. 231 (1918).

Christiansen, Arndt and Wolfgang Kerber. "Competition Policy with Optimally Differentiated Rules instead of '*Per Se* Rules vs Rule of Reason'". *Journal of Competition Law and Economics* 2, no. 2 (2006): 215–44.

Jefferson Parish Hospital District No. 2 v. Hyde, 466 U.S. 2 (1984), n25.

Joskow, Paul L. "Transaction Cost Economics, Antitrust Rules, and Remedies". *Journal of Law, Economics, and Organization* 18, no. 1 (April 2002): 95–116.

Krattenmaker, Thomas G. "*Per Se* Violations in Antitrust Law: Confusing Offenses with Defenses". *Georgetown Law Journal* 77, no. 1 (1988): 165–80.

Leegin Creative Leather Products, Inc v. PSKS, Inc, 551 U.S. 877 (2007).

Northern Pacific Railway v. United States, 356 U.S. 1 (1958) 5.

Reagan, Ronald. "Remarks and a Question-and-Answer Session with the Students and Faculty at Moscow State University", 31 May 1988. Available at <http://www.reagan.utexas.edu/archives/speeches/1988/053188b.htm> (accessed 20 July 2015).

Varney, Christine A. and Jonathan J. Clarke. "Chicago and Georgetown: An Essay in Honor of Robert Pitofsky". *Georgetown Law Review* 101, no. 6 (2013): 1565–85.

8

ENFORCING COMPETITION LAW AGAINST SMEs
Presumptions and Problems

Vince See Eng Teong and Yoshifumi Fukunaga

This chapter argues that, while some states in Southeast Asia favourably treat small and medium-sized enterprises (SMEs), competition enforcement in many other jurisdictions creates difficulties and disadvantages for them. Many different aspects of enforcement contribute to this. Most importantly, some young competition agencies tend to focus their enforcement efforts on SMEs with the presumption that SMEs are more likely to infringe the law due to their lack of understanding. In contrast, state-owned enterprises, which have a variety of opportunities to influence political figures and industry regulators, enjoy a measure of favouritism. SMEs also face difficulties in utilizing competition law to fight larger players, due to their limited financial resources, limited access to proper legal resources, and, sometimes, an inconsistent and non-transparent application of the law by some competition regulators.

Introduction

The treatment of small and medium-sized enterprises (SMEs) in competition law and policy has always been a contentious issue.

SMEs in many countries have, for years, argued that they are placed at a disadvantage in the enforcement of competition law — if not within overall competition policy — and should thus be excluded from the ambit of the law. Some countries have chosen to exclude them from the ambit of the law, whilst others keep them within though subject to the *de minimis* test.[1] Where SMEs are excluded from competition law, it usually takes the form of a blanket exclusion (such as occurs in Article 50 of Indonesia's Law No. 5 of 1999), although some partial exclusions may also be found. This chapter will examine some issues facing SMEs that arise from the enforcement of competition law, such as the presumption of a propensity to infringe the law, enforcement favouritism for large enterprises, the failure to create a level-playing field, and some other disadvantages faced by SMEs in enforcing their rights under competition law. For the purpose of this chapter, the notion of enforcement of competition law is used in its widest sense to include the enforcement of competition regulation by sectoral regulators; the term "competition authorities" here includes both sectoral and general regulators. The geographical focus is Southeast Asia.

The Presumption of Propensity

One common enforcement characteristic of competition authorities — and this is particularly true with young authorities — is to focus their enforcement efforts on SMEs. The official excuse is that SMEs lack understanding of the law and the need for compliance. Statistical surveys, whether conducted by or at the instance of competition authorities, often go to show that SMEs have the highest level of ignorance of competition law (*The Star Online* 2013). The high score amongst SMEs stands in contrast with the low score amongst large enterprises, state-owned enterprises (SOEs), and multinational companies (MNCs). From such survey outcomes, competition authorities often take a quantum leap to reach the conclusion that SMEs are therefore more prone to anti-competitive activities and should thus be the prime target of enforcement (MyCC 2015).

Surely, some enforcement statistics *prima facie* confirm this. For instance, three out of the first four cartel cases found by the Malaysia

Competition Commission (MyCC) to have infringed the Competition Act 2010 involved SMEs, including the Cameron Highlands floriculturists, ice manufacturers in Kuala Lumpur and other cities, and fifteen members of the Sibu Confectionary and Bakery Association. Likewise, virtually all of the parties penalized by the Competition Commission of Singapore (CCS) under the cartel provisions of Singapore's Competition Act 2004 appear to have involved SMEs, including pest control operators, express bus services, electrical and building works, employment agencies, model agencies, Batam ferry operators, and motor vehicle traders.

However, it is debatable whether the right course of action is to focus on SMEs simply on the grounds of their apparent lack of understanding of competition law. After all, an apparent lack of understanding does not necessarily automatically mean that SMEs will infringe it. Moreover, the so-called empirical evidence against SMEs is inherently limited in scope and nature, and to date has been confined in most instances to cartel activities. Competition law is, however, wider than this, and potential breaches can also occur in relation to anti-competitive agreements, abuse of market power, mergers and acquisitions, and, in certain jurisdictions, the granting of state aid. In most of these situations, SMEs are unlikely to be the infringer, since they have low market share or turnover. In cases relating to anti-competitive agreements and abuses of market power, SMEs are often at the receiving end. Merger control is furthermore *ex ante* in nature as opposed to *ex post* assessment of agreements and abusive conduct. State aid is irrelevant to SMEs — and indeed any enterprise — for it has to do with government conduct as opposed to that of a private enterprise.

Another argument against unnecessarily focusing enforcement attention on SMEs is the market impact, if any, of an infringement by an SME. It is undeniable that such market impact is likely to be insignificant and localized, especially when compared to that of SOEs and MNCs, due to the small-scale and localized activities of SMEs (Schaper 2010). As a case in point, the worldwide airfreight surcharge cartel involved many of the state-owned national carriers as well as legacy airlines, but no SMEs.

Even if the enforcement statistics do support the contention that SMEs commit more infringements than SOEs and MNCs, such statistics may simply reflect the realities of enforcement, particularly amongst the young agencies. In reality, SMEs are small market players. They lack political and commercial influence, whether individually or collectively. SMEs also lack financial resources to have access to proper legal advice. For many new competition enforcement agencies squeezed between limited resources and the need to produce quick results, it makes more sense to target small-scale enterprises. SOEs and MNCs are armed with teams of lawyers from international law firms that are well experienced in dealing with competition cases, whereas SMEs are an easy target that does not have ready access to external advisers (Harvie 2001). In jurisdictions where the law is unclear, or enforcement is in general non-transparent or corrupted, there is another valid reason for focusing enforcement on SMEs: the owners of SMEs usually have low level of education, and are unfamiliar with the law, and so may be more prone to paying enforcement officials off than facing some legal proceedings (Mourougane 2012; *Jakarta Post* 2000).

Enforcement Favouritism for Large Enterprises

The focus on SMEs may be compared with the enforcement attitude towards large enterprises, particularly SOEs. Indeed, an examination of the enforcement attitude towards big firms, particularly in regulated industries, often shows a stark contrast to the focus of many competition enforcers on SMEs.

In some countries, a legacy of previous economic activity is that many market sectors may remain dominated by SOEs even after market liberalization or privatization has taken place. As such, the sectors remain monopolistic or oligopolistic — in many instances, the so-called privatization process simply converts a public monopoly into a private one. Due to a long history of state ownership, competition authorities often shy away from competition enforcement in these sectors (Nikomborirak 2006). Where a market sector is characterized by state concessions or ongoing involvement by an arm of government (such as the state fixing fees, rates, or charges), such activities are usually formally exempted and competition law has no role to play.

Where an industry is under the jurisdiction of a specialist industry regulator (such as in utilities or infrastructure), the risk of industry capture of the regulator may also tilt the enforcement balance in favour of large players. It may particularly occur where the fees arising from licensing, for instance, form part of the budget of the regulator (Nikomborirak 2006). As a result of such financial dependency, where the regulator has a choice between invoking its *ex post* competition power and *ex ante* regulatory power, it is likely to resort to the latter. The reason is the regulatory power simply *regulates* the conduct of the market players and is not punitive in nature. On the other hand, the competition power is *punitive* and may, depending on the relevant legislation, open the penalized market players to civil actions for damages arising from breaching the competition provisions. While private rights of action are a useful tool to complement the public enforcement of competition law, the industry regulators' exercise of their *ex ante* regulatory power and failure to exercise their *ex post* competition power creates a rather unsatisfactory and unfair situation: large market players (as the regulated suppliers) may or may not be penalized by the regulatory power, whilst SMEs (as the users and victims of an anti-competitive conduct) suffer damages without an avenue of compensation. Such failure to exercise the regulator's competition power may also create a precedent that fortifies large enterprises' belief that they are above the law, so long as they maintain a good work relationship with the industry regulator. This may in turn lead to industry capture or "lazy" regulators.

Bias towards large enterprises may also stem from the lack of a clear separation between politicians, industry regulators, and regulated large enterprises. As seen in Figure 8.1, in a situation where an individual from a market player may become a member of the industry regulator or of a state decision-making body, or vice versa (such as after the retirement of the relevant individual from the regulatory body or politics), there is a natural inclination to favour regulated large firms in a dispute between large enterprises (as the regulated suppliers) and SMEs (as the users and alleged victims of anti-competitive conduct).

Such bias is also self-evident from the fact that many competition laws do not expressly provide for the appointment of a commissioner with specialized knowledge or expertise in SMEs.[2]

FIGURE 8.1
The Interlocking Relationship

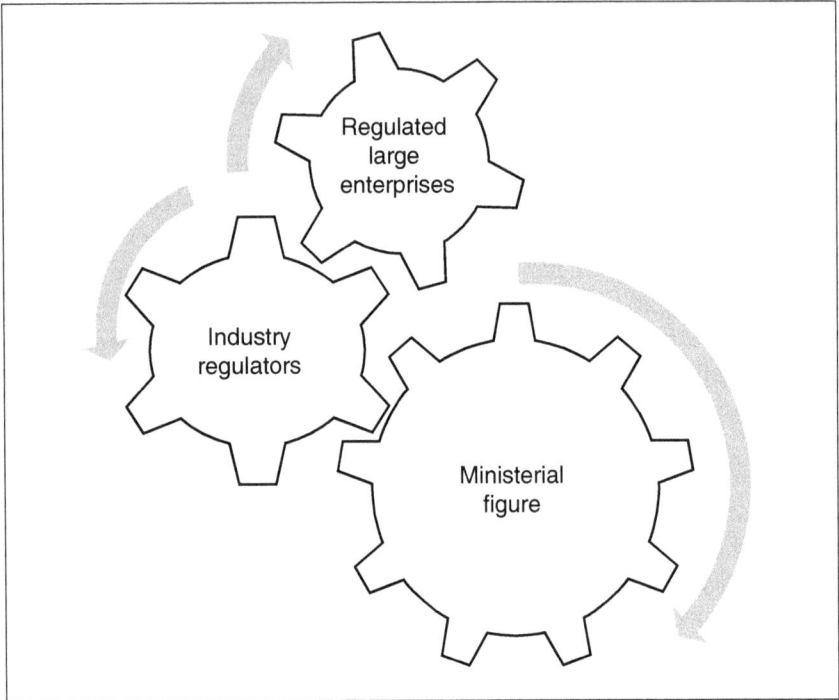

Creating a Level Playing Field

The provision on abuse of market power is a useful weapon to SMEs, particularly in the course of dealing with their large competitors. However, just like any other law, it has some limitations. It only comes into play when a significant market power exists, and thus a central issue is determining the level of market power above which a case of abuse can be founded. While the monopolization provision in the U.S. Sherman Act requires a very high threshold approaching that of a monopoly, the jurisdictions that follow the European Union (EU) model tend to take a much lower threshold, since their laws merely require a dominant position. In the EU, 40 per cent market share suffices. Singapore requires 50 per cent, while Malaysia sets it at a higher threshold of 60 per cent, probably the highest among those jurisdictions that follow the EU style of abuse of dominant position. Indonesia's law defines it at 50 per cent.

What level to set depends to some extent on how liberalized and competitive the domestic economy is, and whether imports serve as a competitive constraint on domestic products. Thailand, for instance, is said to have failed to enforce its provisions on abuse of dominant position due to the lack of definition of its market share threshold (Thanitcul 2013; Nikomborirak 2006). Where a country is plagued with regulatory barriers and where imports do not serve as a well-functioning competitive constraint due to such barriers, setting a high threshold for the finding of the existence of significant market power has the potential effect of rendering the law ineffective. While it is possible to argue that market share by itself does not determine the issue of dominant position, it is certainly the first indication of a competitive relationship among the market players. Where an alleged abuser has a low market share, it may be hard for the complainant to establish a case of an abuse of a dominant position, despite the existence of other market factors that point to the existence of dominance. This may work to the detriment of SMEs where the competition authority is young, inexperienced, or lackadaisical.

The Common Disadvantages

SMEs are also faced with other disadvantages in the course of competition enforcement. Many competition authorities, particularly the younger agencies, insist that the complainant must disclose his or her identity and even substantiate the complaint with evidential proof.[3] Such a requirement is likely to deter, rather than encourage, the exposure of anti-competitive conduct where the regulatory agency lacks legal independence. It is also likely to deter whistle-blowing; in some countries, the state has a record of prosecuting complainants as opposed to the alleged perpetrator of a breach. In the case of cartel activities or abuse of market power, particularly those involving upstream producers whose number is likely to be small if not monopolistic, making an official complaint and disclosing one's identity may simply result in trade reprisals by the complained against the complainant. While an open trade reprisal can constitute a criminal offence in most jurisdictions, it requires the evidence on the criminal standard of proof of reprisal. This may easily be circumvented by the supplier simply ceasing supply without linking the cessation to the complainant's act. Where the investigation is time-consuming, particularly involving an abuse of market power which is more complex and technical than a clear-cut cartel case, the SMEs that have lodged a complaint may have gone out of business by the time a decision finding an abusive conduct is reached.

Public enforcement raises other issues as well. In jurisdictions where the competition authority has an absolute discretion to terminate a case after some preliminary investigation, the exercise of such discretion may not be transparent. Where the law does not require the authority to provide a written explanation of its decision to close an investigation or to make such reasons available to public scrutiny, it may dilute public confidence in the enforcement. In some jurisdictions, political figures (such as the relevant Minister) may have the capacity to issue general directions to the competition authority, which can interfere with the independence of the agency. Such interference may even be made easier where the law provides for such a power without at the same time insisting on publication of such directions. Such potential interference, not to mention the lack of political or commercial influence of SMEs to counter it — coupled with the lack of a legal basis for the independence of the competition authority — simply renders the whole process more dubious.

Would the judiciary be of assistance? While public enforcement in the United States, Australia, and New Zealand in general requires the competition authority to bring cases for determination by the judiciary, those jurisdictions that follow the so-called European commission style or administrative style of enforcement place competition enforcement largely within a separate quasi-judiciary body with limited scope of appeal to the civil courts or judicial review. The avenue of seeking an independent judicial oversight may be curtailed by the relevant law, such as by limiting appeal of the competition authority's decisions exclusively to an appeal tribunal that is not part of the judiciary. Alternatively, the law may limit appeals to certain specific circumstances (e.g. where the competition authority has made a positive finding but not where it has exercised its discretion to close a case without a finding).

Public enforcement aside, private enforcement is also fraught with difficulties. One is where collective redress, such as class actions or representative actions, is not permitted by the law. It is widely recognized that private actions by the victims of competition law infringements against the infringers complement public enforcement, which may be constrained by administrative priority and lack of public resources. Collective redress is particularly significant to some groups of potential victims, such as the indirect purchasers of a good or service that has been controlled by a cartel. Unless they can come together in a class action, or one of them can represent the rest in a representative action, it is hard to imagine a situation where all the indirect purchasers who have been overcharged by the members of a cartel might go to court to sue the latter. Most of the indirect purchasers are likely to have outlaid amounts that are so small that they do not make legal action to recover the lost moneys worthwhile (EC 2008). As for direct purchasers, unless one finds a case like the worldwide airfreight surcharge cartel where the direct, major victims were actually MNCs which couriered their goods on the airlines (EC 2010) or the worldwide bearing cartel case where the direct purchasers were global car manufacturers (EC 2014), the direct purchasers may simply be some SMEs who do not find going to court individually an attractive option (EC 2008). There is also the issue of passing on when the direct purchasers pass on the damages to the indirect purchasers (Petrucci 2008). A failure to facilitate claims by SMEs against large infringing enterprises will result in such damages being left uncompensated, while victims that comply with the law continue to have to absorb the losses (EC 2008).

Even if some SMEs have the will to take their case to the court, they are likely to face some more hurdles. One is financial. Legal fees are likely to be high, particularly where the defendant is an MNC armed with an international law firm and prepared to drag out the case as long as possible so as to rack up the legal costs of their opponent (Mourougane 2012). As Harvie (2001) and Harvie et al. (2010) have pointed out, while cost is a significant factor for enterprises of all sizes, it is of more significance to SMEs due to their small scale of operation and limited access to financial resources. Financial institutions or private lenders are unlikely to be willing to sponsor a private suit, although it is not unheard of. This speaks for the significance of having collective redress by SMEs against large, infringing enterprises. For SMEs, this concern may, to some extent and depending on the relevant legal provisions, be alleviated as a result of the passing of crowdfunding legislation.

Another hurdle is where the relevant competition law permits private rights of action, but it can only take place after the full disposal of the case by the state authorities, as was the case in Singapore (McEwin 2013). While there are arguments in favour of such a stay, namely that competition cases are inherently technical and invariably complicated due to the complex legal and economic analysis involved, such a delay may work to the detriment of the claimants where state authorities are inefficient, or the investigation or court process carries a lot of red tape or is time-consuming. As one author points out, having this kind of legal provision is also evidence of a somewhat paternalistic approach by the state (See 2012).

Conclusion

The lack of understanding of competition law by many SMEs does not necessarily lead to a greater propensity by them to infringe the law — they are two separate issues. There is a missing link and competition authorities do not seem to have any evidence to support any association between the two issues. To the contrary, SOEs and MNCs that are armed with teams of competition lawyers and score high on competition compliance surveys have occasionally also been found to be participants in some of the most serious cartels.

The substance of competition law requires the existence of problematic behaviour which has a significant or appreciable market impact. This impact helps justify legal interference, since markets should generally be permitted to operate freely unless there is a clear rationale for intervention. If there is not a significant market impact, competition law should not intervene. However, this fundamental principle appears to be neglected when it comes to enforcement. SMEs, in comparison with SOEs and MNCs, are unlikely to have much of a significant market impact, yet they are still often the focus of enforcement work by many agencies.

It is debatable whether competition authorities should focus their attention on SMEs. It has been pointed out that taking actions against a few out of the numerous SMEs merely entails a low level of repercussions that are attributed to the low level of publicity (Schaper 2010). Focusing enforcement efforts on SMEs without, on the other hand, providing them with facilitative measures, such as the representative actions and class actions adopted by the European Parliament, is likely to shake the moral basis of the law.

Competition authorities, particularly the young newer ones, should perhaps focus their enforcement efforts on large cases with significant market effects, so as to stamp their authority. Recent examples of such matters include MyCC's imposition of a RM10 million fine on Malaysia Airlines, and CCS's imposition of S$989,000 penalty on SISTIC for abusing their dominant positions. Such actions can send a clear message to all enterprises that they will be penalized regardless of their size. Taking enforcement actions against large firms, dominant SOEs, or MNCs will also establish the law's moral standing, by demonstrating to society that these enterprises are not shielded simply because they are large or state-owned.

NOTES

1. As the protection of SMEs is one of the objectives of Indonesia's Law No. 5 of 1999, Article 50 thereof expressly excludes SMEs from the scope of the law. Another name for the *de minimis* test is the so-called "safe harbour" approach. Under this approach, subject to cartel agreements, an agreement, whether between competitors or non-competitors, is deemed to not have anti-competitive effects if the market shares of the parties to the agreement, whether individually or collectively, are below a certain figure. While this is applicable to agreements only, SMEs are by definition unlikely to be concerned with abuse of market power for the latter is usually premised upon possession of 50 per cent or more of market share. As for merger control, it usually requires a rather significant turnover before it comes into play.
2. A commendable exception may be found in Australia where a Deputy Chair of the Australian Competition and Consumer Commission represents SMEs' interests.
3. This was one issue raised in the review of Vietnam's competition law after ten years in force: *Brief Review Report — Vietnam Competition Legislation*, p. 13.

REFERENCES

European Commission (EC). "Commission Staff Working Paper Accompanying the White Paper on Damages Actions for Breach of the EC Antitrust Rules". SEC (2008) 404. Brussels: Commission of the European Communities, 2 April 2008.

————. "Antitrust: Commission Fines 11 Air Cargo Carriers €799 Million in Price Fixing Cartel". Press release IP/10/1487. Brussels: European Commission, 9 November 2010.

————. "Antitrust: Commission Fines Producers of Car and Truck Bearings €953 Million in Cartel Settlement". Press release IP/14/280. Brussels: European Commission, 19 March 2014.

Harvie, Charles. "Competition Policy and SMEs in Vietnam". Working Paper 01-10. Wollongong: University of Wollongong, 2001.

Harvie, Charles, Sothea Oum, and Dionisius A. Narjoko, eds. "Small and Medium Enterprises (SMEs) Access to Finance in Selected East Asian Economies". ERIA Research Project Report 2010, No. 14 (2010).

Jakarta Post. "What Kind of Intervention is Needed for SMEs?", 31 October 2000.

Malaysia Competition Commission (MyCC). "MyCC's Past Achievements and Way Forward". News Release, 2 March 2015.

McEwin, Ian. "Competition Policy and Law in Singapore". In *Proceeding on AEC and Competition Laws: Opportunities and Challenges*, edited by Sakda Thanitcul and Ian McEwin. Bangkok: Chulalongkorn University, 2013.

Mourougane, Annabelle. "Promoting SME Development in Indonesia". OECD Economics Department Working Papers, No. 995, ECO/WKP (2012) 72. Paris: OECD Publishing, 2012.

Nikomborirak, Deunden. "Political Economy of Competition Law: The Case of Thailand, the Symposium on Competition Law and Policy in Developing Countries". *Northwestern Journal of International Law & Business* 26, no. 3 (2006): 597.

Petrucci, Carlo. "The Issues of the Passing-on Defence and Indirect Purchasers' Standing in European Competition Law". *European Competition Law Review* 29, no. 1 (2008): 33–42.

Schaper, Michael T. "Competition Law, Enforcement and the Australian Small Business Sector". *Small Enterprise Research* 17, no. 1 (2010): 7–18.

See, Vince Eng Teong. "A Decade After the Communications & Multimedia Act 1998 — The Law and Competition". *Competition & Consumer Law Journal* 18 (2010): 139–64.

————. "The Competition Act 2010: The Issues and Challenges". *European Journal of Law and Economics* 40, no. 3 (2012): 587–616.

Thanitcul, Sakda. "Competition Policy and Law in Thailand". In *Proceeding on AEC and Competition Laws: Opportunities and Challenges*, edited by Sakda Thanitcul and Ian McEwin. Bangkok: Chulalongkorn University, 2013.

The Star Online. "Helping SMEs Understand Competition Law", 19 August 2013.

9

HOW COMPETITION LAW MAY AFFECT FRANCHISED SMEs IN APEC ECONOMIES

Jenny Buchan

The business format franchise model has been widely adopted in many nations throughout the Asia-Pacific region because it provides an opportunity for individuals to establish their own small to medium-sized business as a franchisee. It also enables thriving businesses to expand quickly, and without compromising quality, into foreign and domestic jurisdictions as franchisors. Competition law, however, often impacts on franchise operations. The effects arise both from the general impact of competition law on business but also because of the vertical and horizontal structures associated with the franchisor/franchisee relationship. This chapter identifies the relevant competition laws throughout the Asia-Pacific Economic Cooperation (APEC) economies and provides examples of the competition law breaches that franchise networks must avoid. In particular, it examines the difficulties of market definition associated with franchise models and the challenges faced by competition regulators in communicating policy to franchisees and small and medium-sized enterprises (SMEs).

Introduction

Numerous small and medium-sized enterprises (SMEs) throughout the twenty-one Asia-Pacific Economic Cooperation (APEC) economies are operated as business format franchises. Two forms of franchising are widely recognized. In product franchising, a franchisor supplies branded products or services to a franchisee (seller), but does not control all aspects of how the franchisee conducts the retail business. The other form, business format franchising, is more all-encompassing. It involves a franchisor creating a retail business, testing it, and resolving any problems, then documenting every aspect of the business and, finally, advertising for franchisees to purchase and operate franchised clones. The franchisor sells its franchisees a licence, typically for a fixed term. Franchisees then invest their own time and finances in establishing legally independent, but functionally dependent businesses, under the franchisor's brand while following the rules set out by the franchisor. The focus of this chapter is on business format franchising.

This model of franchising is increasingly popular, and has become ever more versatile and sophisticated since the mid-twentieth century. Franchising currently exists along a spectrum, from being a widely studied, highly regulated, and pervasive business model in countries such as Australia and the United States, to an unregulated, data-poor, fledgling activity in countries such as Papua New Guinea. Wherever it exists, and regardless of where on the spectrum the model lies, the independent but dependent nature of the relationship between franchisors and their franchisees poses challenges for the makers of competition policy and the regulators who enforce the laws that flow from that policy.

This chapter outlines the impacts of competition law on business format franchising. It first defines what franchising is, then singles out the areas of competition law that are important to its operation. After this, it analyses a range of competition law responses APEC economies have adopted to deal with franchising. It also reports on the difficulty of defining "the market" in the context of franchising, and the ongoing difficulty competition regulators are facing in communicating policy to SMEs.

What is Franchising?

Any business, or part of a business, that can be cloned and function independently can be franchised. While some franchisors are SMEs, others are large corporations. A franchisor may be a multinational corporation (such as Yum! Brands, Inc. which is listed on the New York Stock Exchange or a private family company such as IKEA), a domestic proprietary company (the usual legal entity for franchisors), a trust, or a sole proprietor. Franchisees are commonly portrayed as SMEs, but they may also become large enterprises over time.

Viewed from the outside, franchisees' businesses are indistinguishable in many respects from any other SMEs. However, there are also some significant differences for the owners of these businesses, and consequently also for regulators. Table 9.1 provides a summary of some key differences between non-franchised SMEs and franchisees.

It should be noted that the reach of franchise law and its terminology differs across APEC economies. For instance, the definition of "commercial franchise" in China catches a wider range of businesses than does the definition in Australia. No matter how "franchise" is defined, however, competition law still applies to the business model.

As a franchisor grows its network, it may appoint an intermediary called a "master franchisee" to populate a large territory with franchisees and service their needs. Either the franchisor or the master may also appoint area developers, whose role is to locate and operate multiple sites, and run one franchise as a demonstration unit for prospective franchisees. Franchisees sign their franchise agreement with the franchisor (in the area developer model), or the master. Both a master and an area developer, on longer fixed term licences than the unit franchisees, have performance targets, and are responsible for developing the franchisor's brand in a region of the world, a country, a state, or a smaller region that is capable of supporting several franchised units.

The franchisor, its master franchisees, area developers, and franchisees are all independent legal entities, not part of the same corporate group. The network of franchisor, master franchisees, area developers, unit franchisees, and third party and related party suppliers is connected by contracts. The franchisor is not the franchisees' employer; it does, however, through contractual obligations, establish a network

TABLE 9.1
Significant Similarities and Differences Between Non-Franchised SMEs and Franchisees

Feature	SMEs	Franchisees
Size by number of businesses	Numerous — typically more than 95% of all firms	Small proportion of overall business population
Number of employees	Limited — frequently no employees other than owner	Range from one to hundreds
Internal governance	Autonomous	Franchisor-mandated and controlled
Terms of trade	Autonomous	Created by franchisor
Supply chain	Autonomous	Created and possibly controlled or owned by franchisor
Ability to negotiate collectively	No	Yes, in some jurisdictions. Once the network achieves critical mass, the franchisor has negotiating power with landlords and other suppliers, akin to the power a large company has.
Market power	No	Possibly, if franchisor is a significant player (for example, McDonalds/Yum! Brands).
Influence with government	Not individually	Yes, through industry representative bodies although conflict exists between franchisors' and franchisees' interests.

Source: Compiled by the author.

governance system that franchisees are bound by. The franchisor is thus able to spread legal and operational risks across a wide range of independent operators whose creditors do not have recourse to the franchisor.

A sense of how enthusiastically the franchise model has been adopted by SMEs operating as unit franchisees throughout the APEC economies can be gained from the data in Table 9.2.

One of the defining features of franchised businesses is a high degree of brand uniformity — Subway's thirty-nine stores in Hong Kong should look and smell the same, and sell the same sandwiches as the 27,000 Subway stores in the United States. Subway does not have franchisor-owned stores; all are franchised SMEs. To enable them to achieve and maintain this standardization, franchisors design franchise agreements to give themselves a high degree of flexibility, while securing maximum control over all other players in their network. Competition law thus becomes relevant, as the franchisor may be able to operate in an anti-competitive way towards both its competitors and its own franchisees.

The Intersection of Competition Law and Franchising

Franchise laws sit alongside competition laws in a regulatory sense. In some jurisdictions, such as Australia, the same regulator is charged with enforcing the competition laws as well as any franchise-specific laws. The Australian Competition and Consumer Commission (ACCC) polices both Australia's Competition and Consumer Act 2010 (Commonwealth) and the mandatory national Franchising Code of Conduct. In other economies, one body regulates competition law, while separate agencies regulate other business trading laws. An example is Peru, where the Institute for the Defense of Competition and Intellectual Property (INDECOPI) regulates competition law, and the country has several laws related to market access which tackle unauthorized and unwarranted barriers to market entry. These are enforced by a separate commission within INDECOPI, the Elimination of Bureaucratic Barriers Commission. In some nations, such as Australia and the United States, franchisors are not seen to be offering franchisees a security, thus the securities regulators cede control of the sector to the competition and consumer protection regulators.

TABLE 9.2
Number of Franchises and Impact across APEC Economies

Apec Economy	Franchisors (estimate)	Franchisees (estimate)	Impact by Employment/Value to Economy of Franchised Businesses (estimate)
Australia[1]	1,160	79,000	Sector turnover $144 billion
Brunei Darussalam	No data	No data	No data
Canada[2]	No data	78,000	No data
Chile[3]	54	250	No data
China[4]	More than 1,000	300,000	No data
Chinese Taipei (Taiwan)	No data	No data	No data
Hong Kong[5]	75 franchisors in HK in 2000	No data	No data
Indonesia	No data	80,000 units	No data
Japan[6]	1,304 in 2014	252,514	Sales amount 234,773 billion yen in 2014
Malaysia[7]	757 in 2014	7,525	2.5 per cent to the gross domestic product in 2014
Mexico[8]	No data	1,600 new outlets opened during 2013	11,200 jobs were created by franchise business in 2013
New Zealand[9]	440 in 2012	22,000	Sector employs over 100,000 people and accounts for 11% of GDP
Papua New Guinea	No data	No data	No data
Peru	No data	No data	No data
Philippines[10]		Over 1,300 franchises in 2011	Sector generated a turnover of US$11 billion
Russia[11]	No data	74,600	Sector contributing 3.5% of GDP
Singapore[12]	600 in 2012	40,000+	Sector contributed 1.6% of GDP in 2012

TABLE 9.2 (*continued*)

Apec Economy	Franchisors (Estimate)	Franchisees (Estimate)	Impact by Employment/Value to Economy of Franchised Businesses (Estimate)
South Korea[13]	3,482 in 2014	194,199 in 2014	Sector employs 1,240,000 people and comprised 7.8% of GDP in 2011
Thailand[14]	250	11,000 in 2011	No data
United States[15]	No data	781,794 units including real estate and automobile	Sector provided 8.569 million jobs in 2014 Generated US$844 billion through franchised units
Vietnam	No data	No data	No data

Notes:
[1] Frazer, Weaven, and Grace (2014).
[2] Canada Franchise Association.
[3] International Business Publications (2009).
[4] China Chain Store & Franchise Association.
[5] Hong Kong Franchise Association.
[6] Japan Fair Trade Commission.
[7] Roslan, Noorashikin (2014).
[8] de Pablo and Algaba (2014).
[9] Flint-Hartle, Frazer, and Weaven (2012).
[10] Philippine Franchising Association.
[11] Franchisopedia.
[12] Lim (2014).
[13] Fair Trade Commission, Republic of Korea.
[14] Bangkok legal blog (2012).
[15] Taylor (2015).

Source: Compiled by the author.

By and large, franchise laws are established to regulate the asymmetries that exist between a franchisor and its franchisees. Little direct reference is made to the roles of master franchisees and area developers. Where countries have enacted specific law regulating franchise relationships, these laws typically focus on one or a combination of three areas: disclosure, relationship laws (including implied terms), and registration requirements. They do not specifically address competition issues. As Table 9.3 shows, almost half of the APEC economies lack

Table 9.3
Competition and Franchise Laws in APEC

APEC Economy	Competition Law Affecting Franchising	Franchise-Specific Legislation/Regulation
Australia	Competition and Consumer Act 2010 (Commonwealth)	Competition and Consumer (Industry Codes-Franchising) Regulation 2014
Brunei Darussalam	Competition order 2015 adopted but not yet in force	No specific regulation
Canada	Competition Act RSC 1985 Consumer Packaging and Labelling Act RSC 1985	Alberta: Franchises Act, R.S.A. 2000. Manitoba: The Franchise Act, S.M. 2010. New Brunswick: Franchises Act, R.S.N.B. 2007. Ontario: Arthur Wishart Act (Franchise Disclosure), 2000. Prince Edward Island: Franchises Act, R.S.P.E.I.,1988.
Chile	Chilean Law No. 19.911, 2003	No specific regulation
China	Anti-Monopoly Law of the People's Republic of China 2007	Measures for the Administration of Commercial Franchise Operations 2004 Regulation on Administration of Commercial Franchises 2007
Chinese Taipei (Taiwan)	Taiwan Fair Trade Act 1992	No specific regulation
Hong Kong	The Competition Ordinance	No specific franchise legislation Pyramid Schemes Prohibition Ordinance 2012
Indonesia	Law of the Republic of Indonesia No. 5/1999 Indonesian Antitrust Authority (Government Regulation 2007)	Franchise Regulation 2007 Ministry of Trade Regulation No. 7 Year 2013 on Partnership Development in Franchise Business Services for Food and Beverages (*Permendag Nomor 7*)
Japan	The Act on Prohibition of Private Monopolization and Maintenance of Fair Trade 1947 Unfair Competition Prevention Act 1993	Companies Act 2005 Medium-Small Business Retail Promotion Act 1973 Guidelines on Franchising 2002
Malaysia	Competition Act 2010	Franchise Act 1998

TABLE 9.3 (*continued*)

APEC Economy	Competition Law Affecting Franchising	Franchise-Specific Legislation/Regulation
Mexico	Ley Federal de Competencia Económica 2014	Industrial Property Law 1991 Article 142 contains a definition of franchise
New Zealand	Commerce Act 1986	No specific regulation
Papua New Guinea	Independent Consumer and Competition Commission Act 2002	No specific regulation
Peru	Act for the Repression of Anticompetitive Behavior 2008	No specific regulation
Philippines	Act No. 3247 (Act to Prohibit Monopolies and Combinations in Restraint of Trade)	No specific regulation
Republic of Korea	Monopoly Regulation and Fair Trade Act 1980	Act on Fairness of Franchise Business Practices 2002 as amended by Fair Franchise Transaction Act 2014
Russia	Russian Competition Legislation 2011	No specific regulation
Singapore	Competition Act 2006 Multi-Level Marketing and Pyramid Selling (Prohibition) Act 2000	No specific regulation
Thailand	Trade Competition Act 1999	*Draft Franchise Act 2011*
United States	Sherman Antitrust Act 1890 Clayton Antitrust Act 1914 Federal Trade Commission Act 1914 Robinson-Patman Act 1936	Disclosure Requirements and Prohibitions Concerning Franchising (The FTC Rule) 1979
Vietnam	Law on Enterprises 2000 Competition Law 2004 and six implementing guidelines (five decrees and a circular).	Decree Number 35/2006/ND-CP regulating franchises came into force on 1 January 2007

Source: Compiled by the author.

specific franchise laws. Any issues that arise in the context of a franchise relationship are regulated under the general laws of those countries.

Anti-Competitive Conduct

As a franchise network consolidates, the franchisor and/or master franchisees will establish a set of relationships with nominated suppliers. By using pre-approved suppliers, the franchisor is able to maintain brand consistency, but runs a risk of acting anti-competitively. It is easy to understand that a franchisor has stronger negotiating power with the supplier when it is representing all of the franchisees in the network with their combined buying power, than if each franchisee negotiated individually. These products or services supplied by or through the franchisor might be key components of the franchisee's offering, such as stock, shop fit contracts, or software contracts, or optional extras such as business finance. Franchisees may be required to source up to 100 per cent of their inputs from, or through, the franchisor or its approved suppliers. Because they are likely to become suppliers to their franchisees, and may also become competitors with each other and with their franchisees, franchisors and international master franchisees must be careful not to become entangled in competition law breaches.

Franchisors and franchisees are both at risk, like any business in a competitive market, of breaches involving conduct with competitors. Franchisors additionally risk engaging in anti-competitive vertical conduct because of the tight supply chains they establish with a group of independent business operators (their franchisees) whose business operations they partly control. Some conduct is illegal *per se* as being anti-competitive, whereas other conduct that may infringe competition laws is only illegal if it would "substantially lessen competition" in a market. This is known as the "rule of reason" test in the United States. As it has matured, franchising has proved increasingly attractive to multinational and domestic public companies; a development that exposes franchisors to the competition law aspects of mergers.

Some countries have had to examine franchising closely and have arrived at solutions that recognize apparent breaches of the competition law, but yet still enable franchisors to operate without fear of prosecution by competition authorities. Examples of this are provided further in the chapter.

Horizontal Agreements

Horizontal agreements exist among competitors at the same level in the market — for example café franchisors that compete for market share as coffee bean importers, as well as for franchisees and retail sites. If a franchisor conducts its own retail trading business without placing contractual requirements on masters and franchisees, it needs to be aware of the risk of breaching the areas of competition laws that proscribe certain horizontal behaviour as being anti-competitive. This includes anti-competitive cartel-related conduct, a misuse of a company's market power, or an anti-competitive contract, as well as boycotting, price signalling, and/or collusion with competitors. The behaviour risks substantially lessening competition in a market and is examined by regulators through the lens of potential detriment to the ultimate consumer.

Vertical Restraints

Vertical restraints are restrictions that a franchisor attempts to place on suppliers, or franchisees, at different levels of a market. They can "include exclusive appointments for a designated territory, tying obligations, resale price maintenance provisions and obligations not to deal in competing products" (Corones 2010, p. 619).

Because each business within the network is independent, franchisors operate in vertical markets of their own creation. They must therefore be careful not to abuse their considerable contractual power over how their franchisees conduct their businesses. A brief elaboration of some types of vertical restraint follows.

Exclusive dealing: This is a practice where one party forces or forbids the other in the business relationship to deal with particular supplier(s). Whether it is illegal depends on whether the arrangement passes a "substantial lessening of competition" test. This test includes an analysis of the economic concept of "market" which is discussed below. Within a franchise relationship, exclusive dealing may arise in relation to customer exclusivity, product exclusivity, and territorial exclusivity. It may not always be to the detriment of franchisees. For example, being allocated exclusive territories may benefit franchisees. Franchisors need to carefully balance the need for consistency and the opportunity to achieve economies of scale with a realistic assessment of what controls are actually essential to retain system quality.

Tying: Tie-in and tying arrangements are types of exclusive dealing. The U.S. court, in Northern Pacific Railway vs United States (1958), described a tying arrangement as a process involving the sale of "one product but only on the condition that the buyer also purchases a different (or tied) product". This may be legitimate if the products only function when purchased together. In some jurisdictions, tying is only seen as illegal if the seller has a financial interest in both products. In other jurisdictions, financial interest is irrelevant. The anti-competitive elements of tying arrangements are that they deprive the buyer of choice and competitors of access to separate markets for the tied products. An example of tying is in the U.S. case of Barber & Ross Co. v Lifetimes Doors, Inc. (1987) where a franchisor attempted to force a franchisee to stock doors it would not otherwise have bought.

Third line forcing: Third line forcing occurs when a party requires its contracting counter party (for example, a franchisor requires its franchisees) to enter into a contract with a third party supplier as a condition of doing business. This third party may be a landlord. In Australia, this conduct is *per se* illegal, as it means the franchisee is not free to source its supplies independently and competitively but must deal with the suppliers dictated by the franchisor.

Resale price maintenance: Resale price maintenance arises when a supplier attempts to dictate the resale price of goods or services. Franchisors in Australia can specify minimum prices of goods and/ or services they have not supplied, but if they are the supplier, they may specify a maximum resale price to their franchisees, although not a minimum. Franchisors may breach the law by, for example, attaching a preprinted price ticket to goods supplied, then requiring the franchisees not to discount. Resale price maintenance can damage franchisees' profits as it prevents franchisees from passing on cost savings to consumers (Corones 2010, p. 619) and from discounting heavily to sell slow-moving stock.

In 2007, the long-held view in the United States that minimum price restraints were automatically illegal, regardless of the impact on competition, was overturned. The Supreme Court decided, by a bare majority (5:4), in Leegin Creative Leather Products, Inc. vs PSKS, Inc. (2007) that franchisors wishing to restrict the depth of discounts for products and services sold by franchisees would be tested on a case by case basis by application of the "rule of reason".

Mergers: It is a breach of many competition laws if a merger will result in a substantial lessening of competition in a market, to the detriment of consumer choice. Several dimensions need to be considered when evaluating whether a market exists. These are discussed below under "market".

It is conceivable that merger issues will arise in the franchising context, as the franchise model is increasingly used by public companies and large private companies. These could occur if, say, two large coffee bean importers, who were franchisors, proposed to merge. Could this merger substantially lessen competition in the wholesale coffee bean market? Similarly if, say, large, multi-brand fast food companies planned a merger then issues might arise in relation to the absence of competitive markets for fast food at freeway-based outlets. It is also worth considering whether a franchisor exercises such tight control over its franchisees that it creates a market within the network. In this context the franchisees are the consumers of the franchisor's business offering. In one of the rare cases where the rights of franchisees has been tested, the merging franchisors argued that there was no injury to the franchisees arising out of the proposed merger as they would be able to charge higher prices. In First and First, Inc. vs Dunkin' Donuts (1990), the Court agreed that the matter had sufficient merit for it to hear the case. However, the franchisees were not successful in halting the merger, partly because the Court refused to consider donuts and coffee as part of the same product market.

Regulating Franchising in the Competition Law Context

The benefits of encouraging people to operate their own small businesses are widely recognized by governments. In recognition of the fact that franchising facilitates small business ownership, a number of APEC jurisdictions deal specifically with franchising matters in the context of their competition laws, as the following examples show.

In Japan, the Act on Prohibition of Private Monopolization and Maintenance of Fair Trade 1947 prohibits businesses from engaging in price maintenance, tying arrangements, and certain other unfair trade practices. According to Japan's Antimonopoly Act Articles 19 and 2, para 9, franchise agreements are not exempt (Shimizu 2014, p. JAP/2).

In Australia, franchisors are clearly subject to the competition law, but individual franchisors may secure authorization to engage in third line forcing if they can satisfy the regulator, the ACCC, that there is an overriding public benefit in them being allowed to breach the law. Arguments that are put to the regulator have stressed the protection of the franchisor's brand, maintenance of product quality, reliability of the supply chain, competitive pricing, business efficiency, compliance with food safety standards, and the provision of a stream of additional income to the franchisor which will be deployed for the benefit of franchisees. Franchising in Australia is specifically regulated under the Franchising Code of Conduct. Under it, franchisors are required to disclose supply chain restrictions to prospective franchisees *ex ante*.

The Peruvian competition authorities take the view that franchises' arrangements do not, of themselves, restrict free competition. Thus, franchising does not attract the attention of the authorities (Del Carmen and Alvarado 2014, PER 10). Similarly, Indonesia specifically exempts franchise-related agreements from being subject to the Competition Law, provided the agreements comply with the guidelines set out by the Commission for the Supervision of Business Competition (Komisi Pengawas Persaingan Usaha or KPPU) (Senen and Ramadhan 2014, INA1).

Singapore's Competition Act 2006 prohibits agreements that prevent, restrict, or distort competition. "The continuing obligation of a franchisee to purchase stock solely from the franchisor could" (Lim 2014, SIN/10) amount to a breach of this legislation. The Act's Third Schedule, however, provides an exemption for vertical agreements. The Competition Commission of Singapore has released guidelines that state that intellectual property provisions — usually a feature of franchise agreements — are normally covered by this "vertical exclusion" provision (Lim 2014, SIN/10).

Factors for SMEs Franchising Through the Lens of Competition Law

Among the factors affecting franchises, and their SME regulators, two stand out as particularly important. Firstly, which market the business is operating in, and secondly, the most effective way to inform the franchisors and franchisees about the relevance of competition law to their businesses.

Some aspects of competition law require "the market" to be identified, as a step towards determining whether particular franchisor conduct could/does substantially lessen competition in that market. A market has four important elements: product, geography, level of function, and time. The definition also acknowledges the possibility of substitution of a cheaper or more readily available product. One widely-accepted Australian judicial definition of a market is:

> ... the area of close competition between firms or ... the field of rivalry between them. ... In determining the outer boundaries of the market we ask a quite simple but fundamental question: if the firm were to "give less and charge more" would there be, to put the matter colloquially, much of a reaction? (Queensland Co-operative 1976).

Each franchise system participates in three markets: the market for sale of franchise opportunities; the local, or online, market that each of its franchisees operates their franchise in; and the market the franchisor creates within its own network. Involvement in the first market is unlikely to lead to a breach of competition law — franchisees are free to select from a wide range of business opportunities. The second market will potentially be scrutinized if franchisees are behaving anti-competitively. The third market remains to be interrogated by regulators.

Conducting this analysis can sometimes be problematic, as recent activity in Malaysia indicates. The Malaysian Competition Act has two main prohibitions. Section 4 prohibits anti-competitive agreements and Section 10 forbids the abuse of a dominant position. Franchise activities are not exempt. One commentator has indeed speculated that an entire franchise chain might be regarded, under Malaysian law, as a single enterprise (Baskaran 2014). If this interpretation is accepted, the restrictive agreements between the franchisor and its franchisees might not be considered anti-competitive. The law in Malaysia is not yet clear on this issue. Neither the Malaysian Competition Commission nor the courts have expressed a view (Baskaran 2014). To view an entire franchise chain as a single enterprise might have unintended consequences, in that franchisees might be construed as being employees with an equity stake in the franchisor's business, and, in the context of competition law, franchisors would be able to price fix, third line force, and impose exclusive dealing requirements on franchisees without being accountable to a regulator.

While some franchisors and franchisees are, without question, big organizations capable of creating or controlling large sections of a market, the majority of franchisees are not running multimillion dollar businesses. A regulator that understands this will not lump all franchisors, or all franchisees, together.

Identifying specific "markets" is becoming increasingly challenging as SMEs, including franchises, adapt to the use of the Internet in their supply chain management and retail operations. This leads to a second factor for the competition regulators dealing with SMEs: how to communicate the law to them.

Despite the many difficulties inherent in communicating with SMEs, regulators need to spend time educating the franchise sector about how competition laws are relevant to them. Breaches, by either franchisors or franchisees, can result in brand damage through negative publicity. They can also result in significant financial penalties.

Effective communication with stand-alone SMEs is notoriously problematic for regulators, but franchise sectors can be accessed through the franchisor and franchisee representative organizations that exist in most countries. Through just one franchisor, a regulator can easily communicate with all of its franchisees. In addition, regulators may establish consultative committees of representatives of several franchise stakeholder groups. An example is Australia's twenty-six-member Small Business & Franchise Consultative Committee, chaired by the ACCC Commissioner whose brief is small business.

Regulators can also set up designated areas of their websites to deal with franchise-related issues. Here they can provide examples of behaviour that would breach, and can provide guidelines for how to obey the law.

Communication with franchised SMEs may be easier in countries where the same regulator has responsibility for enforcing both competition law and the consumer protection laws. The ACCC in Australia and the Commerce Commission in New Zealand are examples of a common regulator. In other jurisdictions, for example Malaysia, a different government agency is in charge of competition laws and consumer protection/franchise laws. Once the agencies are aware of the potential inefficiency these regulatory silos can create, they can devise ways of overcoming any resulting problems.

Conclusion

Franchising is, by its nature, a business model that potentially makes it possible for a brand to expand quickly across many different regions. For example, of the twenty-one APEC economies, only three (Brunei Darussalam, Indonesia, and Papua New Guinea) do not have Subway sandwich franchises. This chapter has identified the main competition issues that a franchise system may confront. Any of the stakeholders in a franchise network may risk breaching competition laws. At every point in the development of its supply chain, and in all business relationships, franchisors, master franchisees, area developers, and franchisees must determine whether competition law risks being breached.

Competition law situations are complex. Franchising is nuanced, and is sometimes regulated by more than one agency or one piece of legislation. Ongoing challenges for competition agencies include keeping pace with the rapidly evolving franchise business model, and getting their message out to the many franchisees who will, inevitably, be widely dispersed geographically within each jurisdiction. Likewise, business operators working under the model need to be aware of their jurisdiction's competition laws. As a growing part of the SME sector, franchise networks will continue to pose a number of interesting challenges for the future regulation of competition law throughout the Asia-Pacific region.

REFERENCES

Act on Prohibition of Private Monopolization and Maintenance of Fair Trade 1947 (Japan).
Bangkok legal blog, by Joel Loo Sean EE, 27 July 2012. Available at <https://bangkoklegal.wordpress.com/2012/07/27/franchising-in-thailand-chapter-1-

things-to-consider-before-buying-selling-a-franchise-in-thailand-with-short-foreword-on-thailand-asean-economy/>.

Barber & Ross Co. v. Lifetimes Doors, Inc. 810 F. 2d 1276 (4th Cir. 1987).

Baskaran, Leela. "Malaysia". In *International Franchising*, edited by Dennis Campbell. New York: Juris Publishing, 2014.

Canada Franchise Association. Available at <http://www.cfa.ca/tools_resources/franchise-researchfacts> (accessed 6 August 2015).

China Chain Store & Franchise Association. Available at <http://www.chinaretail.org/about.asp?typeid=1> (accessed 6 August 2015).

Competition and Consumer Act 2010 (Commonwealth) (Australia).

Corones, Stephen G. *Competition Law in Australia*. Pyrmont: Thomson Reuters, 2010.

de Pablo, Gabriela Campos and Ernesto F. Algaba. "Mexico". In *International Franchising*, edited by Dennis Campbell. New York: Juris Publishing, 2014.

Del Carmen, Maria and Rodrigo Alvarado. "Peru". In *International Franchising*, edited by Dennis Campbell. New York: Juris Publishing, 2014.

Fair Trade Commission, Republic of Korea. *Statistical Yearbook 2014*. Available at <http://eng. ftc.go.kr/bbs.do?command=getList&type_cd=51&pageId=0303> (accessed 6 August 2015).

First and First, Inc. v. Dunkin' Donuts, Inc. Business Franchise Guide (CCH) 9595 (E.D. Pa. 1990).

Flint-Hartle, Susan, Lorelle Frazer, and Scott Weaven. *Franchising New Zealand 2012*. Palmerston North: Massey University Press, 2012.

Franchisopedia. "The Franchise in Russia: Huge Opportunities in a Big Market". Available at <http://franchisopedia.com/global/franchise-articles/franchising-opportunities-and-trends russianmarket/> (accessed 6 August 2015).

Frazer, Lorelle, Scott Weaven, and Anthony Grace. *Franchising Australia 2014*. Brisbane: Griffith University Press, 2014.

Hong Kong Franchise Association. "Franchising in Hong Kong". Available at <http://www.franchise.org.hk/franinhk.asp> (accessed 6 August 2015).

International Business Publications. *Chile Export-import Trade and Business Directory*. New York: International Business Publications, 2009.

Japan Fair Trade Commission. Available at <http://www.jftc.go.jp/e-page> (accessed 6 August 2015).

Leegin Creative Leather Products, Inc v PSKS, Inc 127 S. Ct. 2705, 2712–13 (2007).

Lim, Daniel. "Singapore". In *International Franchising*, edited by Dennis Campbell. New York: Juris Publishing, 2014.

Northern Pacific Railway v. United States, 356 U.S. 1 (1958) 5.

Philippine Franchising Association. Available at <http://www.pfa.org.ph/index.php> (accessed 6 August 2015).

Queensland Co-operative Milling Association Ltd., Defiance Holdings Ltd. (Proposed Mergers with Barnes Milling Ltd.) ATPR 40-012, 1976. Available at <https://www.accc.gov.au/system/files/49%20-%20Queensland%20Co-operative%20Milling%20(1976)%20ATPR%2040-012.pdf>.

Roslan, Noorashikin. "Hasan: Great Year for Ministry". *Franchise News*, 17 December 2014. Available at <http://www.mfa.org.my/newmfa/hasan-great-year-for-ministry> (accessed 6 August 2015).

Senen, Ibrahim and Rivan F. Ramadhan. "Indonesia". In *International Franchising*, edited by Dennis Campbell. New York: Juris Publishing, 2014.

Shimizu, Takenari. "Japan". In *International Franchising*, edited by Dennis Campbell. New York: Juris Publishing, 2014.

Taylor, Kate. "Franchise Industry Not Without Hurdles in 2015". *Entrepreneur*, 8 January 2015. Available at <http://www.entrepreneur.com/article/241597> (accessed 6 August 2015).

10

CHINESE FAMILY FIRMS IN SOUTHEAST ASIA
Special Problems for Competition Law?

R. Ian McEwin

Asian business is different in Southeast Asia. Chinese family companies dominate both big business and small, using organizational forms and practices, such as family conglomerates, that differ from those in the United States and Europe. Little research has been undertaken into the possible anti-competitive effect of such structures. This chapter examines some of these differences and discusses the implications for competition law.

Introduction

Chinese family companies are a major influence in Southeast Asian economies. While family-owned companies dominate small business, as they do in other countries, what is unusual about Southeast Asia is that family companies *also dominate big business*. Big enterprises in Asia are not the large-scale firms run along Western lines, but rather a conglomeration of small and medium-scale enterprises in a variety of markets that are often not even remotely related (see, for example, Gomez and Jomo 1999). In a (now dated) survey of corporate ownership by the World Bank following the Asian Financial Crisis in 1997, Claessens et al. (2000) examined the ownership of almost 3,000 Asian companies and found that a high proportion were family controlled; these firms, in turn, controlled a large part of many Asian economies. For example, the top ten families in Thailand controlled about 46 per cent of assets, whilst their counterparts in Indonesia control an even larger proportion — about 58 per cent (see Table 10.1).

What is perhaps surprising is the high concentration of top family assets irrespective of the level of a country's development or its legal or political system. One likely explanation is the importance of elite patronage networks that not only connect businesses but also link businesses and governments, which are then used to obtain monopoly and other competition-restricting concessions. Business goals and firm characteristics are also important. Family-owned businesses, big or small, may put the interests of the family ahead of profitability, which can have implications for competitive conduct — a family business may be more concerned with preserving the business (to employ family members and to ensure proper succession) and so sustain losses for extended periods of time which may drive even more efficient competitors out of business. Or networks can be used to prevent new entry. Traditionally, most overseas Chinese also formed ethnic Chinese mutual self-help societies, similar to friendly

TABLE 10.1
Family Ownership of Big Business
(% of Total Value of Listed Assets as % of GDP)

Country	Top 1 Family	Top 5 Families	Top 10 Families	Top 15 Families	Top 15 Families
Indonesia	16.6	40.7	57.7	61.7	21.5
Malaysia	7.4	17.3	24.8	28.3	76.2
Philippines	17.1	42.8	52.5	55.1	46.7
Singapore	6.4	19.5	26.6	29.9	48.3
Thailand	9.4	32.2	46.2	53.3	39.3

societies in the West, to regulate particular markets in Southeast Asia — in the name of stability, a fair price, and to provide an employment safety net for members — but these can also facilitate collusion.

Some Chinese big business gained their dominant positions by collaborating closely (or developing patron–client relationships) with the government. Other small and medium-sized Chinese businesses thrived in hostile economic and institutional environments by establishing efficient trading networks based on clan trust, which gave them an advantage over the indigenous population in Southeast Asian countries with undeveloped commercial laws. Chinese business networks also differed in that they were (and still are) based on "personalized business networks, whereas their western counterparts tend to enter into cooperative relationships based upon firm-specific business strategies" (Yeung 2000, p. 409).

The term "crony capitalism" has been applied to the activities of business groups such as the *keiretsu* in Japan, the *chaebol* in South Korea, the overseas Chinese networks, and other family-owned business groups and conglomerates in Southeast Asia. For such business entities, the practice of firms in the group owning each other's shares and lending money to each other on the basis of the relationship rather than on economic merit allows for cronyism. As Hamilton (1999, p. 47) puts it:

> It is at this point that the analysts begin to equate cronyism with *guanxi*, that ubiquitous term meaning, in Chinese, relationship or connection. Equating cronyism and *guanxi* implies that networks based on interpersonal associations look a lot like market distorting cartels.

What do these differences mean for competition law in Southeast Asia? Are there sources of market power in Chinese business networks and organizational forms that are not normally taken into account in simply adapting competition laws based on economic conditions in Europe or the United States? Do business practices that might be seen as anti-competitive but reflect efficiencies given local conditions and practices not be taken into account elsewhere? This chapter considers whether competition law, developed in Western countries, is appropriate for the way Chinese family businesses operate in Southeast Asia.

Why are Chinese Business Organizations and Networks Different?

Witt and Redding (2013, p. 265) argue that "... Asian business systems (except Japan) cannot be understood through categories identified in the West". If business practices are different, the obvious question is: why? Are they due to economic factors such as differing resource endowments, institutional factors like political or legal systems, or because of "culture"? Economists usually ignore culture, because they are mostly concerned with short to medium term issues, whereas culture can be safely assumed to be constant. If, as Witt and Redding (2013) put it, business practices cannot be comprehended through Western models, then cultural differences may be important to understand business practices in Southeast Asia.

Chinese capitalism has its own distinctive cultural features. Family-owned and controlled firms reflect Confucian values and so:

> The fact that a similar pattern of economic behavior emerges whenever governments allow Chinese communities to organize their own affairs suggests that it is in some sense a natural outgrowth of Sinitic culture (Fukuyama 1995, p. 71).

Cultural practices have their roots in historical resource constraints and institutional deficiencies in China. While Confucian influences may be diminishing as competition reduces the importance of differences in culture (because only efficient business organizations and practices survive), they take time to change. But even the 1997 Asian Financial Crisis did not lead to immediate changes in organization and business practices. As Robinson (2009, p. 41) notes:

> Before the crisis, one analyst concluded that 'attempts to transform the informal loosely structured (but highly controlled) Chinese enterprise into a more bureaucratic, Western-style corporation will fail' ... Hesitancy to relinquish family control among overseas Chinese-owned firms ... meant Chinese-owned businesses fiercely resist parting with ownership and management.

However, care needs to be taken in applying explanations in organization and practices based on vague notions of culture, as:

> ... Cultural values, especially when formulated rather vaguely, lend themselves to the development of contradictory theories. This is evident

in the case of Confucian values, which theorists have used to explain both the success of and the lack of entrepreneurship among ethnic Chinese (Carney and Dieleman, 2008, p. 67).

Market economies are based on institutional and legal rules that apply to all, without regard to status. The ideal Confucian state, by contrast, operates through an internal moral code. Confucian moral norms are not universal but depend on five hierarchical relationships: ruler–ruled; father–son; husband–wife; elder brother–younger brother, and friend–friend. Each relationship has mutual obligations. For example, the father protects the son while the son owes filial piety. A harmonious society results from each party fulfilling their obligations.

Of critical importance to Chinese business relations is that there is no moral norm for relationships with strangers. In peasant societies with limited travel, everyone knew everyone. But for Chinese moving to Southeast Asia, everyone was a stranger so there were no personal connections and so no moral obligations. Instead, it could be assumed that others would use strategies to deceive. This meant Chinese businesspeople would naturally favour family businesses and only trust other family members or those from the same clan group. Everyone else was expected to be a rival and untrustworthy, even in collaborative ventures.

On the other hand, institutional factors can be more important than culture, since:

> ... different kinds of business and market organization develop and dominate different market economies as a result of major variations in social institutions and constitute distinctive business systems (Whitley 1992, p. 7).

This approach places greater emphasis on the ability of the overseas Chinese to adapt to, and take advantage of, weak local institutions. An inability to enforce long-term contracts both back in China and in Southeast Asia meant Chinese business operators only dealt with people they could trust. Starting with the family, networks of trust based on clan groups and kinship ties were developed in order to trade successfully (Shapiro et al., 2003). These "trust networks" provided economic advantages such as risk reduction, lower transaction costs, better coordination of inputs within the clan group, and better information between members about short-term opportunities as they arise (which was especially useful in situations where undeveloped markets failed to transmit price information efficiently). These trust networks also facilitated the provision of finance where markets were incomplete and obtaining credit was both costly and time-consuming.

Economic Theories of the Firm

East Asian business structures differ in certain respects from those in the West. Asians are more family- and group-oriented, and respect status and informality much more in business relationships than in the West, where individuality and formal contacts with enforcement mechanisms are more important. While care should be taken not to exaggerate these differences, they are useful in helping to provide an analytical framework. Ruskola (2014), for example, argues that the Western (or liberal model) assumes that the institutional structure of the market starts, bottom-up, from the individual and top down from the political sphere. While the governing logic of the political sphere is a "structure of authority", in the market the governing logic of resource allocation occurs through consensual exchange regulated by contract law. As a result:

> Perhaps the most significant difference between liberal and Confucian worldviews … is that while the former seeks to divide social life into separate spheres, the aspirational norm of Confucianism is *unity*. All aspects of social life are to be regulated by the fiduciary logic of Confucian kinship relations. That is, all of social life ought to constitute one harmonious whole governed by a system of patriarchal norm … (Ruskola 2014, p. 643).

In Confucian societies, it is the kinship group that is the "natural person", not the individual. A similar situation exists with socialism, where the collective is more important than the individual, the institutional structure governing the political, economic, and intimate sphere is the state, and the governing logic is authority. But the impact of Confucian thinking is diminishing, as the following anecdote demonstrates:

> In Singapore until the 1980s government-linked companies formed one of the two officially designated "legs" of development, the other being foreign investment. Government leaders said that Singapore's own Chinese firms could not lead development because they were held down by the "outdated and superfluous" inheritance of traditional Chinese ways (Tipton 2009, p. 427).

Not surprisingly, different world views may lead to differences in the importance of networks and organizational forms such as business groups/conglomerates. These differences are not usually recognized in the microeconomics of organizations or competition law.

But competition law applies to legal forms, not world views. In Europe, for example, competition law frequently refers to businesses as undertakings or economic ventures. But the term "undertaking" is not defined, and instead:

> It is now trite law that a functional approach is taken to the concept of an undertaking ... it has also been long accepted that the term undertaking is not necessarily synonymous with natural or legal personality but denotes "an economic unit for the purpose of the subject-matter of the agreement in question even if in law that economic unit consists of several persons, natural or legal" (Jones 2012, p. 302).

Many countries in Asia have modelled their competition laws on that of the European Union but usually specify to whom the Act applies. Singapore defines an undertaking as "any person, being an individual, a body corporate, an unincorporated body of persons or any other entity, capable of carrying on commercial or economic activities relating to goods or services". This definition is focused on two concepts: entities and economic activity (Townley 2007). In Malaysia, Section 2 of the Competition Act 2010 defines an enterprise as including a parent–subsidiary relationship where "subsidiaries do not enjoy real autonomy in determining their actions on the market". While corporations are clearly economic undertakings, it is important to ask whether subsidiaries and related companies should be considered to be distinct undertakings for competition law purposes. This is particularly important in Southeast Asia, given the importance of networks and business groups/conglomerates.

Economic theories of the firm dominate the analysis of competition law. Traditionally, neoclassical theories of the firm see a business as a set of feasible production options, where a manager maximizes profits by buying and selling inputs and outputs. This approach is useful for many applications, such as forecasting how a firm is likely to behave to changes in the external economic environment. For example, it can model changes in likely price and output as the number of firms (i.e. concentration) in the market changes. Or it can suggest the conditions under which cartels are more likely. But obviously, this approach cannot account for how firms are internally organized, explain why subsidiaries may be preferred to independent operating units, explain why firms merge rather than cooperate, or why there is a preference by some entrepreneurs for business groups or conglomerates.

Transaction Cost Economics (TCE) (see Coase 1937) attempts to deal with organizational form and decisions about whether to bring economic activities within the firm. So firms are seen as the result of decisions about the costs of engaging in transactions versus organizing the same transaction within a firm. Hierarchical authority and control defines the firm. Internal orders replace the market mechanism — obviously the bigger the firm, the greater the market mechanism that is replaced. But as firms grow bigger, the costs of giving a single person (or management team) sole control is likely to lead to more errors and internal firm rigidities.

Williamson (1985) has noted that transaction costs are crucial when relationship-specific investments are involved. Once parties jointly invest they are "locked-in" to each other. In a perfect world, with complete information, they could write a long-term contract in advance that fully details every possible future situation. However, taking account of all possible contingencies is impossible in practice, due to high negotiating and enforcement costs. These terms must be negotiated as the need arises, so the agreement in essence becomes a governance arrangement. Bringing the investment from the market into the firm or into a network can provide that governance arrangement.

Institutional economists see corporations as a way of organizing production in the face of information asymmetries and high transaction costs through trust and authority. So the emphasis of institutional economists on trust and authority parallels the liberal conception of the state (authority) and family (through trust). The Confucian emphasis on family hierarchical arrangements coupled with trust suggests then that institutional economics, with its emphasis on "vertically structured hierarchies", is a methodologically more appropriate approach to examining traditional family conglomerates.

During the 1950s and 1960s in the United States, there was a major debate about the approach competition law should take to conglomerates. Two extreme positions developed. On the one hand, some argued conglomerates were inherently anti-competitive. Others suggested that each case should be examined on its own merits. For example, Stigler (1955, p. 184) noted that:

> ... the exact mechanics by which the total power possessed by the firm gets to be larger than the sum of the parts (in individual markets) escape me, and I am not sure that there are any companies that meet the specifications of the conglomerate firm.

Stigler ignores the ability to lower costs via group subsidies, the ability to access cheaper finance from group banks, or the ability to obtain concessional services from within the group. Market models take outside factors that influence costs and demand as given, whereas they should be considered endogenous in Asian models of competition. Access to considerable resources can give advantages via dictating the terms of competition, both outside the market (lobbying and bribing governments and officials), as well as inside the market. This occurs through cross-subsidization, which lowers costs, which, while not rational for a profit-maximizing firm, is rational where protection of even failing businesses is paramount.

The reality is that markets in Southeast Asia are different. The question then is whether competition law or its enforcement needs to be different. Conglomerates may lead to reduced opportunities for small businesses and new entry. If so, then the question is whether any market or other power created by conglomerates/business groups and networks are best addressed through competition law or other public policies.

Market Power and Conglomerates/Business Groups

In examining potentially anti-competitive practices by corporations, analysts typically assume that companies comprise one class of common stock or shares where each share carries one vote. Control depends on numbers of shares, and shareholders with more shares have greater say in the running of the company than those with fewer. Companies are usually assumed to maximize profits or, equivalently, shareholder value. Usually, companies are assumed to have widely dispersed ownership, thereby creating agency problems between shareholders as principals and management as their agents. But a concern with immediate ownership masks issues of control, which are particularly important in Asia.

Overseas Chinese family businesses usually:

> ... expand by acquiring an ever-increasing number of companies rather than by expanding existing companies. The overall business group may be large, but its individual components may be relatively small. This tends to mean that ethnic Chinese feature strongly in lists of the wealthiest families or entrepreneurs but are under-represented in lists of the biggest companies (East Asia Analytical Unit 1995, p. 153).

La Porta et al. (1999) examined the ownership structure of the twenty largest publicly traded firms in each of the twenty-seven richest countries in the world, where the likelihood of widely-dispersed ownership is high. They found, particularly in countries with poor minority shareholder protection, that even large firms tend to have controlling shareholders, with control held sometimes by the state, but mostly by a family (either the founder or their descendants). Of particular importance is the fact that these controlling shareholders usually have a degree of control greater than their rights to the cash flow or assets of the firm. This is often achieved through pyramid structures or the use of dual class shares.

Claessens et al. (2000) also found that corporate control is mostly exercised through cross-shareholdings, pyramids, and dual-class shares. Dual class equity, where different votes are attached to different classes of shares, helps a shareholder control corporations with less investment than in a single class equity firm. Pyramid control is common in continental European countries and in Asia. Pyramids are usually created through a holding company that has a controlling interest in another holding company that has, in turn, a controlling interest in an operating company. Because both dual-class shares and corporate pyramids are mechanisms to separate cash flow rights and voting rights in a company, they allow a party to control corporate assets while contributing only a small proportion of equity capital. A further way of increasing control is by rights issues. Funds are sought from existing shareholders but if not taken up, then those that do so increase their relative ownership share. As a strategy, this can be used to dilute the shareholding of non-network shareholders.

The economic basis for exercising control through dual-class shares and pyramids is essentially the same as for "trust networks" — they can achieve efficiencies and/or increase market power. They may bring efficiencies where institutions such as equity markets are undeveloped. For example, the business group can serve as an internal financial market where cash from profitable firms within the group supports those that are struggling. Just as importantly, where legal institutions are undeveloped (and thus contracts are difficult to legally enforce), then a business group (or conglomerate or corporate pyramid) can act as an internal substitute for outside contracting, thereby bypassing outside markets and networks. A further advantage is that internal labour resources can be more efficiently employed by moving people between firms and by using trained people in similar roles across the group. A recent empirical study of business groups concluded that "their emergence and early establishment often occur under very difficult institutional conditions and that they played a pivotal role in the early stages of many countries' and regions' economic development" (Carney et al. 2011, p. 454).

Importantly, for competition law purposes, large business groups may also facilitate the exercise of market power. Pyramidal groups, for example, allow for centralized control of interrelated markets. This enables one group member to secretly tie the products of network members or to provide below cost inputs to another member company, allowing the downstream firm to drive competitors out of business. For example, suppose A owns 51 per cent of shares in Company X, a monopolist. A also owns 100 per cent of shares in Company Y. Company X sells an input to Company Y. A could direct Company X to sell the input to Company Y at a 30 per cent discount compared to other buyers. This increases A's overall profits (A receives only 50 per cent of profits from Company X, but 100 per cent of profits from Company Y). Company Y gets a competitive advantage in the downstream market and may be able to drive out other competitors or force the others to join a cartel. If the business group operates across countries, a competition regulator will have difficulty proving predatory pricing, particularly where the chain of companies includes private companies that operate with few records or public scrutiny.

While the resulting market power may be similar, a distinction should be made between conglomerates and business groups. Conglomerates typically are a corporate group, with a parent company and subsidiaries. On the other hand, business groups are an intermediate type of organization lying between market contracting and common-ownership conglomerates. A business group is a collection of legally distinct firms that do business with each other on favourable terms. While they may resemble conglomerates, the companies in a business group are legally independent, i.e. there is no formal control. However, despite this independence they coordinate their long-term strategies. In spite of the formal lack of control, there is still, however, a high degree of informal control within business groups through a family (such as ethnic Chinese groups in Indonesia, Malaysia, the Philippines, and Thailand, or the *Bumiputera/Pribumi* groups in Indonesia and Malaysia); the state (for example, government-linked groups in Singapore or Vietnam); or a financial institution.

What is distinctive about many large business groups in Southeast Asia is that, often, they have been state-created. Following the end of colonial rule, the state in some nations monopolized capital and used it to assist specially selected small groups of local entrepreneurs to buy the assets of the departing colonists, or it nationalized certain firms and transferred control to indigenous entrepreneurs linked to the government. Usually, this state-led strategy was accompanied by the grant of domestic monopolies and protection from foreign competition (both by import protection and restrictions on foreign ownership).

Because business groups control much of the wealth in Southeast Asia, they may represent a particular challenge for competition law, due to close relations with the government. This is more of a problem in the civil law countries where there are usually fewer private remedies available when state regulators do not act on complaints about anti-competitive conduct. Anti-competitive practices within the group can restrict competition through collusion across markets between members of the same group, or the abuse of market power achieved through a coordination of policies and resources.

As far back as 1995, the Australian Government's East Asia Analytical Unit (1995, p. 161) noted that:

> A growing phenomenon among many prominent ethnic Chinese-controlled companies, particularly in South-East Asia, is the degree to which they move together in their quest to jointly dominate markets. This occurs at an international level, emphasising that senior ethnic Chinese business people often treat the region as a single, borderless market.

Market Power and Networks

As Wolf (1968, p. 23) argues, the basis of networks is trust:

> A man not thoroughly embedded in a network of kinship cannot be completely trusted because he cannot be dealt with in the normal way. If he behaves improperly, one cannot discuss his behavior with his brother or seek redress from his parents. If one wants to approach him about a delicate matter, one cannot use his uncle as a go-between to prepare the way. Wealth cannot make up for this deficiency any more than it can make up for the loss of arms and legs. Money has no past, no future and no obligations. Relatives do.

Networks based on trust only work if the benefits of long-term trust exceed the benefits of cheating once (since the network will punish the cheat by ostracizing him or her from the network). Reputation is everything when there are no legal remedies. Traders and others will only deal with those they trust. But it is not the reputation of individuals that counts — rather, it is family reputation, which can be inherited. This may create entry barriers into established networks. New access to a network will depend on sponsorship that vouches for the new entrant's trustworthiness. In most cases, new entrants from an existing family in the network already have the requisite reputational capital.

While trust networks can exist purely by passing on information about those who default on contracts, a network may also have formal mechanisms for punishing those who cheat. If so, the mechanism is potentially an agreement to boycott (refusal to deal with cheats) between competitors; this will breach competition laws in most jurisdictions, and is often *per se* illegal (as occurs in the United States). Amongst the overseas Chinese in Southeast Asia, such arrangements may be conducted through clan associations (such as the Teochew or Hakka). Shunning a cheat without a formal agreement may also be seen as tacit collusion. In the absence of institutions that can properly enforce contracts, collusion to boycott members of a clan group who fail to perform promises can be socially beneficial: without them there would be less contracting and lower output. Hence, such conduct should not breach competition laws, as this kind of boycott is likely to be pro-competitive (assuming there is no other possible courses of action). In fact, such conduct could be justified not by market failure but by:

... a "court failure" justification that would evaluate institutional alternatives in light of a public court's inability to provide the contractual security a merchant group requires. Antitrust law should thus incorporate transaction costs into the efficiency analysis, move beyond the traditional and narrower antitrust inquiry into prices and output, and employ a comparative institutional analysis to determine the relative efficiencies of alternative mechanisms to govern transactions (Richman, 2009, p. 358).

Chinese family companies usually obtain a competitive advantage where relational contracting skills are important, including in the developing markets of Southeast Asia where the legal infrastructure is not always properly developed. However, they nevertheless also retained the relational system in jurisdictions with well-developed laws and institutions, such as Hong Kong and Singapore (Shapiro et al. 2003).

Furthermore:

The flexibility of the Chinese family firm accounts for its prevalence in industries where windows of opportunity open and close quickly, and where start-up costs are relatively low ... the ability to mobilize capital on short notice through one's personal network is also a source of timing advantages. This capability is crucial in businesses like real estate (Shapiro et al. 2003, pp. 111–12).

Yeung (1998) also argues that such networks, have a tendency to preserve themselves as a closed system once they have been successfully established. This, in turn, can perpetuate an existing monopoly.

The difficult issue of business groups has rarely been examined through the lens of actual competition law in Southeast Asia. One exception is a decision of the Indonesian competition regulator. Law No. 5 of 1999 Concerning the Ban on Monopolistic Practices and Unfair Business Competition does not specifically state that the law applies to foreign firms. However, the Commission for the Supervision of Business Competition ("KPPU") has used the single economic entity doctrine to extend the law to foreign firms. The first case involved a holding company (Temasek, owned by the Singapore government) which held shares, both directly and indirectly, in two Indonesian mobile phone companies. Law No. 5 of 1999 prohibits cross-shareholdings that create monopolistic practices or unfair business competition. The question was whether Temasek, as a foreign entity which did not itself operate in Indonesia, was subject to the cross-shareholding prohibition. The KPPU held, in 2007 (Case 07/KPPU-L/2007), that Temasek constituted a single economic entity with two Indonesian companies, because Temasek was: involved in the management of both companies; was authorized to appoint directors or commissioners; and had access to confidential information (Hadiputranto et al. 2013). Because Temasek held only 35 per cent of the capital of Telkomsel (the market leader) and 41.9 per cent of Indosat (the second largest player), this decision caused some consternation, at least in Singapore. Temasek also maintained that the Indonesian government actually held majority stakes in Telkomsel and a golden share in Indosat.

Subsequently, the position has become much clearer in Indonesia with the introduction of Government Regulation No. 57 of 2010, which provides that an entity is regarded as having control over another entity if there is ownership or control of shares or voting rights above 50 per cent; or if ownership is below 50 per cent, the test revolves around whether a company has the ability to influence or determine management policy or actual management.

Undoubtedly, this seems to be a sensible recognition of the potentially anti-competitive conduct of business groups and conglomerates in Southeast Asia.

Some Concluding Comments

Examining legal organizational forms and practices tells us little about the extent to which competition law *should* apply to different kinds of firms and networks. To give the application of competition law substantive content, we need both a *theory* to explain how competition actually works (given the kinds of conglomerate firm and business networks common in Southeast Asia), together with empirical work to assess the effect of any resulting anti-competitive conduct. This is particularly important in ensuring the viability of small businesses that may face being driven out of the market by a conglomerate with considerable resources. To date there has been negligible research work on actual anti-competitive practices in Southeast Asia, and it is an area worth examining further. Hopefully this chapter has provided some suggestions to help spark such work.

REFERENCES

Carney, Michael and Marleen Dieleman. "Heroes and Villains: Ethnic Chinese Family Business in Southeast Asia". In *Theoretical Developments and Future Research in Family Business*, edited by Philip Phan and John E. Butler. Charlotte: IAP-Information Age Publishing, 2008.

Carney, Michael, Eric R. Gedajlovic, Pursey P.M.A.R. Heugens, Marc van Essen, and J. (Hans) van Oosterhout. "Business Group Affiliation, Performance, Context, and Strategy: A Meta-Analysis". *Academy of Management Journal* 54, no. 2 (2011): 437–60.

Claessens, Stijn, Simeon Djankov, and Larry H.P. Lang. "The Separation of Ownership and Control in East Asian Corporations". *Journal of Financial Economics* 58, no. 1–2 (2000): 81–112.

Coase, R.H. "The Nature of the Firm". *Economica* 4, no. 16 (1937): 386–405.

East Asia Analytical Unit, Department of Foreign Affairs and Trade, Commonwealth of Australia. *Overseas Chinese Business Networks in Asia*. Parkes: Department of Foreign Affairs and Trade, Commonwealth of Australia, 1995.

Fukuyama, Francis. *Trust: The Social Virtues and the Creation of Prosperity*. New York: The Free Press, 1995.

Gomez, Edmund Terence and K.S. Jomo. *Malaysia's Political Economy: Politics, Patronage and Profits*. New York: Cambridge University Press, 1999.

Hadiputranto, Hadinoto & Partners. *Guide to Competition Law in Indonesia*. 2013 ed. Available at <http://www.hhp.co.id/files/Uploads/Documents/Type%202/HHP/bk_hhp_competitionlawindonesia_2013.pdf>.

Hamilton, Gary. "Asian Business Networks in Transition: Or, What Alan Greenspan Does Not Know about the Asian Business Crisis". In *The Politics of the Asian Economic Crisis*, edited by T.J. Pempel. Ithaca, New York: Cornell University Press, 1999.

Jones, Alison. "The Boundaries of an Undertaking in EU Competition Law". *European Competition Law Journal* 8, no. 2 (2012): 301–31.

La Porta, Rafael, Florencio Lopez-de-Silanes, and Andrei Shleifer. "Corporate Ownership Around the World". *Journal of Finance* 54, no. 2 (1999): 471–517.

Richman, Barak D. "The Antitrust of Reputation Mechanisms: Institutional Economics and Concerted Refusals to Deal". *Virginia Law Review* 95 (2009): 325–87.

Robinson, Justin. *US-Asia Economic Relations: A Political Economy of Crisis and the Rise of New Business Actors*. New York: Routledge, 2009.

Ruskola, Teemu. "What is a Corporation? Liberal, Confucian, and Socialist Theories of Enterprise Organization (and State, Family, and Personhood)". *Seattle University Law Review* 37, no. 2 (2014): 639–66.

Shapiro, Daniel M., Eric Gedajlovic, and Carolyn Erdener. "The Chinese Family Firm as a Multinational Enterprise". *International Journal of Organizational Analysis* 11, no. 2 (2003): 105–22.

Stigler, George. "Mergers and Preventive Antitrust Policy". *University of Pennsylvania Law Review* 104, no. 2 (1955): 176–84.

Tipton, Frank B. "Southeast Asian Capitalism: History, Institutions, States, and Firms". *Asia Pacific Journal of Management* 26, no. 3 (2009): 401–34.

Townley, Chris. "The Concept of an 'Undertaking': The Boundaries of the Corporation — A Discussion of Agency, Employees and Subsidiaries". In *EC Competition Law: A Critical Assessment*, edited by Giuliano Amato and Claus-Dieter Ehlermann. Oxford: Hart Publishing, 2007.

Whitley, Richard. *Business Systems in East Asia: Firms, Markets and Societies*. London: Sage Publications, 1992.

Williamson, Oliver E. *The Economic Institutions of Capitalism*. New York: The Free Press, 1985.

Witt, Michael A. and Gordon Redding. "Asian Business Systems: Institutional Comparison, Clusters, and Implications for Varieties of Capitalism and Business Systems Theory". *Socio-Economic Review* 11, no. 2 (2013); INSEAD Working Paper No. 2013/05/EPS/EFE. Available at <http://papers.ssrn.com/sol3/papers.cfm?abstract_id=2104088>.

Wolf, Margery. *The House of Lim: A Study of a Chinese Farm Family*. New York: Appleton-Century-Crofts, 1968.

Yeung, Henry Wai-Chung. "Transnational Economic Synergy and Business Networks: The Case of Two-Way Investment Between Malaysia and Singapore". *Regional Studies* 23, no. 8 (1998): 687–706.

———. "The Dynamics of Asian Business Systems in a Globalizing Era". *Review of International Political Economy* 7, no. 3 (2000): 399–433.

11

TRADE ASSOCIATIONS
Competition Law Advocates or Offenders?

Rachel Burgess

For centuries, trade associations throughout the world have played a critical role representing businesses, providing services such as lobbying governments, conducting research and providing various forms of assistance to their members. This chapter argues that trade associations must widen these historic functions. Trade associations are in a special position not only to help educate small and medium-sized enterprises (SMEs) about competition law compliance, but also to assist them in utilizing the rules to their advantage. Their precise role will vary depending on the age and sophistication of the competition regime. In jurisdictions that have recently adopted competition statutes, such as Malaysia and Singapore, trade associations are still often breaching the law, so the focus must be on educating themselves and their members on compliance. In more experienced regimes such as the United Kingdom and Australia, trade associations can bring representative actions or make applications for exemptions on behalf of their members. The question of whether trade associations are resourced to fulfil this widened role is also considered.

Introduction

As small and medium-sized enterprises (SMEs) face an increasingly globalized business world, their ability to remain competitive is essential. In many countries around the world, SMEs make up more than 90 per cent of the number of businesses with the majority of that 90 per cent being micro-businesses (Schaper 2010). Faced with increased regulation, globalization, and competition, many SMEs will need increased guidance and support. Trade associations are well-placed to offer assistance. As competition laws become increasingly widespread and important around the world, this is one area where help is needed.

The number of economies with competition laws has increased dramatically in recent years, with established regulatory frameworks now in place in more than 120 jurisdictions (Dabbah 2010), and several others in the process of introducing their own statutes. Of particular note is the introduction of competition law in ASEAN (Association of Southeast Asian Nations) member countries, which is a target of the ASEAN Economic Community Blueprint.

The complexities of competition law are thus being faced by SMEs around the world. Trade associations provide a forum for SMEs to work collectively rather than face these challenges individually. Ironically, however, such bodies can also provide a forum for competition laws to be breached when competitors meet regularly to discuss business issues. Competition authorities are therefore often understandably suspicious of trade association activities.

This chapter will consider the historic role of trade associations, before looking at the interaction between trade associations and competition law, both good and bad. Examples will be drawn from four main jurisdictions — the United Kingdom, Australia, Malaysia, and Singapore — with occasional reference to other Asia-Pacific countries. The dual role that trade associations can play to assist SMEs, both in relation to education and compliance, and to utilize competition legislation to help their members through enforcement and representative actions, is also examined.

What is a Trade Association?

Trade associations are made up of a number of business organizations, such as companies and sole traders, with common interests that often operate in the same market, sector, or industry. They exist to represent and promote the interests of their members and provide collective services to businesses. They may also deliver a number of commercial services (Chartered Quality Institute 2015). Business associations, industry associations, chambers of commerce and professional associations are all terms commonly used to describe these types of organizations. For ease of reference, the term "trade association" is used in this chapter.

Generally speaking, trade associations are voluntary organizations with businesses joining by paying an annual fee to receive the benefits of membership. (The exception to this rule is professional associations, where membership is compulsory in some jurisdictions.) Perry (2009) notes that "... collective benefits are generally expected to be the mainstay of trade associations" and "given that the results of lobbying may affect members and non-members alike, the option of 'free-riding' exists". A study undertaken by Lee and McGuiggan (2008) of business people in Greater Western Sydney, Australia showed that membership of voluntary business associations is mainly driven by individual gain, rather than collective benefit. So, although the purpose of the trade association may be to achieve outcomes for the collective good, those joining do so for their own purposes.

Trade associations broadly fall into two categories:

(a) **Geographically-based associations** are those that represent any business wishing to join the association within a defined local area. Bennett (1998) classifies this group as "chambers of commerce" and notes that they vary greatly in size, geographic extent, and activities. Examples include the Sydney Business Chamber, the Singapore International Chamber of Commerce (SICC), and the Malaysian International Chamber of Commerce and Industry (MICCI).

(b) **Sector-based associations** represent businesses operating within a particular industry. Bennett (1998) divides this group into six categories: associations of companies; associations of owner-managers; associations of self-employed professionals; professional associations of individuals; mixed associations (a blend of the previous categories), and federations (an "association of associations"). Examples include the Malaysian

Indian Hair-Dressers Owners Association, the Pharmacy Guild of Australia, and the Singapore Electrical Trades Association.

Membership of professional associations is sometimes compulsory, as the professional association sets the standards that must be met by individuals to practise in their profession. Examples include the Malaysian Bar Council (for lawyers), CPA Australia (for accountants), and the British Medical Association (for doctors).

Research into this field of business activity is relatively limited. Bennett (2011*a*) has recently published a comprehensive history of chambers of commerce in Britain, Ireland, and Revolutionary America, but this is one of the few known histories of the sector. Streeck, Grote, Schneider and Visser (2006) edited a book looking at comparative research on business associations facing internationalization in Europe, while Doner and Schneider (2000) have examined which associations tend to be more effective lobbyists than others. Sinha (2005) has investigated the significance of such bodies in India, and Pollitt (1992) has looked at the role that trade associations played in helping SMEs to transition into the European single market in the 1990s. The role that trade associations can play *vis-à-vis* competition law does not seem to have been greatly considered, if at all.

Historic Development of Trade Associations

Trade associations are among the oldest business organizations in the Western world (Bennett 2012*a*). In fact, the first chamber in the world was created in 1599 in the Marseille-Provence region in France (ICC 2015*a*).

Bennett (2011*b*; 2012*b*) suggests that the earliest other chambers of commerce appeared during the period 1767–80 in some seemingly unlikely places (Jersey, Guernsey, Quebec, and Jamaica), as well as the key centres of trade in New York, Liverpool, and Manchester. They were created largely from collective anger sparked by local events, such as the rejection by the British Government of complaints from Jersey about customs duty and the boycott of British taxes in New York. By the 1820s, this had grown into a wider group of chambers. There was a strong Atlantic presence, with trade associations established in big cities or ports, recognizing the importance of trade to these bodies. Today, there are several hundred trade associations in the United Kingdom alone (Chartered Quality Institute 2015).

Trade associations in the Asia-Pacific region developed along similar lines. The SICC was founded in 1837 as a result of objections by Singapore merchants to being excluded from decisions directly affecting their interests. They formed a chamber of commerce as a collective voice to advocate for Singaporean firms and to defend their business interests against the officials of the East India Company (SICC 2014). The MICCI was established in 1837 as an advocate for the business community in Malaysia. It is one of a number of important trade associations operating in that country today; the others being the Federation of Malaysian Manufacturers (FMM), the Associate Chinese Chamber of Commerce and Industry of Malaysia, the Malaysian Association Indian Chambers of Commerce and Industry, and the Malay Chamber of Commerce Malaysia. These associations sit under the umbrella of the National Chamber of Commerce and Industry of Malaysia, which was established in 1962.

The Australian Chamber of Commerce and Industry (ACCI) can trace its history back to 1826 when the Sydney Chamber of Commerce was formed (ACCI 2016). This has since grown into a sizeable cohort of business and employee bodies: an Australian Bureau of Statistics (2006–7) study identified more than 2,000 organizations covering both business associations and union services.

Core Functions of Trade Associations

Regardless of the type of industry organization, there are a number of common core functions. Although trade associations were created as representative bodies to lobby governments in circumstances where individual business people did not have the power to do so (a function that continues today), they very quickly developed a wider range of services. Bennett (2012b) notes the historical significance of physical premises such as libraries, hotels, and coffee houses where members could meet and exchange ideas. Today, almost all of the associations offer the provision of directories, export documentation, business training, and exhibitions, and most also offer some form of workforce training (Bennett 2012a).

The UK Trade Association Forum (Bean 2006) lists trade associations' services as including:

- working proactively to improve members'/sectors' profitability and competitiveness;
- representing member and sectoral interests at all levels of the legislative and regulatory process;
- supplying information and providing advice to members;
- public relations and communications;
- promotion of market opportunities;
- training and education;
- promotion of standards and quality of service; and
- promotion of innovation and technology transfer.

In a recent IBISWorld report, business associations in Australia were reported as providing services such as research on new products, lobbying public officials, publishing newsletters, books and periodicals for distribution to members, and compiling market statistics (Magner 2013). Professional associations were found to have helped keep members up-to-date with new developments, and to have assisted them with employment and business networking opportunities (Magner 2013). Although the report does not emphasize an educational role in the services offered, it notes that associations often employ experts in law and industrial relations to advise on industry-wide issues (which would include new laws and legislative requirements), the results of which are then disseminated to members.

For many individual businesses, a trade association provides a vital source of information, guidance and support on a range of matters from industry best practices to government lobbying, to which it would not otherwise have ready access.

Bennett (2011b) also discusses the importance of early trade associations offering to help government overcome what a 1770s business leader called the "imbecility of entire government administrations". Today, this would be referred to as overcoming information asymmetry which is the "inbuilt weakness of all government regulation of the economy: politicians and administrators are ignorant of daily business practices and careless about the practicalities and costs of implementation" (Bennett 2011b). This role is often championed by trade associations and is highly significant to the interplay between SMEs and competition law and policy.

SMEs and Competition Law

The challenges faced by SMEs in complying with law and regulation are widely accepted: a shortage of resources, time, and money that is often required to comply with an increasingly regulated market. These challenges arise equally in relation to compliance with competition law. Small businesses may think that competition law is not relevant to them and may struggle to understand its complexities. SMEs are also often reluctant to make complaints about a large supplier or customer for fear of retaliation.

In countries with newer competition regimes, such as Malaysia and Singapore, many SMEs are still trying to understand the new law, with some believing that it does not (or should not) apply to their businesses. The position in Malaysia is discussed in more detail elsewhere in this book. In 2007, the Competition Commission of Singapore (CCS) noted that there were two main challenges in dealing with SMEs. These were a lack of awareness or understanding of competition law and a need to change age-old business practices. Trade associations had traditionally protected members by recommending prices, a practice which is now problematic (CCS 2007).

Storey (2010) notes a number of key differences between SMEs and large firms in relation to competition law and policy. He argues that SMEs view legislation as a disproportionate burden, because their unit cost of compliance is so much higher than larger businesses. Some SMEs respond to this problem by ignoring the issue, others are simply unaware of the changes, and a third category respond by joining an organization (such as a small business lobby organization or a trade association) that can make them aware of current and expected changes. This emphasizes the critical role that trade associations can play in this area.

Trade Associations and Competition Law

The role that trade associations can positively play in relation to competition law is discussed below, but it is important to recognize that competition authorities are often suspicious of the activities of industry bodies, since they can sometimes provide a forum for anti-competitive behaviours. Many people view trade associations as mediums through which firms can collude. As Adam Smith has been oft-quoted, "People of the same trade seldom meet together, even for merriment and diversion, but the conversation ends in a conspiracy against the public, or in some contrivance to raise prices" (Smith 1776, para 82). Competition concerns most frequently arise in relation to exchanges of information on pricing or other commercially sensitive information at association meetings, membership rules that unfairly exclude some businesses, and the imposition of standard terms and conditions that can chill or retard the competitive tension between firms. Issues also arise in relation to the setting of scale fees by professional associations such as doctors and lawyers.

A number of competition authorities have already begun to engage directly with industry groups. For example, both the ACCC and the UK Office of Fair Trading (OFT) have published guidlines on competition law issues relevant to trade associations (ACCC 2011; OFT 2004). These documents, perhaps understandably, focus on the responsibilities of a trade association to comply with competition law and do not provide practical commercial advice for trade association members. With the right legal advice, trade associations could provide this practical advice for their members.

Trade Associations as Advocates of Competition Law

Competition authorities have an opportunity to utilize trade associations to help them in their work. Particularly in relation to SMEs, trade associations can play a significant role in supporting competition regimes to implement and enforce competition law and to help businesses to utilize competition law to their advantage. This can be achieved in a number of ways.

Public Supporters of Competition Law

Trade associations can sometimes publicly support and champion competition law and policy. In Australia, for example, competition law has been part of the legal landscape for more than forty years, and many trade associations publicly support competition law and the role of the ACCC. For example, both the Council of Small Business Australia and the ACCI lodged submissions in response to the

Competition Policy Review Issues Paper (Commonwealth of Australia 2014) supporting the work of the national competition regulator and arguing for more, not less, active competition regulation.

In the international arena, the International Chamber of Commerce (ICC) has a dedicated Commission on Competition that provides expertise and training on competition law issues to its members. It has published internationally recognized documents including the ICC Antitrust Compliance Toolkit and holds regular competition law events (ICC 2015b).

In countries where competition law is still developing, it is less clear whether trade associations are being publicly supportive of competition law. The CEO of the Singapore Business Federation (SBF), Ho Meng Kit, has publicly acknowledged the importance of competition law compliance (CCS 2012). However, as discussed elsewhere in this book, some industry associations have condemned the introduction of competition law in Malaysia, blaming it for upsetting the market and causing "everything to go wild". Given the number of trade associations that have been involved in competition law breaches in such countries, it seems that there is still some way to go in this area.

Educators

Trade associations can play an educational role in assisting SMEs to understand and comply with competition law. This is of particular relevance in the newer competition regimes.

As SMEs rely on information provided to them by their associations, a lot of positive work can be achieved in this area. A good example is the role that trade associations in Britain played in the early 1990s, by distributing information regarding joining the European Union (EU). It was recognized that representative organizations were especially important for SMEs who did not have the resources or the time to monitor EU matters (Pollitt 1992). Pollitt suggested that associations could help their members deal with the large amount of information and legislation relating to the single market by publishing briefing materials or bulletins. He argued that they should also be available to respond to specific queries from members and either provide, or facilitate, training (Pollitt 1992). These ideas work equally well for competition law.

In Singapore, the SBF has engaged in outreach and awareness events in conjunction with the CCS and considers itself to be a platform to reach the broader business community, particularly SMEs (CCS 2012). The SCCI has also been active in this area. In 2014, it ran a workshop in conjunction with one of Singapore's law firms on competition law across ASEAN.

In Malaysia, the FMM has attempted to fulfil this role by regularly conducting training sessions on the Malaysian Competition Act for their members, as well as working alongside the Malaysian Competition Commission (MyCC) to produce a compliance checklist for their members. This work is to be commended.

A Representative Role

Trade associations occasionally extend their representative role beyond lobbying to governments on regulatory and policy issues, to one of acting on behalf of businesses in the application or enforcement of competition law.

An example can be found in Australia, where the Competition and Consumer Act permits exemptions from competition law through either the authorization or notification process. The ACCC can authorize a particular agreement or conduct (other than misuse of market power) where it believes that the public benefit outweighs any public detriment. In relation to certain types of conduct (exclusive dealing, collective bargaining, supplier arrangements, and pricing information), a notification may alternatively be made to the ACCC. Collective bargaining proposals are an important tool for SMEs dealing with larger suppliers or customers as, if approved, they allow two or more competitors to collectively negotiate the terms and conditions of supply, including price. In relation to both authorizations and notifications, the ACCC expressly states that industry associations can lodge an application on behalf of its members. This tool has been widely used in Australia, with seventeen out of forty-five applications for authorization made by trade associations in 2014 alone. In the most recent *Small Business in Focus* publication, the ACCC gives three examples of collective bargaining proposals submitted by associations on behalf of their members: the Tasmanian Farmer and Graziers Association to collectively bargain with vegetable processors; the TAB Agents Association of New South Wales to collectively negotiate terms and conditions of service for gambling related matters; and the Australian Newsagents' Federation to negotiate with a range of suppliers on behalf of its members (ACCC 2014).

In the United Kingdom, the Consumer Rights Act 2015 is introducing some positive changes in this area. The UK competition regime allows for actions for private law damages to be brought by persons who have suffered loss or damage as a result of an infringement of competition law. Previously, these actions could only be brought by individuals or by a specified body in relation to a consumer claim. It was not possible for a representative action to be brought on behalf of small businesses. In the decade since these provisions were introduced, only one consumer representative action has been completed and the system has largely been considered a failure. The amendments, which came into force from October 2015, will allow opt-out collective proceedings to be brought. The Explanatory Notes state that the purpose of this is "to allow consumers and businesses to easily achieve redress for losses they have suffered as a result of breaches of competition law" (UK Parliament 2015). The amendments also provide for a "fast-track" procedure with the stated purpose of enabling simpler cases brought by SMEs to be resolved more quickly and at a lower cost (UK Parliament 2015). It will therefore be possible for trade associations to commence proceedings for damages for breaches of competition law on behalf of businesses. The option for "opt-out" proceedings means that not all businesses need to be identified, making it far more practical.

The potential role of trade associations in helping to enforce competition law has also been recognized for some time in the United Kingdom. In the OFT Guidelines on *Involving Third Parties in Competition Act Investigations* (OFT 2006), trade associations were recognized as likely to be materially affected by potentially anti-competitive agreements or conduct if some or all of its members were (or were likely to be) materially affected. This meant that the trade association could make a complaint to the OFT on behalf of its members and be recognized as a Formal Complainant, which gave it certain procedural rights.

The OFT (which was replaced by the Competition and Markets Authority in 2013) regularly receives input from trade associations in relation to their merger inquiries, as well as other consultations.

Industry associations have also provided assistance in drafting guidance and reviewing competition in the professions (OECD 2008). In the concluding paragraphs of its submission to the OECD (Organization for Economic Cooperation and Development) Policy Roundtable on Trade Associations, the UK government states:

> A competition authority's relationships with trade associations can be mutually beneficial: the authority may better understand the markets it encounters while the associations may influence and inform policy and legal debates that are of interest to them. ... Trade associations are also ideally placed to facilitate increased compliance across their markets (OECD 2008, p. 209).

Limitations

Although there is significant opportunity for trade associations to assist their members with competition law in the manners described above, there are also potential limitations. Associations rely heavily on membership fees for funding. Although more and more bodies are undertaking commercial activities, it is still the case that many are poorly funded and may have limited ability to provide the support identified above. Increased government funding for industry associations could be utilized to support an increased representative role.

The issue of standing will also need to be considered if trade associations are able to bring representative actions on behalf of their members. The UK Consumer Rights Act 2015 makes specific provisions for collective proceedings and the role of a representative such as an industry association. In Australia, representative actions may be brought in the Federal Court by the ACCC in relation to certain consumer protection provisions of the Competition and Consumer Act. Representative actions may also be brought by other groups (such as trade associations) if the conditions set out in Section 33C of the Federal Court of Australia Act 1976 are met. These require at least seven persons to have a claim against the same person; the claims must have arisen out of the same, similar, or related circumstances; and the claims must have given rise to a substantial common issue of fact or law. As "opt-out" proceedings are available in both the United Kingdom and Australia, not all claimants need to be identified.

Trade Associations as Offenders of Competition Law

There are times when trade associations are responsible for breaches of competition law, either in their own right (for example by imposing discriminatory membership criteria) or by their members (for example, where members agree to a price rise at a trade association meeting).

Trade associations were involved in five out of the six cases decided by the MyCC in the first three years of operation of competition law in Malaysia. Almost all of the parties involved were SMEs and all of the cases involved price-fixing. The decision to fix prices took place at association meetings or following the recommendation of an association, with announcements subsequently being made in the press. The members of the trade association were found to be in breach of the law, but not the trade associations themselves.

In Singapore, where competition law has been in force since 2004, trade associations have also been involved in several breaches of competition law. In 2009, the CCS found sixteen coach operators guilty of colluding with their trade association to fix the prices of coach tickets on routes between Singapore and Malaysia. At a meeting of the Express Bus Agencies Association, a minimum selling price was agreed and price increases were later imposed through a fuel and insurance surcharge.

In Australia, the ACCC has taken action against several industry bodies. For example, in 2003 it launched an enforcement action against the Tasmanian Salmonid Growers Association, for facilitating an agreement between Atlantic salmon farmers to cull their salmon stocks in order to avoid oversupply and consequential price cuts (ACCC vs Tasmanian Salmonid Growers Association Ltd). Unfortunately, the parties' legal advisers had told them that the agreement did not raise competition issues.

In the United Kingdom, trade associations have also been found to be in breach of competition rules. There are a number of examples under the old Restrictive Trade Practices legislation, such as Re Yarn Spinners' Association's Agreement where the association bound its members not to sell yarn at prices lower than those fixed by the association (OECD 2008). There are more recent examples arising under the Competition Act 1998. In the Northern Ireland Livestock and Auctioneers Association case, a non-binding recommendation of the association as to the amount of commission to charge was considered to be a decision by the OFT but no fine was imposed because of exceptional circumstances (OECD 2008). In the Notification by the Film Distributors' Association of its Standard Conditions for Licensing the Commercial Exhibition of Films, the OFT found that the standard conditions were a decision and objected to the provision which restricted the cinemas' ability to set their own prices.

In many cases, particularly in the newer competition regimes, it is likely that the breach of competition law by trade associations and their members has arisen out of ignorance of the law. Competition authorities are not sympathetic to ignorance as an excuse for competition law breaches; trade associations have a responsibility to themselves and their members to ensure compliance with competition law.

What of the Future?

Since their inception, trade associations throughout the world have played a critical role liaising between individual businesses on the one hand and the government and established regulatory structures on the other. In the area of competition law, trade associations can become a powerful advocate for competition law and policy in several ways. They can publicly support competition law and the actions of competition authorities in their jurisdiction. They can help their members understand and comply with the law by carrying out (or facilitating) relevant training. In more developed competition regimes, trade associations are increasingly taking a representative role in the competition law field. For example, in Australia, trade associations regularly make applications for authorizations and notifications (including collective bargaining) on behalf of their members. Trade associations will also now be able to bring collective actions for damages in the United Kingdom on behalf of groups of businesses that have suffered as a result of a competition law breach.

In newer competition regimes, trade associations are, perhaps inadvertently, leading their members into competition law breaches. In these jurisdictions, trade associations must take responsibility for educating themselves and their members on the new rules to ensure compliance. With the passage of time, these trade associations may also be able to represent SMEs in enforcing the competition rules, either by making complaints to the regulator or, where the legislation allows, making exemption applications or taking private actions.

There are a number of steps that competition authorities may wish to consider to assist trade associations with these roles. A committee dedicated to working with trade associations may be helpful. This could include a staff exchange to facilitate a sharing of ideas and information between the competition authority and the association to help overcome information asymmetry. The trade associations chosen for such activities will need to be carefully selected, to ensure that time and resources are well invested and conflicts of interest are avoided.

With the continued expansion of competition regulation throughout the world, it is clear that neither trade associations nor their members can afford to ignore the existence of such laws. The positive steps taken by the more developed competition regimes to involve trade associations in compliance and enforcement activities may well provide useful guidance for the newer regimes.

REFERENCES

Australian Bureau of Statistics. *Interest Groups, Australia, 1995–6*. Cat. no. 8639.0. Canberra: Australian Bureau of Statistics, 2001.
———. *Not-for-profit Organisations, Australia (Re-Issue)*. Cat. no. 8106.0. Canberra: Australian Bureau of Statistics, 2006–7.
Australian Chamber of Commerce and Industry (ACCI). "Our History", 2016. Available at <https://www.acci.asn.au/our-history> (accessed 8 May 2016).
Australian Competition and Consumer Commission (ACCC). *Industry Associations — Competition and Consumers*. Canberra: Australian Competition and Consumer Commission, 2011.
———. *Small Business in Focus: Small Business, Franchising and Industry Codes*. Half Year Report No. 9, July–December 2014. Available at <https://www.accc.gov.au/system/files/953_Small%20business%20in%20focus%20no.%209_FA.pdf> (accessed 15 June 2015).
Bean, Stuart. "A 'Best Practice Guide' for Trade Associations". Trade Association Forum 2006. Available at <http://www.taforum.org/a-> (accessed 22 June 2015).

Bennett, Robert J. "Business Associations and Their Potential Contribution to the Competitiveness of SMEs". *Entrepreneurship and Regional Development* 10, no. 3 (1998): 243–60.

————. *Local Business Voice: The History of Chambers of Commerce in Britain, Ireland, and Revolutionary America, 1760–2011*. Oxford: Oxford University Press, 2011*a*.

————. "Anger as a Binding Force, in Chambers of Commerce and Elsewhere". *Harvard Business Review*, 7 October 2011*b*. Available at <https://hbr.org/2011/10/anger-as-a-binding-force-in-ch> (accessed 22 June 2015).

————. "Chambers of Commerce: From Protesters to Government Partners". *British Academy Review Issue* 20 (2012*a*): 37–40.

————. Podcast based on the "Local Business Voice book" from a seminar at the British Academy, 2012*b*. Available at <http://www.britac.ac.uk/cmsfiles/assets/11091.mp3> (accessed 14 June 2015).

Chartered Quality Institute. "Industry Associations". Available at <http://www.thecqi.org/Knowledge-Hub/Knowledge-portal/Compliance-and-organisations/Industryassociations/> (accessed 14 June 2015).

Commonwealth of Australia. *Competition Policy Review*, 2014. Available at <www.competitionpolicyreview.gov.au> (accessed 22 June 2015).

Competition Commission of Singapore (CCS). *Competition Law and SMEs in Singapore*. Presentation at 3rd Training Course on Competition Policy, Singapore, 1–3 August 2007.

————. "Opening Address by Mr Ho Meng Kit, CEO, SBF for CCS-SAL Conference — 'Competition Compliance: Part of Good Corporate Governance'", 27 July 2012. Available at <https://www.ccs.gov.sg/media-and-publications/speeches/opening-address-by-mr-ho-meng-kit-ceo-sbf-for-ccssal-conference---competition-compliance--part-of-good-corporate-governance>.

Dabbah, Maher M. *International and Comparative Competition Law*. Cambridge: Cambridge University Press, 2010.

Doner, Robert F. and Ben Ross Schneider. "Business Associations and Economic Development: Why Some Associations Contribute More Than Others". *Business and Politics* 2, no. 3 (2000): 261–88.

International Chamber of Commerce (ICC). "History of the Chamber Movement", 2015*a*. Available at <http://www.iccwbo.org/chamber-services/chamber-resources/history-of-chamber/> (accessed 3 July 2015).

————. "Commission on Competition", 2015*b*. Available at <http://www.iccwbo.org/about-icc/policy-commissions/competition/> (accessed 16 June 2015).

Lee, Geoffrey and Robyn McGuiggan. "Why do SMEs Attend Business Association Events?". Paper presented at the Australia and New Zealand Marketing Academy (ANZMAC) 2008 Conference, Sydney, 2008.

Magner, L. *IBISWorld Industry Report S9551: Industry Associations in Australia.* Melbourne: IBISWorld, 2013.

Office of Fair Trading (OFT). *Trade Associations, Professions and Self-regulating Bodies: Understanding Competition Law.* London: Office of Fair Trading, 2004.

―――. "OFT Urges SMEs to Report Anti-Competitive Practices". Press release 129/05, 21 July 2005. Available at <http://webarchive.nationalarchives.gov. uk/20100202100434/http://oft.gov.uk/news/press/2005/129-05> (accessed 14 June 2015).

―――. *Involving Third Parties in Competition Act Investigations: Incorporating Guidance on the Submission of Complaints.* London: Office of Fair Trading, 2006.

Organisation for Economic Co-operation and Development (OECD). *Policy Roundtables: Trade Associations 2007.* DAF/COMP (2007) 45. Paris: Organisation for Economic Co-operation and Development, 2008.

Perry, Martin. "Trade Associations: Exploring the Trans Tasman Environment for Business Associability". *Journal of Management and Organization* 15, no. 4 (2009): 404–22.

Pollitt, David and Colin Mellors. "Preparing for the Single Market: The Role of Trade Associations and Professional Bodies". *European Business Review* 92, no. 2 (1992): 22–25.

Schaper, Michael T. "Competition Law, Enforcement and the Australian Small Business Sector". *Small Enterprise Research* 17, no. 1 (2010): 7–18.

Singapore International Chamber of Commerce (SICC). "SICC Present and Future", 2014. Available at <http://www.sicc.com.sg/SICC/About_Us/Who_ are_we/SICC/AboutUs/SICC_Present_and_Future.aspx?hkey=6161ddd9-34ab-44e1-98a2-8225ff77f3e4> (accessed 30 May 2015).

Sinha, Aseema. "Understanding the Rise and Transformation of Business Collective Action in India". *Business and Politics* 7, no. 2 (2005).

Smith, Adam. *The Wealth of Nations*, Volume 1, Book 1, Chapter 10, 1776.

Storey, David J. "The Competitive Experience of UK SMEs: Fair and Unfair". *Small Enterprise Research* 17, no. 1 (2010): 19–29.

Struck, Wolfgang, Jurgen Grote, Volker Schneider, and Helle Visier, eds. *Governing Interests: Business Associations Facing Internationalisation.* London/ New York: Rutledge, 2006.

UK Parliament. *Consumer Rights Act 2015 Explanatory Memorandum 2015.* Available at <http://www.legislation.gov.uk/ukpga/2015/15/notes/ contents> (accessed 14 June 2015).

SECTION 3

Country Studies

12

COMPETITION LAW, REGULATION, AND TRADE
Implications for Productivity and Innovation in Singaporean Manufacturing SMEs

Azad Singh Bali, Peter McKiernan, Christopher Vas, and Peter Waring

This chapter explores the nexus between competition and productivity in the context of small and medium-sized enterprises (SMEs) in Singapore's manufacturing sector. Drawing on a study involving 215 in-depth surveys with SME leaders and managers, we explore questions of competition, regulation, and trade, and their implications for productivity and innovation. We find that there is considerable concern among SMEs that the market power of some large competitors is stifling efforts to enhance productivity and innovation. This suggests an important role for competition law and the competition regulator, the Competition Commission of Singapore (CCS), in boosting productivity and innovation. We also find that while SMEs support efforts to broker free trade agreements, they see a strong role for government in helping to identify the opportunities so generated and in building the capabilities needed to take advantage of these.

Introduction

This chapter considers the impact that competition law, regulation, and trade have on productivity and innovation among small and medium-sized enterprises (SMEs) in the manufacturing sector of Singapore. SMEs account for more than two-thirds of all employment, and 99 per cent of all businesses registered in Singapore (Department of Statistics Singapore 2014). Singapore's industrial and manufacturing focus has evolved since the founding of the Republic in 1965. Its industrial emphasis shifted from labour-intensive products that had limited value-added in the 1960s to export-oriented and semi-automated products in the 1970s. The 1980s saw the rapid expansion of the services sector, as well as a transition to high value-added manufacturing. However, over the past two decades, the share of the manufacturing sector in gross domestic product (GDP) has diminished, crowded out by a rapidly growing services sector. The manufacturing sector, and SMEs especially, have recorded weak total factor productivity (TFP) growth while maintaining a high dependence on foreign labour. Singapore has sought to explicitly address these challenges by raising productivity and wages of the resident labour force. As over two-thirds of the labour force is employed in SMEs, initiatives to increase the productivity of SMEs have received significant policy attention.

The chapter commences by explaining the rationale for the current productivity drive in Singapore and the importance placed on lifting the performance of SMEs. Following this, it examines the nexus between competition law, productivity, and innovation, paying particular attention to the key features of the competition law regime in Singapore. The third section presents the research strategy and methodology and the key findings of our study. The fourth and concluding section argues that competition law is a strong lever for promoting productivity and innovation, although it is not singularly sufficient. It is therefore vital that reform of competition law, and the architecture of national competition frameworks, explicitly reflects productivity and innovation considerations.

Singapore's Productivity Imperative

Singapore is typically regarded by experts and global authorities as having a highly competitive economy. As the nation's Senior Minister of State for Trade and Industry, Lee Yi Shyan, recently noted, the World Economic Forum Global Competitiveness Report 2013–14 ranked Singapore second behind Switzerland for competitiveness. However, Lee also noted that the same authority had ranked Singapore 19th in the world for the intensity of local competition (CCS 2014). This rather modest ranking may go some way to explaining the apparent disconnect between Singapore's reputation as a competitive economy and its rather bleak record in recent years on most measures of productivity and innovation.

Over the last decade, Singapore has experienced low productivity growth, and it now lags by a considerable margin in productivity and innovation levels when compared to the economies of the United States, Japan, and its neighbours in the region (see Table 12.1).

TABLE 12.1
Global Productivity Growth Rates 2012–13

Regional Indicators	2012	2013
North America		
Labour productivity growth	0.90%	0.90%
GDP growth	2.80%	1.90%
Total Factor Productivity	0.70%	0.40%
Euro region		
Labour productivity growth	−0.10%	0.40%
GDP growth	−0.07%	−0.30%
Total Factor Productivity	0.80%	−0.60%
Labour productivity growth in ...		
Brazil	−0.40%	0.80%
China	7.30%	7.10%
India	3.10%	2.40%
Japan	1.20%	0.80%
Poland	5.60%	1.40%
Russia	3.10%	1.60%
Singapore	−2.50%	1.60%
United Kingdom	−1.80%	0.50%
United States	0.70%	0.90%

Source: Conference Board (2013).

With predictions that low to no productivity growth would persist, the Singapore Government has taken difficult decisions to purposefully slow the growth in its foreign workforce. This decision has been taken in acknowledgement of the fact that the "sectors which are most dependent on foreign workers are also the ones furthest behind international standards of productivity" (Budget Singapore 2013, p. 18).

Figure 12.1 illustrates the trends in total labour productivity, including the manufacturing sector, in Singapore during the period 2001–13. Singapore's total labour productivity grew annually by 1.6 per cent between 2008 to 2013, marginally higher than the 1.1 per cent recorded annually during the previous five years. While there have been advances in labour productivity in particular sectors of the economy, a structural shift in employment away from these productive sectors has resulted in declining total labour productivity (Goh 2013). Such sectoral changes are not unique to Singapore, and are also prevalent in economies such as Finland, Japan, Netherlands, and Germany that are also undergoing structural changes to their economy.

FIGURE 12.1
Labour Productivity in Singapore, 2001-13

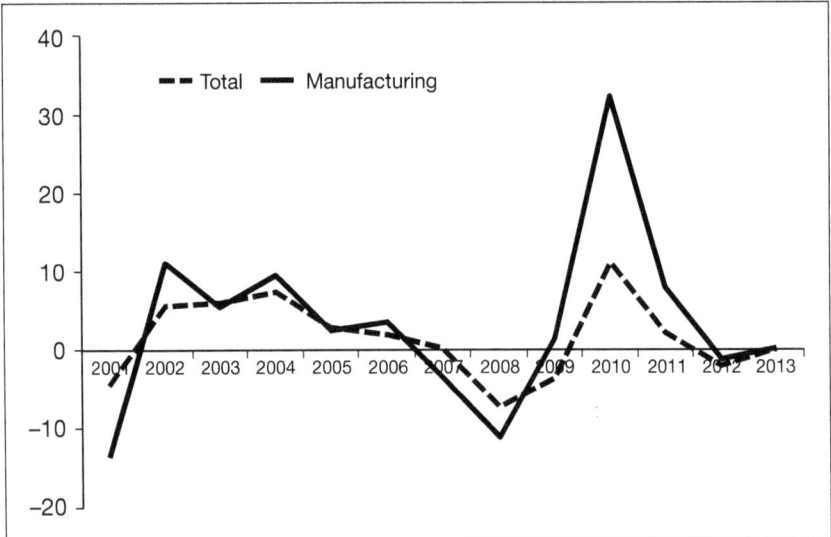

Source: Singapore Yearbook of Manpower Statistics (2011; 2014).

As the figures represent year-on-year changes in productivity, the sharp increase in labour productivity during 2009–10 must be viewed in the context of a gradual decline since 2005, resulting in a low base. For most of the time period illustrated in Figure 12.1, labour productivity in the manufacturing sector has trended total labour productivity in the economy. This is particularly interesting, given the declining share of the manufacturing sector in the economy over the past decade. The value-added to GDP share of the manufacturing sector declined from 27.55 per cent in 1980 to 18.76 per cent in 2013 (see Table 12.2).

Despite the declining share of manufacturing output in its economy, Singapore has witnessed unprecedented increase in income levels. Its per capita income has increased from US$23,000 in 2000 to US$55,000 in 2013 (World Bank 2014).

In his 2013 Budget speech, Deputy Prime Minister and Minister for Finance Tharman Shanmugaratnam underscored the importance of productivity growth for sustaining economic growth and living standards in Singapore. He declared:

> Raising productivity is not just our most important economic priority, but enables us to build a better society. Higher productivity is the only sustainable way to raise incomes for ordinary Singaporeans, and provide jobs that give people a sense of responsibility and empowerment (Budget Singapore 2013, p. 13).

The Minister further commented on the important role to be played by SMEs in the country's productivity drive, noting that "... we

TABLE 12.2
Sectoral Contribution in Value-Added to GDP, 1980–2013

Sector	1980	1990	2000	2010	2013
Services	62.2	67.32	65.07	72.33	74.86
Industry	36.23	32.34	34.83	27.63	25.11
Manufacturing	27.55	25.58	27.75	21.36	18.76
Agriculture	1.57	0.34	0.1	0.04	0.03

Source: World Bank (2014).

must help our SME sector revitalise itself. There are however wide divergences in efficiency amongst SMEs even in the same industries" (Budget Singapore 2013, p. 18).

In Singapore, the focus of this nationwide effort to improve productivity has tended to overshadow the role to be played by contestable markets and the competition authority. Instead the focus has tended to dwell on reducing foreign labour dependencies and upgrading capital vintages through the provision of government grants and tax incentives (see, for instance, the Singapore Government's Productivity and Innovation Credit Scheme). While the importance of these policy levers cannot be understated, we assert that lifting multi- or total factor productivity requires a multipronged effort and a focus on setting the right business climate in which productivity and innovation can flourish. In the next section we address this by examining the role that can be played by an effective competition law regime.

The Competition Law, Productivity, and Innovation Nexus

There is a compelling body of research that underscores the positive relationship between competitive markets, productivity, and innovation. A key strand of the productivity literature focuses especially on the organization (vertical and horizontal integration) of the firm, in response to market access and competition. Melitz and Ottaviano (2008), for instance, in their study find that both market size and trade have an impact on competition and productivity. Restrictions in market access — whether explicit or implicit — impose transaction costs on the firm and can lower productivity. Krishna and Mitra (1998) observed increased competition and productivity in a panel of Indian firms after the removal of structural economic barriers in that country in 1991. Similarly, Barseghyan and DiCecio, (2011, p. 1) found in their research that "… higher entry costs lead to greater misallocation of productive factors and lower Total Factor Productivity (TFP) and output". They found that "countries in the lowest decile of the entry costs distribution have 1.32 to 1.45 times higher TFP and 1.52 to 1.75 times higher output per worker than countries in the highest decile". Similarly, Nicolleti (2013, p. 2) argues that the "distribution of labour productivity growth rates across countries, industries and periods skewed towards higher rates in high competition countries and in industries with low regulatory burdens".

These findings impute a strong role for competition law to promote the contestability of markets, by reducing market barriers and checking abuses of market power. The Organization for Economic Cooperation and Development (OECD 2005) has confirmed this pivotal role, arguing that competition law raises productivity by spurring efficiency, disciplining managers, increasing investment by removing barriers, reinforcing incentives for innovation, and speeding up the adoption of new technology. Similarly Dowdle (2014, p. 14) has stated that competition law promotes "... productive efficiency, which refers to a market's ability to maximise output from a given quantity of input (in practical terms, this means producing goods at their lowest possible costs)". Likewise, Nicolleti (2013) has asserted that, "there is pervasive evidence that anti-competitive regulations inhibit growth via productivity through various channels including its effect on ... capital formation and the effectiveness of the creative destruction process".

The most significant means by which competition impacts productivity is by "naturally" rewarding the most efficient firms with larger market shares. This is due to the forces fostered in contestable markets, which exert continuous downward pressure on prices and consequently on unit costs. Firms respond to these challenges by truncating costly production processes, opening up room for more efficient firms to dominate the market. A competitive market should create pressure on firms to consciously raise their productivity to gain a competitive (cost) advantage in the market. In a review of the literature, Foster et al. (2001) found a positive correlation between productivity and firm survival as well as growth. The adoption of productivity-enhancing technology and the upgrading of managerial skills is also more likely to occur in competitive markets, according to Nicolleti (2013, p. 3) where there are stronger incentives to act. Weaker competition between firms also results in difficulty of "moving resources to the most productive firms and the propagation of inefficiency via intersectoral linkages".

The literature also presents persuasive evidence that exposure to international competition through the dismantling of trade barriers also has the effect of improving productivity growth. Lileeva and Trefler (2010), in a study of Canadian firms, found that firms that increased exports in response to dismantling trade barriers witnessed increased labour productivity, engaged in more innovation, and adopted newer manufacturing technology.

While the line of causality between competition and productivity is unwavering within orthodox economic theory, it is less so in accounts of the key drivers of firm-level innovation. *The Oslo Manual* (OECD 2005, p. 10) defines innovation as "the implementation of a new or significantly improved product, or process ... marketing method, organizational method in business practices, workplace organization". Innovation has long been recognized as a cornerstone of efficiency in markets, and a source of competitive advantage. A dominant research orthodoxy in many studies is that innovation happens in markets, and essentially concerns non-state actors. Under this approach, the role of government in promoting innovation is to vouchsafe competitive markets and reduce regulation that could diminish competition. The 2004 World Development Report lends credence to this view, noting that firms reporting strong competitive pressure were more likely to introduce either a new product, upgrade an existing product, or adopt new technology (World Bank 2004). On the other hand, highly competitive markets where there is little prospect of earning supernormal profits may dissuade market entry and inhibit the investment required to engage in innovation. As Evans (2014, p. 24) has noted, quoting the U.S. Supreme Court, "the opportunity to charge monopoly prices is what attracts business acumen in the first place; it induces risk taking that produces innovation and economic growth". The challenge for competition law and regulators is to balance the need for contestability of markets while also preserving the incentive for market entry and innovation.

Shapiro (2002, pp. 8–9), in his review of the linkage between competition law and innovation, is similarly cautious when he states that "competition regimes are conducive to innovation and act gradually over time as companies learn new rules regarding licensing and collaboration, so dramatic effects in the short-or-medium-term resulting from changes in competition policies are unlikely". Shapiro is careful not to argue in favour of a straight line of causality from competition, instead advancing the more modest claim that the "impact on competition policy on innovation is more pronounced in efforts to commercialise new science and technology, to diffuse innovations more broadly throughout the economy and to extend, or build upon existing inventions".

Recent explanations of innovation activity raise important and sometimes vexed questions for competition regulators. One example of this surfaces in the body of research known as "cluster analysis"; a reputable area of investigation within modern innovation theory. Porter (2004, p. 5) describes clusters as:

> geographically proximate groups of interconnected companies, suppliers, service providers, and associated institutions in a particular field, linked by commonalities and complementarities.

Cluster studies include work on natural, resource-driven clusters, designed government-sponsored clusters, regional knowledge clusters, competition and cooperation within industry concentrations, and the "competitive advantage" of industry clusters (Feser and Bergman 2000). The increased productive value generated in industry innovation clusters is well established: they include expanded economies of scale and economies of scope, by identifying and optimizing global value chains, efficient supply chain models, increased labour productivity derived through networks and collaboration, and resultant growth in new firms. In fact, the concept of geographically-based clusters first emerged over a century ago in the work of Alfred Marshall in 1890 (Marshall 1890). Since then clusters have evolved and have taken different forms.

The potential for industrial clusters to create "competitive advantage" has been supported by a growing body of research (De Jong and Marsili 2006). SMEs can benefit from increased collaboration and networking that results in the sharing of technical and marketing expertise, and subsequent participation in new supply chains. These activities enable firms operating within clusters to share some associated risks, thereby helping increase the level of trust across firms.

Since "clustering" inevitably involves close collaboration, information exchange, and joint business activities, competition regulators need to judge whether some activities are contrary to competition principles or are indeed legitimate responses by SMEs to larger firms with greater market power. The experience of clusters draws attention to the tension that may exist between innovation and competition.

Another significant and related area of tension for competition law regimes in Asia pertains to the type of capitalism that is frequently observed in Asian countries. Dowdle (2014, p. 42) and Redding (2004) among others have shown that there is greater evidence of relational or networked capitalism in Asia as a result of high inter-firm interdependence, relational contracting, and government-linked firms (often through the ownership or equity stakes of sovereign wealth funds). This type of capitalism is deeply embedded in Asian culture, history, and political economy but may occasionally clash with competition law principles.

In spite of these tensions, the past decade has witnessed a proliferation of antitrust and competition commissions in Asian economies, largely spurred by globalization and the convergence of competition law and practices. In Singapore, the competition law regime is relatively young, having only been developed over the last ten years. The Competition Commission of Singapore (CCS) was established in 2005 as a statutory board charged with enforcing the Competition Act of Singapore (Han 2014). The CCS has declared its philosophical approach to regulating competition in which there is a clear articulation of the relationship between competition, productivity, and innovation.

Economic regulation is challenging in an environment such as Singapore's, where the government has historically adopted a laissez-faire approach in organizing its economic system. As with any regulation, its economic impact will depend on the costs it imposes on businesses to comply with the regulation, and the benefits it yields for the economy. The Competition Act 2004 and the CCS's oversight of market transactions will increase the cost of doing business. The government's philosophy, however, is that these increased costs should not encumber business practices. To ensure that Singapore's competition laws do not choke business practices, the government has ensured that they reflect domestic imperatives. Singapore's competition laws depart from those of the European competition law, which are largely driven by internal market imperatives within Europe and represent an "orthodox view of global antitrust policies" (Pollard 2014, p. 2). For instance, the CCS considers no cut-off thresholds to establish "market dominance", nor does it use the AKZO presumption of dominance, where a 50 per cent market share absent accentuating circumstances, would be evidence of market dominance (Monti 2006; Pollard 2014). Vertical agreements (that is, arrangements between businesses at different levels in the supply chain) are also exempt from CCS scrutiny.

As will become evident over the following sections, SMEs in the manufacturing sector are in broad accord with this philosophy. However, they are also concerned that the market power wielded by larger firms may be inhibiting improvements to productivity and innovation.

Research Strategy and Methodology

The authors were commissioned by the Singapore Innovation and Productivity Institute to conduct a year-long study (2014) on productivity and innovation among SMEs in the Singapore manufacturing sector. The research objective was to discover the key drivers of total factor productivity in this sector and to examine the performance of SMEs across these key drivers.

The study collected primary data productivity and innovation practices from Singaporean SMEs in identified subsectors. In the study, twenty SME leaders across the Singaporean manufacturing subsectors were interviewed to understand the policy context and challenges that they faced. This was followed by a Delphi study where the views of global and local experts and thought leaders (including academics, government officials, and policymakers) were sought on the drivers of productivity and innovation in SMEs. A Delphi study is a structured communication technique in which a panel (or panels) of experts is consulted in order to access informed opinion on a subject. The objective is to move towards group convergence and an agreed answer based upon "collective intelligence". Interaction in Delphi is anonymous and questions are presented to the group in such a way as to suppress any identification and thus remove any inhibitions or other constraints often felt by participants in face-to-face interactions.

The approach identified six thematic determinants of productivity in SMES: technology and capital utilization; pay and performance management; training, development and organizational learning; innovation culture; government policy, markets, and regulation; and leadership and management quality. Reflecting on the aforementioned approach, a survey instrument containing forty-one multiple-choice questions across these six themes was subsequently designed. A stratified random sample based on the share of economic output to the manufacturing sector was drawn from the Accounting and Corporate Regulatory Authority of Singapore which maintains information on businesses, using Singapore Standard Industrial Classification (SSIC) classification codes. These are listed in Table 12.3. These subsectors account for more than 80 per cent of the manufacturing output in Singapore.

The main survey data was collected through a face-to-face interview with the person most familiar with productivity and innovation issues in the firm — usually the CEO or other senior manager. Data was captured on a tablet computer and uploaded to a cloud-based survey administrator in real time. To improve the response rate, this approach was complemented with a "snow-balling" approach inviting SME respondents that completed the survey to introduce the survey to other SMEs within their network. The number of firms surveyed across subsectors is illustrated in Figure 12.2.

Table 12.3
Industrial Subsector and SSIC Classification Codes

Industrial Subsector	SSIC Classification — Two-Digit Level
Chemicals & Chemical Products	C20
Pharmaceuticals & Biological Products	C21
Computer, Electronic & Optical Products	C26
Fabricated Metal Products	C25
Food & Beverage	C10; C11
Machinery and Equipment	C28
Other Transport Manufacturing/Engineering	C30

FIGURE 12.2
Distribution of Firms Surveyed

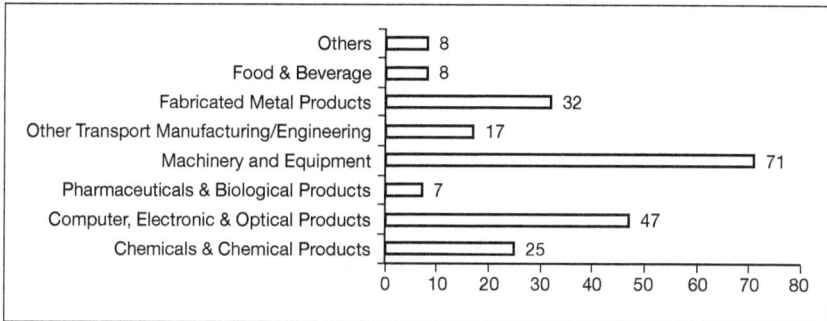

Key Research Findings

The results of the Delphi study underscore the pivotal role to be played by competition and regulatory authorities in enhancing productivity and innovation in the national economic systems. For instance, one Delphi respondent stated that what was needed was:

> An openly competitive environment which provides the opportunity for large and small firms to gain access to both public and private contracts — small firms should not be blocked out through institutional barriers.

Similarly, another respondent suggested that productivity and innovation among SMEs could be improved through:

> ... Increased competition within a broad macro environment. Secondly, removal of government regulations that "lock up" particular activities — the legal profession, medical, construction, and transport are often overprotected and over-regulated (largely for the benefit of insiders).

This theme of creating the conditions through which firms can participate in open and contestable markets was also strongly tied to building innovation capabilities. A Delphi respondent claimed that one of the key factors constraining innovation was a "lack of strategic awareness which may come from inexperience, from being in a 'comfort zone', from lack of competition, etc., but the effect is to limit motivation to innovate". Another respondent continued along these lines when stating that:

> My answers to the first four questions seek to convey a belief that productivity and innovation only happen when management are committed to making it happen and have the skills and capacity to make it happen. That in turn depends on the incentives they face (in particular, competition) and their capacity to respond to those incentives, their own abilities, and those of their employees, and the extent to which public policy blunts or distorts incentives, inhibits managements' capacity to respond to those incentives, and which adds to the stock of knowledge on which managements can draw.

This statement points to an important insight: that competitive market conditions alone are insufficient to drive productivity and innovation. Rather, it is the capacity of the management of the firm to respond effectively to competitive signals which results in these improvements.

The results of our Delphi study were largely supported by the large-scale survey of 215 SMEs in the manufacturing sector. SME leaders were asked to consider the extent to which each of the following statements (in Figure 12.3) was true for their firms.

The vast majority of respondents (almost 83 per cent) agreed with the contention that "Competition drives productivity and innovation in our markets", with less than 7 per cent disagreeing with the statement. In conversation with SME leaders, a number referred to their perception of Singapore as being "small and intensely competitive". Similarly a number also referred to the large population of multinational corporations (MNCs) in Singapore as both presenting an opportunity and a competitive threat to SMEs in the manufacturing sector.

While competition was widely seen as a driving force for productivity and innovation, the majority of respondents (55 per cent) perceived the small size of the Singapore market as being a natural restraint on the capacity of firms to improve. A number of SME leaders complained that Singapore's relatively small market tended to limit the size of orders and the ability to scale operations, thereby reducing the incentive to invest in capital-intensive production technologies.

One interesting finding was that related to the statement, "Market domination by a few large players restricts our productivity and innovation". Just over 45 per cent of respondents agreed with this

FIGURE 12.3
To What Extent is the Following True for Your Firm?

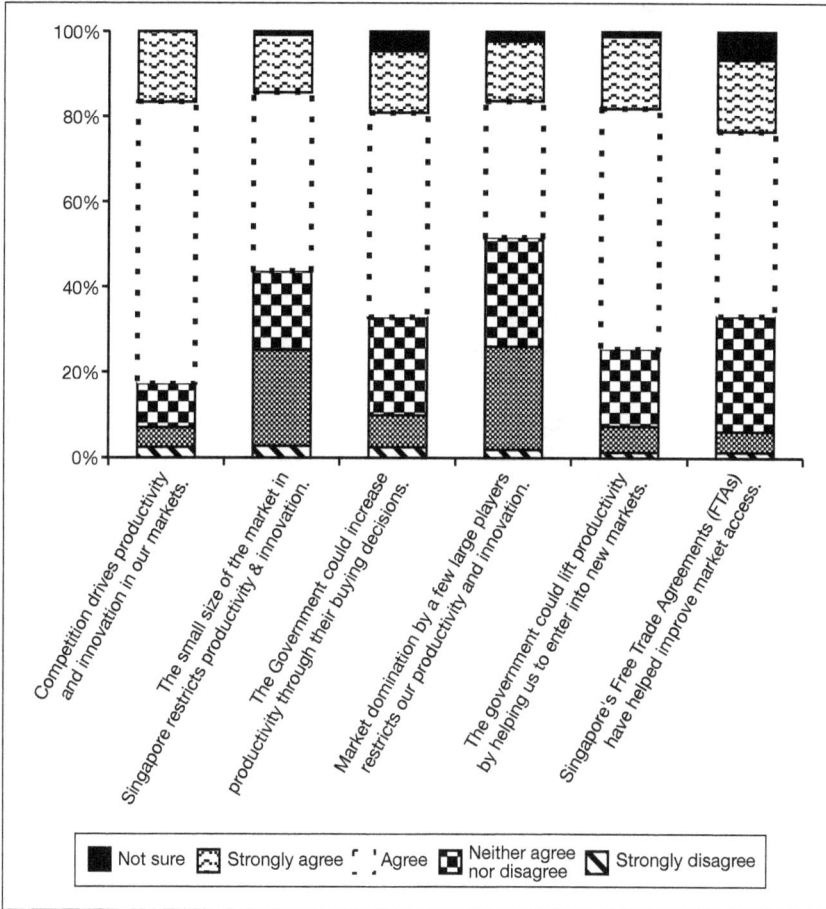

assertion, while a little over 26 per cent disagreed. This result points to at least the perception that market power wielded by larger manufacturers was having the effect of stifling improvements to productivity and innovation. The finding also further highlights the clear nexus between competition, productivity, and innovation, and the pivotal role to be played by the competition law authorities. Market domination or market abuse by a small number of large providers not only reduces competition but also competition's positive consequences — innovation and productivity growth.

It is widely recognized that access to global markets and integration into global supply chains foster competition, and can yield advances in firm-level productivity, which in turn create an environment that fosters innovation. Integration with the global economy has been a key pillar to Singapore's long-term growth strategy, and has been enabled through generous Free Trade Agreements (FTAs). As of 2013, Singapore had over twenty regional and bilateral FTAs with thirty-one trading economies (IE 2014). These agreements have allowed Singapore to rapidly integrate into global financial and real markets and improve market access. Its current total trade to GDP ratio exceeds 250 per cent (World Bank 2014). In our sample, 60 per cent of SME respondents agreed with the statement that Singapore's FTAs have helped improve market access. This suggests that trade that brings opportunity as well as exposure to fair competition is perceived favourably by SMEs. A majority of SME leaders (73 per cent) indicated that productivity could be further raised if the Singapore Government could assist SMEs to enter into new markets. This is further evidence that greater economies of scale and exposure to market opportunity can be used as levers to drive productivity and innovation.

Overall, the results of this study do point to some lingering concerns within SMEs in the manufacturing sector, related to the market power of larger participants in their industry. This suggests a need for close monitoring of the sector by the CCS.

Conclusion

As this chapter has demonstrated, there is a near consensus on the positive relationship between an effective competition law regime and productivity enhancement. This was evident not simply from the review of the extant literature but also from our Delphi and main survey results. There is also broad support to be found in the literature and in the industry for a similar relationship between competition law and innovation. However, support for this second relationship was more measured and qualified, and there is an awareness of the observable tensions between competitive markets and innovation activity.

According to the former head of the competition authority in the United Kingdom, Sir John Vickers (cited in Evans 2014, p. 22), competition policy at its heart is "judicious regulation to bring out the best in laissez-faire". In the Singapore context, competition policy and law has a pivotal role to play in bringing the best out of the economy by helping to foster lagging total factor productivity and innovation. The concept of "judiciousness" that was referred to by Sir John is one that resonates in the context of any exposition of competition law and its relationship to productivity and innovation. Judiciousness, or the exercise of caution to avoid harm, is required by states and competition authorities in our view, to ensure that the quest to improve market access and curb the abuse of market power does not infringe upon or reduce the incentive to invest in innovation. It is also necessary for competition regulators to support initiatives such as clustering among SMEs, as a means of enhancing productivity and innovation and their ability to compete globally.

From the vantage point of SMEs in the Singapore manufacturing sector, we found that there was a strong awareness of the positive role to be played by competition law in the drive for productivity improvement. However, it was also apparent that SMEs believed that more could be done to curb the market power of larger firms, which could in turn encourage SMEs to invest in innovation. Finally, in the context of Singapore's national drive to improve productivity, our findings point to the strong need for policymakers to harness all the relevant policy levers in establishing the optimal business climate to incentivize producers in ways that raise the welfare and living standards of all.

REFERENCES

Barseghyan, Levon and Riccardo DiCecio. "Entry Costs, Industry Structure, and Cross-country Income and TFP Differences". *Journal of Economic Theory* 146, no. 5 (2011): 1828–51.

Budget Singapore. "A Better Singapore: Quality Growth, an Inclusive Society", 25 February 2013. Available at <http://www.singaporebudget.gov.sg/budget_2013/pb.html> (accessed 9 September 2013).

Competition Commission of Singapore (CCS). "Opening Address by Mr Lee Yi Shyan, Senior Minister of State for Trade & Industry and National Development, at The CCS-SAL Competition Law Conference 2014", 28 November 2014. Available at <https://www.ccs.gov.sg/media-and-publications/speeches/opening-address-by-mr-lee-yi-shyan-senior-minister-

of-state-for-trade--industry-and-national-development-at-the-ccssal-competition-lawconference-2014>.

Conference Board. "Total Economy Database", 2013. Available at <https://www.conference-board.org/data/economydatabase/index.cfm?id=30565> (accessed 6 June 2015).

De Jong, Jeroen P.J. and Orietta Marsili. "The Fruit Flies of Innovations: A Taxonomy of Innovative Small Firms". *Research Policy* 35, no. 2 (2006): 213–29.

Department of Statistics Singapore. "Profile of Enterprises in Singapore", 2014. Available at <https://www.singstat.gov.sg/docs/default-source/default-document-library/statistics/visualising_data/profile-of-enterprises-2014.pdf> (accessed 17 June 2015).

Dowdle, Michael W. "On the Public-Law Character of Competition Law: A Lesson from Asian Capitalism". NUS Law Working Paper 2014/004. Singapore: National University of Singapore, 2014.

Evans, David. "Competition Policy and Economic Development". Keynote address of CCS-SAL Competition Law Conference, Singapore, 21 August 2014.

Fabrizio, Kira R., Nancy L. Rose, and Catherine D. Wolfram. "Do Markets Reduce Costs? Assessing the Impact of Regulatory Restructuring on US Electric Generation Efficiency". *American Economic Review* 97, no. 4 (2007): 1250–77.

Feser, Edward J. and Edward M. Bergman. "National Industry Cluster Templates: A Framework for Applied Regional Cluster Analysis". *Regional Studies* 34, no. 1 (2000): 1–19.

Foster, L., J. Haltiwanger, and C.J. Krizan. "Aggregate Productivity Growth: Lessons from Microeconomic Evidence". In *New Developments in Productivity Analysis*, edited by Charles R. Hulten, Edwin R. Dean, and Michael J. Harper. Chicago and London: University of Chicago Press, 2001.

Goh Tee Wei. "A Shift-Share Analysis of Singapore's Labour Productivity Growth, 1998–2013". *Economic Survey of Singapore 2013* (2013), pp. 70–77.

Han, Li Toh. "Singapore: CCS". In *The Asia Pacific Antitrust Review 2014*. London: Law Business Research Ltd., 2014.

International Enterprise (IE) Singapore. "IE Singapore's Global Footprint Singapore", 2014. Available at <http://www.iesingapore.gov.sg/About-Us/Overview> (accessed 15 February 2015).

Knittel, C. "Alternative Regulatory Methods and Firm Efficiency: Stochastic Frontier Evidence from the US Electricity Industry". *Review of Economics and Statistics* 84, no. 3 (2002): 530–40.

Krishna, Pravin and Devashish Mitra. "Trade Liberalization, Market Discipline and Productivity Growth: New Evidence from India". *Journal of Development Economics* 56, no. 2 (1998): 447–62.

Lileeva, Alla and Daniel Trefler. "Improved Access to Foreign Markets Raises Plant-level Productivity ... for Some Plants". *The Quarterly Journal of Economics* 125, no. 3 (2010): 1051–99.

Marshall, Alfred. *Principles of Economics: An Introductory Volume*. 8th ed. London: Macmillan & Co. Limited, 1890.

Melitz, Marc J. and Gianmarco I.P. Ottaviano. "Market Size, Trade, and Productivity". *Review of Economic Studies* 75, no. 1 (2008): 295–316.

Ministry of Manpower, Government of Singapore. *Singapore Yearbook of Manpower Statistics*, various years. Available at <http://stats.mom.gov.sg/Pages/Home.aspx>.

Monti, Giorgio. "The Concept of Dominance in Article 82". *European Competition Journal* 2, no. 1 (2006): 31–52.

Nicolleti, Giuseppe. "Regulation, Competition and Growth". Hearings of the WP2 of the OECD Competition Committee, 23 October 2013. Available at <http://www.oecd.org/daf/competition/Item%204.3_CLP%20hearings_Nicoletti.pdf> (accessed 10 December 2014).

Organisation for Economic Co-operation and Development (OECD). *The Oslo Manual: Proposed Guidelines for Collecting and Interpreting Technological Innovation Data*, 2005. Available at <http://www.oecd.org/science/inno/2367580.pdf> (accessed 8 December 2014).

Pollard, M. "More than a Cookie Cutter: The Global Influence of European Competition Law". *Journal of European Competition Law & Practice* 5, no. 6 (2014): 329–30.

Redding, Gorden. "The Conditional Relevance of Corporate Governance Advice in the Context of Asian Business Systems". *Asia Pacific Business Review* 10, no. 3 (2004): 272–91.

Shapiro, Carl. *Competition Policy and Innovation*. OECD Science, Technology and Industry Working Papers, 2002/11. Paris: OECD Publishing, 2002.

World Bank. *World Development Report 2004: Making Services Work for Poor People*. Washington, D.C.: World Bank, 2004.

———. "World Development Indicators", 2014. Available at <http://data.worldbank.org/data-catalog/world-development-indicators> (accessed 26 March 2015).

13

SME LAW AND ABUSE OF A SUPERIOR BARGAINING POSITION IN JAPAN

Shuya Hayashi and Kunlin Wu

Japan's policy towards small and medium-sized enterprises (SMEs) has gone through several major changes in its philosophy and practices over the last century. In the period immediately after World War I, Japanese government strategies were principally aimed at developing a well-ordered market and encouraged the grouping of enterprises. In the aftermath of World War II, this policy changed to be essentially focused on pro-competitive policy settings during the post-war Occupation Period. However, under the 1963 SME Basic Act, national SME policy changed once more, this time to focus on deterring the abuse of superior bargaining position. Japanese SMEs have often suffered from such abuses and, as a result, several pieces of law (including the Antimonopoly Act and the Subcontract Act) have been enacted to deal with the issue. This chapter gives a review of these regulations, and discusses some cases arising from its application.

Japanese SME Policy

Japan, an island country with a population of approximately 126 million, has a political system similar to that of many Western nations, but has evolved its own unique set of competition laws and small and medium-sized enterprise (SME) policy responses.

Some institutional structures are very similar to those in most other developed nations. For example, the nation is a constitutional monarchy with a parliamentary system of government. Japan's elected legislature, the Diet, consists of two elected chambers: the House of Representatives and the House of Councillors. The head of the executive branch of the Japanese government, the Prime Minister, holds office with the approval of the Diet. Of all the nation's administrative organizations, the Ministry of Economy, Trade and Industry (METI) is the most significant body in terms of its influence on the nation's economic and industrial policies. Japan also has a Small and Medium Enterprise Agency (the SME Agency), which was established under METI, and is responsible for SME policy. The courts operate independently of the executive branch and are largely corruption-free.

In Japan, a SME is defined in one of several ways under Article 2 of the Small and Medium-sized Enterprise Basic Act. In the manufacturing, construction, or transportation sectors, it is a firm whose capital does not exceed 300 million yen, or whose number of employees does not exceed 300. In the wholesale sector, it is an organization whose capital does not exceed 100 million yen, or a company or an individual whose number of employees does not exceed one hundred. In the service industry, it means any business entity whose capital does not exceed 50 million yen, or whose number of employees does not exceed one hundred. Finally, in the retail industry, it is an enterprise whose capital does not exceed 50 million yen, or with no more than 50 employees.[1] Using such definitions, SMEs account for 99.7 per cent of all companies in Japan, and hire 70 per cent of all employees (SME Agency 2013, p. 6).

Japan's policies towards SMEs have gone through several major changes in philosophy and practice over time. The genesis of Japan's SME policy is still somewhat debated, and two main different theories have been proposed. One suggests that it can be traced back to the middle Meiji Period (Kawakami 2004, pp. 207–9), and, given its wide historical span, is not discussed further in this chapter. The other holds that Japan's SME policy was initiated in the Depression after World War I. During the war, Japan's economy boomed due to wartime demand: because most European countries were incapable of exporting many of their goods and services, Japanese companies seized this opportunity to enter into Asian markets they had not previously operated in. However, these markets were recaptured by European companies after the war. As a consequence, many Japanese SMEs attempted to maintain their domestic market share by fierce price competition. They were inadvertently trapped in a vicious cycle, where they had to slash prices repeatedly to attract customers. In view of this excessive competition, the Japanese government established a system of export associations, aimed at both restraining cheap but poor quality goods and bringing stability and order to marketplace dynamics. This system is often regarded as the origin of Japan's modern SME policies (Yasuda 2009), yet it can also be considered as a form of competition policy.

During World War II, the nation's economy was largely under government control. Resources were poured into producing materials for the war industry, and munitions industry enterprises and their subcontractors formed a manufacturing *keiretsu* system. The Japanese government aggressively encouraged such groupings of enterprises (Yasuda 2009), and from the viewpoint of SMEs, this constituted a kind of SME policy, although an anti-competitive one.

In the immediate aftermath of World War II, governance and administration was overseen by the occupying Allied Forces, who instituted a number of reforms. SME policy was administered by the Antitrust and Cartel Division, and the Act for Establishment of the Small and Medium Enterprise Agency was enacted in 1948 (Act No. 83 of 1948). The purpose of the law, as Article 1 stated, was to encourage "... sound and independent SMEs, which prevent economic concentration and ensure fair opportunities for those who intend to operate a business". Almost at the same time, the Antimonopoly Act (the AMA) came into effect in 1947. These two pieces of legislation thus formed a package: the AMA acted as a deterrent to anti-competitive economic concentration, and the SME Agency helped alleviate the negative effects of market concentration or monopoly by providing assistance for SMEs (Yasuda 2009).

Competition among large enterprises, SMEs, and even new entrants was legislatively supported irrespective of their scale, size, or market share. Such competition was seen as a necessary countervailing power to the prior economic power exercised by certain large firms and *keiretsu*. SMEs, as one of the main sources of such countervailing power, were expected to compete with large enterprises. The same line of thought can be found in Galbraith (1952).

Geroski (1995) has suggested that the response by market incumbents to the threats posed by a new entry are selective. Incumbents are inclined to ignore entrants under certain conditions, at least until those new entrants become well-established. A corresponding phenomenon can be observed in Japan. Like most start-ups around the world, many new ventures in Japan had only a few employees, and it would be unrealistic to assume that new entrants could compete on par with incumbent large-scale enterprises.

The Subcontract Act (Act No. 120 of 1956), which prohibits abuse of a superior bargaining position, was also introduced. The Japan Fair Trade Commission (JFTC) and the SME Agency have concurrent jurisdiction over claims under the Subcontract Act, and collaborate to promote compliance with its provision amongst firms. They also hold regular training courses and seminars on the Act.

The pre-existing SME Basic Act was replaced by the Small and Medium-sized Enterprise Basic Act (Act No. 154) in 1963, which had two especially notable features. For the first time, a clear definition of what constituted an SME was provided under Article 2. In addition, the Preamble as well as Article 1 of that Act explicitly stated that its objectives included that of dissolving "two-tier structures" formed by large enterprises and SMEs.

The term "two-tier structure" indicates a disparity in productivity and wages between large enterprises and SMEs. Large enterprises were presumed to abuse their superior bargaining position over SMEs. In order to eliminate such a disparity, SME policy began to put an emphasis on enhancing SME productivity and on strengthening their price bargaining power. This led to the introduction of provisions regarding abuse of a dominant position, both in the AMA and in the Subcontract Act.

The promotion of SMEs during the Occupation Period was largely pro-competitive in focus, whilst under the 1963 SME Basic Act, SMEs were not perceived as competitors to large enterprises; and new entrants might be undesired because they might intensify competition among incumbents, which would be against the purpose of controlled competition. Unions and trade associations were thus allowed to be organized due to their effects on restraining excessive competition. The primary focus of the 1963 SME Basic Act was to control, restrain, or even prevent competition. Its priority was to deter abuse of a superior bargaining position. The SME policy was thus not pro-competitive, but rather anti-competitive. A stark difference can be observed in the relationship between SME policy and competition policy during the Occupation Period, and that under the 1963 SME Basic Act. Accordingly, there may not always be perfect harmony between SME policy and competition policy.

Market conditions gradually changed in the period after the passing of the 1963 SME Basic Act (Yasuda 2009, p. 18). A significant new factor was the emergence of foreign competitors, which made it difficult for the SME Agency to stringently enforce the Act, due to a fear that it might lead large enterprises to relocate their production bases overseas. Another changed condition was that more Japanese SMEs had adopted a range of innovative technologies and management practices that now gave them significant market share. Unlike large firms, many of them were likely to try new tools and approaches in the marketplace and in their product offerings.

Competition among SMEs, new entrants, and large enterprises often differs from textbook models. Economics literature suggests that the market entry and exit are determined based on average cost and price. However, in the case of new services, Japanese SMEs were often able to enter a new emerging market first, while large enterprises subsequently followed in due course. As Schumpeter's "creative destruction" theory indicates, it was vital for an enterprise whose goal is to generate profits to target a strategic niche market where the enterprise can dominate and obtain a monopolistic position. For many Japanese SMEs, this strategy was based around creating and monopolizing a new market instead of competing in an existing one.

The 1963 SME Basic Act was fundamentally amended in 1999. The 1999 SME Basic Act has two primary goals: one is to promote start-ups (Article 13), and the other is to facilitate innovation in management and business activities within existing firms (Articles 12 and 14).

In brief, the relationship between the SME policy and competition regulation has undergone a process of evolution over several decades. Japanese SMEs were once deemed "too many and too small". There was a common consensus that the number of SMEs in the nation would decrease over time, and that new entries would be deterred from forming. As a result, state policy put an emphasis on preventing abuse of a superior bargaining position by large enterprises. To some extent, these concerns were accurate: the exit rate of SMEs actually exceeded the entry rate in 1989 for the first time in history (Nakata 2013, pp. 45–8). This phenomenon was considered a desired result at the time, since it reduced the number of "excess" SMEs. Today, on the contrary, SME policy has changed drastically to highlight the necessity of increasing the number of SMEs.

Abuse of a Superior Bargaining Position

The regulation on the abuse of a superior bargaining position is contained in Article 2, paragraph (9), item (v) of the AMA. The substantive content was originally stipulated in 1982 in Article 14 of the Designation of Unfair Trade Practices (Public Notice No. 15 of 1982), promulgated by the JFTC and later combined into the AMA in 2009. Prior to the 2009 amendment, the original 1953 legislation had contained an Article which stated that no entrepreneur shall deal with its counterparty by unjustly using its bargaining position.

The purpose of the original 1953 legislation was to address the apparent oppression of SMEs by large-scale enterprises, which can arise from a disparity between the bargaining positions of the two parties. One firm may be subject to terms and conditions less favourable than those enjoyed by its counterparty. Such disparities and inequality of terms are common and not problematic in most cases. However, a problem arises when a firm with a superior bargaining position unjustly takes advantage of that position to the detriment of its counterparty (usually a smaller, weaker firm). This can impede fair competition by affecting the counterparty's acceptance of the offer and the terms and conditions of a contract. Abuse can happen in the context of a large firm's dealings with many clients (counterparty businesses) or even in its dealings with just a single or very limited number of firms. When a firm with a superior bargaining position abuses its position systematically with a number of its clients, it may be necessary to invoke the abuse clause in order to maintain fair competition.

Tables 13.1 and 13.2 spell out the various current provisions that exist in Japanese law regarding abuse of a dominant position. Those shown in Table 13.1 may be subject to an administrative surcharge, or infringement notice, issued by the JFTC, whereas those in Table 13.2 do not.

TABLE 13.1
Relevant Provisions Regarding Abuse of a Superior Bargaining Position

Provisions		Typical Conduct
Article 2, paragraph (9), item (v) of the AMA	The term "unfair trade practices" as used in this Act means an act falling under any of the following items: (v) Engaging in any act specified in one of the following by making use of one's superior bargaining position over the counterparty unjustly, in light of normal business practices:	
	(a) Causing said counterparty in ongoing transactions (including a party with whom one newly intends to engage in ongoing transactions; the same applies in (b) below) to purchase goods or services other than those to which said transactions pertain.	Coercion to purchase
	(b) Causing said counterparty in ongoing transactions to provide money, services or other economic benefits.	Unjust coercive collection for monetary contributions, and coercion on its counterparty into dispatching employees.
	(c) Refusing to receive goods in transactions with said counterparty, causing said counterparty to take back such goods after receiving them from said counterparty, delaying payment to said counterparty or reducing the amount of payment, or otherwise establishing or changing trade terms or executing transactions in a way disadvantageous to said counterparty.	channel stuffing, unjustly low price purchase, unjust request for a discount, etc.
Article 2, paragraph (9), item (vi) (e) of the AMA	The term "unfair trade practices" as used in this Act means an act falling under any of the following items: (vi) Any act falling under any of the following items, which tends to impede fair competition and which is designated by the Fair Trade Commission, other than the acts listed in the preceding items: (e) Dealing with the counterparty by making use of one's superior bargaining position unjustly.	Unjust delay in payment, unjust refusal to receive goods, and unjust return of goods.
Article 13 of the DUTP	Causing a corporation which is one's transaction counterparty to follow one's instruction in advance, or to get one's approval, regarding the appointment of officers of the said corporation (meaning those as defined by Article 2, paragraph (3) of the AMA (The same shall apply hereinafter)), unjustly in light of the normal business practices by making use of one's superior bargaining position over the counterparty.	Unjust interference with appointment of officer, and trading (loans) on the terms related to the appointment of officer.

Table 13.2
Prohibited Conduct Under the Subcontract Act and
Special Designations

The General Field of Subcontracting	Prohibited Conduct Designated by the JFTC in Different Industries
《The Subcontract Act》 – including manufacturing contract, repair contract, information-based product creation contract and service contract (excluding subcontract in construction industry) – refusal to receive goods, return of goods, delay in payment of proceeds, reduction of payment, taking back the goods which have been accepted by a counterparty, setting unjustly low proceeds, coercion to purchase, sanctions, request for payment prior to the date of payment of proceeds when supplying raw materials, request to dispatch employees, delivery of a negotiable instrument difficult to be discounted, coercive collection for monetary contributions and coercion to redo an order.	《Designation of Specific Unfair Trade Practices by Large-Scale Retailers Relating to Trade with Suppliers》 Fair Trade Commission Notification No. 11 of 2005 – unjust return of goods, unjust ex-post price reduction, unjust consignment sales contract, coercion on suppliers into lowering prices for bargain sales, refusal to receive specifically-ordered goods, coercion to purchase, unjust assignment to employees of suppliers, unjust receipt of economic benefits, and unfavourable treatment in response to refusal of requests or notification to the JFTC.
	《Specific Unfair Trade Practices when Specified Shippers Entrust the Transport and Custody of Articles》 Fair Trade Commission Notification No. 1 of 2004 – delay in payment of proceeds, reduction of payment, setting unjustly low proceeds, coercion to purchase, delivery of a negotiable instrument difficult to be discounted, coercive collection for monetary contributions, coercion to redo an order, and sanctions.
	《The JFTC, Specific Unfair Trade Practices in the Newspaper Business》 Fair Trade Commission Notification No. 9 of 1999 – providing a distributor with more copies of newspapers than the distributor actually ordered, coercing a distributor into ordering a specific number of newspapers and actually providing such number of copies to the distributor.

Abuse of dominance has a number of different adverse effects on the process and operation of fair competition (Tansou 2006). Firstly, a large enterprise can unjustly strengthen its market position relative to that of its competitors. Secondly, it also restrains competition, for the counterparty cannot exercise its freedom and discretion so as to compete effectively. Finally, it undermines one of the foundation stones of free competition — the right of each transacting party to determine and settle on terms and conditions based on their independent own judgement.

This third point is a particularly important one (Negishi 2009), and is also partly adopted by the JFTC. In its Guidelines Concerning Abuse of Superior Bargaining Position under the Antimonopoly Act (issued in November 2010), the JFTC expressed its official view on this issue:

> However, if a party whose bargaining position is superior to that of the counterparty makes use of such a position to impose a disadvantage on the counterparty in a way that is unjust in light of normal business practices, it hinders transactions from being based on the free and autonomous judgment of the counterparty [underlined by the authors], and puts the counterparty in an unfavorable position compared to the counterparty's competitors. It also puts the party with the superior bargaining position in a favorable position compared to the party's competitors (JFTC 2010, Section I, 1).

The definition and meaning of "a superior bargaining position over the counterparty" does not mean that the potential offender needs to be a market-dominant firm, or one with significant market power. A relatively superior bargaining position compared to the counterparty will suffice. When judging whether an entrepreneur has a superior bargaining position, the main focus is on the degree of the counterparty's dependence on the transaction, and the following factors should be taken into account on a case-by-case basis: the capacity of the counterparty to choose other business partners; the disparity between the two firms' overall business capabilities; market conditions and the characteristics of the relevant goods or services.

What constitutes "unjust" behaviour is to be based on a comparison with "normal business practices". Whether conduct is unjustly disadvantageous "in light of normal business practices" should be determined by comparison with appropriate business practices that conform to the fundamental principles of the AMA. The terms and conditions under examination should be compared with those which would be set out if the transaction were conducted on an equal footing basis. Such terms and conditions need not be analysed on the basis of economic rationality. So-called "normal business practices" are not necessarily either practical or existing business practices, but rather those that would be permitted from the perspective of fair competition (Tanaka 1982).

Abuse of a superior bargaining position often emerges in transactions between subcontracting enterprises and their SME subcontractors. In Japan, such abuse is regulated under the Subcontract Act, a complementary law to the AMA. The Subcontract Act and special designations promulgated by the JFTC specify what may constitute a superior bargaining position and illustrate typical examples of prohibited conduct. Conduct prohibited under the Subcontract Act and its special designations are summarized in Table 13.2.

Cases in Japan

A number of cases to date illustrate the application of abuse of dominance laws. The Mitsukoshi case (1979) was the first matter in which the old provision prohibiting abuse of a superior bargaining position was solely applied. In April 1979, the JFTC found that Mitsukoshi, a well-known large-scale retailer in Japan, had taken advantage of its superior bargaining position over its suppliers to conduct transactions on unjustly unfavourable terms and conditions, compared to normal business practices. Mitsukoshi's abusive conduct covered a number of different activities. In order to push up sales of advance movie tickets, firework show tickets and overseas travel packages, Mitsukoshi forced its suppliers to pre-purchase these tickets. In another arrangement, Mitsukoshi had coerced its suppliers into paying the costs of remodelling its selling space without reasonable grounds. And when Mitsukoshi held commercial fairs, it forced its suppliers to pay for the expenses of holding such events, even though they had no direct relation to the fairs.

The Sanyo Marunaka matter (2004) was another well-known case. Sanyo Marunaka was a large-scale retailer operating a major chain of local supermarkets across the country. It conducted business with various suppliers in different sectors, including those in the food, grocery, clothing, and accessories industries. Using its superior bargaining position, Sanyo Marunaka made an unjust request for discounts, and even returned goods after it purchased them from the suppliers. It also required suppliers to use their own employees to help run Sanyo Marunaka's retail business, and coerced the suppliers into purchasing men's clothes.

Scepticism about the Regulations Concerning Abuse of a Superior Bargaining Position

Not all commentators support the use of an "abuse" provision by competition regulators. For example, Ryuhei Wakasugi, a noted Japanese economist, has questioned the rationale of the regulations (Wakasugi 1999, p. 105):

> [Translated by the authors] It is undeniable that in fact the regulation criteria is ambiguous. ... The ambiguity of regulation derives from the inherent fundamental problem that it is unclear what abuse of a superior bargaining position indicates and why it impedes fair and free competition. ... According to the definition, a degree of obscurity still remains with regard to ... in what circumstances a superior bargaining position will emerge between parties having ongoing transactions, and in what way we should grasp the relationship between this position and the fact that the transactions are actually concluded.

Wakasugi (1999, p. 115) offered a persuasive reason why economists have been antagonistic to the regulations, stating that:

> It is not unequivocal that by what kind of mechanism economically desirable results can be achieved through government intervention or regulation. ... Even granted that a party has a superior bargaining position over its transacting counterparty, the conclusion of transaction should not be regarded as an abuse of such a position because it was the result of optimal choice made by the transacting parties.

On the other hand, Wakasugi also points out that the regulations may be effective to some extent when a subcontracting enterprise seeks to employ a strategy to the detriment of its subcontractors by taking advantage of "the hostage". Wakasugi (1999, pp. 121–23) notes that the "... efficient allocation of resources may be achieved by the prohibition against an *ex post* unfavorable modification of the terms and conditions imposed on an inferior party (e.g., a subcontractor) in ongoing transactions." He goes on to state (Wakasugi 1999, pp. 125–26):

> Government intervention ... is unable to adjust income distribution to the benefit of the weak. If the primary aim were to protect economically weak parties, we should adopt a more straightforward policy measure, such as an income transfer mechanism, including subsidy and tax-relief system, rather than applying government intervention in private contracts such as the regulations concerning abuse of a superior bargaining position.

Conclusion

The history of SME and competition policy in Japan is complex, and has evolved over many years. Today, the major focus is on preventing abuse of a dominant position, and several regulations and laws have been enacted to deal with this issue. After decades of experience in the application of laws concerning this issue, it is worth noting that the regulations still seem to put a stress on fairness rather than economic efficiency.

On the surface, this seems a logical policy response, as SMEs are usually presumed to be in a much weaker bargaining position than the larger firms they often deal with as suppliers, manufacturers, retailers, and wholesalers.

Ironically, though, such relationships may not always be the main competition concern. The SME Agency conducted market surveys of small enterprises in 1984 and 2002, and in both surveys asked the following question: "Who is your main competitor?" While large enterprises replied that their competitors were existing large companies, SMEs answered that their main competitors were incumbent SMEs. According to the surveys, in practice, most Japanese enterprises did not actively compete with rivals of varying sizes, but rather focused their efforts on competitors who were the same size as them (SME Agency 1984, 2002). It goes to show that the relationship between SME policy and competition law is often more complex and less obvious than it may appear to be at first glance.

NOTE

1. At the time of writing, JP¥119 = US$1.

REFERENCES

Galbraith, John Kenneth. *American Capitalism: The Concept of Countervailing Power*. Boston: Houghton Mifflin, 1952.

Geroski, Paul A. "What Do We Know About Entry?". *International Journal of Industrial Organization* 13, no. 4 (1995): 421–40.

Kawakami, Yoshiaki. "Nihon Ni Okeru Chusho Kigyo Kenkyu No Atarashii Shiten (i) Nibunhou No Jirenma: Senzenki" [A Study of New Viewpoint of SMEs (1): Dilemmatic Dichotomy in Prewar Period]. *Fukuoka University Review of Commercial Sciences* 49, no. 2 (2004): 203–25.

Nakata, Tetsuo, ed. *History of Japan's Trade and Industry Policy (12): Small-and Medium-sized Enterprises 1980–2000*. Tokyo: Research Institute of Economy, Trade and Industry, 2013.

Negishi, Akira. *Chushaku Dokusen Kinshihou* [Explanatory Notes Upon the Antimonopoly Act]. Tokyo: Yuhikaku, 2009.

SME Agency. "Chusho Kigyo Keiei Katsudou Jittai Chosa" [A Field Study on the Business Operations of SMEs], 1984. Available at <http://www.chusho.meti.go.jp/pamflet/hakusyo/H15/Z02-01-15-00.htm> (accessed 15 June 2015).

―――. "Keiei Senryaku Ni Kansuru Jittai Chosa" [A Field Study on Business Strategy], 2002. Available at <http://www.chusho.meti.go.jp/pamflet/hakusyo/H15/Z02-01-15-00.htm> (accessed 15 June 2015).

―――. "Japan's Policy on Small and Medium Enterprises (SMEs) and Micro Enterprises", 2013. Available at <http://www.chusho.meti.go.jp/sme_english/outline/04/20131007.pdf> (accessed 15 June 2015).

Tanaka, Hisashi, ed. *Hukouseina Torihiki Houhou* [Unfair Trade Practices]. Tokyo: Shouji Houmu, NBL Bessatsu No. 9, 1982.

Tansou, Akinobu and Jyouji Atsuya, eds. *Shin Gendai Keizaihou Nyuumon* [A New Introduction to Modern Economic Law]. 3rd ed. Kyoto: Horitsu Bunka Sha, 2006.

Wakasugi, Ryuhei. "Hukouseina Torihiki Houhou Ni Kansuru Kisei (1): Futourenbai Oyobi Yuuetsuteki Chii No Ranyou • Shitauke Torihiki" [Regulations on Unfair Trade Practices (1): Below-cost Sale, Abuse of a Superior Bargaining Position and Subcontract]. In *Nihon No kyosou Seisaku* [Competition Policy in Japan], edited by Akira Gotou and Koutarou Suzumura. Tokyo: University of Tokyo Press, 1999.

Yasuda, Takehiko. "Sinkisannyu No Tachiba Kara Mita Kyoso Seisaku — Nihon No Kesu" [Competition Policy from the Perspective of New Entry — A Case of Japan]. *Kousei Torihiki* 702 (2009): 17–22.

14

COMPETITION LAW, POLICY, AND SMEs IN SOUTH KOREA

Sun Hyung Sonya Kim and Yong Jung Kim

Small and medium-sized enterprises (SMEs) have played a significant role in the process of Korea's successful economic development. This is the result of various governmental policies that have been enacted to foster SMEs. As economic circumstances (both internal and external) have changed, the focus of Korean SME law and policies has shifted from unilateral protection or support of SMEs to reinforcing the economic significance and competitiveness of SMEs. Consequently, the importance of competition policies to SMEs has also grown. The main body of competition law in Korea, the Monopoly Regulation and Fair Trade Act (MRFTA), contains certain exceptions applying to SMEs and provisions for their protection. Other legislations have been enacted to ensure fair transactions for SMEs and franchisees. The MRFTA and related laws aim to create a free competitive market to address the anti-competitive and unfair transactional structures that small firms may be exposed to.

Overview

In the process of Korea's rapid and successful economic development, small and medium-sized enterprises (SMEs) have played a major role.

This is the result of both specific stipulations in the Constitution, and due to various SME promotion and support policies that have been successfully implemented. But against a backdrop of government-led economic policies that have traditionally prioritized large conglomerate (*chaebol*) growth, Korean SME policies may be considered relatively lacking, especially when considering the earlier stages of Korea's economic development.

For much of the last few decades, Korean SME policies had been focused on protection policies or on policies in which SMEs played a supplemental role to large conglomerates. More recently, the Korean government has succeeded in amending its policies in response to internal and external changes in national economic circumstances. It has been moving towards reorganizing its legal system to promote and support SMEs so that the economic roles and competitiveness of small firms can be strengthened.

The significance and value of SMEs can vary in different ways, depending on the stage of economic development of the nation involved. SMEs can be considered to have major significance for a rapidly developing country, since promoting them may help build an industrial base, expand employment opportunities, balance development in different regions of the country, and establish a stable social infrastructure. On the other hand, for economically-advanced countries, the issue may be approached in terms of improving the sophistication of SMEs in order to form a stable and healthy industrial base (Lee 2006).

In this sense, the focus of Korean SME policies has shifted according to different stages of the nation's economic development. Prior to the 1980s, in the early stages of economic development, SME policies concentrated on raising the level of industrial competitiveness and solving issues of disparate growth between SMEs and large conglomerates that arose from the pursuit of large conglomerate-centred pressured-growth economic policies. But since the 1990s, in line with economic open-door policies and widespread concern over the strength of Korea's industrial base, national SME policies have focused on strengthening the competitiveness of small firms. In this process, there has been a gradual shift to approaching small business issues from a competition policy perspective.

Definition of SMEs and Current Status

Small firms are defined under Article 2, paragraph 1 of the Framework Act on Small and Medium Enterprises (1966) which stipulates the scope, size, and independence requirements to qualify as an SME.[1] These standards are utilized to evaluate the applicability of various laws and policies related to the protection and promotion of SMEs.

As of 2012, SMEs in Korea represented 99.9 per cent (3.3 million) of the total number of businesses in all industries. Persons employed by SMEs composed 87.7 per cent (13 million people) of the total number of employees in all industries. In the manufacturing sector, SMEs' share of total production and total value added amounted to 45.7 per cent and 47.6 per cent, respectively (Korean Federation of SMEs 2014). As can be seen through these figures, SMEs form the foundation of the Korean economy. Hence, continuous efforts to raise the level of SME international competitiveness and support its underlying infrastructure are critical.

SME and Competition Policies in Korea: Objectives

Generally, SMEs have less access to funds, personnel, technology, business management, information, and bargaining power compared to large conglomerates. This is a common experience in many countries. More specifically in Korea, SMEs have suffered from a long history of export-oriented compressed growth policies that led to an economic structure in which many major industries were largely monopolized. As economic polarization increasingly intensified, a small firm's ability to develop a successful business relationship with large conglomerates became a decisive factor in its ultimate survival and success.

In response, the Korean government has incorporated SME policies in its industrial policies. Hence, various SME law and policies have been implemented to protect and support SMEs with the ultimate goal of achieving balanced economic growth across the industrial base.

Prior to the 1980s, SME policies were primarily focused on promoting specialization, with SMEs designated to play a supplemental role to large conglomerates. But since the first Oil Shock (1973), and through a series of internal and external changes in the economy, SME policies have shifted their focus to developing small firm sustainability and raising the level of their competitiveness.

SME and Competition Policies in Korea: The Development of Policies and Laws

Currently in Korea, there are approximately eighteen laws being enforced in support and promotion of SMEs. Fundamentally, these statutes are based on Article 123 of the Constitution that stipulates that the state shall "protect and foster small and medium enterprises", and also "foster organizations founded on the spirit of self-help among businessmen engaged in small and medium industry and shall guarantee their independent activities and development".

The developmental process of SME-related policies and laws can be chronologically categorized according to how the government at the time sought to deal with the SME issues it faced (Park 2010).

Governmental policies for SME promotion were first implemented in the early 1960s, as part of the national economic growth plan initiated at the time. The Framework Act on Small and Medium Enterprises was enacted in 1966 to improve the relatively inferior infrastructure of SMEs. This Act specifically defined the scope of SMEs and obligated central and regional governments to implement SME growth policies, while at the same time requiring small businesses to cooperate with such measures. The Small and Medium Enterprise Cooperative Act (1961) was also enacted at this time.

Through such laws, the government implemented various policies to help the establishment of SMEs as a valid component of the nation's industrial structure, including measures to promote venture companies and regional companies, business area protection, business rationalization, internationalization, cooperation among SMEs, improvements in business structures, fair competition, and collaborative growth between SMEs and large conglomerates.

As a result of successful economic development policies, the Korean national economy started to experience substantial growth in the 1970s and 1980s. But such growth was concentrated in large conglomerates, and severely disproportional growth within major industrial categories and companies started to have a detrimental effect on the overall economy. As one of the policy responses to this problem, SME policies were refocused to develop a more sophisticated industrial structure with balanced SME growth.

Specific measures to protect SME business territories were implemented, along with other policies to promote collaborative growth between SMEs and larger companies. Other strategies and laws were also introduced at this stage to deal with undue delays in payments and to address SME financial funding issues.

At a later point still, the resilience and adaptability of SMEs surfaced as a critical issue when the Korean economy experienced significant turmoil from the first Oil Shock. Accordingly, the policy focus shifted onto enhancing SME competitiveness, rather than encouraging them to simply remain in a supplemental role to large conglomerates.

For this purpose, the Promotion of Small and Medium Enterprises Act (1978) and the Support for SME Establishment Act (1986) were enacted. These statutes established the Small & Medium Business Corporation and various SME funds, and provided governmental funding and administrative support. Also, to counter persisting monopolistic market structures, the main body of statutory competition law, the Monopoly Regulation and Fair Trade Act (MRFTA), was enacted in 1980, along with the Fair Transactions in Subcontracting Act in 1984.

In the early 1990s, market liberalization measures and frequent labour-management disputes led to serious difficulties for SMEs. In response, the government once again changed its drive to focus on improving the productivity and research and development (R&D) capacities of SMEs, while reorganizing SME laws to improve, restructure, and stabilize corporate structures and management.

In 1997, the Asian Financial Crisis hit Korea, wreaking havoc on the industrial base for SMEs, and causing numerous bankruptcies and a severe economic downturn. The government responded by introducing various short-term financial support measures. Both the Act on the Promotion of Technology Innovation of Small and Medium Enterprises (2001) and the Special Act on Support for Human Resources of Small and Medium Enterprises (2003) were passed during this period.

By the late 1990s, SME policies had fully moved away from industrial policies intending to protect and support SMEs, and instead began to promote their independence and competitiveness.

In the latest turn of policies, as disproportional growth between SMEs and large conglomerates has become an increasingly serious issue, the Act on the Promotion of Collaborative Cooperation between Large Enterprises and Small-Medium Enterprises (2014) was enacted. This law aimed to foster collaborative growth between SMEs and large conglomerates, created a new Collaborative Growth Commission and earmarked certain industries deemed appropriate for SMEs.

SME and Competition Policies in Korea: The Relationship Between Competition Policies and SME Policies

Until now, there has been a relative lack of discussion in Korea on the most effective ways to establish SME-related policies in relation to competition policies. Since protection and promotion still remains a critical part of the nation's SME policy approach, the issue of conflict persists. Consequently, barriers-to-entry or business adjustments may be set up in conflict with general competition policy objectives. Such conflicts are also often evident in measures that seek to protect certain categories of business, or in the policy of supporting SME entry into certain designated industry sectors. On the other hand, although SME-related provisions have been included in the MRFTA, they may still be seen to be lacking in providing sufficient support for SMEs.

Despite this, SME policies have been able to break away from previous protection-focused policies and have become refocused on raising the level of SME competitiveness. In doing so, SME policies have been brought in line with competition policies. This is based on an understanding that the goals of SME policies and competition policies are alike: securing SME competitiveness (the main purpose and drive of SME policies) helps establish competitive markets and helps regulate transactional imbalances between firms of different sizes (the main purpose and drive of competition policies).

Competition policies for SMEs in Korea can be largely divided into three categories. The first set treats SME–large conglomerate relationships as horizontal relationships and attempts to establish fair competition in the market by regulating exclusionary anti-competitive conduct by large conglomerates. This approach protects SMEs indirectly by regulating large conglomerates that take advantage of their market dominant positions, and thus, levels the playing field for SMEs.

The second category of policies views SME–large conglomerate dealings as vertical relationships. This set of policy and law regulates unfair transactional conduct in which large conglomerates abuse their superior position and force disadvantageous terms onto SMEs.

The last category does not view SME–large conglomerate relationships as horizontal or vertical, and instead takes an entirely different approach. One approach excludes any application of the MRFTA to SME policies, relying on SMEs to advance to a certain level of competitiveness without such legislative support. Another approach focuses on solving structural issues of monopolistic markets rather than regulating specific business conduct.

SME-related Provisions in the MRFTA

The MRFTA was enacted in 1980 and Article 1 (the "Purposes" section) stipulates that the Act shall prevent abuse of market-dominating positions, excessive concentration of economic power, unjust concerted practices (cartels), and unfair trade practices. These provisions aim to establish and maintain competition in the market, while restricting excessive expansion by large conglomerates (from both horizontal and vertical perspectives), in order to indirectly help SMEs compete. More directly, provisions in the MRFTA carve out exceptions for SMEs or regulate unilaterally disadvantageous terms in transactions to establish fair transactional order and guarantee the opportunity for SMEs to compete and trade on an equal standing.

The Korea Fair Trade Commission (KFTC) is the principal government agency in charge of enforcing the MRFTA and other laws related to SME protection (including the Fair Transactions in Subcontracting Act, Fair Franchise Transactions Act, and the Large-Scale Retail Fair Trade Practices Act). It has been established in the form of an independent regulatory commission, and has both quasi-legislative powers (that is, it has the authority to establish various laws, legal standards, and guidelines) and quasi-judicial powers (the authority to require corrective measures to be taken for any proven violations).

The MRFTA contains a number of special features relevant to SMEs, including (and as discussed in the following sections):

- Exclusions for SMEs in MRFTA;
- Presumption of anti-competitiveness for mergers in SME-dominated markets;
- Provisions restricting economic concentration;
- Provisions restricting unfair trade practices.

Exclusions for SMEs in MRFTA

In certain cases, the MRFTA does not apply to SME conduct that would otherwise be deemed in violation of the Act. Relevant provisions include Article 60 (which excludes certain cooperatives) and Article 19 (which excludes some cartels).

Article 60

Article 60 of the Act states that the provisions of the MRFTA do not apply to any conduct of a cooperative (including a federation of cooperatives) satisfying certain requirements, unless the conduct amounts to unfair trade practices or a price increase by unjust restriction of competition. Under this Article, to be considered a cooperative, the following conditions must be satisfied: the cooperative must be established for the purpose of mutual aid among small-sized undertakings[2] or among consumers; the cooperative must be established voluntarily, and voluntary and open membership must be guaranteed; each member must have an equal right to vote; and if a cooperative distributes profits to its members, the articles of the cooperative must set limits on such distribution.

This exclusion helps small-sized undertakings (who may be too small to counter large conglomerates) cooperate and band together to become a valid unit capable of competition in the market.

SMEs and Unjust Concerted Practices (Cartels)

Article 19 Clause (1) of MRFTA prohibits unjust concerted practices (cartels) among companies by stating that firms "… shall neither agree with [any] other undertaking [business] to engage in any of the following conducts by contract, agreement, resolution, or any other mean, nor cause other undertaking to engage in such conduct".

However, Clause (2) states that "Clause (1) does not apply to the concerted conduct that has certain purposes, satisfy the requirements as specified in the Presidential Decree, and been authorized by the

Korea Fair Trade Commission." These certain purposes are stipulated as the following six categories: industry rationalization; research and technological development; overcoming economic depression; industrial restructuring; rationalizing terms of trade; and perhaps most importantly, for the purposes of enhancing the competitiveness of SMEs.

To qualify as an excluded cartel under this last category, the cartel must meet a number of conditions: it must have a significantly positive effect on the productivity of SMEs (such as improvements in quality and technology) or strengthening SME bargaining power; all of the cartel participants must be small firms; and no other means exist to effectively compete with or counter large-scale companies, other than forming a cartel.

The legislative purpose of such exclusion for cartels is to help SMEs band together to overcome the disadvantages inherent in their competition with large conglomerates.

Presumption of Anti-Competitiveness for Mergers in SME-dominated Markets

MRFTA also prohibits anti-competitive mergers, according to Article 7 Clause (1). In addition, under Clause (4) of the same article, in certain cases of mergers, competition is presumed to be materially restricted. More specifically, under Article 7 Clause (4) Item 2, if a large company, either directly or through a person with a special interest, combines enterprises in a particular business area where SMEs (as defined under the Framework Act on Small and Medium Enterprises) occupy not less than two-thirds of the whole market share, such merger is presumed to suppress competition in that particular business area.

This provision attempts to limit large companies from entering markets or industries in which SMEs comprise a majority of the market.

SMEs and Restricting Economic Concentration

MRFTA also includes provisions aimed at restricting excessive economic concentration in large conglomerates, while also prohibiting cross-shareholding among large company groups, limiting debt guarantees among affiliated companies, requiring public disclosure, and improving corporate governance structures. Such provisions were introduced into MRFTA in 1986 when economic concentration in large corporate groups became a major social and economic issue, and has garnered significant success since then.

While such provisions may not benefit SMEs directly, they do help limit the excessive expansion of large corporate groups and expand the range and opportunities of SME business activities, thus helping lay the groundwork for SMEs and large conglomerates to compete independently and equally.

SMEs and Unfair Trade Practices

MRFTA also includes provisions prohibiting unfair trade practices against SMEs. It deals with a firm unjustly using its superior bargaining position, and the practice of large conglomerates providing unfair subsidies to their related persons or entities.

Prohibitions against Abuse of Superior Bargaining Position in a Transaction

Article 23 Clause (1) Item 4 prohibits "... trading by unjustly using a superior bargaining position" as a form of unfair trade practice. The purpose of this provision is to promote fair trade by guaranteeing equal status between principals in a transaction who may have disparate economic power. Accordingly, this provision prohibits a party with superior bargaining position (or at least in a position to wield substantial influence on the other party's business activities) from abusing that position and causing disadvantage to the other party.

Specific prohibited practices in this category include coercion to purchase, coercion to provide benefits, imposing sales targets, forcing disadvantages, and interference in management.

Strictly speaking, the primary focus of these provisions is not solely about SME–large conglomerate relationships. But in the process of Korea's economic development, large conglomerates have long carried out unfair trade practices by abusing their superior bargaining power against SMEs. Hence, these provisions have in practice helped establish more equitable dealings in typical transactions between large conglomerates and SMEs.

Unfair Subsidizing

Article 23 Clause (1) Item 7 prohibits the practice of providing "... advanced payment, loan, human resources, real estate, stocks, bonds, goods, services, intangible property, or considerably advantageous trading terms" as a form of unfair trade practice. This is intended to regulate unjust intra-group transactions between affiliated companies in large conglomerate groups, which usually take the form of especially generous subsidies for affiliates or other trading arms of the large enterprise.

While such intra-group transactions may sometimes be characterized as valid dealings between legally separate companies, they are more troublesome in the Korean context, because intra-group transactions are considered to intensify excessive economic concentration and monopolistic market structures for large conglomerate groups. They threaten the economic health of the entire corporate group by allowing large firms to sustain marginal companies and harm consumer welfare with their anti-competitive effects. Further, from the perspective of SMEs, unjust subsidizing amounts to insider trading within a conglomerate group that inherently excludes third party companies and deprives SMEs of business opportunities.

Special Competition Policies for Large Conglomerate-SME Relationships

Various special laws have also been separately enacted to regulate certain unfair trade practices that may occur in vertical transactions among large conglomerates and SMEs. Although they can be considered to be part of the general umbrella of competition policies and laws, these statutes are somewhat distinguishable from traditional competition policies that prioritize protecting competition itself. The Fair Transactions in Subcontracting Act, the Large-scale Retail Fair Trade Practices Act, and Fair Franchise Transactions Act fall under this category.

The Fair Transactions in Subcontracting Act

In Korea, SMEs commonly provide subcontracting services to large conglomerates, a practice which has grown out of the nation's history of disproportional economic development. On the positive side, subcontracting transactions between large conglomerates and SMEs enable both parties to share the benefits of growth. On the other hand, serious issues arise when large conglomerates take advantage of their superior position and force unfair or disadvantageous terms onto SMEs.

To deal with such issues, unfair acts in subcontracting were addressed as a subcategory of unfair trade practices under MRFTA in 1982, and the Fair Transactions in Subcontracting Act (the "Subcontracting Act") followed in 1984. This enactment was part of the various governmental SME protection and promotion policies that were implemented when concerns were raised about the intensification of economic concentration and weakening of the SME base across the country.

In the early stages of enactment of the Subcontracting Act, the focus was on financial issues, such as non-payment and late payments. But lately, the Act has been expanded to focus on establishing balanced transactional relationships between large conglomerates and SMEs in this category.

The Subcontracting Act applies to transactions in which firms deal with subcontractors that are smaller than them. The Act covers cases of subcontracting in production or repair, construction, or any assignment of service. Main contractors are required to put their agreement with subcontractors in written terms, and also required to pay subcontractors within sixty days of delivery. The Act also prohibits the main contractor from setting subcontracting fees unreasonably lower than market rates, cancelling subcontracts without reason, or unduly reducing payments.

When a violation of the Subcontracting Act occurs, a corrective measure ordering payment of the subcontracting fees to be paid or surcharges up to a maximum of twice the subcontracting fees (punitive damages) can be imposed. Apart from KFTC enforcements, the Subcontract Dispute Settlement Council has been established to encourage voluntary settlements of disputes and provide appropriate damage relief. As at the time of writing this chapter, the KFTC has imposed corrective measures in 23,000 cases.

The Large-scale Retail Fair Trade Practices Act

Unfair trade practices between large conglomerates and SMEs stand out even more prominently in the large-scale retail industry. In Korea, the retail-distribution industry is considered substandard, complicated, and inferior compared to the manufacturing industry. Within this industry, small-to-medium scale suppliers are at a serious disadvantage when dealing with large-scale retailers. This is especially significant since a small number of large-scale retail stores dominate existing retail distribution networks.

The KFTC has undertaken various measures to improve unfair trade practices in this sector. Prior to 2013, the KFTC relied on Regulatory Announcements for the Large-scale Retail Industry to promote healthy development in the retail-distribution industry. But as unfair trade practices continued to thrive and new forms of unfair trade practices emerged, the Regulatory Announcements were elevated to become the Large-scale Retail Fair Trade Practices Act in 2013.

Under the Large-scale Retail Fair Trade Practices Act, large-scale retailers are required to put their agreements with suppliers in written terms. In addition, the Act prohibits large-scale retailers from taking undue advantage by unreasonably reducing payments for goods, unreasonably delaying payments for goods, unreasonably refusing to accept goods, unreasonably returning goods, unreasonably transferring promotional costs, forcing exclusive dealings, or demanding the disclosure of business information.

The KFTC had succeeded in ordering corrective measures in more than 200 cases up until 2013, using the Regulatory Announcements for the Large-scale Retail Industry.

The Fair Franchise Transactions Act

As the economy began to mature in Korea, the franchise industry became very popular and experienced rapid growth. Yet unfair trade practices have often prevailed in this industry, as franchisors (typically larger companies) frequently abused their superior positions and forced unilaterally disadvantageous terms on, or unfairly terminated contracts with, franchisees (who are almost always SMEs).

The KFTC originally relied on Regulatory Announcements for the Franchise Industry to regulate unfair trade practices. In 2002, the Fair Franchise Transactions Act was enacted. Under the Act, franchisors are required to provide prospectuses and franchise agreements to franchisees. The Act also prohibits specific types of unfair trade practices, such as unreasonable termination of supplies by a franchisor and abuse of superior position in a transaction. In order to protect franchisees from arbitrary termination by a franchisor, the Act stipulates that franchisors must notify franchisees in advance before terminating a franchise agreement. It also sets certain restrictions when terminating a franchise agreement.

A Franchise Dispute Settlement Council has been installed within the Korea Fair Trade Mediation Agency. This body provides a forum to settle disputes in franchise transactions. If a settlement fails to be reached at this council, the case can then be transferred to the KFTC and be processed in accordance with the agency's usual case handing process.

Since the enactment of the Fair Franchise Transaction Act, the KFTC has imposed corrective measures in approximately 1,000 cases of violations.

Conclusion

SME policies in Korea have evolved over time, reflecting different needs and priorities, and producing different laws as a result. Today they focus on promoting the competitiveness of small firms, and as such, competition policy and law now have a new significance for all small-scale enterprises. For this purpose, MRFTA has incorporated a number of special provisions for SMEs. At the same time, a number of other complementary laws have also been passed that deal with other related matters and industrial sectors, such as those dealing with subcontracting, large-scale retailing, and franchising. Each of these has had a significant impact on the nation's small business sector. Today, Korea has perhaps many more SME-specific laws than most countries, and these policies and laws will no doubt also change in the future.

NOTES

1. Under this Act, SMEs are defined as the following: for-profit enterprises satisfying conditions specified in the related law, which include requirements for sales, total assets, actual independence of ownership, and management; social enterprises not in pursuit of profits satisfying conditions specified in the related law; and cooperatives or federations of cooperatives.

2. Small-sized undertakings are to be distinguished from SMEs, and is generally used for a business that is considerably smaller than what is generally considered an SME. But the article itself and relevant rulings fail to provide a concrete standard for determining what qualifies as a small-sized undertaking for the exclusion to apply.

REFERENCES

Hwang Lee, Sun Hyung Kim, Yong Jung Kim, Woo Sik Jung, Hyun Jung Yun et al. *2013 Modularization of Korea's Development Experience: Korea's Developmental Experiences in Operating Competition Policies for Lasting Economic Development* (Knowledge Sharing Program, 2014).

Fair Transactions in Subcontracting Act.

Fair Franchise Transactions Act.

"Framework Act on Small and Medium Enterprises". Available at <http://elaw. klri.re.kr/eng_mobile/viewer.do?hseq=22787&type=part&key=28>.

Korea Federation of SMEs. *2014 Current Status of Korean SMEs*. Seoul: Seongjimunhuasa, 2014.

Large-scale Retail Fair Trade Practices Act.

Lee, Gyung Eui. *Theories on SME Policies*. Seoul: Jisiksanupsa, 2006.

"Monopoly Regulation and Fair Trade Act". Available at <http://eng.ftc.go.kr/ files/static/Legal_Authority/Monopoly%20Regulation%20and%20Fair%20 Trade%20Act_mar%2014%202012.pdf>.

Park, Jung Goo. "Problems and Improvement Measures for SME Policies". LEG Working Paper, no. 2010-1 (2010).

15

COMPETITION LAW IMPLEMENTATION AND SMEs
Singapore's Experience

Wee-Liang Tan and Lip-Hang Poh

This chapter provides a ten-year review of the Singapore Competition Act from its introduction in 2005 up until 2014. The Competition Commission of Singapore (CCS) was established in 2005 to administer and enforce the Act. The CCS had the immediate task of helping businesses, especially small and medium-sized enterprises (SMEs), make the transition towards competition law compliance. However, CCS's enforcement experience and stakeholder engagement surveys over the last decade have revealed that most SMEs continue to be unaware of the prohibitions of the Act. CCS has had to modify its SME engagement strategy, innovating along the way. In the decade of its existence, the CCS has learnt some important lessons that may prove helpful to other competition authorities.

Introduction

Singapore is a recent entrant to the fold of countries subscribing to competition law. It has been ten years since the Singapore Competition Act was introduced and it is timely to review its introduction and implementation. How was competition law received by the small and medium-sized enterprises (SMEs)? What steps have been taken by the Competition Commission of Singapore (CCS) — established in 2005 to administer and enforce the Act — to address SME concerns, especially as they are the ones least able to adapt to changes in regulation?

Singapore is a small and open economy. Its nominal gross domestic product (GDP) in 2014 was S$390 billion[1] (Statistics Singapore 2014) and its trade to GDP ratio was 351 per cent (World Bank 2016), one of the highest in the world. SPRING Singapore (2014), the government agency responsible for SMEs, reported in 2014 that 99 per cent of businesses in the country were considered to be SMEs, contributing almost 50 per cent of GDP. SMEs are defined as:

- Enterprises with annual sales turnover of not more than S$100 million; or
- Enterprises with an employment size of not more than 200 workers.

This chapter begins by introducing the rationale for competition law in Singapore. As a small and open economy, Singapore does not quite fit the "typical profile" of a country that needs competition law. We next describe how Singapore prepared the business community for the implementation of the Act. The subsequent sections of the chapter discuss how the Act was rolled out in the country, the events that ensued, and the changes in CCS's approach in engaging SMEs over the last ten years. We conclude with some lessons that other competition authorities can learn from the Singaporean experience.

Rationale for Introducing Competition Law

The decision to introduce a competition regime in Singapore took many by surprise. After all, Singapore had some potentially valid reasons for resisting its adoption.

For a small economy, competition law enforcement might be regarded as a potentially difficult subject to police. This has been the experience in a number of other countries: by way of example, an International Competition Network report on some other small economies (Swiss Competition Commission and Israel Antitrust Authority 2009) noted that competition agencies in open and small jurisdictions experience more difficulties in ensuring that a competition authority is sufficiently equipped to achieve an adequate enforcement of the rules. Sometimes, small economies face higher expenses than larger ones when enforcing the law, and smaller competition agencies may struggle to achieve minimum efficient scale. However, the fundamental argument against implementing competition law in small economies is rooted in the fact that competition law does not necessarily lead to more efficient economic outcomes in small markets *vis-à-vis* larger markets. Gal (2003) examined the three main economic characteristics of small economies: high levels of industrial concentration, high entry barriers, and below minimum efficient scale levels of production. These features suggest that in small economies, market structures need to be more concentrated (that is, fewer competitors in any given industry for small economies) to exploit minimum efficient scale. Gal (2003) noted further that small economies could overcome the consequences of their small size by opening their economies to trade. Singapore has, from its inception, been at the forefront of free trade. It has opened its market to new entrants and products. Trade policy can enlarge production scope and scale for businesses in a small economy, but will expose domestic firms to "competition discipline" from foreign firms.

That being said, Gal has argued that there is an interaction between trade policy and competition policy (a wider concept that encompasses competition law and regulation of natural monopolies and oligopolistic markets). When trade barriers are reduced, competition policy can facilitate trade by reducing barriers to entry by foreign firms. Gal (2003, p. 41) opined that "the freer the trade, the stronger the incentives of firms to re-erect barriers" in order to retain market shares.

Competition policy can certainly help level the playing field so that it is possible for foreign firms to enter a market. However, efficiency gains from trade may be eroded by foreign firms abusing their market power or colluding in cartels. Competition law is therefore needed as a tool to prevent such conduct. Gal (2003, p. 42) concluded that:

> ... even in a small market with a liberal trade policy, competition policy has a crucial role for increasing efficiency in the market by reducing or eliminating abuses of dominant positions and the incentives of firms to collude, and by ensuring that domestic firms will have incentives to achieve productive and dynamic efficiency in light of aggressive international cooperation.

The factors above were carefully considered by the Singapore Economic Review Committee (SERC) in 2003 when it recommended the introduction of the Act in its report:

> Singapore does not have a generic competition law to prevent cartel activities like price-fixing and market division, and abuse of dominance by significant market players. We have enacted such rules only for specific sectors, like energy and telecommunications, which are more prone to anti-competitive behavior. A generic competition law that covers all sectors will institutionalize and give teeth to the Government's longstanding pro-competition policy. It will form part of our enabling infrastructure for entrepreneurship and ensure fair play between all enterprises, including MNCs [multinational corporations], GLCs [government-linked companies] and SMEs (SERC 2003, p. 129).

A similar view was espoused by Ong (2007), who argued that the introduction of competition law could help create a pro-enterprise business environment in Singapore and so further enhance the nation's international competitiveness, by making markets more efficient.

Another often-cited reason for the Act was the conclusion of the United States–Singapore Free Trade Agreement in 2003: that it was a condition imposed by the United States. That being said, the idea that competition policy is needed to complement trade policy still applies. The Act has an extraterritorial reach which allows CCS to take enforcement action against foreign firms, in so far as their anti-competitive conduct adversely impacts the Singapore economy and local businesses.

Introducing and Implementing the Act

Two rounds of public consultations were convened when the Competition Bill was drafted in 2004. The business community in Singapore generally echoed the SERC's view that the law was a positive, pro-enterprise initiative that could help SMEs.

The American Chambers of Commerce (2004, p. 9) submitted that the Act would:

> ... also serve to protect the many Singaporean SMEs who are doing business here ... Their ability to contribute their products and ideas into the marketplace, where consumers will ultimately judge them through their spending power, depends heavily on a market which is structured to ensure that competing firms can do so fairly and without restrictive and anti-competitive practices.

One Raymond Choo (2004, p. 6) commented during the public consultation that:

> ... the Competition Commission is there to make sure that a more level playing field is developed between the small players and the big boys in a competing or related industry. Small businesses can also take comfort that bigger companies cannot engage in anticompetitive conduct in the name of marketing strategies to shore up their business or unfavourably capture market share from the smaller businesses.

The Competition Bill was passed by the Parliament in October 2004 and assented to by the President in November 2004.

It became apparent during the consultation process that businesses in Singapore needed time to amend their existing business agreements, and to ensure that they did not run afoul of the Act. The Singapore Manufacturers' Association and the Singapore International Chamber of Commerce (2004, p. 9), in their joint submission during the public consultation period, observed that "in situations of co-operations between members of associations, it is not unusual that horizontal agreements will arise". Further concerns that SMEs might lack the necessary resources to navigate and understand competition law were also raised. The American Chambers of Commerce (2004, p. 16) submitted that "smaller firms with limited financial resources who might be the victims of anti-competitive practices would be less likely to file appeals, knowing that they would need to go through the extra time and expense of a lengthened process."

The Act was implemented in phases in order to give businesses sufficient time to understand the law and renegotiate existing business agreements that might have infringed it. Vivian Balakrishnan, then Senior Minister of State for Trade and Industry (2004, p. 4), noted during the second reading of the draft Competition Bill in Parliament that:

> The phased approach will allow time for the Commission and for businesses to prepare for the implementation of the law ... There will be a 12-month transition period before the provisions on anti-competitive agreements, decisions and practices; abuse of dominance; enforcement; appeals processes; and the other miscellaneous areas which will take effect on 1st January 2006. This would be the second phase. In the third phase, which is likely to be 12 months thereafter, the remaining provisions relating to mergers and acquisitions, which are more complex and technical, will come into force.

Hence the enforcement of the key prohibitions were phased. The Section 34 prohibition against anti-competitive agreements and Section 47 prohibition against abuse of dominant position came into force on 1 January 2006, whilst the Section 54 prohibition against mergers and acquisition that substantially lessened competition came into force on 1 July 2007. The transition period was subsequently extended by a further six months so that businesses had more time to ensure that their business practices are in compliance with the Section 34 prohibition. The Competition Regulations (Transitional Provisions for Section 34 Prohibition) provided that CCS would not impose any penalty on agreements made before 31 July 2005 and businesses were given until 1 July 2006 to renegotiate these agreements.

CCS was set up on 1 January 2005 to administer and enforce the Act. The agency has the power to investigate anti-competitive activities, and also has adjudicative powers (i.e. determining if the investigated activities are anti-competitive or not). In addition, CCS is empowered to give directions and/or impose financial penalties on undertakings that infringe the Act.

The Commission was officially launched by the Ministry of Trade and Industry on 2 August 2005 at the inaugural Competition Law Conference. In order to provide legal certainty to businesses, it began issuing public guidelines on how it would interpret and enforce the law before the prohibitions came into force. These guidelines described the types of anti-competitive conduct that CCS would enforce against. To ensure that the principles laid out in the draft guidelines were clear and understandable, public consultations were held to gather feedback on them. CCS also partnered with the Singapore Business Federation, organizing a series of seminars for businesses in order to solicit targeted feedback from them.

Apart from allowing CCS time to work on the guidelines, the phased implementation of the Act also allowed the agency to embark on a series of outreach programmes to raise awareness about the law. CCS conducted over twenty outreach sessions to businesses, government officials, and legal practitioners in 2006 alone. Over 1,300 people attended these sessions, where CCS discussed the prohibitions of the Act and their implications for existing and future business conduct. CCS also collaborated with umbrella business associations such as the Singapore Business Association, the Singapore International Chamber of Commerce, and the Singapore Chinese Chamber of Commerce and Industries (SCCCI), as they had extensive networks with other associations and businesses. For example, SCCCI had links to another 130 trade associations and 4,000 corporate entities from diverse industries. CCS also engaged with individual business associations. The 2007 outreach strategy was aimed at helping SMEs understand the Act: how the Act could benefit them and how they might alert CCS to anti-competitive practices in the market. CCS spoke to association members from the Cement and Ready-Mixed Concrete Association Singapore, Singapore Motor Tyre Dealers Association, Singapore Noodles Manufacturers Association, and Singapore Bakery and Confectionery Trade Association.

Table 15.1 documents the number of representatives (categorized by stakeholder groups) who attended the various outreach sessions conducted by CCS from 2006 to 2009.

TABLE 15.1
Number of Individuals who Attended CCS Outreach Sessions,
2006–9

Year	General Outreach	Business	Government
2006	235	1,060	39
2007	73	825	NA
2008	NA	620	361
2009	564	206	365

Implementation Experience

Whilst the initial comments on the Act indicated that businesses would be receptive to competition law (provided suitable education about the law was also provided), the implementation experience did not proceed as smoothly as anticipated.

CCS commissioned a study in 2009 to determine the extent of consumer, business, and other stakeholders' awareness of the Act, and to assess their familiarity with CCS. Over 1,100 questionnaires were collected from respondents drawn from government agencies, legal practitioners, trade associations, MNCs, SMEs, and the general public.

The survey identified that CCS's major challenge was to communicate the benefits of competition law to consumers and businesses. Four in ten of the businesses surveyed did not believe that Singapore businesses played by the rules, whilst only 39 per cent believed that businesses operated on a level playing field. Those surveyed also noted that CCS did not have a visible track record; 80 per cent of respondents believed that CCS could do more to make itself more visible to Singaporeans and businesses. Awareness of CCS and the Act was the lowest amongst SMEs, with only 17 per cent of those surveyed stating that they knew about CCS. When business owners were asked if they would like to find out more about what the agency did, only 16 per cent expressed a strong interest in doing so; noticeably, the interest level amongst SMEs owners was lower than amongst the owners of middle or large-sized firms.

Until 2014, all of CCS's Section 34 prohibition decisions were made against SMEs. In CCS's first price-fixing infringement decision, which was made against a group of express bus operators, one of the infringing SMEs, Regent Star, claimed ignorance and argued that it did not know that price-fixing was against the Act. The decision was issued in 2009 and news of the decision against the cartel was covered extensively by the local media. Yet despite this media coverage, ignorance continued to be raised as a defence or mitigating factor by SMEs involved in subsequent cartel investigations. Following the case against the express bus operators cartel, CCS also enforced the Section 34 prohibition against electrical works contractors, ferry operators, foreign domestic worker agencies, and modelling agencies.

The enforcement experience highlighted the fact that some stakeholders, especially SMEs, were paying little attention to competition law. Small firms appeared to have adopted a "wait and see what CCS does; until then, business as usual" attitude regarding implementation of the Act. This attitude may help explain why some SMEs were being caught for flagrant infringements such as price-fixing, and then subsequently pleading ignorance as a defence. The SMEs surveyed also opined that they were not "protected" by competition law. It seemed that the earlier pre-implementation sentiment (namely, that competition law was good for SMEs) could not be relied upon. On the contrary, the sentiments expressed by SME respondents to the CCS survey indicated that they were taken unaware by competition law requirements when enforcement commenced.

Having learnt that the ground was not as sweet as CCS was led to believe, and that its efforts at education were not yet sufficient, the Commission adjusted its approach and embarked on new initiatives. The next section discusses CCS's SME engagement strategies, how the agency responded to the problems identified above, and what proved to be the most effective tools.

Engaging with SMEs: CCS's Assist, Communicate, and Facilitate Strategies

CCS had already acknowledged that businesses, especially SMEs, needed assistance with understanding competition law. It also recognized that they required help in determining whether or not they might be breaching it in their daily business practices. It began to put into place a notification system to help businesses ascertain if their business agreement(s) or conduct infringed the prohibitions of the Act. Businesses in doubt could also refer their situations and agreements to CCS for review. During the period of review by CCS, such agreement(s) and conduct are immune from financial penalties. However, most notifications to CCS till 2009 involved non-SMEs. The 2009 survey and subsequent editions of the survey revealed that SMEs did not understand competition law and that they lacked the resources to understand and comply with the Act. It was therefore not surprising that most SMEs did not consider the notification system a useful tool to help them with compliance.

CCS then launched two initiatives in 2012 to assist small enterprises. The first initiative was an e-learning tool which was launched on the CCS website (CCS 2012b). The online training module provides a clear overview of the Act, including the dos and don'ts for businesses. It also explained some of the ways businesses can develop a compliance strategy, with users assuming the role of CEO (chief executive officer), procurement officer, or legal counsel in the programme. This helped them understand competition compliance from different perspectives and essentially served as a "ready-made" compliance training course for SMEs.

A handbook titled *Better Business with Competition Compliance Programme* was published in 2013 to encourage businesses to entrench competition compliance as part of good corporate governance (CCS 2013). The handbook discussed the key features of, and lays out the basic principles of, an effective compliance programme. A ready-made "competition compliance programme" poster summarizing how competition compliance leads to "better, smarter, and safer business" was also included in the handbook.

From CCS's enforcement cases and survey findings, it was clear that SMEs did not understand how the law applied specifically to them and what adjustments they needed to make in order to comply. Instead of communicating with trade/business associations sporadically and on an ad-hoc basis, CCS decided to launch a "relationship manager" system in 2012.

Officers in the Business and Economics Division of the Commission were assigned as relationship managers to individual business associations. Relationship managers were responsible for organizing regular meetings and exploring ways to increase contact time and engagement opportunities with these organizations and their members. A series of workshops on competition law and compliance were conducted in conjunction with the introduction of the "relationship managers".

The relationship manager system gave a "face" to CCS but this manager's role went beyond mere communication. Relationship managers also facilitated broader interactions. The associations now knew who in CCS to go to for a particular issue, and could quickly make contact with CCS regarding complaints or any industry/trade association-led initiatives. This close contact with industry bodies also allowed CCS to gather first-hand information on possible anti-competitive practices in a particular sector, and provided associations with a ready avenue to discuss regulatory impediments.

CCS also contributed feature articles to the newsletters of various industry associations. These articles explored competition law issues specific to the business operations of that particular industry. For example, CCS wrote an article on competition compliance for the National Association of Travel Agencies Singapore, whilst in another article published by the Franchising and Licensing Association, CCS discussed the interface between intellectual property and competition law.

CCS also revamped its publicity materials, graduating from a basic compliance-focused message on the key prohibitions of the Act to a more sophisticated "competition law protects your business" message. The Section 47 prohibition brochure was designed to help SMEs identify abusive business conduct by large players in the market, and explained how it harms their business, whilst the Section 34 prohibition brochure message was targeted at helping SMEs identify cartel activities and cautioned their involvement in such agreements. In order to reach out to Chinese-speaking SME owners, all of CCS's new publicity materials were also published in Mandarin.

CCS also utilized social media platforms, such as Facebook and YouTube, to reach out to businesses. The Commission's official

Facebook page was launched in 2010, enabling subscribers to receive first hand updates on competition law developments.

An online game titled "Sumo Marathon" was also launched on the Facebook page to educate players on the Section 47 prohibition. Players assumed the role of CCS to protect small sumo wrestlers from obstacles flung into their paths by the Big Sumo. The Big Sumo wrestler represented the dominant player in a market, abusing its position and abusing the smaller players in the market (small sumo wrestlers). The game aimed to give players a good understanding of CCS's role in preventing dominant players from abusing their dominance in the economy.

In 2012, CCS launched its Digital Animation film contest. Participants were challenged to create competition law-themed animations. By running this contest, CCS not only educated the public and generated more general interest in its work, but it also crowdsourced a number of good quality educational videos. CCS has since archived these videos, and made them available on its YouTube channel.

These videos help explain difficult competition law concepts to the layperson and are used at CCS's business outreach events. Since 2012, CCS has organized three editions of the contest, attracting more than seventy entries altogether. These YouTube videos, apart from engaging the young minds who participated in the contests, also helped CCS bring its message to "netizens". As at May 2015, CCS had garnered 4,000 fans on its Facebook page and over 100,000 views of its YouTube videos.

Lastly, CCS's leniency programme has helped to raise firm awareness about cartels. Under this scheme, CCS can grant immunity from prosecution to leniency applicants who provide information about a cartel they may have been involved in. For example, in the collusive tendering in electrical and building works case in 2010, CCS accepted a leniency application from Arisco, one of the fourteen companies involved in an electrical works cartel. Arisco was also granted complete immunity from financial penalties.

CCS's SME Experience: Key Points

What lessons can other competition agencies learn from the CCS experience? There are at least three significant ones.

(1) Regular evaluation is important. Had there not been a stakeholder survey conducted in 2009, CCS would not have discovered that SME sentiments following the implementation of the Act were far from expected. CCS would have continued using an inaccurate perception, when the reality was quite the opposite. Since then, an ongoing series of stakeholder surveys has provided CCS with the opportunity to track the effectiveness of its new initiatives and inform CCS of any future steps it needs to take when engaging with SMEs. Such measures already appear to be paying rewards. In more recent surveys, the awareness level of CCS and the Act amongst businesses has increased from 31 per cent to 59 per cent. Businesses reported in the 2014 survey that the quality of outreach and advocacy had also improved since 2012. They indicated that they now found CCS's outreach sessions more effective, and also asked for these outreach sessions to be more tailored to specific business contexts. Such findings help CCS verify if it is taking steps in the right direction when engaging with businesses at the industry/trade association level.

CCS also commissioned a paper in 2013 on post-enforcement evaluation methodologies, which it will use to make post-enforcement evaluations. The paper also set out indicative findings of the impact of CCS's past enforcement actions. One example involved SISTIC, Singapore's largest ticketing services company. In the SISTIC abuse of dominance case, CCS's enforcement had led to some initial positive outcomes for the industry, as smaller ticketing operators have increased their market shares and new operators have entered the market.

(2) Competition agencies need to continue to communicate. The survey findings also provided some useful insights into the necessary changes that CCS needed to take with regard to advocacy. For example, the 2009 survey found that "successful enforcement" is a key plank to communicating the importance of competition law — strong enforcement raises awareness and drives interest in competition law. Until stakeholders saw the impact of enforcement, they were not likely to appreciate the importance of competition law and CCS's enforcement role. As a result of this finding, a series of one page infringement-themed publicity materials was launched at the

15th Annual SME Conference and SME Expo 2013 (the former being the longest-running Mandarin business conference in Singapore, while the latter is an SME-solution and information hub that offers SMEs business solutions and services) (CCS 2013a). The prohibitions of the Act were presented in "case-study" formats where the "what, outcome, and impact" of a CCS infringement decision were discussed. The characters featured in these one-page publicity materials were based on the animation video contests described earlier.

(3) Working with business associations is important. Apart from giving a "face" to CCS, the relationship manager system has also served as an interface with industry, allowing CCS to gain insights on business practices and sentiments. Such interactions are invaluable, as CCS can gather information promptly and at the same time disseminate competition law related updates.

Conclusion

The Singapore experience offers a number of lessons for countries undergoing the initial years of competition law introduction. Firstly, one should not take comments that the introduction of competition law will be "all ok" for businesses at face value. CCS's experience illustrates the need for policymakers to treat such comments with caution: the pre-implementation and post-implementation sentiments about the Act in Singapore were contradictory.

It also demonstrates the value of using evaluation studies. There is a need to include an objective assessment soon after the implementation of competition law, to accurately gauge the reactions and responses from constituencies affected by the law. Once such studies have been put in place, ideally they should continue to be conducted periodically in future.

Next, one should allow adequate time for preparations, so that businesses can adjust to the changes in the business environment that result from introducing competition law. Although Singapore initially created a one-year transition period, an additional half year was ultimately needed before the Section 34 prohibition took effect, following feedback from businesses that they needed more time to renegotiate existing business agreements.

Sticks and carrots also matter. Singapore's experience demonstrates that the astute utilization of the proverbial "stick" of successful enforcement is a useful tool that raises awareness and drives interest in competition law. As competition law concepts are not immediately obvious to the layperson, successful enforcement helps to contextualize competition law concepts, pointing out what is unacceptable business conduct that falls foul of the Act. As discussed earlier, the one-page enforcement case study publicity material was very well received by SMEs. However, such enforcement needs to be coupled with a relationship strategy with businesses, adding the element of persuasion and assistance (the proverbial "carrot").

Lastly, the success of competition law implementation ultimately depends on all stakeholders, not only businesses, subscribing to a competition culture. Tools such as social media, seminars, traditional media, and third party organizations have all helped CCS to reach out to the wider community and consumers. Entrenching a competition culture throughout both the private and public sectors, which facilitates the creation of a pro-competitive business and regulatory environment, remains the ultimate goal and is an ongoing endeavour. This account only provides Singapore's progress in achieving the goal thus far.

NOTE

The views expressed in this chapter are personal and do not represent the official position of the Competition Commission of Singapore (CCS). The views shall not in any way restrict or confine the ability of CCS to carry out its duties and functions as set out in the Competition Act (Cap. 50B).

1. At the time of writing, S$1.40 = US$1.

REFERENCES

American Chamber of Commerce. "Comments on the Singapore Competition Act of 2004", 29 May 2004. Available at <https://www.mti.gov.sg/legislation/Documents/app.mti.gov.sg/data/pages/90/doc/frm_LEG_2competition_submission_amcham.pdf> (accessed 20 June 2015).

Balakrishnan, Vivian. "Second Reading Speech for the Competition Bill by the Senior Minister of State for Trade and Industry", 19 October 2004. Available

at <https://www.ccs.gov.sg/~/media/custom/ccs/files/media%20and%20
publications/speeches/second%20reading%20speech%20for%20the%20
competition%20bill%20by/19oct042ndreadingspeechfinal.ashx> (accessed
20 June 2015).

Choo, Raymond. "Submission to the Ministry of Trade and Industry
on the Second Public Consultation of the Draft Competition Bill",
20 August 2004. Available at <https://www.ccs.gov.sg/public-register-
and-consultation/publicconsultation-items/~/media/custom/ccs/files/
public%20register%20and%20consultation/public%20consultation%20items/
second%20round%20of%20public%20consultation%20on%20the%20competi/
frmleg2competitionsubmissionraymondchoo.ashx> (accessed 27 March
2015).

Competition Commission of Singapore (CCS). Annual Reports 2009/10,
2010/11 and 2012/13. Available at <https://www.ccs.gov.sg/media-and-
publications/publications/annual-reports> (accessed 12 March 2015).

————. *Better Business with Competition Compliance Programme.* Available at
<https://www.ccs.gov.sg/~/media/custom/ccs/files/education%20and%20
compliance/conducting%20a%20compliance%20programme/better20
business20with20competition20compliance20programme20english.ashx>.

————. "Price Fixing of Coach Bus Services for Travelling Between Singapore
and Destinations in Malaysia from 2006 to 2008", 3 November 2009.
Available at <https://www.ccs.gov.sg/public-register-and-consultation/
public-consultation-items/price-fixing-of-coach-bus-services-for-travelling-
between-singapore-and-destinations-in-malaysia-from-2006-to-2008>
(accessed 12 March 2015).

————. "Collusive Tendering (Bid-rigging) in Electrical and Building Works",
4 June 2010. Available at <https://www.ccs.gov.sg/public-register-and-
consultation/public-consultation-items/collusive-tendering-bidrigging-in-
electrical-and-building-works> (accessed 12 March 2015).

————. "Price fixing of monthly salaries of new Indonesian Foreign Domestic
Workers by Employment Agencies", 30 September 2011. Available
at <https://www.ccs.gov.sg/public-register-and-consultation/public-
consultation-items/price-fixing-of-monthly-salaries-of-new-indonesian-
foreign-domestic-workers-by-employment-agencies> (accessed 12 March
2015).

————. "Price Fixing of Rates of Modelling Services in Singapore by Modelling
Agencies", 23 November 2011. Available at <https://www.ccs.gov.sg/
public-register-and-consultation/public-consultation-items/price-fixing-of-
rates-of-modelling-services-in-singapore-by-modelling-agencies> (accessed
12 March 2015).

————. "CCS Imposes Financial Penalties on Two Competing Ferry Operators
for Engaging in Unlawful Sharing of Price Information", 18 July 2012*a*.

Available at <https://www.ccs.gov.sg/public-register-and-consultation/public-consultation-items/ccs-imposes-financial-penalties-on-twocompeting-ferry-operators-for-engaging-in-unlawful-sharing-of-priceinformation?type=public_register> (accessed 12 March 2015).

————. "Competing on Merit: Getting to Know the Competition Act", 2012*b*. Available at <https://www.ccs.gov.sg/Custom/CCS/content/e-learning/index.html>.

————. "Case Study: First Abuse of Dominance Case in Singapore", 2013*a*. CCS one-page publicity material. Available at <https://www.ccs.gov.sg/~/media/custom/ccs/files/education%20and%20compliance/educational%20resources/corporate%20brochures/case%20study-first%20abuse%20of%20dominance%20case%20in%20singapore.ashx>.

————. "Post-Enforcement Evaluation Methodologies and Indicative Findings", 26 August 2013*b*. Available at <https://www.ccs.gov.sg/~/media/custom/ccs/files/media%20and%20publications/publications/occasional%20paper/ccs%20post%20enforcement%20evaluation%20-%20uploaded%20270813.ashx> (accessed 12 March 2015).

Department of Statistics Singapore. "2014 Gross Domestic Product", 2014. Available at <http://www.singstat.gov.sg/statistics/latest-data#1> (accessed 25 March 2015).

Gal, Michal S. *Competition Policy for Small Market Economies*. Cambridge: Harvard University Press, 2003.

Ministry of Trade and Industry. "Report of the Entrepreneurship and Internationalisation Subcommittee Economic Review Committee", 13 September 2002. Available at <http://www.mti.gov.sg/ResearchRoom/Documents/app.mti.gov.sg/data/pages/507/doc/6%20ERC_EISC.pdf> (accessed 27 March 2015).

Ong, Beng Lee. *Promoting Competition: The CCS Perspective Regulation and the Limits of Competition Symposium 2007*. Civil Service College Singapore, Institute of Policy Studies and Economic Society of Singapore, 2007.

Singapore Economic Review Committee. *New Challenges, Fresh Goals — Towards a Dynamic Global City*. Singapore: Ministry of Trade and Industry, February 2003. Available at <http://www.mti.gov.sg/ResearchRoom/Documents/app.mti.gov.sg/data/pages/507/doc/1%20ERC_Main_Committee.pdf> (accessed 9 July 2015).

Singapore International Chamber of Commerce. "Comments on Draft Competition Bill", 29 May 2004, p. 9. Available at <https://www.ccs.gov.sg/public-register-andconsultation/public-consultation-items/~/media/custom/ccs/files/public%20register%20and%20consultation/public%20consultation%20items/first%20round%20of%20public%20consultation%20

on%20the%20competit/frmlegcompetitionsubmissionsicc.ashx> (assessed on 20 June 2015).

Singapore Manufacturers Federation. "Comments on the Singapore Draft Competition Bill by the Singapore Manufacturers' Federation (SMa)", 2004, p. 9. Available at <https://www.ccs.gov.sg/public-register-and-consultation/public-consultation-items/~/media/custom/ccs/files/public%20register%20and%20consultation/public%20consultation%20items/first%20round%20of%20public%20consultation%20on%20the%20competit/frmlegcompetitionsubmissionsma.ashx> (accessed 20 June 2015).

SPRING Singapore. "SME Centres are Helping Businesses Seize Opportunities for Growth", May 2014. Available at <http://www.spring.gov.sg/Inspiring-Success/Enterprise-Stories/Pages/Bringing-Assistance-Closer-to-SMEs.aspx> (accessed 27 March 2015).

Swiss Competition Commission and Israel Antitrust Authority. "Special Project for the 8th Annual Conference: Competition Law in Small Economies". International Competition Network Conference, 2009. Available at <http://www.internationalcompetitionnetwork.org/uploads/library/doc385.pdf> (accessed 27 March 2015).

World Bank Data. "Trade (% of GDP)", 2016. Available at <http://data.worldbank.org/indicator/NE.TRD.GNFS.ZS> (accessed 25 April 2016).

16

COMPETITION LAW AND SMEs IN INDONESIA

Tulus T.H. Tambunan

The major form of competition regulation in Indonesia is to be found in the Competition (Anti-Monopoly) Law of 1999. A number of other regulations also have an impact on the sector. The Competition Law is intended to help small and medium-sized enterprises (SMEs) by ensuring that they have an equitable opportunity to participate in the economy, fostering a healthy business environment, and protecting them from unfair business practices by larger firms. Current competition issues facing SMEs today include the imbalance and abuse of a dominant position by large chain stores in the retail sector; the conflict between traditional and modern market stores; legacy issues and market distortions from the Soeharto era; and implementation of competition principles at the local and regional levels.

Introduction

Indonesia is not only the largest economy in Southeast Asia, but it is also one of the largest democracies in Asia. As a country with a very big population of more than 250 million people, creating employment has been a persistent policy challenge. For this reason, small and medium-sized enterprises (SMEs) are considered very crucial to the national economy, as they are the largest employment creator, especially amongst women and the ranks of the lowest skilled. Successive Indonesian governments have provided a wide range of programmes to assist small-scale enterprises, and since the 1997–98 economic crisis, SMEs in Indonesia have received more serious attention, as they turned out to be more resilient than larger firms in responding and thriving in difficult times. This government support is also reflected in Article 50h of Indonesia's Competition Law No. 5/1999, which exempts small-scale enterprises from the provisions of the Law (KPPU 2007).

This chapter provides an overview of the current competition environment for SMEs in the Republic of Indonesia. It begins by defining and explaining some of the contemporary features of its SME sector, and then outlines the main elements of the national competition (antimonopoly) law. It examines some of the current problems and cases being dealt with, and concludes with a suggestion for future research into this new field.

MSMEs in Indonesia: Definition and Key Characteristics

One common definition of SMEs in Indonesia is based on the National Law (No. 20 of 2008) on Micro, Small and Medium Enterprises (MSMEs). It categorizes MSMEs as those enterprises which have an annual turnover of no more than Rp 50 billion,[1] and whose fixed investments (excluding land and building) are worth less than Rp 10 billion. Another method that is often used to define firms is provided by Statistics Indonesia (*Badan Pusat Statistik*, or BPS), which is based on the total number of workers: microenterprises (MIEs), small enterprises (SEs), and medium enterprises (MEs) are units with 1–4, 5–20, and 20–50 workers respectively.

In addition to these financial and employment measures, the various subcategories of MSMEs in Indonesia also differ in a number of other characteristics, such as their degree of formality, market orientation, production processes, networks, and location (see Table 16.1). These are important when talking about market competition or when assessing the impact of the Competition Law on MSMEs. For example, most Indonesian microenterprises generally operate in local markets

TABLE 16.1
Main Characteristics of MIEs, SEs, and MEs in Indonesia

Aspect	MIEs	SEs	MEs
Formality	Usually informal sector; unregistered; pay no taxes	Mixture of both formal and informal sectors	All operate in formal sector; registered; pay taxes
Location	Majority in rural areas/villages	Many in urban areas/cities	Mostly in urban areas/cities
Organization & management	Run by the owner. No internal labour division. No formal management & accounting system	Run by the owner. Majority have no formal management or accounting system	Run by either professional managers, owner or family members. Formal organizational structures accounting systems
Nature of employment	Majority use unpaid family members	Some hired wage labourers	All employees are hired wage labourers.
Nature of production process	Very low degree of mechanization. Low levels of technology employed. Manual production frequently used	Some use of modern technology	High degree of mechanization and access to modern technology
Market orientation	Local markets; low-income consumers	National or foreign markets; middle to high-income consumers	National or foreign markets; middle to high-income consumers

Educational background of owners	Generally low	Mixture of both low and highly-educated	Generally well-educated managers
Sources of inputs	Majority use local raw materials and use own money	Some import raw materials; some have access to bank and other formal credit institutions	Use both local and imported raw materials; have access to formal credit sources
External networks	Majority have no access to government programmes and no business linkages with LEs	Many have good relations with government and have business linkages (such as subcontracting) with LEs.	Majority have good access to government programmes and linkages with other LEs
Women entrepreneurs	Ratio of female to male entrepreneurs is high	Ratio of female to male entrepreneurs is high	Ratio of female to male entrepreneurs is low
Main sector	Agriculture; retail; trade	Trade; manufacturing	Trade; manufacturing

Source: Tambunan (2014).

that are not affected by modern firms or large enterprises (LEs). As a result, the level of market distortion or unfair competition practised by LEs in such markets can be assumed to be zero, or very close to it; competition law thus has very little effect on many micro firms. Unfair or illegal competition still can happen in these market segments, but it will usually be between MIEs themselves, rather than between MIEs and larger enterprises. But unfair MIE-to-MIE behaviour is largely beyond the reach of Indonesian competition law, because (as will be discussed later in this chapter) Section 50h of that Law exempts many small-scale enterprises, including MIEs.

Most businesses in Indonesia are MSMEs, and their number has steadily increased every year, as Table 16.2 demonstrates. However, most of these entities are MIEs set up by poor households or individuals who cannot find employment elsewhere, or who operate the venture as a secondary (supplementary) source of income. The majority of SMEs in Indonesia are engaged in the agricultural sector: industries such as animal husbandry, forestry, and fisheries collectively account for 51 per cent of all firms. The second largest groups of SMEs are to be found in the trade, hotel, and restaurants sector (29 per cent). They are also the biggest single contributor to national gross domestic product (GDP), as Figure 16.1 indicates.

All of this has taken place in the context of a rapidly changing national economy. Indonesia was one of Asia's so-called "tiger economies" (along with Thailand, Malaysia, and Singapore) before the Asian Financial Crisis hit in 1997/98. That crisis hit the country deeply: its economy underwent a deep recession, and it only began to recover after 1999. By 2014, however, the country's GDP had reached Rp 10,542.7 trillion (or around US$811 billion based on the then exchange rate of Rp 13,000 per U.S. dollar), equivalent to about Rp 41.8 million per capita. Before and during the Soeharto era, the Indonesian economy had been heavily dependent on agriculture and mining, but it has since undergone a rapid structural change. In 2014, the biggest sector was manufacturing with 20 per cent of GDP, followed by agriculture and trade, each with 13 per cent of GDP (BPS 2015).

TABLE 16.2
Total Enterprises by Size Category in All Economic Sectors in Indonesia, 2000–12

(in thousand units)

Size Category	2000	2003	2005	2007	2009	2010	2011	2012
SEs	39,705	43,372.9	47,006.9	47,720.3	52,723.5	53,781.1	55,162.2	56,485.6
MEs	78.8	87.4	95.9	120.3	41.1	42.6	44.2	48.997
LEs	5.7	6.5	6.8	4.5	4.7	4.8	4.95	4.97
Total	39,789.7	43,466.8	47,109.6	49,845.0	52,769.3	53,828.5	55,211.4	56,539.6

Sources: Processed data from Menegkop & UKM (<www.depkop.go.id>) and BPS (<www.bps.go.id>).

FIGURE 16.1
GDP Shares of SEs, MEs, and LEs in Indonesia, 2011 and 2012 (%)

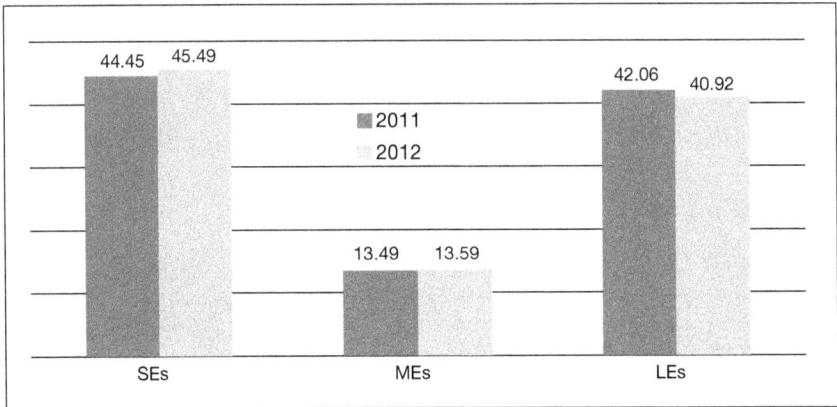

Source: Processed data from Menegkop & UKM (<www.depkop.go.id>) and BPS (<www.bps.go.id>).

Current Developments

The nation has had a highly variable economic and political history over the last century. A long-standing Dutch colony, it gained independence in 1945. After a brief period of somewhat chaotic democratic governance, the country fell into a form of authoritarian rule under President Soeharto's so-called "New Order" regime from 1966 to 1998, after which the *reformasi* movement saw the reinstallation of democracy. Although Indonesia experienced rapid economic development during the Soeharto era, the development of private business in that period was marred by many kinds of inefficient government policies that caused market distortions. There were numerous informal and formal unfair market practices; corruption; and monopolistic or oligopolistic practices by a small group of big companies or conglomerates with close links to the Soeharto regime. Excessive market concentration emerged in multiple markets, providing some businesses with very substantial aggregate economic power (OECD 2012).

After the Asian Financial Crisis (1997–98) and with the re-emergence of democratic government, there was strong recognition of the need to ensure equal business opportunities for all commercial players. This gave rise to the National Competition (or Anti-Monopoly) Law (No. 5/1999), one of the first in the ASEAN region. The Law is actually a synthesis of two separate initiatives, one launched by the Parliament and the other by the executive branch. Parliament's proposed law responded primarily to popular demands for democracy and more equal economic opportunity, whilst the government sought primarily to improve the performance of the economy. The enacted law combines these considerations (OECD 2012).

Competition Law

The Competition Law contains eleven chapters (see Table 16.3) and fifty-three articles, and took effect in March 2000. The various chapters cover a wide variety of issues, including prohibited agreements (which covers oligopoly, price-fixing, price discrimination, resale price maintenance, market allocation, boycott, cartels, trust, oligopsony, vertical integration, and exclusive dealing/closed agreements); prohibited activities (including monopoly, monopsony, market control, predatory pricing, conspiracy); dominant positions (covering interlocking directorates, share ownership issues, and mergers and

TABLE 16.3
Chapters of the Indonesian Competition Law

Chapter	Content
I	General Provisions
II	Underlying Principles and Objectives
III	Prohibited Contracts
IV	Prohibited Activities
V	Dominant Position
VI	Supervisory Commission for Business Competition
VII	Case Handling Procedures
VIII	Sanctions
IX	Miscellaneous Provisions
X	Transitional Provisions
XI	Concluding Provisions

Source: Maarif (2001).

acquisitions); the structure of the competition regulator, the *Komisi Pengawas Persaingan Usaha* or KPPU (including its membership, duties and authority); procedural rules; sanctions and punishments; and some miscellaneous provisions. It is intended to help SMEs by ensuring that they have an equitable opportunity to participate in the economy, fostering a healthy business environment, and protecting them from unfair business practices by larger firms (Iwantono and Budjianto 2007).

The Law has two key policy-related features. Firstly, although it is applicable to all economic sectors and to companies of all sizes, it also provides selective support to some forms of enterprises through various exemptions and exclusions. These exemptions are very broad and not limited to only SMEs: they can also be granted for social, economic, and political reasons. According to Article 50 of Chapter IX (miscellaneous provisions), small enterprises, as well as cooperatives, are excluded from the provisions of this Law. Thus, any agreement made by a small firm are exempted, arguably to allow them to develop and grow further. In 2008, the KPPU was given a new mandate to supervise partnerships amongst SMEs, and between SMEs and LEs, under Law No. 20 of 2008 (Anggraini 2009).

The main focus of the Indonesian competition regulation (and, indeed, of competition law in most jurisdictions) is to prevent anti-competitive behaviours and activities such as cartels, monopolization, the abuse of a dominant market position, and mergers and acquisitions that lessen competition. Besides economic objectives, such laws also help promote a number of non-economic or social objectives, such as promoting consumer interests, enhancing equity and wealth redistribution, and encouraging the development of SMEs. As with competition laws in other countries, the Indonesian law does not prevent a company from becoming dominant through economies of scale and scope. Rather, it prevents dominant firms from abusing their dominant positions. It targets firms with a relatively high market share, and so (indirectly) promotes and protects the interest of SMEs (Ahamat and Rahman 2013).

To enforce the Competition Law, the Supervisory Commission for Business Competition (usually referred to by its Bahasa Indonesia acronym, KPPU) was established in June 2000. KPPU is a state body independent of the executive and legislature, whose members are appointed by the President. Its main tasks are to examine allegations relating to the Competition Law, issue guidelines for implementation and interpretation of the Law, and to apply administrative sanctions (subject to court control) where appropriate. In theory, it is a quasi-judicial body with wide-ranging powers, but subject to court control. In practice, it is the dominant player in developing and applying the Law (Hadiputranto et al. 2013). It is also worth noting that the agency has produced some material specifically for SMEs (see, for example, Iwantono and Budjianto 2007).

In addition to the Anti-Monopoly Law, Indonesia has several other statutes that also touch upon issues relating to the promotion of fair competition. These include a trademark law, patent law, copyright law, criminal code, civil code, company law, and the Consumer Protection Law (No. 8/1999). Law No. 20 of 2008 on SMEs authorizes the government to promote a business climate which is conducive to the development of small firms, and to prevent the formation of market structures which create unfair competition in the forms of monopoly, oligopoly, and monopoly that are detrimental to SMEs. It also encourages the establishment of business partnerships between SMEs and larger enterprises.

Major Issues

The Competition Law, and associated legislation, have not necessarily been enough to completely remove some of the legacy issues of the Soeharto period. Unfortunately, according to many observers, a substantial legacy of anti-competitive legislation adopted during the New Order era still remains in place (UNCTAD 2009; KPPU 2011; OECD 2012). The United Nations Conference on Trade and Development (UNCTAD 2009), for example, has noted that most competition problems in Indonesia directly or indirectly stem from government actions. Many state-created monopolies which were ubiquitous in the New Order period have continued into the current era, even though by 2010 the KPPU had put forward more than sixty policy recommendations to forestall the creation or do away with monopolies created by government regulation. This obviously suggests that some fundamental challenges remain in embedding awareness of competition principles into various ministries and departments. One of the biggest problem areas was that of transportation, which alone comprised around 25 per cent of all KPPU's policy recommendations.

The telecommunications and trade areas accounted for about 13 per cent, followed by the finance and investment sectors (11 per cent). Unfortunately, as the UNCTAD study also noted, many of these policy recommendations were not followed with any concrete responses by the government. Aside from a possible lack of political will, this could be due to the fact that many public policymakers and regulators in Indonesia (especially at the regional and district levels, where much power has now been devolved to) are unfamiliar with the goals or benefits of competition policy, and do not incorporate competition issues into their decision-making.

Of the problematic areas identified by the KPPU above, it is the trade sector that contains the most SMEs. Of the many complaints that the KPPU have investigated in this sector, there are two cases that have had significant impacts on competition with SMEs. The first one was a case of abuse of dominant position by Carrefour Indonesia towards its small supplier; the second was the expansion into modern minimarkets by the largest retailer in the country, P.T. Indomaret.

The French-owned Carrefour chain of hypermarkets started to expand rapidly in major Indonesian cities after the Asian Financial Crisis. According to Indonesian investment law, all foreign hypermarkets must have business linkages with local suppliers, which it proceeded to establish. However, firms supplying to Carrefour began to argue that the trading terms were difficult to meet. A particular issue was related to fees and margins, and a requirement that suppliers would provide guarantees to Carrefour that their product selling price was the lowest available. For example, if Carrefour obtained written evidence that its competitor could sell the same product with a cheaper price than Carrefour's purchasing price, the hypermarket had the right to seek compensation from its own suppliers, based on the difference between Carrefour's purchasing price and competitor's selling price. This was often done automatically, without giving suppliers the chance to discuss or contest the matter. Carrefour also used its bargaining power to pressure suppliers to accept other trading terms, by techniques such as withholding payments due, not issuing purchase orders, or decreasing the quantities ordered in future (KPPU 2007, pp. 11–2).

The Indomaret case was different but still significant. In order to protect traditional markets, in July 2001, the KPPU brought an action against this large retail chain for competing unfairly with smaller traditional retailers in the greater Jakarta region. The major allegation was abuse of a dominant position or a violation of Article 2 and Article 3 of the Competition Law. However, the KPPU did not find a strong case for predatory pricing, and no obvious violation of the Competition Law could be found. Nevertheless, perhaps under political pressure, the KPPU ruled that P.T. Indomaret should not continue to expand in markets where they were in direct competition with traditional sellers. It has been argued that the KPPU had determined the conduct of Indomaret to be illegal because of a provision in the Law which directs the state to promote and protect MSMEs. The Indomaret case became a landmark decision in competition jurisprudence, establishing a principle that the protection of MSMEs is more important than maintaining free competition. This decision was a blow to large retailers who might otherwise have undertaken further expansion into large urban markets such as Jakarta. It was also somewhat damaging to consumers, who might have benefited from the large scale economies that such retailers bring (e.g. WalMart chain in the United States) (Thanitcul 2005; Dowling 2006).

These two cases are probably the most important examples of the current state of competition in the retail sector. It is indicative of the competition and tensions between modern supermarket offerings provided by several large enterprises (such as Indomaret and Carrefour, as well as others like Alfamart, Hero Supermarket, Ramayana, 7-Eleven, Mitra Adi Perkasa, Matahari, and Lotte) and traditional markets (known as *pasar rakyat*) in Indonesia. The well-known newspaper *Kompas* (2012) reported that the uncontrolled rapid increase of modern retailers (minimarkets) and wholesalers in regions outside Jakarta in the past ten years has reduced the incomes of many local traditional retailers (who are mainly micro or small enterprises). Modern retailers have expanded into villages not only in Java, but also in Sumatera, Kalimantan, and other provinces in the eastern part of the country, and drawing customers away from traditional markets and stalls, which are largely occupied by small and micro firms.

The traditional market and individual retail units within it seem to be losing the battle against their modern competitors. The modern minimarket in Indonesia has grown by around 400 per cent in the past ten years, and in January 2014, there were 16,000 such units compared to 750,000 traditional units (*Kompas* 2014*a*). According to a survey conducted by AC Nielsen, cited by *Kompas* (2014*b*), in 2013, the modern market in Indonesia grew at around 31 per cent, whilst traditional markets declined by about 8 per cent. The number of traditional markets in the country has dropped from about 13,500 in 2007 to just under 10,000 in 2011 (*Kompas* 2014*b*).

Regional issues are also an important matter in the nexus between Indonesian competition regulation and the small business sector. Currently, one concrete problem relating to market competition at the regional/local level is that of business licensing. In many countries, this constitutes a pervasive form of regulation and it raises particular competition policy issues, since it can act as a barrier to entry into an industry. A report from Steer (2006), cited by OECD (2012), notes that the implementation of regional autonomy in Indonesia has created additional problems in business licensing and given rise to market distortions. Since local governments are now free to adopt their own arrangements, licensing processes and procedures diverge from one jurisdiction to another. Many local authorities have also used their new powers to create additional licences and permits, often as a form of revenue generation. Although the Indonesian government has made a serious effort to improve its current licensing system by establishing national single window for licences, there are still more districts having "many-stop services" than those having a "one-stop service" for such permits. According to the World Bank's *Ease of Doing Business* report, it can take, on average, fifty-two days to start a new enterprise, although in many districts in the country, there may be even more procedures and costs (World Bank 2014).

According to UNCTAD (2009), another problem facing Indonesia (and the KPPU, in particular) in the enforcement and implementation of the law occurs at the regional/district level. In the first several years after its establishment, the KPPU was focused solely on the competitive impacts of national legislation. In more recent years, however, it has begun to provide advice on local rules, advocating competition policy principles at the subnational government level; it has also established a small number of regional offices which focus on local legislation and rules. However, the KPPU faces serious resource constraints in seeking to deal with local government laws. Most of the problems relating to regional or district competition rest with local governments, and the KPPU does not have the capacity to address the myriad of local government-created monopolies. This should not come as a surprise, given that the implementation of political and fiscal autonomy since 2001 has made local governments more independent, leaving the KPPU and the central government with little power to intervene.

Conclusion

Has the Indonesian system of competition regulation provided a fair market opportunity to all enterprises from all size categories? It is not easy to have a definitive conclusion at this stage. On one hand, there is very limited evidence on open conflicts between small/traditional and large/modern companies in cases handled by the KPPU thus far. On the other hand, national data shows that the number of SEs has grown whilst that of medium- and large-sized enterprises have declined. Of course, the rise in the number of new enterprises is not always a result of the current quality or degree of free market competition. Market competition also gives opportunities for existing firms to expand their production or market share or to grow into larger size. In other words, a transformation of firm from small into larger size may also reflect the degree of market competition.

There is a need for much more research into competition issues in the country, and of the situation of SMEs. Are they aware of the Competition Law and do they really understand it? What types of business relationships do they have with large enterprises, if any? Have they ever experienced "unfair" treatments from their business partners or competitors; and if so, what form has it taken? These and many other questions would help scholars, policymakers, and regulators better understand the issues facing SMEs in the country today, and is sorely needed.

NOTE

1. At the time of writing, Rp 14,000 = US$1.

REFERENCES

Ahamat, Haniff and Nasarudin Abdul Rahman. "Delimiting the Social Boundaries of Competition Law in ASEAN: A Common Approach?". Paper presented at the International Conference on International Relations and Development, Chulalongkorn University, Bangkok, 22–23 August 2013.

Anggraini, A.M. Tri. "Indonesian Competition Law: Past and Beyond". Mimeograph. Jakarta: KPPU, 2009.

Badan Pusat Statistik (BPS). *Laporan Bulanan. Data Sosial Ekonomi* [Monthly Report. Social Economy Data], edisi 57. Jakarta: BPS, February 2015.

Dedie S. Martadisastra. "Persaingan Usaha Ritel Modern dan Dampaknya Terhadap Pedagang Kecil Tradisional" [Modern Retail Business Competition and Its Impact on Traditional Small Trader]. *Jurnal Persaingan Usaha*, edisi 4 (2010): 65–88.

Dowling, John Malcolm. "Competition Policy in Indonesia". SMU Economics & Statistics Working Paper Series No. 08-2006. Singapore: Singapore Management University, February 2006.

Hadiputranto, Hadinoto and Partners. "Guide to Competition Law in Indonesia". 2013 ed. Jakarta: Hadinoto Hadiputranto and Partners, 2013.

Hallberg, Kristin. "A Market-Oriented Strategy for Small and Medium-Scale Enterprises". International Finance Corporation (IFC) Discussion Paper No. 40. Washington, D.C.: The World Bank, 2000.

Iwantono, Sutrisno and Murman Budjianto. "The Benefit of Competition Law to SME". Jakarta: KPPU, 2007. Available at <http://www.kppu.go.id/id/wp-content/uploads/2011/11/ACC-Session-2-Murman.pptx> (accessed 10 May 2014).

Komisi Pengawas Persaingan Usaha (KPPU). "Competition Policy and SME in Indonesia". Presentation at 3rd Training Course on Competition Policy, Asia-Pacific Economic Cooperation (APEC), Singapore, 1–3 August 2007.

————. "Annual Report on Competition Policy Developments in Indonesia". Report to the OECD Competition Committee (DAF/COMP/AR(2011)42). Jakarta: KPPU, 10 October 2011.

Kompas. "Operasional Minimarket. Kenyamanan yang Terusik" [Minimarket Operational. Disturbed Comfortable], 21 June 2012.

————. "Triliunan Rupiah di Pasar Rakyat" [Trillion Rupiah in People Market], 11 August 2014a.

————. "Ritel Modern Tumbuh" [Modern Retail Grows], 3 February 2014b.

Maarif, Syamsul. "Competition Law and Policy in Indonesia". Draft report, the ASEAN Competition Law Project, 2001.

Organisation for Economic Co-operation and Development (OECD). "Indonesia: Competition Law and Policy". OECD Reviews of Regulatory Reform. Paris: OECD, September 2012. Available at <http://www.oecd.

org/indonesia/chap%203%20-%20competition%20law%20and%20policy.pdf>
(accessed 10 May 2014).

Tambunan, Tulus T.H. *The Readiness of MSMEs in Facing ASEAN Economic Community 2015*. New York: Nova Science Publishers, 2014.

Thanitcul, Sakda. "SMEs and Competition Law: A Case Study on Suppliers of Goods to Large Retail Store". Paper presented at the International Expert Seminar on Mapping Policy Experience for SMEs in Phuket, 19–20 May 2005.

United Nations Conference on Trade and Development (UNCTAD). "Voluntary Peer Review on Competition Policy: Indonesia". Report. New York & Geneva: United Nations Committee on Trade and Development, 2009. Available at <http://unctad.org/en/Docs/ditcclp20091_en.pdf> (accessed 10 June 2013).

World Bank. "Doing Business 2015: Going Beyond Efficiency — Indonesia". Report No. 92043. Washington, D.C.: World Bank Group, 2014.

You, Joung-Il. "Small Firms in Economic Theory". *Cambridge Journal of Economics* 19 (June 1995): 441–62.

17

SMEs AND MALAYSIA'S NEW COMPETITION LAW
Experiences to Date

Shila Dorai Raj and Rachel Burgess

On 1 January 2012, the Competition Act 2010 came into operation in Malaysia. The Malaysia Competition Commission (MyCC) has faced significant challenges educating Malaysia's small and medium-sized enterprises (SMEs) on the need to comply with this new law.

Despite petitioning to the contrary, the Malaysian Government did not exempt SMEs from application of the law. However, the MyCC has since adopted a helpful position to the small business sector in its guidelines. Agreements, other than serious cartels, entered into by businesses with low market shares are considered to not affect competition so the Act does not apply. It is likely that many agreements entered into by SMEs will benefit from these rules.

Most of the cases investigated by the MyCC to date have involved SMEs. In many cases, trade associations have facilitated the illegal arrangements. Notwithstanding the significant advocacy efforts of the MyCC, there is still a worryingly low awareness and understanding of the law. The MyCC has experienced substantial difficulties in disseminating information to the widespread, multilingual SME community. Even those businesses aware of the law have been slow to undertake compliance. Trade associations and business groups have a key role to play in helping SMEs to understand and comply with the law.

This chapter briefly explains the early policy considerations, examines the cases decided to date, and the advocacy work undertaken by the MyCC, and finally considers what more needs to be done to improve SMEs' understanding of Malaysia's competition law.

Introduction

As part of its commitment to become a self-sufficient industrialized nation by the year 2020 (Vision 2020), Malaysia has recently adopted a competition law regime. The Competition Act (CA) was passed by the Federal Parliament in April 2010, and came into force on 1 January 2012. Being new is not all bad — there is a plethora of case law and experience available from all around the world from which the Malaysia Competition Commission (MyCC) can learn. However, there are also significant challenges for a new, inexperienced competition authority to meet the expectations of the business and government communities in enforcing the new legislation.

The MyCC is an independent statutory body created by the Competition Commission Act 2010 with responsibility for enforcing the Act. Its main role is to protect the competitive process for the benefit of consumers and businesses. It is an adjudicating body, with powers to receive complaints, investigate, issue infringement decisions, and impose fines and penalties. It is also empowered to issue guidelines, act as advocate, and grant both individual and block exemptions. The Federal Government and the MyCC are institutionally connected, as there are four public sector officials appointed as members of the Commission.

A number of key decisions have been made by the MyCC in its first few years, most of which have involved small and medium-sized enterprises (SMEs). The MyCC has come under some criticism for targeting small players, with many people in Malaysia still believing that the Act should not apply to SMEs. Whilst discussions during the drafting stages of the competition law involved SMEs and sought to address their concerns, the Malaysian government has remained firm, refusing to provide any exemptions from the Act based only on the size of the businesses concerned.

The MyCC has been working hard to assist SMEs to understand and comply with the new legislation. But the challenge is a tough one. At the first MyCC Competition Law Conference held in Kuala

Lumpur in September 2013, MyCC Commissioner S. Sothi Rachagan reported that only 6–7 per cent of those that responded to the Baseline Study on Awareness of CA 2010 in Malaysia undertaken by the MyCC knew about the law (Rachagan 2013). The study showed that knowledge of the law was highest amongst large businesses and decreased as businesses became smaller (RKA Consulting Group 2013). It is highly likely that many of the businesses who are unaware of the law are SMEs. More recently, a 2014 survey conducted by the federal government's SME Corporation revealed that only 27 per cent of the sample size SMEs surveyed (some 2,280 firms) were aware of the Act (SME Corporation of Malaysia 2014). There were also significant differences within the SME respondents. The study found that medium-sized businesses had a greater awareness (36 per cent) than small (27 per cent) and micro (21 per cent) enterprises. Awareness has clearly improved but there is still a long way to go.

This chapter examines the application of the Act to SMEs in Malaysia, looking in particular at the early policy considerations and consultation with Malaysia's SME community; the decisions of the MyCC (so far) that have involved SMEs; how the MyCC has sought to assist SMEs to understand the Act; and what more can be done going forward.

Background

Malaysia is located in Southeast Asia, and comprises two similarly sized regions, Peninsular Malaysia and East Malaysia. The country is multi-ethnic and multicultural, with Islam as the national religion. It has a population of about 30.3 million, approximately 67 per cent of whom are Malay, 24 per cent Chinese, 7 per cent Indian, and 2 per cent others. The official language is Bahasa Malaysia, but English remains an active second language widely used both in the public and private sectors.

Divided into thirteen states and three federal territories, Malaysia is a federal constitutional monarchy. Malaysia's system of government is closely modelled on the Westminster parliamentary system, including a common law regime. The Federal and State Parliaments are responsible for passing, amending, and repealing acts of law within their remit.

Malaysia's gross domestic product (GDP) has grown at an average of 5 per cent per annum and while historically it has been highly dependent on its natural resources, over the years it has grown into a newly industrialized market economy. The services sector remains the largest contributor to growth, followed by the manufacturing sector.

A SME is defined in Malaysia as a business:

- in the manufacturing sector, with sales turnover not exceeding RM50 million[1] OR full-time employees not exceeding 200 workers; and
- in the services and other sectors, with sales turnover not exceeding RM20 million OR full-time employees not exceeding 75 workers (SME Corporation of Malaysia 2013).

This new definition, which substantially increases the turnover and full-time employee thresholds, came into effect on 1 January 2014. It is reported to have brought the number of SMEs in Malaysia to 653,000 or 98.5 per cent of all businesses (SME Corporation of Malaysia 2013). This number is not surprising when compared with many other Asia-Pacific jurisdictions where SMEs account for more than 97 per cent of all businesses (Schaper 2012). About 90 per cent of Malaysia's SMEs operate in the services sector, while the remaining 10 per cent operate in manufacturing (5.9 per cent), construction (3 per cent), agriculture (1 per cent), and mining (0.1 per cent).

As is the case in other parts of the world, SMEs in Malaysia are often small family-based businesses. However, it needs to be stressed that in Malaysia, many of the businesses that fall under the umbrella of SMEs are very basic and unsophisticated. Often the business consists simply of a sole proprietor operating his or her business from a shared shop lot. In most cases, these businesses are much less sophisticated than those in most developed countries.

Many of Malaysia's SMEs are unlikely to have access to the sort of information and/or technology that businesses in more developed countries take for granted. The SME Corporation Census of 2011, for example, found that although 67 per cent of respondents did have Internet access, only 27 per cent of businesses actually used ICT (information and communications technologies) in their business operations (SME Corporation of Malaysia 2011).

The Decision to Apply Competition Law to SMEs

Malaysia's competition law had a long gestation period. The first mandate was given in the 8th Malaysia Plan (2001–5) to formulate a policy and law relating to the Fair Trade Practices Policy (FTPP). This mandate continued into the 9th Malaysia Plan (2006–10). Finally, the FTPP was tabled and deliberated in Cabinet on 26 October 2005. The key policy issues included the promotion of the right of SMEs to participate in the market and a prohibition on unfair trade practices in the economy.

Shortly after the approval of the Cabinet FTPP Paper, the Ministry of Domestic Trade, Cooperatives and Consumerism formed a consultative group known as the CG25, comprising representatives from key government agencies, several business chambers, industry associations and civil society (non-profit organizations). Bodies such as the National Chambers of Commerce and Industry, the Malay Chambers of Commerce, the Associated Chinese Chambers of Commerce and Industry, and the Malaysia Associated Indian Chambers of Commerce and Industry helped to represent the interests of SMEs.

Several consultations on the draft legislation were held with this body. Whilst the feedback was generally receptive to the introduction of the law, the key concerns raised by various SME groups were that unfair trade practices (such as profiteering), misleading conduct (such as false advertising claims), intimidating conduct by large enterprises, and imposing unfair burdens should be addressed. The SME community also sought a *de minimis* clause to make it clear that SMEs of a certain size would be automatically excluded from the application of the law.

Ultimately, the government decided that an enterprise should not be exempted based only on size, especially in so far as the law related to hard-core cartels. This decision was consistent with the approach taken by many other competition law regimes: throughout the world, less than 25 per cent of competition laws exempt SMEs, either directly or indirectly (Qaqaya 2013).

However, the scope of the draft legislation was changed to remove the provisions on unfair trade practices. The Malaysian Government took the view that the existence of laws such as the Consumer Protection Act 1999 (in operation since 1 October 1999) and the Trade

Descriptions Act 1972 (subsequently replaced by the Trade Descriptions Act 2011) were adequate to deal with these issues. The Consumer Protection Act covers matters including misleading and deceptive conduct, false representations, unfair contract terms, and safety of goods. The Trade Descriptions Act prohibits false trade descriptions and false or misleading statements, conduct, and practices relating to the supply of goods and services.

Malaysia's Competition Law

The goal of competition policy has been the subject of debate in competition law circles for decades. Should competition policy protect consumers, should it protect small businesses, or should it protect the process of competition, relying on market forces to ensure that the best businesses survive, offering the best products at the lowest prices? It is beyond the scope of this chapter to attempt to fully answer this question. However, it is worth noting that Malaysia seems to have taken an economic approach to competition policy. The Act is stated to be:

> An Act to promote economic development by promoting and protecting the process of competition, thereby protecting the interests of consumers ...

This approach is consistent with that of the European Union, which now takes an economic approach to this question, meaning that the focus of competition law should be to protect the process of competition itself (although this is not always borne out in the case law). The result should be that consumers benefit, as an efficient market should eliminate poor performing businesses, leaving more efficient firms to offer new products at competitive prices.

The Act applies to all commercial activities in Malaysia and may apply to commercial activities outside Malaysia where there is an effect on competition in a market in Malaysia. A "commercial activity" is defined broadly as "any activity of a commercial nature", so the activities of SMEs will certainly be covered. However, activities in the exercise of governmental authority, those based on the principle of solidarity, and purchases which are not for the purposes of economic activity, are excluded under Section 3(4) of the Act.

The Malaysian legislation deems certain types of agreements to have the *object* of preventing, restricting, or distorting competition. This is defined in Section 4(2) to be price fixing, market sharing, limiting production, and bid rigging — referred to in this chapter as cartels. This means that if the MyCC can show the existence of a cartel, it is not necessary to show any *effect* on competition. These agreements automatically breach the law. (It is possible that a party to a Section 4(2) agreement could relieve itself of liability if it can satisfy the individual exemption criteria set out in Section 5, although this is unlikely in the case of cartels.)

Where parties enter into other types of potentially anti-competitive agreements, the MyCC will need to show an effect on competition. In paragraph 3.4 of its *Guidelines on Anti-Competitive Agreements* (MyCC 2012*a*), the MyCC has stated that where an agreement is reached between competitors, it is unlikely to have a significant effect on competition if the *combined* market share of the parties is less than 20 per cent. Where the parties are non-competitors, the agreement is unlikely to have a significant effect on competition if *each* of the parties has a market share of less than 25 per cent.

So although there are no express provisions excluding SMEs, this is an extremely helpful position. Most small-scale enterprises will have small market shares, so it is likely that many of the agreements entered into by SMEs in Malaysia will fall outside of the Act.

However, as the cases discussed below illustrate, many SMEs and their industry associations are still falling foul of the cartel provisions, largely due to a lack of awareness or understanding, despite the MyCC's significant advocacy efforts.

What are SMEs Doing Wrong?

The Malaysian press has reported a number of proposed price rises agreed by associations and their members (most of whom are SMEs) in markets as diverse as flowers, hairdressing, lorry transportation charges, ice, bread, and bus services.

The Cameron Highlands Floriculturist Association (CHFA) case (MyCC 2012*c*), the MyCC's first infringement decision (non-penalty), came to the agency's attention because of an announcement in the local press. It involved an agreement between members of the CHFA to increase the price of cut flowers by 10 per cent. The price rise was announced in the newspaper by the president of the CHFA. As this was the MyCC's first decision and it was taken during an initial so-called "soft touch" period (2012), the Commission did not impose a penalty. However, the CHFA was required to cease the price fixing, give an undertaking that its members would not engage in anti-competitive practices, and issue a statement to that effect in the newspapers (MyCC 2012c).

In February 2013, the Malaysia Indian Hairdressing Saloon Owners Association (MIHSOA) announced in *The Star* newspaper that "Indian barbers in the country have decided to raise prices for haircuts by RM2 effective today." The president of the MIHSOA was reported as saying "a unanimous decision was made at a meeting here on Wednesday" (*The Star Online* 2013). The MyCC launched an investigation which culminated in the MIHSOA giving an undertaking in January 2014 that the decision to increase prices would be withdrawn and that their members would not engage in anti-competitive conduct in the future (MyCC 2014a).

The announcement of the Pan-Malaysian Lorry Owners Association (PMLOA) to increase transportation charges by 15 per cent came to the MyCC's attention, again through the press, and a formal investigation was launched in September 2013. The Commission quickly imposed interim measures (provided for under Section 35(2) of the Act to prevent serious and irreparable damage, or to protect public interest) under which the PMLOA, its members, and the lorry enterprises were ordered to not comply with the decision to increase prices and not to agree to any further changes to the transportation charges (*New Straits Times* 2013). In May 2014, the PMLOA gave an undertaking to the MyCC to publish an apology for the anti-competitive behaviour in major newspapers in four languages, provide a copy of the undertaking to all of PMLOA's members, and to ensure that its Central Committee Members (those involved in the original agreement) do not engage in anti-competitive conduct in the future (MyCC 2014b).

The cases explained above were the result of decisions by an association. However, another interesting case involving a group of ice manufacturers was investigated by the MyCC. The group (not registered as an association) led by a major ice producer announced a plan to increase the price of edible tube ice by RM0.50 per bag and the price of block ice by RM2.50 per bag from 1 January 2014. Once again, these announcements were made in local newspapers. Following an investigation, the MyCC issued a draft decision in February 2014 stating that it intended to impose fines ranging from RM1,200 to RM106,000 on the manufacturers. An oral hearing was held where some manufacturers pleaded ignorance of the law and undertook not to be involved in this type of arrangement again. Some of the fines were reduced based on principles of equality and proportionality, while others were upheld because of the significant role played in fixing the prices.

Such instances of price fixing do not only occur in Peninsular Malaysia. Across the country in the state of East Malaysia, in November 2013, the *Borneo Post* reported that the Sibu Confectionary and Bakery Association (SCBA) had announced a 10–15 per cent price increase to offset spiralling costs (Boon 2013*b*). The MyCC issued a proposed decision in this case in September 2014. The Commission found that twenty-four enterprises, all members of the SCBA, had infringed the Act by entering into the agreement to raise their prices. The agreement was reached at the SCBA Annual General Meeting (AGM). Only sixteen of the twenty-four enterprises were present at the AGM; however, the remaining eight became aware of the agreed increase in prices and implemented the change. During the oral hearing, four parties admitted liability while eleven contested the finding as they had not actually raised prices, despite their attendance at the meeting. The MyCC reduced the penalties for these eleven parties. Total penalties of RM247,730 were imposed.

An interesting case which demonstrates the effects of deregulation came about in the latter half of 2014, when the fare structure of school bus operators was deregulated by the federal Land Public Transport Commission (SPAD); prior to this, school bus tariffs had been set by SPAD. Following deregulation, the Federation of Malaysian School Bus Operators announced a 30 per cent rise in bus fares from January 2015. The MyCC intervened and has since actively worked with the bus operators (most of whom are SMEs), explaining to them why their announcement was against the law. The Federation was unaware of the law, the role of the Commission, and the fact that price-fixing was now illegal under the Act. However, worryingly, these discussions have proved ineffective: almost every day, individual bus operator associations continue to announce impending price increases in the press.

In all of these cases, most of the parties involved were SMEs. These examples seem to suggest that many of Malaysia's SMEs, and perhaps more importantly their trade associations, do not yet understand the most basic dos and don'ts of competition law. Most breaches of the law by SMEs are not taking place in secret, contrary to expectation. Not only are businesses reaching these illegal price-fixing agreements, they are then announcing them in the local press, illustrating either a lack of awareness of the law or a complete lack of understanding that it applies to them.

Resisting the Law

Based on informal feedback received by the MyCC at its various advocacy events, many Malaysians still think that the Act should not apply to their business. This attitude is especially prevalent amongst SMEs.

The authors believe further significant cultural change is required to successfully implement competition law in Malaysia. The types of behaviours that are now prohibited by the Act have been common business practice for decades. By way of example, the outgoing chairman of the Kapit Coffee Shop and Restaurant Owners' Association complained that the Act had caused the price of food and drinks to fluctuate rather significantly. He was reported in the *Borneo Post* in March 2013 as complaining that "... the Act, while noble, prevented the association from standardising prices of goods thus causing 'everything to go wild'" (Boon 2013a). Teaching these businesses that the old way of doing things is no longer allowed (more than that, it is illegal) will take some time.

As part of its enforcement process, the MyCC has held detailed discussions with SMEs under investigation to clarify what aspects of their behaviour are now prohibited. During those discussions, SMEs have complained that they struggle to determine their own pricing, as they have little or no experience of doing so. Many have historically relied on their respective trade associations to determine what prices they should be charging and whether an increase is required. The MyCC has explained to the individual businesses involved that they need to determine for themselves whether an increase in price is required and, if so, how much. The MyCC has pointed out the harmful effects of an unjustified price rise, as it often brings about a knock-on effect throughout the supply chain, increasing prices at every level of the production or distribution network.

The lack of sophistication in the way the SMEs conduct their businesses leads to this reliance on trade associations, and a belief that such bodies should collectively make pricing decisions on their behalf. Many SMEs do not keep orderly records of their transactions, some or most are family owned and run, and their turnover is very small, often just enough to sustain their daily business costs.

There is also a lot of work to be done to help educate the SMEs about how the Act can help them in their business. Although many SMEs are subjected to anti-competitive practices by larger players in the market, there is a reluctance to complain to the competition regulator, based on a fear of retaliation from the larger players.

Reaching Out to SMEs

It has to be recognized that introducing new laws is a challenging process, as those that are trying to enforce them, together with those that must comply with them, struggle to understand how the law will apply on a day-to-day basis. Many Malaysian SMEs have little time and resources to comply with yet another piece of legislation. Even where seminars or information sessions are provided free of charge, businesses often cannot afford for their one or two staff members to be away from the business.

In addition to the resistance to the new law, the cultural diversity in, and geographic spread of, Malaysia's SMEs poses a challenge for the MyCC. SMEs are spread throughout Peninsular and East Malaysia, and reaching out to educate them on their rights and obligations is an enormous task. It is one that the MyCC has taken very seriously.

Between April 2011 and November 2014, the agency conducted 120 advocacy sessions. In 2013, it ran a series of newspaper articles in a widely read newspaper, *The Star*, explaining key aspects of the Act (Dorai Raj 2013*a*; 2013*b*). It has also produced a range of publications, including a *Handbook for the General Public* (MyCC

2012*b*), a FAQ brochure for SMEs (MyCC 2013*b*) and a *Guide for Business* (MyCC 2013*a*). In 2014, it published a series of articles aimed specifically at SMEs in the *Malaysia SME* magazine (Dorai Raj 2014*a–f*).

In spite of the efforts made by the Commission, the impact of the outreach is still negligible. Only those who want to know about the implications of the law pay any attention to the lessons outlined in these publications. Part of the problem is language. Most of the MyCC publications are in English, with only a small number translated into the national language, Bahasa Malaysia. Translation is an area where MyCC has encountered further substantial challenges. The concepts involved in competition law are often difficult to explain, and the additional complexity of translating these legal concepts into multiple languages has become onerous and in many cases impossible. The other main languages of Malaysia (Bahasa Malaysia, Mandarin, and Tamil) often do not have equivalent words or concepts to explain some of the complexities of competition law as initially set out in English. As a result, translations have not been attempted and many Malaysians are not able to access the MyCC publications in their own tongue.

In all of the cases investigated so far, it was found that the SMEs and their associations were not aware of the law, and even when it was explained to them, they were not keen to understand it in any detail. Only 31 per cent of those surveyed in the 2014 SME Survey thought that prices could no longer be agreed. Less than half of the respondents were aware of the existence of the MyCC or its role. In practice, when asked to submit a written representation in response to an allegation raised against them, SMEs have often looked to MyCC staff to assist them, showing a complete lack of understanding of the role of the Commission and suggesting that sources of external professional advice are hard for them to access.

What More Can Be Done?

Schaper (2010) argues that a lot more research needs to be undertaken to assess the effect that competition policy has on SMEs. This is certainly true, especially in countries with more developed systems.

However, in the newer regimes in Asia where a decision has (rightly) been made to apply the laws to SMEs, the focus needs to remain on education. Innovative ways to reach SMEs, especially those that are microbusinesses, need to be considered.

Australia's online education programme for small business is one such innovative solution, and which is discussed elsewhere in this book. Although the SME Census suggests that few Malaysian SMEs use ICT in their business, it did find that 67 per cent had Internet access, so this is a plausible approach. This is supported by the Baseline Study that found 82 per cent of those surveyed said they would look to the Internet for further information on the Act, followed by newspapers (49 per cent), and TV/radio (40 per cent) (Rachagan 2013). Focused SME communications, like the Australian Competition and Consumer Commission (ACCC) *Small Business in Focus* brochure may also help (ACCC 2014).

The Competition Commission of Singapore publishes pamphlets in simple, non-legal terms, summarizing cases that have been decided in Singapore. Similar brochures may be a useful tool to help explain where, and why, businesses in Malaysia are breaching the Act. Perhaps the MyCC's initiative in publishing a series of articles in 2014 in the *Malaysia SME Magazine* is a positive step to directly communicating with SMEs about how competition law issues apply to them.

Experience, to date, shows that a more focused communication strategy or outreach programme targeted specifically at SMEs is needed. While MyCC has conducted a substantial number of outreach programmes with the Federal Government (briefings, seminars, advisory opinions), it has not yet targeted the many state governments. Moreover, the agency does not currently have an internal staff group dedicated to SME issues and this may be an area worth considering.

Conclusion

There are still a very large proportion of businesses that are unaware of the existence of the Act. This is worrying, given the law was enacted more than six years ago, and has been in force since 1 January 2012. Even where businesses are aware of its existence, there is a general reluctance to accept either that the law applies or that it is relevant to them. The MyCC has a tough task ahead of it to change entrenched attitudes and behaviours. A lot of good work has been done in their first years of operation to educate businesses, but clearly there is still a long way to go.

In Malaysia, as in many Asian countries, a cultural shift to the way that business is being conducted is required if enterprises are to become competition law compliant. The idea that firms can meet to discuss prices or products is often part of the business culture. Businesses are daunted by the prospect of having to compete against each other. The case of the school bus operators is a good example where the bus operators had previously relied on a regulator to determine the rates for them, and now struggle to know how to set their own fares. No doubt similar challenges will be faced in other industries as deregulation in Malaysia continues.

It is not just SMEs who have to be mindful of the law and how it affects them. Their representatives also have to do so. In Malaysia, where SMEs have fallen foul of the competition legislation, it is often the case that their trade associations have been involved. For SMEs with limited time and resources to access advice, it is perhaps not surprising that they are still falling foul of this relatively new law. There is a real need for trade and business associations to assist in the education process, as these bodies have greater access to the SME audience.

SMEs cannot expect to be treated differently by the MyCC and if they continue to infringe the law, particularly the cartel provisions, the Commission will have to take action. No doubt all businesses (big and small) in Malaysia will learn from the ongoing decisions of the MyCC.

NOTE

1. At the time of writing, RM1 = approximately US$0.27.

REFERENCES

Australian Competition and Consumer Commission (ACCC). *Small Business in Focus: Small Business, Franchising and Industry Codes.* Half Year Report No. 9, July–December 2014. Available at <https://www.accc.gov.au/system/files/953_Small%20business%20in%20focus%20no.%209_FA.pdf> (accessed 15 June 2015).

Boon, Peter. "Competition Act 2010 Aims to Stamp Out Cartel-like Practices". *Borneo Post Online*, 7 March 2013*a*. Available at <http://www.theborneopost.com/2013/03/07/competition-act-2010-aims-to-stamp-out-cartel-like-practices/> (accessed 9 December 2014).

———. "Announcement of Price Hike Draws Attention of MyCC". *Borneo Post Online*, 20 November 2013*b*. Available at <http://www.theborneopost.com/2013/11/20/announcement-of-price-hike-draws-attention-of-mycc/> (accessed 9 December 2014).

Dorai Raj, Shila. "Competition Act — Ignorance is No Excuse". *The Star*, 11 March 2013*a*. Available at <http://www.thestar.com.my/Business/Business-News/2013/03/11/Competition-Act--ignorance-is-no-excuse.aspx/> (accessed 9 December 2014).

———. "Helping SMEs Understand Competition Law". *The Star*, 19 August 2013*b*. Available at <http://www.thestar.com.my/Business/Business-News/2013/08/19/Helping-SMEs-understand-competition-law.aspx/> (accessed 9 December 2014).

———. "Does the Competition Act 2010 (CA 2010) Apply to You?". *Malaysia SME*, Kuala Lumpur, 3 May 2014*a*.

———. "A Question of Competition". *Malaysia SME*, Kuala Lumpur, 14 June 2014*b*.

———. "A Question of Competition". *Malaysia SME*, Kuala Lumpur, 26 July 2014*c*.

———. "A Question of Competition". *Malaysia SME*, Kuala Lumpur, 6 September 2014*d*.

———. "A Question of Competition". *Malaysia SME*, Kuala Lumpur, 18 October 2014*e*.

———. "A Question of Competition". *Malaysia SME*, Kuala Lumpur, 1 November 2014*f*.

Economic Planning Unit, Prime Minister's Department Malaysia. *Eighth Malaysia Plan 2001–2005*. Available at <http://www.epu.gov.my/en/eighth-malaysia-plan-2001-2005> (accessed 9 December 2014).

———. *Ninth Malaysia Plan 2006–2010*. Available at <http://www.epu.gov.my/en/ninth-malaysia-plan-2006-2010> (accessed 9 December 2014).

Malaysia Competition Commission (MyCC). *Guidelines on Anti-Competitive Agreements.* Kuala Lumpur: MyCC, 2012*a*.

————. *Handbook for the General Public*. Kuala Lumpur: MyCC, 2012*b*.

————. "Finding of Infringement under Section 40 of the Competition Act 2010 — Infringement of Section 4(2)(a) of the Competition Act 2010 by Cameron Highlands Floriculturist Association", 6 December 2012*c*. Available at <http://mycc.gov.my/sites/default/files/Cameron%20 Highlands%20Floriculturist%20Association.pdf> (accessed 20 January 2016).

————. *Guide for Business*. Kuala Lumpur: MyCC, 2013*a*.

————. *FAQs for SMEs*. Kuala Lumpur: MyCC, 2013*b*.

————. "Undertaking by the Persatuan Pengusaha Jurugaya Rambut India Malaysia", 30 January 2014*a*. Available at <http://mycc.gov.my/sites/ default/files/Persatuan%20Pengusaha%20Jurugaya%20Rambut%20India%20 Malaysia.pdf> (accessed 20 January 2016).

————. "Undertaking by the Central Committee Members of the Pan Malaysia Lorry Owners' Association (PMLOA)", 7 May 2014*b*. Available at <http://mycc.gov.my/sites/default/files/PMLOA.pdf> (accessed 20 January 2016).

New Straits Times. "MyCC Imposes Proposed Interim Measures to Pan-Malaysia Lorry Owners Association", 20 September 2013.

Qaqaya, Hassan. "Does Competition Law Pose as a Hurdle to SMEs". Paper presented at the 1st MyCC Competition Law Conference "New Standards for Business in Malaysia", Kuala Lumpur, 25–26 September 2013.

Rachagan, Sothi. "An Overview of Competition Law in Malaysia". Paper presented at the 1st MyCC Competition Law Conference "New Standards for Business in Malaysia", Kuala Lumpur, 25–26 September 2013.

RKA Consulting Group. "Final Report: Baseline Study on Awareness of CA2010 in Malaysia" for MyCC, 25 June 2013 (not published. Referred to with permission of MyCC).

Schaper, Michael T. "Competition Law, Enforcement and the Australian Small Business Sector". *Small Enterprise Research* 17, no. 1 (2010): 7–18.

————. "Do Competition Laws Help the Small Business Sector?". Presented at MyCC Workshop "Does the Competition Act Help or Hinder SMEs?", Kuala Lumpur, 5 November 2012.

SME Corporation of Malaysia. *SME Corporation Census 2011*. Kuala Lumpur: SME Corporation of Malaysia, 2011.

————. *Guideline for New SME Definition*, October 2013. Available at <http:// www.smecorp.gov.my/images/guideline_0.pdf> (accessed 20 January 2016).

————. *Detailed 3Q 2014 SME Survey Findings*, 2014 (not published. Referred to with permission of SME Corporation of Malaysia).

Storey, David J. "The Competitive Experience of UK SMEs: Fair and Unfair". *Small Enterprise Research* 17, no. 1 (2010): 19–29.

The Star Online. "Barbers Raise Their Rates", 1 February 2013. Available at <http://www.thestar.com.my/News/Nation/2013/02/01/Barbers-raise-their-rates/> (accessed 9 December 2014).

18

COMPETITION POLICY AND SME DEVELOPMENT IN VIETNAM

Viet Le and Charles Harvie

Vietnam embarked on an economic reform programme in 1986 aimed at transitioning from a centrally-planned to market-oriented economy. Since then, market competition has steadily increased with the participation of non-state owned enterprises, together with state-owned enterprises which dominated the economy during the period of central planning and, indeed, for much of the post-reform period. This has been the case particularly since the year 2000, when a breakthrough Enterprise Law was introduced resulting in strong growth of new business registrations. At the same time, the Vietnamese economy has taken significant steps towards closer economic integration with regional and international markets through its membership of ASEAN (Association of Southeast Asian Nations), APEC (Asia-Pacific Economic Cooperation), and the WTO (World Trade Organization).

The introduction of a Competition Law in 2005 further provided a legal framework with which to promote business development in Vietnam. This Law aimed to provide a fair competition environment for all businesses and types of ownership operating in Vietnam. This chapter discusses the basis, and the process, for the introduction of the Competition Law of Vietnam. It describes key features of the Law including specific provisions given to small and medium-sized enterprises (SMEs). It highlights the challenges in implementing the Law in general and to SMEs in particular. It also discusses the roles of key stakeholders in the implementation process, including the Vietnam Competition Authority. The chapter concludes with some suggestions as to how the Competition Law can be made more effective and relevant.

Introduction

Vietnam has attained significant achievements in economic performance since launching the package of economic reforms known as "Doi Moi" in 1986. The economic base has been greatly diversified with the participation of domestic state and private enterprises as well as foreign invested enterprises. The country has become economically integrated as a member of ASEAN (Association of Southeast Asian Nations), APEC (Asia-Pacific Economic Cooperation), and the WTO (World Trade Organization), having one of the highest trade-to-GDP (gross domestic product) ratios. It has also negotiated and concluded a number of bilateral free trade agreements as well as multilateral agreements. These economic reforms unleashed a burst of entrepreneurial energy that enabled Vietnam's economy to grow by 7–8 per cent annually for nearly two decades (Brown 2015).

In order to maintain the 7–8 per cent annual economic growth rate and achieve the eight million new jobs targeted under Vietnam's Socio-Economic Development Strategy 2011–20, a healthy level of private investment is required. Increasingly, such a contribution is expected to come from the domestic private sector, which is largely composed of small and medium-sized enterprises (SMEs) which are defined as firms with less than 300 employees. Since the implementation of the revised Enterprise Law in 2005, the government of Vietnam has greatly assisted the development of SMEs with the establishment of a regulatory framework conducive to private enterprise (ADB 2012). As a result, by the end of 2010, nearly 550,000 enterprises were registered in Vietnam, up from only 14,500 in 2000. SMEs represented 97 per cent of the country's total number of firms and 46 per cent of GDP. The domestic private sector accounted for 59 per cent of total employment in 2010, up from 29 per cent in 2000. Growth in the number of private companies has been followed by sustained increases in the average size and productivity of firms. From 2000 to 2010, the average capital per firm increased six-fold, and the average net revenue per employee tripled. However, the average SME size remains quite small at twenty-two employees per enterprise and average capital of VND17.6 billion (MPI 2012). The contribution of SMEs to tax revenue is increasingly important. By the end of 2010, of the 336,000 enterprises paying taxes in Vietnam, 318,000 were private enterprises, 13,000 were foreign-owned enterprises, and about 5,000 were state-owned enterprises (SOEs) (ADB 2012).

This chapter shows, first, that the Competition Law ("the Law") in Vietnam was developed in response to both the complexities of domestic economic reality and demand from increased economic integration in regional and global markets. It then describes the process through which the Law evolved before being approved in 2005. It provides an overview of the contents of the Law, before discussing specific provisions for SMEs and some issues regarding the implementation of the statute. It also includes a description of the key competition agencies in Vietnam, including the Vietnam Competition Council (VCC) and the Vietnam Competition Authority (VCA), and their activities. The chapter concludes by offering some recommendations.

Background and Economic Context

Economic reform was officially launched in Vietnam in 1986 to herald the transition from central planning to a market economy. This resulted in a significant increase in economic activities. Vietnam's GDP expanded by almost 6,000 times over the 1986–2014 period in current value terms (GSO 2014). The economy has become more diversified with the participation of private domestic enterprises and foreign invested enterprises in addition to SOEs, which dominated during the central planning period and, indeed, for much of the subsequent reform period. Changes in the domestic commercial environment and an increase in the number of businesses produced more competition among, and between, businesses in both the state and non-state sectors.

The Vietnamese economy originally contained many sectors characterized by state monopolies, which restricted the development of non-state enterprises and negatively impacted the competitive environment. The rapid development of many industries and services during the reform period created competitive pressure on enterprises, but the predominant position of SOEs and discrimination against non-SOEs in many key sectors remained. Unfair competition acts or anti-competitive acts became increasingly apparent during the late 1990s, when the Asian Financial Crisis exposed structural weaknesses. In addition, for much of the 1990s, growth came from the SOEs and large foreign multinational corporations (MNCs) focusing on import substitution, both of which were highly capital intensive and did not generate much employment growth (Harvie 2004). These economic realities required a new growth and development paradigm to achieve high and sustainable rates of economic growth, employment generation, and a competitive market-driven economy. Thus, there was a fundamental shift in the development strategy toward non-SOEs, and in particular, private sector SMEs, beginning in 2000, with the introduction of the Enterprise Law.

In the early 1990s Vietnam started to open up its economy, promote external trade, and welcome foreign direct investment (FDI). In 1995, Vietnam joined ASEAN in its first step to participate in the regional and global economy. It also made the commitment to be part of the ASEAN Economic Community. As part of this community, all ASEAN economies were required to put in place a competition law by 2015. This is to ensure a healthy and fair competitive environment and create a basis for coordination and cooperation among ASEAN competition authorities (Trinh 2013). In its effort to open the economy further, Vietnam joined APEC in 1998 and concluded a Bilateral Trade Agreement with the United States in 2000.

Vietnam applied for membership to the WTO in 1995. During the process of negotiating accession to the WTO, it came under pressure to make a strong commitment to build a transparent legal framework, introduce effective competition policies, and establish an independent competition agency. These were to ensure a level playing field for both local and foreign enterprises operating in the country. After many rounds of bilateral and multilateral negotiations over a period of eleven years, Vietnam's accession package was accepted in November 2006 and it became the WTO's 150th member in January 2007. This happened after the Vietnamese Competition Law was put in place in 2005.

The above developments in both the domestic market and the process of international economic integration created a demand to build a legal framework that would facilitate an economic environment based on competition. However, it was not until the late 1990s that the formulation process for the competition law started, with discussions in workshops and events within domestic academic circles, think-tanks, and state agencies. The process was also aided by technical assistance efforts from international institutions like the United Nations Development Programme (UNDP), the World Bank, and the International Monetary Fund (IMF). A notable issue during this period was the "unequal playing field" between the state and non-state sector, with claims of favourable treatment and easy access to key resources by SOEs. In addition, there was increased participation by foreign companies, most often transnational corporations operating in the domestic market, as well as problems arising from domestic and cross-border anti-competitive practices (Pham 2006).

Observers have noted that the rationale for Vietnam to adopt formal competition regulation was to support its developing market-based economy, with the hope that Vietnam's economy and its people might benefit from the law. Its introduction was also meant to satisfy the demand from international organizations, such as the WTO, as Vietnam became more and more integrated into global trade (Dang and Pham 2008). Thus, the enactment of the Law in Vietnam was neither exclusively bottom-up/internally driven nor top down/externally driven. Rather, both internal and external influences played critical roles in the shaping of policy outcomes (Tran 2013).

Development of Competition Law

Business laws were initiated soon after economic reform was formally introduced in 1986, but it was not until 2000, when the breakthrough *Enterprise Law* was introduced that business registrations, mostly SMEs, increased sharply (Le and Harvie 2012). At this point, anti-competitive acts or monopolies were regulated by separate and scattered provisions in a number of different pieces of legislation, such as the Ordinance on Price, the Ordinance on Telecommunications, the Law on Credit Institutions, Commercial Law, and Electricity Law. The implementation of this type of legislation was not really effective, partly due to the lack of a complete and consistent legal framework, lack of state management competency in competition and monopoly control, and a lack of sanctions for non-compliance (Trinh 2013).

A competition law in Vietnam was included in the agenda for lawmaking by the National Assembly in 1998. It assigned the then Ministry of Trade (MOT) to take the lead in drafting the legislation. The MOT issued a Directive for this task in the year 2000, which emphasized that:

> competition and monopoly are basic concepts of a market economy, therefore regulations on competition and monopoly would be an important part in the legal system on economic matters contributing to create a legal corridor and ensure that economic activities will take place in a fair, healthy, highly effective manner and at the same time will bring about strict management by the State, protection of public welfare, legitimate rights and interests of traders doing business (MOT 2000).

The new law had to encourage fair competition, strengthen economic development, and restrict unfair competition practices, as well as deal with competition restraints.

After numerous seminars and drafts, and with substantial comment from business and both domestic and international experts, the first Competition Law was passed in December 2004 by the National Assembly after a four-year drafting process. It referenced the statutes of nine nation-states and territories and the model laws promoted by international institutions such as the United Nations Conference on Trade and Development (UNCTAD) and the World Bank. It was also influenced by the enforcement practices and experiences of several other countries. The Law became effective on 1 July 2005 (Pham 2006).

Promulgation of the legislation marked a significant milestone in the evolution of the national market economy, and the Law now plays an important role in facilitating the effective performance of the market economy. It has a broad scope in its application and covers every individual and organization doing business in Vietnam, irrespective of ownership form (VCA 2014a). This is in line with the revised Enterprise Law and Investment Law approved in 2005.

Key Features of the Competition Law and Enforcement Agencies

Vietnam's statute consists of 123 articles and is divided into six chapters, including General Provisions (Articles 1–7); Control of

Competition Restriction Acts (Articles 8–28); Unfair Competition Acts (Articles 39–48); Competition Management Agency, Competition Council (Articles 49–55); Investigation, Handling of Competition Cases (Articles 56–121); and Implementation Provisions (Articles 122–123) (Fruitman 2013).

After the National Assembly passed the Law in 2004, the national government also issued a number of decrees in 2005 guiding its implementation. Most recently, a new decree (No. 71) in 2014 revised penalties for breaches of the Law. It was issued to reflect the VCA's experience to date in enforcing the legislation, and to overcome some of the difficulties they have encountered (DFDL 2014).

The Law applies to all business enterprises and professional and trade associations in Vietnam, overseas enterprises and associations registered in Vietnam, public utilities and state monopoly enterprises, and state administrative bodies. It has supremacy over all other enacted laws of Vietnam regarding restrictive business practices and unfair trade practices (Pham 2006). According to the Law, competitive practices in Vietnam must be undertaken on the principle of honesty while not infringing upon national interests, public interests, or the lawful rights and interests of other businesses and consumers. Pursuant to the Law there are two broad categories of competitive practices that are regulated: (a) *practices in restraint of competition*, including: agreements in restraint of competition (collusion), abuse of a dominant market or monopoly position, and economic concentration; and (b) *unfair competitive practices* (Dang 2008).

The Law prohibits five broad types of anti-competitive practices: (1) competition restriction agreements; (2) abuse of a dominant or monopoly position; (3) concentrations of economic power that substantially restrict competition; (4) acts of unhealthy competition; and (5) anti-competitive behaviour/decisions by officials or State administrative agencies taking advantage of their authority. The Law also sets certain procedures for complaints and investigations of alleged abuses (Pham 2006). A notable feature of Vietnam's competition regime, which is different from that of the European Union, is that regulation of agreements in restraint of competition in Vietnam appears to be limited to horizontal agreements (i.e. agreements between competitors, often referred to as cartels), with vertical arrangements being regulated solely under provisions relating to abuse of dominant market position (Dang and Pham 2008).

The enforcement apparatus in Vietnam has been built and formed by two key agencies — the VCC and the VCA. The legal basis for the operation of the VCC and the VCA was included in Articles 49–55 of the Law and subsequent Government decrees in 2006. In relation to competition restriction agreement cases, the VCA is authorized to accept and organize investigations, while the VCC has the function of handling the cases. Under this model, both the investigation and handling of competition restriction agreement cases is independent of each other.

The VCC is an independent body and is primarily responsible for hearing and resolving cases of practices in restraint of competition. The Council consists of eleven to fifteen members appointed by the Prime Minister (Nguyen 2014). Although it is nominally independent, VCC members are current officials from different ministries and include three deputy ministers from the Ministry of Industry and Trade, Ministry of Justice, and Ministry of Finance (VCC 2015). It does not appear that any current members of the VCC have backgrounds in dealing with SMEs.

The VCA is an organization under the Ministry of Industry and Trade. It has its headquarters in Hanoi, along with branches in Ho Chi Minh City and Da Nang. The VCA structure consists of six boards (the Antitrust Investigation Board, Competition Policy Board, Unfair Competition Investigation Board, Consumer Protection Board, Trade Remedies Board, and the International Cooperation Board) which reflect its responsibilities. The VCA is headed by a Director General and five Deputy Director-Generals (VCA 2014b).

The VCA has the power to:

- control economic concentration;
- accept applications for exemptions and to advise the Ministry of Industry and Trade, or the Prime Minister;
- conduct investigations into anti-competitive conduct; and
- handle or sanction unfair competitive practices (Nguyen 2014).

Thus, the VCA investigates and adjudicates matters related to unfair competition. It also investigates competition restriction allegations but leaves the adjudication of these matters to the VCC.

With its broad coverage to include enterprises across all types of ownership, the Law and the accompanying decrees have the potential to greatly influence business practices and contribute to fairer competition among different types of enterprises, including private SMEs. Nevertheless, some practical challenges remain in enforcing the Law, especially in relation to small-scale enterprises operating in certain sectors, as discussed below.

Provisions for SMEs under the Law and Implementation Issues

It is commonly recognized that the position of smaller firms in competition and in a fair trading legal regime can be overlooked, despite their large share of the total population of businesses in an economy. In addition, smaller firms have less available resources and suffer from both information asymmetry and knowledge imperfections. They have limited access to specialized legal and economic advice on competition matters (Schaper 2010). In the context of Vietnam, observers have previously noted the need for a competition policy that can also encourage the growth and development of private sector SMEs (Harvie 2001). Many of these issues were taken into consideration when the Law was drafted, and today the Vietnamese Competition Law contains several special provisions regarding SMEs in relation to competition restriction agreements and economic concentrations.

The Law identifies and addresses eight types of competition restriction agreements in Article 8: (1) agreements on the price-fixing of goods or services; (2) agreements on distributing outlets, sources of supply of goods, provision of services; (3) agreements on restricting or controlling produced, purchased, or sold quantities or volumes of goods or services; (4) agreements on restricting technological development and on restricting investments; (5) agreements on imposing conditions on the signing of goods or services purchase or sale contracts or forcing other enterprises to accept obligations not related to such contracts; (6) agreements on preventing, restraining, disallowing other enterprises to enter the market or develop a business; (7) agreements on excluding enterprises other than the parties of the agreements from the market; and (8) agreements on conniving to enable one or all of the parties of the agreement to win bids for the supply of goods or provision of services.

The Law does not allow any exemptions for agreements prescribed in Clauses 6, 7, and 8, above, while remaining agreements (Clauses 1 to 5) are prohibited only if the parties involved have a combined market share of 30 per cent or more in the relevant market (Article 9). Once this market threshold is met, the parties can apply for exemption for a specified period if the agreements are to: (a) restructure the organization, change the business model, and improve business efficiency; (b) promote technical and technological advances, and improve goods and service quality; (c) promote the uniform application of quality standards and technical norms of products of different kinds; (d) unify business transaction terms, delivery and payment conditions, not related to prices and pricing factors; (e) enhance the competitiveness of SMEs; or (f) enhance the competitiveness of Vietnamese enterprises in the international market (Article 10).

Thus, under condition (e) in Article 10, SMEs can undertake certain agreements with regards to price-fixing, market division, and output, or technology and investment restriction, if they can justify that these agreements are to improve their competitiveness.

Apart from competition restriction agreements, another area where the Law contains SME-specific provisions is with regard to economic concentration. "Economic concentration" is defined in Article 16 of the Law to include mergers, consolidations, acquisitions and joint ventures. Under the Law, economic concentration is prohibited where the parties' combined market share exceeds 50 per cent (Article 18). However, an exemption can be granted if the resulting business is still an SME after economic concentration. It has the potential to encourage smaller businesses to increase their scale and move from being micro- or small-sized to a medium-sized enterprise.

In addition, SMEs are exempted from having to notify the VCA if the relevant parties' market shares are between 30–50 per cent before economic concentration, according to Article 20 of the Law. If the parties involved can work out that their resulting business after the economic concentration is still an SME, they can go ahead with that concentration without having to inform the VCA.

The Law does not specify what constitutes an SME; as a result, both the VCA and VCC have adopted working definitions of small firms that are based on the various decrees issued by government from time to time.

However, despite the potential of the Law to support their development, SMEs have not taken advantage of the opportunities accorded to them under the Law. As in other countries, it has been noted that SMEs have a poorer understanding about the law compared to their larger counterparts (Nguoi Dua Tin 2013).

The VCA has been trying to improve awareness about the Law through advocacy activities aimed at enterprises and associations. This has included seminars, workshops, and other indirect forms of communication, such as brochures and online information. However, these activities have been mainly conducted in larger cities such as Hanoi, Ho Chi Minh City, and Da Nang (VCA 2014a). Although education and advocacy activities have contributed somewhat to building the image and the recognition of the VCA, it has not been sufficiently effective. The VCA recognizes that more practical and direct advocacy activities should be undertaken in future (VCA 2013). Indeed, SME-specific advocacy activities have been almost absent from the activities conducted by the VCA.

The VCA also has difficulty in getting information from businesses during their investigations, as they are not willing to share information with the VCA investigators. Most enterprises are not active in detecting and reporting violations of the competition law and in protecting their own legitimate interests and rights, because of their poor knowledge about it (VCA 2014a). These issues are further impeded by the lack of resources among SMEs. Thus, they do not have key information such as market share data to apply for exemptions or provide to the VCA staff. They tend to devote resources and give priorities to the day-to-day operations of the business. These issues are also common among SMEs in other countries, all of which tend to have low awareness about competition law and difficulty in detecting breaches and non-compliance (Schaper 2010).

Paperwork is also an issue. SMEs have to formally apply for the exemptions applicable to them. The requirements for the application dossier include an application form, business registration certificates, financial reports, and market share reports for the last two years from all parties involved, justification of the applicable exemption clause, and authorization from other parties for the applicant. These can be a major hurdle for SMEs to prepare, due to their limited resources or simply due to their inability to provide the information required.

Hence, they may end up not applying for the exemptions and/or not participating in the agreements altogether.

There is still a low awareness, and scepticism, about the relevance of competition law in Vietnam (Pham 2006). This is the case almost a decade after the law became effective (VCA 2012; VCA 2014a). As a case in point, a survey conducted by the VCA in 2013 with 500 enterprises showed that only 2 per cent of them believed they had a good knowledge about the Law, and 93 per cent responded that they had little knowledge about it. The survey also revealed that 31 per cent had not heard about the VCA before the survey.

Limited resources pose a challenge for the enforcement of competition legislation. Investigators for competition restriction cases are expected to have good investigation skills, but a majority of the VCA staff lack practical expertise and case handling skills (VCA 2014a). This limits the ability of the Authority to manage cases submitted to them in a timely manner. Moreover, neither the VCC nor the VCA have members experienced in dealing with SMEs. This has further restricted their ability to deal with this important sector.

The Law, despite its broad coverage, is not without limitations. The implementation of the Law to date has revealed inadequacies in the provisions contained in it, such as the regulations on determining the relevant market, market share, and sanctions for violations of anti-competitive behaviour. A comprehensive review of the Law was conducted in 2012 which also proposed some recommendations for amendment, but have not yet been enacted (VCA 2012).

It may well be that most Vietnamese SMEs are not active in participating in agreements that could restrict competition, or in engaging in activities with other SMEs that contribute to greater economic concentration. Instead, economic concentration is often conducted by larger players in the market, and SMEs are the objects rather than being the final outcome of such activity. For this reason the exemptions provided in the Law and discussed above have not been widely used by SMEs. There has not been much evidence that the Law has made a significant impact on the development of SMEs in Vietnam in the past ten years, despite the provisions in the Law meant to support their development.

Enforcing the Competition Law

In the early years after the introduction of the Law, the VCA focused more on advocacy and promotion of the Law than in enforcing it. Adopting a gradualist approach, the VCA seems to have stepped up their enforcement from 2010, according to statistics on the number of cases undertaken (see Tables 18.1 and 18.3). Although the VCA has limited power to issue fines, the fines and fees collected have increased with the number of cases (see Table 18.2). The fines imposed by the VCA have tended to be at the lower level of possible

TABLE 18.1
Unfair Competition Cases, 2006–13

Types	2006	2007	2008	2009	2010	2011	2012	2013	Total (2006–13)
Advertising for unfair competition purposes	0	0	0	5	20	33	37	2	97
Sales promotion for unfair competition purposes	0	0	0	2	2	0	0	0	4
Discrediting other enterprises	0	1	0	4	1	2	0	0	8
Misleading indications	0	1	1	0	1	0	0	0	3
Illegal multilevel sales	0	2	10	3	4	1	3	1	24
Disturbing business activities of other enterprises	0	0	1	0	0	0	1	0	2
Total by year	0	4	12	14	28	36	41	3	138

Source: VCA Annual Reports (VCA 2013; VCA 2014c).

TABLE 18.2
Unfair Competition Cases, Fines and Fees during 2006–12
(VND million)

	2006	2007	2008	2009	2010	2011	2012	2013	Total
Fines and fees	0	85	805	1,081	1,080	1,425	990	650	**6,116**

Source: VCA Annual Reports (VCA 2013; VCA 2014c).

TABLE 18.3
Investigation of Competition Restriction Cases, 2006–13

	2006	2007	2008	2009	2010	2011	2012	2013	Total
Initial investigation	5	3	4	8	10	10	12	12	**64**
Investigation	0	1	2	0	1	2	4	0	**10**
Decision	0	0	0	1	2	0	0	1	**4**
Total by year	**5**	**4**	**6**	**9**	**13**	**12**	**16**	**13**	

Source: VCA Annual Reports (VCA 2013; VCA 2014c).

amounts, as their purpose has largely been about educating rather than penalizing.

Since the introduction of the Law, more unfair competition violations have been dealt with than competition restriction violations. The most common violation is advertising for unfair competition purposes, such as false or misleading advertising. Most of the companies conducting false advertisements were manufacturers and distributors of dietary supplements. These products are often advertised with many functions which are inconsistent with the product dossier registered at authorized agencies, and are not the same as the actual benefits of the product (VCA 2014a).

This can be partly explained by the nature of the Vietnamese economy, as common unfair competition violations — such as misleading indications and false advertising — are more prevalent in an emerging market where new goods and services are increasingly being introduced. Another reason for this is the fact that such unfair competition violations are relatively easy to uncover and deal with. The lack of experience as well as insufficient resources makes it harder for the VCA to monitor competition restriction practices and uncover these violations (Nguyen 2014).

With regard to competition restriction cases, the number of investigations conducted by the VCA has increased gradually every year (see Table 18.3). Most of them are only in the initial investigation stage and relate to price-fixing agreements (Nguyen 2014). In 2012 and 2013, the number of competition restriction cases was equal between the goods and services sectors, while the formation of a cartel was a more frequent behaviour than other types of restriction behaviour (see Table 18.4). The first major case of competition restriction involved an SOE, Vietnam Air Petrol Company (Vinapco), which was found to have abused its dominant position and was fined by the VCC in 2009. This was an important matter that raised public awareness of the Law, as was the fact that it included enforcement action against an SOE (Fruitman 2013).

Unfair competition cases tend to be related to smaller domestic private enterprises, while competition restrictions and economic concentration matters have often involved large domestic enterprises, SOEs, and foreign invested enterprises.

The advocacy strategy pursued by the VCA has focused on certain economic sectors. For example, in 2013, the VCA targeted the pay TV, construction, pharmacy, and marine transportation industries. Nevertheless, neither the VCC nor the VCA has had any specific activities focusing on businesses according to their size, such as SMEs. The lack of such targeted activities means that SMEs have not been made fully aware about the consequences of violating the Law.

Clearly, there is a need to put in place advocacy activities for the SME sector. They need to be educated about the exemptions available to them under the Law, which might permit them to undertake agreements and economic concentration to improve their competitiveness and scale. These will give them a more equal footing relative to larger firms in the market.

Table 18.4
Competition Restriction Cases, 2012–13

Year	Cases by Sector		Cases by Behaviour		Cases by Outcome		Total
	Goods	Services	Cartel	Abusive Behaviour	Investigation	Continuing Observation	
2012	6	6	11	1	1	11	12
2013	6	6	7	5	0	12	12

Source: VCA Annual Reports (VCA 2013; VCA 2014*c*).

Conclusion

Domestic economic reality and international economic integration provided the *raison d'être* for the formulation of the Competition Law in Vietnam. The introduction of the Law in 2005 provided an important legal mechanism which has contributed to a potential level playing field for all forms and types of businesses.

It is important for the VCA to continue building its capacity and to provide advocacy activities to SMEs. The VCA could work together with relevant SMEs business associations in these tasks. SMEs should be given access to legal assistance to prepare exemption dossiers. The VCC and the VCA should include members and staff with background and experience in dealing with SMEs. This will ensure that SME development is well and truly supported under the Competition Law in Vietnam.

Although the Law contains special provisions for SMEs in recognition of their important contribution in Vietnam, and provides them with favourable exemptions, these have not had a significant impact on the development of SMEs. The lack of awareness among SMEs about the Law in general, and the limited use of the exemptions applicable to them, still remains an issue more than a decade after the introduction of the Law. In addition, the lack of resources available for competition agencies and SMEs themselves has also made it harder for the Law to exert a significant impact on the sector. There exists a significant gap between the aspirations of the Law and its implementation in practice, especially among SMEs.

REFERENCES

Asian Development Bank (ADB). "Socialist Republic of Viet Nam: Supporting the Second Small and Medium-Sized Enterprises Development Program". Technical Assistance Report. Manila: ADB, October 2012.

Brown, David. "Vietnam Looks for Renewal in an Intensely Political 2015". East Asia Forum, 6 January 2015. Available at <http://www.eastasiaforum.org/2015/01/06/vietnam-looks-for-renewal-in-an-intensely-political-2015/> (accessed 6 February 2015).

Cao, Xuan Hien. "Competition Law and Policy in Vietnam". Presentation at the 4th East Asia Conference on Competition Law and Policy, Hanoi, 3 May 2007.

Dang, The Duc and Tri Hung Pham. "Competition Law and Policy in Vietnam". *The Singapore Law Gazette*, November 2008.

DFDL. "Changes coming quickly to Vietnam's Competition Law Penalties". *Lexology*, 2014. Available at <http://www.lexology.com/library/detail.aspx?g=d2492912-b98d-4373-a43f-e17f3d541de2> (accessed 7 February 2015).

Fruitman, David. "Vietnam". In *The Political Economy of Competition Law in Asia*, edited by Mark Williams. Cheltenham: Edward Elgar, 2013.

General Statistical Office (GSO) of Vietnam. "National Accounts", 2014. Available at <https://gso.gov.vn/default.aspx?tabid=715> (accessed 18 December 2014) [in Vietnamese].

Harvie, Charles. "Competition Policy and SMEs in Vietnam". Working Paper Series No. 01-10. NSW, Australia: University of Wollongong, 2001.

————. "The Contribution of SMEs in the Economic Transition of Vietnam". *Journal of International Business and Entrepreneurship Development* 2, no. 2 (August 2004): 1–16.

Le, Viet and Charles Harvie. "Regulatory Reform and the Growth of Private Entrepreneurship in Vietnam". In *Government, SMEs and Entrepreneurship Development: Policy, Practice and Challenges*, edited by Robert Blackburn and Michael Schaper. Surrey: Gower/Ashgate, 2012.

Ministry of Planning and Investment (MPI). "White Paper on Small and Medium Sized Enterprises in Vietnam 2011". Hanoi: MPI, 2012.

Ministry of Trade (MOT). Directive No. 11/2000/CT-BTM on drafting the Law on Competition and Preventing Monopoly. Hanoi: Ministry of Trade, 12 May 2000.

Nguoi Dua Tin. "92,8% doanh doanh nghiệp chưa nắm rõ Luật cạnh tranh" [92.8% of Businesses unclear about Competition Law], 2013. Available at <http://www.nguoiduatin.vn/928-doanh-nghiep-chua-nam-ro-luat-canh-tranhkhi-loi-chua-thaydung-battoi-quan-tam-a87250.html> (accessed 4 December 2014).

Nguyen, Anh Tuan. "Vietnam: Overview". *The Asia-Pacific Antitrust Review 2014*. Available at <http://globalcompetitionreview.com/reviews/60/sections/206/chapters/2351/vietnam-overview/> (accessed 4 December 2014).

Nguyen, Thanh Tu. "Vietnam's Competition Law and Policy Development in the Process of Integration into the World Economy". Paper presented at UNCTAD Regional Seminar on Competition Policy and Multilateral Negotiations, Hong Kong, 16–18 April 2002.

Pham, Alice. "Development of Competition Law in Vietnam in the Face of Economic Reforms and Global Integration, The Symposium on Competition Law and Policy in Developing Countries". *Northwestern Journal of International Law and Business* 26, no. 3 (2006): 547–63.

Schaper, Michael. "Competition Law, Enforcement and the Australian Small Business Sector". *Small Enterprise Research* 17, no. 1 (2010): 7–18.

Tran, Thi Minh Phuong. "Enactment of Vietnam Competition Law 2004: A Case Study of Harmonizing Internal and External Factors". Master thesis in International Relations, Victoria University of Wellington, 2013.

Trinh, Anh Tuan. "Developments in Vietnamese Competition Law and Policy". *Antitrust Chronicle* 2, no. 1 (2013). Available at <https://www.competitionpolicyinternational.com/developments-in-vietnamese-competition-law-and-policy/> (accessed 1 December 2014).

Vietnam Competition Authority (VCA). *Review Report on Vietnam Competition Law*. Hanoi: VCA, 2012.

———. *Annual Report 2012*. Hanoi: VCA, 2013.

———. *Review of Competition Related Regulations in Sectoral Regulatory Laws*. Hanoi: VCA, 2014a.

———. "Organisational Chart", 2014b. Available at <http://www.vca.gov.vn/Organization.aspx> (accessed 16 December 2014).

———. *Annual Report 2013*. Hanoi: VCA, 2014c.

Vietnam Competition Council (VCC). "Introduction about Vietnam Competition Council" [in Vietnamese], 2015. Available at <http://www.hoidongcanhtranh.gov.vn/?page=news&do=detail&category_id=2&id=41> (accessed 16 February 2015).

19

CHINA'S ANTI-MONOPOLY LAW AND THE SME SECTOR

Mark Williams

The small and medium-sized enterprise (SME) sector has not been a primary focus of anti-monopoly policy in China. However, it does make up a large and growing part of the domestic economy. The Anti-Monopoly Law (AML), enacted in 2007, does not contain any specific exemptions for SMEs. Industry associations often play an important role in undertaking activities that potentially breach the AML, and a number of different enforcement actions have already been undertaken against such arrangements by some of the different regulatory agencies responsible for ensuring compliance with the law. The adoption of more even-handed enforcement of the competition law against state sector monopolists and SME cartels would likely benefit the SME sector as a whole, enhance consumer welfare, and assist in China's stated policy aim of encouraging the growth of the domestic consumer market.

Introduction

The small and medium-sized enterprise (SME) sector has not traditionally been a priority concern for most competition agencies globally, for the trite reason that small enterprises generally do not possess market power and, therefore, cannot exercise it to distort competition. Only in the narrowest of markets, or where the small enterprises combine with other enterprises to engage in collaborative anti-competitive acts (usually through the agency of a trade association) (Këllezi et al. 2014), do small enterprises register on a competition agency's "radar" screen.

Small enterprises are more often considered to be the victims of the aggressive use of market power. Upstream sellers with market power (input suppliers), or downstream distributors who have monopsony power or who control access to the ultimate customers (for example, supermarkets), are often seen as more likely targets of antitrust enforcement than SMEs. Moreover small retail enterprises may be required to enter into vertical arrangements with manufacturers or wholesalers that might be disadvantageous to them.

However, as mentioned above, it is usually through hard-core cartel-like practices on price, quantities, or market division (often coordinated by a trade association or through bid-rigging agreements) that the SME sector is likely to receive the attention of antitrust agencies.

In China, due to its particular history and political economy since 1949, the private SME sector was negligible until the reform and opening process began in 1978. Since that time, however, there has been an explosion in the SME sector, and the nation has seen the creation of millions of small businesses. Originally, there was no constitutional recognition and no legal framework to recognize sole trader businesses, partnerships, or private limited companies. At the beginning of the reform era, de facto private business had to be disguised by the use of so-called "red hat" pseudo-cooperatives, which were initially linked to farming enterprises or the processing of agricultural products, since privately-owned enterprise was seen as potentially politically subversive at that time. Domestic small-scale private businesses were not permitted until 1988, some ten years after the commencement of the economic reform process.

Subsequently, in the 1990s and 2000s, the Communist Party of China (CPC) adopted a new ideology centred on the notion of a "socialist market economy". In parallel with the new political dispensation, the Constitution was amended on various occasions to adopt the new economic orthodoxy and to provide protection for private property rights. Additionally, a raft of new laws established several legally permissible forms of private business and provided for their registration and regulation. In particular, the General Principles of Civil Law (1986) allowed the creation of "individual and house hold enterprises", whilst the Sole Proprietorship Enterprise Law (1999), the Partnership Enterprise Law (2006), and the Company Law (2005) provided the legal basis for private enterprise SMEs in China. Moreover, in June 2002, the twenty-eighth session of the Ninth NPC (National People's Congress) Standing Committee published the SME Promotion Law. The law provided, *inter alia*, certain protections for SME assets and income. The Product Quality Law (1993, amended 2000) and the Protection of Consumer Rights and Interests Law (1993) were also adopted as part of the more market-oriented economic structure that the CCP now sanctioned.

The private sector of the economy was further boosted by the privatization of hundreds of thousands of the smaller state-owned enterprises (SOEs) in the 1990s (Williams 2005). As a result, this sector (in terms of both manufacturing and services) has been the most dynamic part of the Chinese economy. This has especially been the case in relation to the provision of employment and economic growth, whereas the SOE sector has shrunk comparatively as a percentage of total economic output.

As part of the completion of the legal infrastructure to ostensibly support a fully functioning socialist market economy, the nation adopted an Anti-Monopoly Law (AML) in 2007.[1] Consequently, this chapter will consider a number of issues pertinent to the interaction of the SME sector and the AML, including China's definition of SMEs, the primary purposes for which the AML was enacted, and the relevant substantive legal provisions applicable to SMEs. The role of industry and professional associations in the context of competition regulation is also discussed, followed by an examination of the AML's enforcement mechanisms and their use in a selection of SME competition cases.

Background: The Chinese Economy and Its SME Sector

At the risk of stating the glaringly obvious, China is now an economic giant. Its economy ranks second globally after the United States (World Bank 2015). China is also a giant in terms of geographical size (it has a land area of approximately 9.5 million square kilometres) and by virtue of its enormous population of some 1.37 billion people. Gross domestic product (GDP) per capita now makes China a middle-income country, but there remains substantial income and wealth disparities, with a very high Gini coefficient. There are stark differences in levels of economic development between city and countryside, and between the relatively developed east and south and the poorer interior and western provinces (Xie and Zhou 2014).

Whilst China has adopted major economic reforms and has created the legal infrastructure needed to support private enterprise, it has not undertaken any significant political reforms. The nation remains a one-party state, and the power and influence of the CPC over the formal institutions of government and the state-sector of the economy remains absolute. The Party controls policymaking, the government, the legislature, and the judiciary. Most facets of the media are also firmly under state, and so Party, control. These institutional arrangements can both positively and negatively affect the creation, operation, and growth of the SME sector, but the dominance of political factors in economic management can create an uncertain environment for SMEs.

However, one significant and positive way that economic inequality has been addressed is the empowerment of farmers and individuals to set up and expand private SMEs. Those with business acumen have been able to generate significant wealth; they have also been, by far, the most dynamic sector of the domestic economy, and made a very large contribution to providing employment, especially in small-scale manufacturing, the retail sector, and in certain service industries. SMEs have also made a large contribution to China's stratospheric export growth in manufactured goods in the last thirty years.

In China, in defining an SME, the categorization of SMEs is sector specific and is divided between small and medium segments. Table 19.1 lists some of these. For example, in the industrial sector, those employing between 200–2,000 people and having sales of between CNY30–300 million, or assets in the range of CNY40–400 million, are considered small; those above this point are categorized as medium sized enterprises.[2]

A slightly different definition is used in the construction industry, which is one of the largest employers of unskilled labour. Enterprises with 600–3,000 employees, and sales and assets of CNY30–300 million

Table 19.1
Definitions of SMEs in China

Size Category	Industries	Employment-based	Total assets	Business revenue
Small	Industry	<300	≤> 40 million	≤> 30 million
	Construction	<600	<40 million	<30 million
	Wholesale	<100		<30 million
	Retail	<100		≤ 10 million
	Transport	<500		≤ 30 million
	Post	<400		≤ 30 million
	Hotel & restaurant	<400		<30 million
Medium	Industry	300–200	≤ 40 million–400 million	≤ 30 million–300 million
	Construction	600–3,000	<40 million–400 million	<30 million–300 million
	Wholesale	100–200		<30 million–300 million
	Retail	100–500		≤ 10 million–1,500 million
	Transport	500–3,000		≤ 30 million–300 million
	Post	400–1,000		≤ 30 million–300 million
	Hotel & restaurant	400–800		≤ 30 million–150 million

Note: SME should meet one or more of the conditions; ME should meet three conditions; the others are SE.
Source: SME Promotion Law of China, 2003.

and CNY40–400 million respectively, are considered small and those having more than that are medium sized.

The SME sector in China is economically very important both to maintaining economic growth and providing employment. It may also be pivotal in helping the government to achieve its major economic goal of restructuring the economy away from its current reliance on exports and capital intensive infrastructure investment, and focusing instead on a more consumption-orientated economy.

What was China's AML Enacted to Do?

The enactment of the AML was a long and convoluted process. Drafting of the law began in 1994 and was only finally enacted in 2007 (Wu 2013). After China acceded to the World Trade Organization (WTO) in 2001, the economy boomed both domestically and in export markets. As part of the accession agreement, China committed to open many of its previously closed or highly protected domestic markets in specified ways and in particular sectors, to allow greater participation of foreign firms.

The government, academics, and many in the domestic business sector were worried that domestic businesses, especially the large SOEs, would not be able to compete with Western multinational companies (MNCs); a means had to be devised to strategically ensure the continued viability of state control of the major economic sectors, such as financial services, energy, iron and steel, petrochemicals, transport, and communications. A suitably drafted and enforced competition law could, on the one hand, be a defining statement of state commitment to an open market-based economy regulated by rules that conform to international practices. But, on the other hand, such a law might also allow domestic economic interests to be protected by the selective enforcement of open-textured rules that were subject to a wide degree of interpretation.

The creation of a competition law was thus seen (by pro-market reformers) as a basic requirement for a market-oriented economy, but for the more "conservative" hawkish factions, this law could be used for ulterior motives.

The AML was, therefore, primarily conceived as a means to manage the Chinese domestic economy in a way that comported to the government's view of how the economy should be structured, rather than being a tool to promote open markets policed by the competitive process. The impact of the AML has only become apparent as a result of the promulgation and implementation of subsidiary legislation several years implementation of the law by the three enforcement agencies.

AML Provisions Relevant to Small Firms

As the title of the statute suggests, the main focus of the AML targets the actual or potential exercise of monopoly power. To be able to exercise such monopoly power, an absolute legal or de facto monopoly is not required by the law, and instead some lesser degree of market power exercised in an anti-competitive fashion is all that is required. Such an exercise of market power must take place in relation to a specifically identified product market in a nominated geographical space. As has been previously mentioned in the introduction, SMEs are unlikely to individually have such market power, other than in very unusual circumstances. However, SMEs in combination may form a cartel, fix prices, agree on quantitative restrictions, divide up markets, or rig bids. Such "hard-core" anti-competitive agreements are usually automatically illegal, as an anti-competitive outcome can be easily inferred in such cases; in many jurisdictions they constitute *per se* or "object" offences, with little or no need for a competition assessment of the impugned conduct. It is very rare that a competition law provides exemptions for such conduct, although historically, cartel-like activities have been immunized for a plethora of policy reasons in various jurisdictions (such as professional sports in the United States or ocean shipping in Australia).

The AML reads like many other competition laws. It prohibits four distinct types of anti-competitive activity: monopoly agreements (Article 13); abuse of market dominance (Article 17); anti-competitive concentrations (Article 20); and abuse of administrative power (Article 32).

The last iterated conduct is a peculiar provision that deals with particular conduct by state authorities in China, and is effectively an alternative way to attempt to deal with acts that would otherwise be more correctly condemned in administrative courts as being ultra vires. However, in China, the administrative court system is weak and ineffective in dealing with such conduct. Article 32 is similarly a very weak provision, enforceable only by the discretionary exercise of power by the defaulting organ's superior administrative or political body; to date there are no reported instances of it being used.

The agricultural sector is entirely excluded from the ambit of the AML under Article 56, and SOEs are given special status, although they are not specifically exempted from the AML. No specific exemptions for SMEs are provided and no safe harbour or *de minimis* provisions are included in the statute.

As can be appreciated, the SME sector was not a priority issue for legislators when the AML was enacted; the law primarily focused on "monopoly conduct" and "monopoly agreements" and by definition, SMEs normally do not have the market power to be dominant (save in very narrowly defined product or geographical markets). Moreover, anti-competitive agreements that fall short of "hard core" agreements again generally cannot create collective market power absent barriers to entry or a very wide spread and efficiently enforced collective agreement. Lastly, mergers between SMEs similarly rarely cause competition concerns, as the resulting entity is very unlikely to have market power.

Industry Associations and Collective Behaviour

Most Chinese SMEs belong to an industry association. These bodies often have close affiliation to the local government and the CPC, usually with a Party cell in de facto control.

The government and the CPC are very wary of any type of independent non-government organization for political reasons. Direct participation by the Party and government, often amounting to direction or control of business or professional organizations, is not unusual. The interface between business and government or Party is much closer than is usually the case in Western jurisdictions. As a result, industrial policy and political considerations may form part of association decisions. Inevitably, such matters are not often found in the public domain. But in a recent case, the government was directly involved in organizing a cartel. The Ministry of Commerce (MOFCOM) was concerned that the low prices charged by Chinese vitamin producers might provoke an anti-dumping action by the U.S. authorities. To forestall this, MOFCOM arranged for the Chinese producers to agree to fix higher prices for the U.S. market. Unfortunately, when this cartel was discovered, legal action was taken against the producers, who then sought to defend the action based on the doctrine of sovereign state compulsion. This failed, as MOFCOM was not acting under any legally enforceable mandate (Re Vitamin C. Antitrust Litigation, 13-4791, U.S. Court of Appeals for the Second Circuit (Manhattan)).

AML Article 11 somewhat ambiguously states that "[a] trade association shall intensify industrial self-discipline, guide business operators to lawfully compete, safeguard the competition order in the market". However, Article 16 reinforces the ostensible prohibition by explicitly stating that "[a]ny trade association may not organize the business operators in its own industry to implement the monopolistic conduct as prohibited by this Chapter". The reasons for the adoption of Article 16 was that during the passage of the Bill, a noodle manufacturer's association announced that its members had collectively agreed to raise their prices due to poor profitability and to ensure an "orderly market" (Wang 2009). The move generated media attention just as the AML legislation was being discussed by the NPC Standing Committee, causing some embarrassment and forcing the adoption of a late amendment. It is suspected that such conduct has not ceased since the adoption of the AML. Indeed, some similar cases have been uncovered and prosecuted by Chinese enforcement agencies in the last few years, though the small number of such cases probably means that there are many more that have not been uncovered.

There is often a good reason for such collective behaviour by small enterprises. SMEs often complain about the predations of local government officials. They allege that officials seek corrupt payments or unjustified fees and charges to make up local revenues. SMEs argue that the predations of some local officials make taking collective action a justifiable defensive measure. Furthermore, SMEs often also see themselves as disadvantaged when compared to the favoured treatment of SOEs in respect of protected markets, local protectionist policies, and access to favourable financing from state banks or via an IPO (initial public offering) on the state controlled stock exchanges. Collective action is, therefore, unsurprisingly seen as the SME sector's only rational response to such a business environment. Arguably it assists them in self-preservation, and helps reduce the significant business risks they are inevitably subject to in the domestic market.

Furthermore, many SME associations are closely intertwined with local government organs that were previously part of the state economic planning mechanism. These organizations have often changed their legal form from being government bureaus to being industry associations, whilst still retaining very close informal links to the government. Government economic policy decisions are often implemented via such informal contacts with trade associations. Thus, collective action by SMEs is a common business practice in China, either as a defensive response to negative environmental factors or as a collaborative effort with the government to implement economic development policies.

Enforcement of the AML

The enforcement machinery of the AML includes the AML Commission, which acts as the coordinating national body that has nominated three state agencies to undertake the task of operational enforcement.

MOFCOM is tasked with administering the merger regime and acts as the Commission's secretariat. It also often deals with international collaboration issues, transnational mergers, and broader policy issues. The National Development and Reform Commission (NDRC) has been tasked with enforcing the "price monopoly" provisions, which includes price-related infractions of the abuse of dominance and monopoly agreement articles. The State Administration of Industry and Commerce (SAIC) is allocated the "non-price monopoly" infractions of the AML to administer.

This tripartite division of AML enforcement is suboptimal and the majority of competition cases inevitably include some impact on prices, whether directly or indirectly. Thus, the allocation of enforcement responsibility is opaque and potentially riven with interdepartmental rivalries. Overlapping jurisdiction, different enforcement priorities and procedures, and varying levels of expertise and competition competence all combine to undermine confidence in the robustness of the enforcement system.

However, despite these organizational imperfections, AML enforcement, by MOFCOM in particular, has become very important globally. The size of the Chinese domestic market and the need for Chinese approval of most MNC mergers has made MOFCOM's decisions important in global commerce (Sokol 2013).

In the Chinese domestic market, SAIC and NRDC have also been active in AML enforcement, although their targets have predominantly been large foreign players who have market power in specific sectors of the domestic economy. Some cases have been follow-ons from earlier overseas decisions where the same participants have operated anti-competitively in the Chinese market or which have involved the specific trade practices of large MNCs in China. It is notable that there has been little action against the large SOEs that dominate many sectors of the Chinese domestic economy (Tan 2015). However, some smaller regional SOEs, industry associations, and small firms have been the subject of investigation and penalty proceedings, as is discussed in the next section.

SME Enforcement Cases

The following cases are illustrative of various types of anti-competitive behaviour discovered and punished by the NDRC and the SAIC in the last few years. SMEs have both been the perpetrators and the victims of anti-competitive cartels and the abuse of dominance by upstream suppliers. A striking feature of many of the reported sanctioned cases is the prevalence of coordinating industry associations, often working in parallel with government or quasi-government bodies to fix prices, limit supply, or to artificially divide markets.

These are examples only and do not necessarily present a complete picture of the competitive environment faced by SMEs in China. Also, the number of reported cases is very small compared to the size of the Chinese goods and services markets. As a result, the true level of anti-competitive conduct is almost certainly much greater in the economy as a whole than the reported cases suggest.

It should also be noted that the published case decisions or reports in the news media are generally very brief and lack a great deal of detail as regards the particular factual matrix, the precise nature of the infraction alleged, the reasoning process of the enforcement agency, or the method of calculating the fine imposed. Given the lack of detail in the reports, the companies cited may or may not fall within the Chinese definition of an SME. Nevertheless, the cases do represent the type of anti-competitive conduct that smaller companies have engaged in or have been subject to in China.

NDRC Cases

In March 2010, a rice noodles cartel was uncovered in Guangxi province. Eighteen rice noodle manufacturers were involved. They held a series of meetings to discuss profit sharing and business integration and to set market prices. The Guangxi Price Bureau ruled that this behaviour violated the Price Law and the Antimonopoly Law. The bureau fined three of the leading companies RMB100,000 (US$16,256) each, and ordered fines of RMB30,000–80,000 (US$4,877–13,005) for other manufacturers depending on the gravity of their actions.

In August 2010, the Fuyang Paper Manufacturing Industry Association held five meetings where more than twenty member companies discussed sales pricing in respect of white paperboard. The Zhejiang Price Bureau ruled that the conduct violated both the Price Law and Antimonopoly Law, and ordered the Association to pay fines of RMB500,000 (US$81,281). Individual members were not apparently sanctioned.

In March 2012, the Guangdong Sea Sand Association and several of its member companies agreed to set resource fees for mining sea sand. The Guangdong Price Bureau determined these actions violated Article 16(2) of the AML and issued fines and warnings to members of the association. Three members of the association — Guangdong Baohai Sand and Stone, Dongguan Jianghai, and Shenzhen Donghai Century Information Consulting — were collectively fined RMB759,200 (US$123,417). Other members were issued with warnings not to repeat similar behaviour.

In February 2013, the Kweichow Moutai Group sought to fix the minimum resale price to third party distributors since 2012, taking punitive measures against those who did not implement the price. The bureau ruled that such activities violated Article 14 of the AML as a resale price maintenance (RPM) agreement, and fined Kweichow Moutai RMB247 million (US$40.2 million), or 1 per cent of the "related" sales revenue in the previous year. This case illustrates that small retailers can be subject to imposed RPM restrictions by upstream dominant suppliers.

In a similar case also involving a well-known liquor producer, the Wuliangye Group, the Sichuan Development and Reform Commission found that between 2009 and 2013, Wuliangye signed agreements with over 3,200 independent dealers to limit the lowest resale price for its products. It then enacted punitive measures against those who did not implement the minimum retail price. The commission ruled that such activities violated Article 14 of the AML as a RPM agreement. It fined Wuliangye RMB202 million (US$32.8 million), or 1 per cent of the "related" sales revenue in the previous year. This case illustrates the scale of RPM conduct that affects SME retailers.

In August 2013, the Shanghai Price Bureau ruled that Shanghai Laofengxiang and several other gold jewellery stores had sought to set retail prices within strict bounds for gold jewellery products under the umbrella of the Shanghai Gold & Jewellery Trade Association. The bureau ruled that this behaviour violated Articles 13 and 16 of the AML and fined the association RMB500,000 (US$81,281) and the five stores a total of RMB10.09 million (US$1.6 million), or 1 per cent of their previous year's sales. This case illustrates again the role of a trade association of SME retailers acting together to injure consumers of gold products.

In December 2013, Hunan Loudi City Insurance Industry Association and twelve domestic insurance-related companies agreed to set unified prices for new car insurance discount rates, divide the market, and sign exclusive agreements with the association-organized automobile service centre. The Hunan Price Bureau found that this behaviour violated the AML and fined the association and six of the insurance companies RMB2.19 million (US$256,011). The other five companies were exempted from penalties because they had cooperated with the authorities.

SAIC Cases

In August 2010, Lianyungang Construction Material and Machinery Association and sixteen member companies were found to have agreed in 2009 to monopolize the market. The deal prohibited all involved from independently signing contracts with buyers. The Jiangsu Administration of Industry and Commerce (AIC) ruled that this behaviour constituted an illegal monopoly agreement under the AML. It confiscated illegal profits of more than RMB136,481.20 (US$22,187) and fined five participants in the cartel a combined total of RMB530,723.19 (US$86,275).

In January 2012, SAIC found that a group of three second-hand auto dealerships in Anyang, Henan formed a cartel and signed an agreement to set a uniform price and to divide up the market in 2007. By 2009, the cartel had expanded to include eleven further dealerships. SAIC ruled that these activities violated Article 13 of the AML. It then confiscated RMB1.468 million (US$238.641) in illegal profits and imposed a fine of RMB265,000 (US$43,071) on the participants.

In August 2012, the Liaoning Construction Material Industry Association's Cement Committee and twelve member companies from central Liaoning were found to have signed agreements in 2010 to monopolize the market, control production, and set market shares. The Liaoning AIC ruled that their behaviour constituted an illegal monopoly agreement under the AML and imposed fines of RMB16.37 million (US$2.7 million) on the association and the twelve participating members.

In November 2012, SAIC found that the Yongzhou (Hunan) Insurance Industry Association and twelve insurance companies in October 2011 had signed an agreement establishing a new car insurance service centre. This centre served as a clearing house for consumer purchases of new car insurance. SAIC decided that the agreement was an illegal monopoly agreement under the AML, and fined the Association RMB400,000 (US$65,025) and the twelve companies a combined total of RMB972,000 (US$158,010).

In April 2013, the Xishuangbanna Tourism Association (XTA) was found to have launched a new "information platform" in 2003, as a mode of coordinating the offering of tourist services. Between 2009 and 2011, the Association convinced more than eighty other firms including hotels, attraction operators, passenger car service providers, and travel agencies to conform with the platform requirements to sell their services. The agreement promoted specific tours to specific stops, with punitive action taken against those who deviated from these "recommendations". Furthermore, the XTA and twenty-four individual travel agencies signed agreements to fix prices and itineraries for travel. The Yunnan AIC found the behaviour of the Association and the firms had violated the AML and a fine of RMB800,000 (US$130,000) was imposed.

These cases illustrate the behaviour that involves the SME sector both as perpetrator and victim. Such cases are typical not only in China but in many other countries. The only significantly distinctive feature of these cases is the widespread involvement of industry associations, which are effectively quasi-government organizations. The collaboration between governmental-type entities and local SMEs in particular sectors may be more prevalent in China than in Western jurisdictions due to a long history of government involvement in all aspects of economic development.

Conclusion

In this chapter, the particular characteristics of the SME sector in China and its relatively recent evolution have been considered. It is clear that SMEs will continue to be one of the most dynamic sectors of the Chinese economy. Recent policy changes to emphasize domestic consumption, instead of an over-reliance on infrastructure and the export sector, is likely to be very positive for the development and expansion of SMEs in China.

Generally, the SME sector has low barriers to entry. Except for instances of cartel behaviour, and given the general absence of market power, the SME sector should be more innovative and grow faster than the SOEs which have dominated much of the domestic economy in the past. SMEs are more likely to be able to anticipate or react to consumer preferences, so aiding the growth of the consumer economy.

However, in some SME sectors, industry associations are likely to continue to emphasize the advantages of "self-discipline" for collective profitability. It is also likely that governmental or quasi-governmental bodies will maintain some form of direct involvement in many of these associations.

SMEs and their associations may well see such collective action as legitimate in defence of their markets, especially when faced with competition from foreign MNCs and national SOEs with market power. However, the self-interest of producers and suppliers is not normally the primary objective of a competition law. Instead, consumers are ultimately supposed to be the primary beneficiary.

China is a very large country with a large, diverse economy. But AML enforcement resources are very limited, with the NDRC and SAIC having only small numbers of staff at their head offices devoted to its enforcement. Furthermore, government "buy in" with regard to a pro-competition agenda is often scant at the policy level. Other motives often appear to drive the enforcement agenda, such as industry policy and the effective protection of large SOEs. If the AML was more rigorously and evenly applied, the SME sector would likely be a net beneficiary, since input costs might be reduced and various closed markets might be opened up for SME participation.

However, at present such considerations of SME sector welfare do not appear to be a priority issue for Chinese anti-monopoly authorities. Hopefully this stance will change in the future.

NOTES

1. An English translation of the AML is available at <http://english.mofcom.gov.cn/article/policyrelease/Businessregulations/201303/20130300045909.shtml.>
2. At the time of writing, CNY1 = approximately US$0.16.

REFERENCES

China.org.cn. "Law of the People's Republic of China on the Protection of Consumer Rights and Interests", 1993. Available at <http://www.china.org.cn/china/LegislationsForm2001-2010/2011-02/14/content_21917139.htm>.

Këllezi, Pranvera, Bruce Kilpatrick, and Pierre Kobel, eds. *Antitrust for Small and Middle Size Undertakings and Image Protection from Non-Competitors*. Heidelberg: Springer, 2014.

Ministry of Science and Technology of the People's Republic of China. "Product Quality Law of the People's Republic of China (Amended on 7/8/2000)", 8 July 2000. Available at <http://www.most.gov.cn/eng/policies/regulations/200501/t20050105_18422.htm>.

Re Vitamin C. Antitrust Litigation, 13-4791, U.S. Court of Appeals for the Second Circuit (Manhattan).

Sokol, D. Daniel. "Merger Control under China's Anti-Monopoly Law". *New York University Journal of Law & Business* 10, no. 1 (2013). Available at <http://www.nyujlb.org/wp-content/uploads/nyb_10-1_1-36_Sokol.pdf>.

Tan, Wei. "SOEs and Competition Policy in China". *Competition Policy International*, 17 August 2015. Available at <https://www.competitionpolicyinternational.com/assets/Columns/cpi-asia-antitrust-column-tanFINAL.pdf>.

Wang, Xiaoye. "Comments on the Anti-Monopoly Law of the People's Republic of China". *Front Law China* 4, no. 3 (2009): 343–75.

Williams, Mark. *Competition Policy and Law in China, Hong Kong and Taiwan*. Cambridge: Cambridge University Press, 2005.

World Bank. "GDP Ranking", 1 July 2015. Available at <http://data.worldbank.org/datacatalog/GDP-ranking-table> (accessed 15 August 2015).

Wu, Qianlan. *Competition Laws, Globalization and Legal Pluralism: China's Experience*. Oxford: Hart Publishing, 2013.

Xie, Yu and Xiang Zhou. "Income Inequality in Today's China". *Proceedings of the National Academy of Sciences* 111, no. 19 (2014): 6928–33.

Zhong, Nan and Zhang Jin. "Smaller Firms to Benefit from New Definition of SMEs". *China Daily*, 27 October 2010. Available at <http://www.chinadaily.com.cn/business/2010-10/27/content_11463340.htm>.

20

A NEW COMPETITION AGENCY LEARNS TO DEAL WITH SMEs
The Case of the Hong Kong Competition Commission

Knut Fournier

This chapter describes the evolution of competition law in recent years in the Hong Kong Special Administrative Region. It discusses the reasons giving rise to the implementation of the Competition Ordinance, its major features, and the reaction of the small business sector to the new law. A number of enforcement actions have already been undertaken by the Hong Kong Competition Commission against small and medium-sized enterprises (SMEs), and it is suggested that a focus on small enterprises is a logical and somewhat predictable step by the new agency.

Introduction

The Hong Kong Special Administrative Region (HKSAR) is a small jurisdiction whose economy is currently in transition from an entrepôt trade to a service-based economy. Since China's accession to the World Trade Organization (WTO) in 2001, Hong Kong's role as an international trade and services centre has increased. The SAR's economy is largely supported by low taxes, an educated workforce, and the rule of law. Major groups in the shipping, logistics, transportation, energy, telecoms, and retail markets have secured dominant positions through massive infrastructure investments and government deals. Yet 98 per cent of Hong Kong companies are small and medium-sized enterprises (SMEs) and serve the local market, which consists of some 7 million people population with a gross domestic product (GDP) per capita comparable to the United Kingdom or Japan. In 2014, Hong Kong's SMEs (defined by the government as a manufacturing business which employs fewer than one hundred persons in Hong Kong; or a non-manufacturing business which employs fewer than fifty persons in Hong Kong) employed 48 per cent of the local workforce (Trade and Industry Council 2014).

Over the years, businesses have played a significant role in shaping the governance of Hong Kong. In Hong Kong's political system, the Chief Executive is the head of the Executive Council, which comprises of members of government as well as non-official members. The Chief Executive is elected by a 1,200-strong election committee, of which a majority is returned by selective categories of professions. This system favours the business community, as the election committee is heavily influenced by pro-Beijing business people and long-established business interests. Among the Executive Council, a substantial number of people have extensive business experience.

The legislative branch, known as the Legislative Council, consists of a single chamber. Out of its seventy members, thirty-five are returned by "Functional Constituencies", which selectively represent some of the professions of Hong Kong, including the industrial, commercial, medical, teaching, legal, and financial sectors. This unusual system of closed and indirect elections, in which professional interest groups select their own political representatives, gives particular weight to the voice of the business community. If one considers democracy to be a competitive system of government selection, Hong Kong is governed by a political cartel.

Until very recently, the legislative and regulatory context in Hong Kong did not raise any concern for small and medium-sized businesses. This changed in the summer of 2012 when the Chief Executive signed the Competition Ordinance (cap 619), the first cross-sector competition law to be enforced in Hong Kong. The Ordinance is closely modelled after the European Union competition law. It provides for a prohibition on anti-competitive agreements (the First Conduct Rule) and on abuses of dominance (the Second Conduct Rule). It also provides for a merger control mechanism, although it is so far limited to the telecoms sector, where a system has been in place since the early 2000s. The Ordinance provides for a prosecutorial system in which the independent Hong Kong Competition Commission (HKCC), headed by Commissioners, investigates and brings cases to the Competition Tribunal.

When the government floated the idea of a cross-sector competition regime in 1997, SMEs were among the most vocal opponent of the project. The Ordinance, as finally adopted now, reflects some of the concerns that were voiced by SMEs. For instance, it contains *de minimis* provisions excluding certain practices from the scope of the law if these practices are conducted by SMEs. However, these exemptions, which are detailed later in this chapter, are limited in scope. Now that the HKCC has been appointed and staffed, several of the possible first enforcement actions that have been hinted by the new institutions may affect SMEs, including a possible crackdown on price-fixing among gold retailers and on bid-rigging in the construction and real estate maintenance sectors.

The first part of this chapter deals with the cases which formed part of the background to the adoption of the Competition Ordinance, with a particular attention to the HKSAR vs Chan Wai Yip case, in which stalls at a market were pre-allotted by the bidders. The second part offers a look at a possible regional trend that may be relevant to the Hong Kong situation: new competition authorities in Asia have apparently focused on SMEs and trade associations first, before turning to more complex cases involving bigger companies. The third part details the provisions of the Competition Ordinance and the Guidelines that are relevant to SMEs, and analyses these provisions in the context of the legislative debates that lead to the adoption of these rules. The fourth section discusses some possible developments for Hong Kong SMEs in relation to competition law, and pays particular attention to the efforts already undertaken by the HKCC to reach out to, and raise awareness among, SMEs and their representatives. Finally, it examines how the Competition Ordinance and the enforcement efforts that accompany it may potentially contribute towards a change of culture in the traditionally non-competitive economic environment of Hong Kong.

SMEs in Hong Kong Before the Advent of the Competition Ordinance

Hong Kong SMEs have long had a history of engaging in anti-competitive practices, including in bid-rigging, and was one of the reasons that lead to the ultimate introduction of a competition law for the HKSAR. Since bid-rigging practices are inherently anti-competitive, it has also been one of the reasons why SMEs are likely to be in the crosshairs of the HKCC.

Several bid-rigging matters involving SMEs were prosecuted before the introduction of the Ordinance, including some which went all the way to the Court of Final Appeals (CFA). In 2010, the CFA heard a bid-rigging case in which certain small stall owners were accused of prearranging the result of an auction for the allocation of stalls at a market by a lottery. The CFA ruled in HKSAR vs Chan Wai Yip (2010) that the defendants were not guilty of conspiracy to defraud. The court's reasoning starts from the definition of conspiracy to defraud, which requires dishonesty. Because agreements among bidders are legal, the court said, they cannot be "dishonest" for the purpose of the common law offence of conspiracy to defraud. SMEs who pre-allotted the stalls prior to the auction organized by the Food and Environment Health Department (FEHD) were charged with conspiracy to defraud, instead of the more obvious offence under Section 7 of the Prevention of Bribery Ordinance (POBO Section 7). Under POBO Section 7, a person who offers an advantage to another person in exchange for refraining from bidding at a public auction commits an offence. The fact that the prosecution did not rely on POBO Section 7 to bring charges against the defendants, but instead chose the more complicated route of the common law offence of conspiracy to defraud, reflected the inexperience of the Department of Justice in dealing with cases of bid-rigging. Several troubling elements emerged from the case. First, the FEHD could not possibly have ignored the fact that the stalls had been secretly pre-allotted by the auction participants: all the stalls attracted only one bidder and stalls were knocked down at the 75 per cent of the reserve price.

Sir Antony Mason NJP, writing for the court, considered that the agreement to pre-allot the food stalls among bidders must have been obvious to the FEHD officer-in-charge of the auction. The judge cited this as evidence of the lack of dishonesty of the auction participants, considering that the auction rules did not bind the government into accepting the offers and entering into a contract (Chan Wai Yip 2010, p. 852).

The judgment's reference to the rules of the auction is particularly illustrative of the teleological approach taken by the court, and may indicate that the court was looking for a way to restrict judicial remedies against bid-riggers. Indeed the same rules, containing a provision specifically referring to the text of POBO Section 7 which could have been used against the defendants, had been considered irrelevant by the court since the rules were not read to the bidders by the officer-in-charge of the auction. Finally, among the many issues that arise from the Chan Wai Yip case, the most favourable to bid-riggers was certainly that the court found the agreement to be legal, even though it was actionable under POBO Section 7 (in Hong Kong) and under competition rules (in the United Kingdom, where all of the authorities cited by the court have been ruled). In the court's reasoning, an agreement to rig a public tender where participants merely promised each other to not bid in a specific auction, in exchange for the same promise, was legal. The court's mistake lay in considering that these two promises "cancel out each other" (Chan Wai Yip 2010, p. 853), while on the contrary they accumulate. Government services may only protect themselves against this practice by refusing to sign a contract with the winner of the auction. Sadly for the public of Hong Kong, the ineptitude of government to prevent bid-rigging also limited the judicial remedies against such practices.

This was not the only case involving SMEs that fuelled the debate over the need for substantial competition legislation in Hong Kong. Although this was the only one that went all the way to the CFA, in the years that preceded the drafting of the Competition Ordinance, three other events involving SMEs also illustrated the need for a competition regulator. Simultaneous and coordinated price increases were publicly announced in the noodle manufacturing market in April 2004, in laundry shops (November 2004), and in the market for driving lessons (April 2005). In all these cases, the lack of a competition law left the government powerless. It could only send the perpetrators a copy of the competition guidelines which had been drafted shortly before, effectively confirming to SMEs and their trade associations that price-fixing was not yet unlawful (Ho 2005).

All these cases and incidents created a momentum for competition law reform in Hong Kong, and indicated the central role of SMEs in the debate over the design and the implementation of such a statute.

Enforcement Against Smaller Players as a Training Ground for Young Competition Authorities

The need for a cross-sector competition regime in Hong Kong was first hinted at in 1997, when a Competition Policy Advisory Group (a toothless mockery of competition authority) was appointed by the Chief Executive and placed under the supervision of the Financial Secretary. From there, it took nearly twenty years to draft, pass, and enact a competition law.

Part of the reason why it took such an extended period of time for Hong Kong to enter the large group of competition-enforcing jurisdictions was the opposition to the project by small firms and their representative organizations. Local small enterprises complained that they were at risk of being targeted unfairly by the law, that their business model would be threatened, that competition law was not needed in Hong Kong, and that they should be exempt from the new ordinance all-together (FHKI 2007). These claims may appear irrational to the competition professional used to enforcement headlines against Google, Gazprom, and other behemoths of the European or U.S. economies. Yet the fears about the impact of a competition regime were not completely unfounded. Part of the reason why the HKCC, appointed in 2013 and which began enforcing competition rules in mid-2015, can be seen as a threat against SMEs are tied to the Singaporean and Malaysian competition authorities' tendency to focus on small businesses. The Competition Commission of Singapore (CCS), a relatively recent institution, had already been very active against SMEs. In its defence, it had also issued infringement decisions against big businesses, but a look at the enforcement priorities and patterns of the CCS suggested that the regulator built its skill set and the knowledge it needed to address more serious anti-competitive conducts and agreements by first focusing on SMEs and trade associations. One of the first decisions of the CCS concerned bid-rigging in pest-control and termite treatment contracts (CCS 2008). This was followed by a case in the bus operators sector, in which bus tickets between Singapore and Malaysia were fixed among sixteen companies and the Express Bus Agencies Association (CCS 2009). The following year, the CCS issued decisions against fifteen bid-riggers in the electrical works sector, including a high number of SMEs (CCS 2010). Also in 2010, the CCS issued its Guidelines for Medical Fees, a non-binding document that nevertheless had an impact on individual medical practitioners. In 2011, motor traders and car-part resellers were fined a total of S$179,000[1] for price-fixing at public auctions, and eleven modelling agencies were fined for fixing the rate of modelling services (CCS 2011).

The list of enforcement actions against SMEs and trade associations goes on, although a clear trend emerges from the analysis of enforcement patterns at the CCS: SMEs have provided the CCS with a tremendous training ground in terms of skills and knowledge, and these skills have recently been put to use by the CCS to enforce competition rules against more serious conducts and actors. In 2014, the CCS cracked down on an international ball-bearing manufacturers cartel (S$9 million) and very recently against the freight-forwarders cartel (S$7 million). To someone conscious of the cultural and economic proximity between Singapore and Hong Kong (both small Asian economies oriented towards trade and transitioning from entrepôt trade to a service-based economy), Singapore looks like a possible example for the Hong Kong Competition Commission. SMEs and their trade associations have proven to be low-hanging fruits for competition authorities in Singapore and Malaysia: they have weak compliance mechanisms and a very low understanding and knowledge of rules and regulations. As such, Hong Kong SMEs might be presumed to be the first obvious target for the young HKCC.

In Malaysia, an even younger competition authority also distinguished itself by its early focus on SMEs. In 2012, the Malaysia

Competition Commission (MyCC) issued its first-ever enforcement decision against a small business group, the Cameron Highlands Floriculturist Association (MyCC 2012). However, the MyCC attempted to settle the case and to obtain commitments from the trade association, acknowledging that it was more interested in changing behaviours than in a crackdown on SMEs. More recently, MyCC settled with shipping companies in an alleged abuse of dominance case, in which the two targeted companies agreed to modify their customer contracts to remove any exclusivity clause (MyCC 2014).

The Competition Ordinance and SMEs: A Programmed Conflict

Given the enforcement history in other Southeast Asian economies, it is perhaps not surprising that Hong Kong's small business sector was among the most virulent opponents to the Competition Ordinance. Some of these fears, though, proved to be ultimately unfounded. For example, one of the principal arguments brought by the Hong Kong Federation of Industries in its 2007 submission to government was that SMEs would be unfairly targeted by the new law. It was suggested that the Ordinance would be utilized by big businesses, eager to seize this new opportunity to crush SMEs under enormous litigation costs (FHKI 2007). A few years later, when the Ordinance was finally passed in 2012, the right of private action had been excluded from the law and SMEs appeared less likely to be targeted by major industry players.

While SMEs advocated for a complete exemption under the new regime, legislators instead devised a partial exemption from competition rules. Among all the possibilities studied, the legislature settled for the proposal formulated by Professor Lin and Professor Chen in their government-funded review of competition policy in Hong Kong (Lin and Chen 2008). As a result, under Schedule 1 Section 5 of the Ordinance, agreements of "lesser significance" are excluded from the rule prohibiting anti-competitive agreements if they do not constitute serious anti-competitive conduct such as price fixing. These include agreements and concerted practices between firms whose combined turnover is less than HK$200 million.[2] For abuses of substantial market power, the "lesser significance" turnover threshold is HK$40 million.

Two lessons emerge from an analysis of these rules. Firstly, the purely turnover-oriented rule is unusual by international standards. In comparison, the notice issued by the European Commission (EC) on *de minimis* agreements (agreements of such a small importance that they are excluded from competition rules) is strictly focused on endogenous conditions to determine if an agreement between undertakings should be exempted. The EC takes into account the market share of the undertakings: agreements between companies amounting to less than 10 per cent of market share (15 per cent if the companies are not active on the same markets) are considered harmless (EC 2001). Additional elements, such as the structure of the market and the existence and effect of agreements between third parties, help the EC in determining if SMEs should be shielded from competition rules. It should be noted here that the definition of *de minimis* agreements by the EC has been complicated by the extensive debate over market definition (Kaplow 2010). The Hong Kong approach to agreements of lesser importance (i.e. the adoption of a turnover threshold), seems in part to aim at avoiding these complex and consuming debates. In terms of compliance cost, and predictability, the Hong Kong approach presents a clear advantage for SMEs. However, while the notion of market is irrelevant to the determination of the *de minimis* thresholds, the Guidelines provide that the turnover will take into account the total gross revenues, obtained both within and outside Hong Kong (Competition Authorities 2015, p. 58). Overall, the European *de minimis* doctrine and practice demonstrates a high level of flexibility, and decision-making based on a maximum of elements, while eliminating irrelevant factors. In light of the European example, the combined turnover of the undertakings, retained as the sole factor in the Competition Ordinance, would certainly be considered irrelevant.

The Guidelines published by the HKCC and the Communications Authority in July 2015 offer very little additional provisions concerning SMEs, although they do assert that vertical agreements between small and medium sized enterprises "would rarely be capable of harming competition".

The second lesson is that these relatively clear thresholds would allow for most of the SME cases which preceded the passage of the Ordinance to fall under the jurisdiction of the new law because they would constitute serious anti-competitive conduct. The Chan Wai Yip case, for example, would have clearly been caught under the Ordinance.

What Future for SMEs in a Competitive Hong Kong?

The HKCC has signalled that it may focus some of its time and resources on SMEs, despite having only been appointed in May 2013 and staffed for less than one year at the time of writing.

The HKCC's website clearly shows an interest in getting SMEs to understand and comply with the Ordinance. For example, out of the six "seminars & workshops" organized by the HKCC between June and December 2014, four were training seminars for SMEs. One of the two files published on the HKCC website's "resources" section is a thirty-seven-slide presentation to SMEs. More recently, the HKCC has published a brochure for trade associations in June 2015, which focuses on practices relating to information exchanges and price recommendations.

Two recent events reinforce the perception that the HKCC will turn its attention to SMEs. The first one concerns price-fixing in the gold retail and chicken markets, a practice that was revealed in reports by unions and trade associations of these two sectors shortly after the HKCC started hiring senior executives. The newly recruited enforcers immediately reacted in a series of interviews and media comments, making clear that price-fixing by trade associations would be one of the first priorities of the HKCC (Nip 2014a, 2014b). In this exchange of statements in the press, the gold retailers expressed their fear that "small companies will be forced out of business if the competition law bans the current system in which two trade associations set a daily price across the industry" (Nip 2014b). Thomas Cheng, a former competition lawyer and member of the HKCC, publicly replied by arguing that the end of the current practice of daily price-fixing among gold retailers would not mean that small businesses would be priced out of the market, since big businesses cannot price below costs under the Ordinance (Nip 2014b). Following the publication of their practices and the realization that this would qualify as price-fixing, the two gold trade associations approached the HKCC to apply for an exemption. However, as the Ordinance had not yet been enacted, the agency was not able to assess an application for exemption (Nip 2014a).

In a second series of events, another issue heralded a possible future priority for the HKCC. Following a city-wide mandatory renovation scheme voted in 2011, more than 3,200 buildings began to be renovated in Hong Kong. It became apparent as renovation work and contracts increased in number that bid-rigging in the construction and building maintenance industry was rampant, driving the costs of renovation to unreasonable highs (SCMP Editorial 2014). Shortly after the beginning of a public outcry over the contractors' anti-competitive practices, the Property Owners' Alliance Against Bid Rigging was formed. In the summer of 2014, the Alliance staged a demonstration in front of the HKCC and was received by the Commission. This incident paints a new picture of the competition landscape of Hong Kong: next to SMEs, big businesses, and the regulators, civil society invited itself and made clear that it was a force to count with. Highlighting the seriousness of the issue, several members of the Property Owners' Alliance Against Bid Rigging received death threats following the media coverage of their actions (Robertson and Yau 2014).

These two separate series of events, combined with the HKCC's efforts to engage early on with SMEs, point to a possible focus on SMEs and trade associations on the part of the HKCC. The freshly staffed Hong Kong regulator needs public support, which it may well find in addressing the issues that are perceived as harmful to the public, to consumers, to the economy, and at the same time are obvious (e.g. gold retailers) or perceived as notorious (e.g. building management bid-rigging).

Concluding Remarks: Choices and Cultural Changes

This chapter has attempted to describe and analyse the picture of a possible focus on SMEs and trade associations by the HKCC. The background evolution of competition policy in Hong Kong, broader regional trends in enforcement by new agencies in Asia, the limited exemptions provided for SMEs in the Ordinance and its Guidelines, and finally the first movements of the HKCC, all indicate that the Commission may target SMEs in order to build the skills and the public support it needs to make the implementation of the Ordinance a success in Hong Kong.

It is also worth noting that the HKCC does not have many alternative targets to SMEs. In its initial years of enforcement, it may prove too challenging for the HKCC to establish a track record of success going after the large conglomerates of Hong Kong. Furthermore, commentators have criticized the composition of the HKCC, as the business community is heavily represented among the Commissioners. In the utilities section, for instance, the two electricity providers do not compete against each other, since the Hong Kong government granted each of them the right to provide electricity on an exclusive part of the territory, along with a contractually guaranteed rate of return (Consumer Council 2014).

Finally, the passing of the Competition Ordinance, and the appointment and staffing of the HKCC, are just the first steps of a major cultural change needed in Hong Kong's business practices. This evolution will only occur if the enforcement of competition law is a success, and if it applies across the board. In a city where 98 per cent of businesses are SMEs, it does not seem possible for SMEs to escape this change, although they will certainly attempt to resist it.

NOTES

1. At the time of writing, S$1 = US$0.71.
2. At the time of writing, HK$1 = US$0.13.

REFERENCES

Cheng, Thomas. "Competition Law Enforcement in the Television Broadcasting Sector in Hong Kong: Past Cases and Recent Controversies". In *World Competition, Law and Economics Review*, edited by José Rivas (The Netherlands: Kluwer Law International, 2010).

Competition Authorities: Hong Kong Competition Commission and Hong Kong Communications Authority. *Guideline on the First Conduct Rule*, July 2015.

Competition Commission of Singapore (CCS). "Collusive Tendering (Bid-rigging) for Termite Treatment/Control Services by Certain Pest Control Operators in Singapore". Case number CCS 600/008/06, 9 January 2008.

————. "Price Fixing of Coach Bus Services for Travelling Between Singapore and Destinations in Malaysia from 2006 to 2008". Case number CCS 500/003/08, 3 November 2009.

————. "Collusive Tendering (Bid-rigging) in Electrical and Building Works". Case number CCS 500/001/09, 4 July 2010.

————. "Price-fixing in Modelling Services". Case number 500/002/09, 23 November 2011.

Consumer Council. "Searching for New Directions: A Study of the Hong Kong Electricity Market", December 2014. Available at <http://www.legco.gov. hk/yr14-15/english/panels/edev/papers/edev20141216cb4-231-2-e.pdf>.

European Commission (EC). "Commission Notice on Agreements of Minor Importance Which Do Not Appreciably Restrict Competition under Article 81(1) if the Treaty Establishing the European Community (de minimis)". 2001/C368/07, 2001, Article 7.

Federation of Hong Kong Industries (FHKI). "Public Consultation on the Way Forward for Competition Policy in Hong Kong: Submission to the Hong Kong Economic Development and Labour Bureau", 2007.

HKSAR v. Chan Wai Yip (2010) 13 HKCFAR.

Ho, John D. "From Free Port to Competition: Is Asia's World City Playing Catch-up?". In *The Hong Kong Special Administrative Region in Its First Decade*, edited by Joseph Y.S. Cheng. Hong Kong: City University of Hong Kong Press, 2005.

Kaplow, Louis. "Why (Ever) Define Markets?". *Harvard Law Review* 124 (2010): 443–47.

Lin, Ping and Edward K.Y. Chen. *Fair Competition under Laissez-Faireism: Policy Options for Hong Kong*. Hong Kong: Lingnan University of Hong Kong, 2008.

Malaysia Competition Commission (MyCC). "Decision on an Infringement by the Competition Commission against the Cameron Highland Floriculturist Association". Case number: MyCC/0003/2012(ACA), 6 December 2012.

————. "MyCC Accepts Undertakings from Logistics Providers". News Release, 7 October 2014.

Nip, Amy. "Watchdog Set Sights on Price-fixing". *South China Morning Post*, 24 May 2014a.

————. "Gold Traders Concerned Competition Could Force Small Firms to Close". *South China Morning Post*, 28 April 2014b.

Robertson, Benjamin and Elaine Yau. "Beating the Bid-riggers: Angry Homeowners Use Competition Law to Battle Price-fixing". *South China Morning Post*, 15 September 2014.

SCMP Editorial. "Flat Owners Responsible for Management Reform". *South China Morning Post*, 17 November 2014.

Sung, Timmy. "Watchdog Urged to Investigate Maintenance Bid-rigging". *South China Morning Post*, 28 August 2014.

Trade and Industry Council. "A Report on Support Measures for SMEs", 2 December 2014.

Tsang, Emily. "Anti-graft Campaigners Receive Death Threats After Standing-up Against Bid Rigging". *South China Morning Post*, 1 June 2014.

21

THE REGULATION OF TELEVISION PROGRAMME PRODUCTION CONTRACTS UNDER JAPAN'S SUBCONTRACT ACT

Iwakazu Takahashi

Small and medium-sized enterprises (SMEs) make up more than three-quarters of Japan's corporate landscape. Fostering these small and medium-sized businesses is one of the most important goals of Japan's Antimonopoly Act (AMA). The Act Against Delay in Payment of Subcontract Proceeds, etc. to Subcontractors (The Subcontract Act of 1956) was enacted as a complement to the AMA to enable Japan's Fair Trade Commission to regulate the abuse of superior bargaining positions. In this chapter, the broadcasting industry is used as a case study of how the Subcontract Act can affect SMEs in a particular industry.

Introduction

Japan's Antimonopoly Act (AMA), introduced in 1947, has been used as a means of regulating the transactions between big corporations and small and medium-sized enterprises (SMEs) in many industrial fields.

The purpose of the Act is to institute a framework for competitive behaviour in which SMEs are not merely the object of government protection, but are also encouraged to acquire competitive power by their own efforts.

SMEs make up more than three-quarters of Japan's corporate landscape, and fostering these small and medium-sized businesses has been one of the most important parts of the AMA. The legislation prohibits "unfair trade practices" (Article 19), such as the abuse of a superior bargaining position, and is one of the most important provisions in the Act relevant to SMEs.

The Act Against Delay in Payment of Subcontract Proceeds, etc. to Subcontractors (also known as the Subcontract Act of 1956) is a statute that was enacted as a complement to the AMA, in order to enable immediate action by Japan Fair Trade Commission to regulate the abuse of superior bargaining position. The most important point of this legislation is a requirement that an enterprise has to immediately deliver to its subcontractor a written statement setting forth key parts of the contractual arrangements that have been agreed upon. This can include items such as the nature and contents of work to be performed, the amount to be paid, the date of payment, and the method of payment. This Act also prohibits certain conducts, such as delays in payment (without a valid reason) by main subcontracting entrepreneurs.

The Subcontract Act applies to: (1) manufacturing contracts (e.g. machine parts manufacturing, metal mould production); (2) repair contracts; (3) information-based product creation contracts; and (4) service contracts (e.g. transportation services, building maintenance services).

The third category — for "information-based product creation contracts" — covers broadcasting programme production contracts for television programme production; it also covers software development and commercial messages for television productions. Television stations, which not only broadcast television programmes, but also produce television programmes by themselves, contract out two-thirds of the production to subcontractors.

Whilst most chapters of this book have examined the role of principal competition laws on SMEs, it is also worth noting that subsidiary laws like the Subcontract Act can also affect competitive dynamics and relationships between big and small firms. So what impact does this law have on the relationship between larger enterprises and their subcontractors?

The Japanese Television Broadcasting Industry

There are two kinds of television stations in Japan. One group consists of public broadcasting stations, carried out by the NHK, a quasi-state-run broadcasting body. There are also a large number of private broadcasting stations. NHK started its television broadcasts in 1953, whilst Japan's first private broadcasting station, Nippon Television, also started its services in the same year. Today, there are 127 private television stations in operation around the country.

Television stations in Japan both develop and produce movies and have production staff such as producers and directors. A detailed history of the industry can be found in the work of Shigemura (2010).

When the broadcasting industry was introduced in Japan, there were five major film production companies and they were critical of television. They called it "electric picture-story show". These film companies concluded an agreement to prohibit their actors from television appearances and by contract, movie actors were only permitted to appear in their employers' films. For this reason, television stations were compelled to create their own production organizations and to hire actors from fields other than moviemaking. But this proved to be beneficial for the growth of television stations. Supported by theatre actors and by the people who left the movie industry because of their dissatisfaction with the state of moviemaking at that time, these people were assigned to train new production personnel and actors (Shigemura 2010).

Japan's television broadcasting industry, during the last sixty years, has evolved into a structure where television programme production and television broadcasting are both integrated into the television station. This contrasts with many countries, where the broadcasting station and programme production companies are separate entities. In Western countries, film production companies that possessed production capabilities did not change its policy toward television stations (Shigemura 2010).

Given this situation, only a small number of programme production companies can maintain their independence against television stations. Most programme production companies are in a weak position in relation to television stations. This problem is related to the ownership of copyrights and other rights regarding programme marketing.

The exception is animation. In the past, animation was not an attractive avenue for advertisement sales because its main target audience was children. For this reason, the production scheme for animation very often consisted of the television station paying only for broadcast rights and the production costs were covered not only by the film company but also by advertising agencies and toy manufacturers. Television stations did not hold the copyright to animations created under contract with film companies and the film companies actively marketed these animation productions. This resulted in Japanese animation becoming developed in the global market (Shigemura 2010).

Amongst the 127 private television stations, five are based in Tokyo and are called "Network Key Stations". The television stations in Osaka and Nagoya are called "Quasi Key Stations", because these television stations have the capability to produce television programmes in specific genres such as comedy in Osaka. Other television stations are called "Local TV Stations". Most of them produce some local programmes which are only broadcast in the local area (see Figure 21.1).

Power is highly centralized in Japan. Both central government ministries and agencies, as well as the head offices of large companies, are all located in Tokyo. This means that most television programme sponsors are in Tokyo; so too are major actors, actresses, and musicians. Because of these factors, only five key television stations in Tokyo have the capability to produce television programmes. Tokyo's "Network Key Stations" constitute its television broadcast network over almost every region in Japan and supply almost every kind of programme.

Tokyo's "Network Key Stations" and "Local TV Stations" enter into contracts on "TV Program Organization" and "TV News Organization". In these arrangements, local television stations of each Tokyo key station network must broadcast the same programme produced by a network key station at the same time, such as the so-called "golden time", running from 6 p.m. to 10 p.m. every evening. The broadcasting of another programme at this time by local stations is strictly restricted by the contract. In the case of television news organization contracts, local television stations of each Tokyo key station network are prohibited from supplying the local news it has produced to another key broadcast Tokyo station network.

FIGURE 21.1
Major Terrestrial Television News Networks

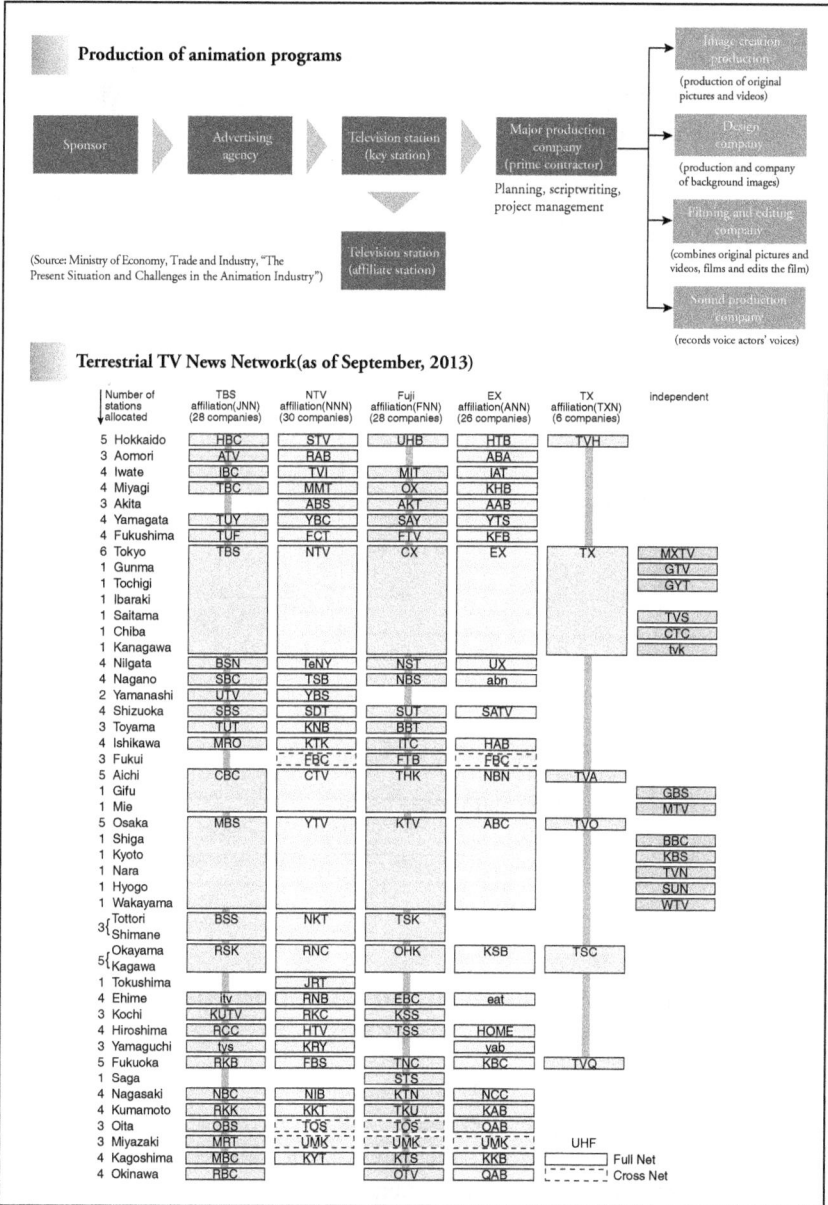

Production of animation programs

Sponsor ▶ Advertising agency ▶ Television station (key station) ▶ Major production company (prime contractor)

Planning, scriptwriting, project management

Television station (affiliate station)

(Source: Ministry of Economy, Trade and Industry, "The Present Situation and Challenges in the Animation Industry")

→ Image creation production (production of original pictures and videos)
→ Design company (production and company of background images)
→ Filming and editing company (combines original pictures and videos, films and edits the film)
→ Sound production company (records voice actors' voices)

Terrestrial TV News Network (as of September, 2013)

Number of stations allocated	TBS affiliation(JNN) (28 companies)	NTV affiliation(NNN) (30 companies)	Fuji affiliation(FNN) (28 companies)	EX affiliation(ANN) (26 companies)	TX affiliation(TXN) (6 companies)	independent
5 Hokkaido	HBC	STV	UHB	HTB	TVH	
3 Aomori	ATV	RAB		ABA		
4 Iwate	IBC	TVI	MIT	IAT		
4 Miyagi	TBC	MMT	OX	KHB		
3 Akita		ABS	AKT	AAB		
4 Yamagata	TUY	YBC	SAY	YTS		
4 Fukushima	TUF	FCT	FTV	KFB		
6 Tokyo	TBS	NTV	CX	EX	TX	MXTV
1 Gunma						GTV
1 Tochigi						GYT
1 Ibaraki						
1 Saitama						TVS
1 Chiba						CTC
1 Kanagawa						tvk
4 Niigata	BSN	TeNY	NST	UX		
4 Nagano	SBC	TSB	NBS	abn		
2 Yamanashi	UTV	YBS				
4 Shizuoka	SBS	SDT	SUT	SATV		
3 Toyama	TUT	KNB	BBT			
4 Ishikawa	MRO	KTK	ITC	HAB		
3 Fukui		FBC	FTB	FBC		
5 Aichi	CBC	CTV	THK	NBN	TVA	
1 Gifu						GBS
1 Mie						MTV
5 Osaka	MBS	YTV	KTV	ABC	TVO	
1 Shiga						BBC
1 Kyoto						KBS
1 Nara						TVN
1 Hyogo						SUN
1 Wakayama						WTV
3 { Tottori / Shimane	BSS	NKT	TSK			
5 { Okayama / Kagawa	RSK	RNC	OHK	KSB	TSC	
1 Tokushima		JRT				
4 Ehime	itv	RNB	EBC	eat		
3 Kochi	KUTV	RKC	KSS			
4 Hiroshima	RCC	HTV	TSS	HOME		
3 Yamaguchi	tys	KRY		yab		
5 Fukuoka	RKB	FBS	TNC	KBC	TVQ	
1 Saga			STS			
4 Nagasaki	NBC	NIB	KTN	NCC		
4 Kumamoto	RKK	KKT	TKU	KAB		
3 Oita	OBS	TOS	TOS	OAB		
3 Miyazaki	MRT	UMK	UMK	UMK	UHF	
4 Kagoshima	MBC	KYT	KTS	KKB		
4 Okinawa	RBC		OTV	QAB		

Full Net
Cross Net

Contract of Television Programmes Production

There are two ways of producing television programmes. One is for television stations to produce their own material; the other is by television stations placing an order for television programmes (such as drama, pop song shows, and documentary programmes) with other programme producing companies. In many cases, the programme producing companies (which are called "parent company") consign their programme production to other production companies called "subcontractors" (see Figure 21.2).

FIGURE 21.2
Outsourcing Contracts in Television Programme Production

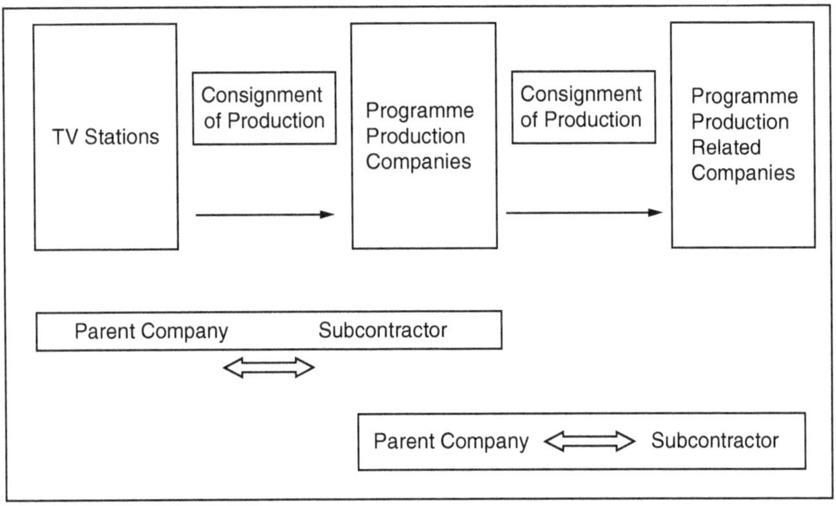

The Relationship Between Broadcasting Programme Production and the Subcontract Act

The purpose of the Subcontract Act is to ensure that transactions between main subcontracting entrepreneurs and subcontractors are fair and, at the same time, protect the interests of subcontractors, thereby contributing to the sound development of the national economy.

The Subcontract Act has, in response to a trend towards a service-centred and post-heavy industry economy, been amended in 2003 (effective from April 2004) so as to additionally target the commission of "information-based product creation". This includes computer software and "TV programmes", as well as of the provision of services including "transportation, building maintenance, etc." (JFTC 1997). The Subcontract Act is applied to a subcontract transaction if the transaction fulfils a number of specific conditions, as shown in Figure 21.3.

A key point of this Act is that a main firm ("parent enterprise") has to immediately deliver to the subcontractor a written statement setting forth: (1) the contents of work of the contract; (2) the sales amount; (3) the date of payment; and (4) the method of payment (Article 3). The parent enterprise is also obliged to prepare and preserve documents or electromagnetic records, to fix the date of payment

FIGURE 21.3
Application of the Subcontract Act

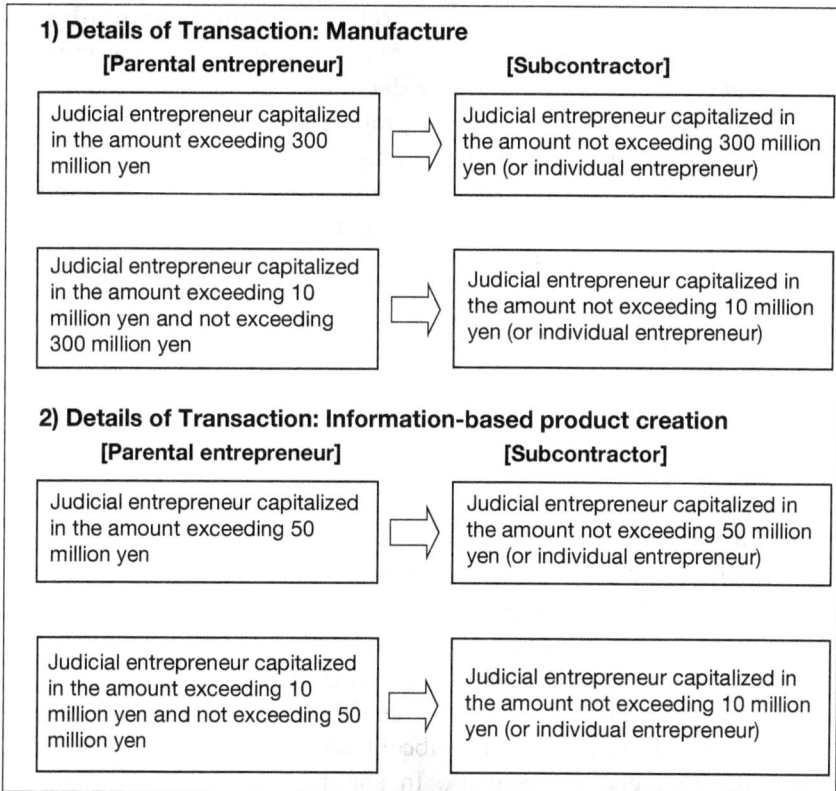

1) Details of Transaction: Manufacture

[Parental entrepreneur]		[Subcontractor]
Judicial entrepreneur capitalized in the amount exceeding 300 million yen	⇒	Judicial entrepreneur capitalized in the amount not exceeding 300 million yen (or individual entrepreneur)
Judicial entrepreneur capitalized in the amount exceeding 10 million yen and not exceeding 300 million yen	⇒	Judicial entrepreneur capitalized in the amount not exceeding 10 million yen (or individual entrepreneur)

2) Details of Transaction: Information-based product creation

[Parental entrepreneur]		[Subcontractor]
Judicial entrepreneur capitalized in the amount exceeding 50 million yen	⇒	Judicial entrepreneur capitalized in the amount not exceeding 50 million yen (or individual entrepreneur)
Judicial entrepreneur capitalized in the amount exceeding 10 million yen and not exceeding 50 million yen	⇒	Judicial entrepreneur capitalized in the amount not exceeding 10 million yen (or individual entrepreneur)

of subcontract proceeds within sixty days, and to pay the interest for any delayed payments longer than sixty days (this is spelt out in Articles 5, 2-2, and 4-2).

The Subcontract Act also prohibits certain conduct by the parent enterprise. These include (unless there is a valid reason): (1) the refusal to accept work from a subcontractor; (2) the failure to make payment after the due date of payment; (3) reducing the amount of subcontract proceeds; (4) the power of a subcontractor to take back the goods after receiving them from the said subcontractor; (5) unjustly fixing a conspicuously lower amount of subcontract proceeds than the price ordinarily paid for the same or similar content of work; (6) coercing the subcontractor to purchase designated goods or to use designated services; (7) causing a subcontractor to provide cash, services, or other economic gains for oneself; (8) causing a subcontractor to effect changes to the work, or to re-work after the receipt of the work (Takahashi 1994).

These conditions also arise in relation to information-based product creation contracts. Information-based product means; (1) computer programmes (e.g. video game software, accounting software, household appliance-control programme, customer-management system); (2) artefacts composed of images, voice, and other acoustics such as movies, broadcasting programmes, etc. (e.g. television programmes, television advertisements, radio programmes, movies, animations); and (3) artefacts composed of characters, figures, signs, any combination thereof, or the combination thereof with colour (e.g. design drawing, poster design, product/container design, consulting report, magazine advertisement).

When television stations, as a programme producer, contracts out two-thirds of that production to subcontractors, there is a multi-layered transaction structure between main subcontracting entrepreneurs and subcontractors. In 40 per cent of cases for such transactions, there was a written contract between the television stations and subcontractors. The remaining 60 per cent of subcontracted production was by way of an oral contract in the past.

In the past, in some cases, subcontractors' payments were reduced by more than 10 per cent because of poor management by the main subcontractors. Delays in payment could be of the order of 20 per cent, with about 60 per cent of subcontractors being required to redo work after delivery of the work. In about 10 per cent of cases, the subcontractor was forced to cover additional costs (JFTC 2004). Today, this situation has improved, but to some extent, the same conditions remain. The cases which will violate the subcontract act are as follows:

Placing orders and delivery of a written statement. In a television programme production contract, the parent enterprise has to immediately deliver to the subcontractor a written statement setting forth: (1) the contents of work of the contract; (2) the amount of subcontract proceeds; (3) the date of payment; and (4) the method of payment. This requirement is spelt out in Article 3 of the Subcontract Act. Sometimes, a written statement is not delivered on the day of order, and instead arrives much later. There are still oral contracts in some cases, in which the date of payment and the method of payment are not clear. Although payment is required within sixty days of receiving the television programme, according to the Subcontract Act, there is a custom where the payment date is calculated from the broadcast day or from the day the television station receives a bill, which is often much longer. These customs, which violate the Subcontract Act, are no longer allowed.

The ownership of copyright. It also seems that sometimes, there is a custom whereby, if a television station covers the whole budget to produce a television programme, the television station holds the total copyright of the programme. But the Copyright Act stipulates that copyright should belong to the programme production company (a subcontractor), without consideration as to who covered the cost of producing the programme. In this case, the television station may violate the Subcontract Act because of its "Beating down Prices (by using superior bargaining power of television station)" (Art. 4, para. 1, item 5). It seems that sometimes, there is a custom by which the material content gained in the process of producing the final television programme belongs to the television station. This contract clause may violate the Subcontract Act because it involves "[r]equesting a subcontractor to provide unjust economical benefits (by using superior bargaining power of TV station)" (Art. 4, para. 2, item 3).

Other conduct. There are also other behaviours which may violate the Subcontract Act in the transactions between the television station and the programme production companies, or between programme production companies and programme production-related companies.

Examples include "[r]efusing to receive TV programme" in circumstances where no reason is given to the subcontractor; unjustly coercing the subcontractor into reworking the contents of the product delivered; reducing the amount of the subcontractor's proceeds; and coercing the subcontractor into purchasing goods or using services.

The AMA and Broadcasting Programme Production

With reference to the relationship between the Subcontract Act and the AMA, the Subcontract Act, Article 8 provides that, in the case that the Japan Fair Trade Commission (JFTC) has rendered a recommendation to the main subcontracting entrepreneur, to the extent that the entrepreneur has complied with the recommendation, Article 20 of the AMA (elimination measures against unfair trade practices) shall not apply to the act of that entrepreneur. If the main subcontracting entrepreneur does not take the measures to protect the interests of the subcontractor against the recommendation, JFTC may order the entrepreneur to cease and desist from the said act (AMA Art. 20, para. 1). The main subcontracting entrepreneur can make a request for a hearing for rescission or modification of the order and the Tokyo district court shall commence hearing procedures regarding the order (AMA Art. 85).

Conclusion

Most television programme production companies and television programme production-related companies are SMEs in Japan. Along with the recognition of the importance of producing television programmes, it is becoming more important to ensure that the transactions between television stations and programme production companies are fair and free. The Subcontract Act (amended in 2003) covers transactions related to information-based product creation contract including broadcasting programmes which have become more important in Japan.

In the transactions between television stations and television programme production companies, the television stations need to pay more attention to the Subcontract Act and the AMA. To do so, it is important that the character of the programme to be ordered (for a "TV station initiated programme" or a "TV programme production company initiated programme") be made very clear. There is also a need for television stations to explain to television programme production companies the order in greater detail, including the ownership of copyright.

REFERENCES

Japan Commercial Broadcasting Association. "The Commercial Broadcasting Industry in Japan", p. 7.

Japan Fair Trade Commission (JFTC). "Kigyo Torihiki Kenkyukai Hokokusho" [Report of the Research Group on Corporation Transaction], 1997, p. 3 [Only in Japanese].

————. "Terebi-bangumi Seisaku-gyo niokeru Shitauke-torihiki no Jittai" [Report on the Situation of Subcontract Transaction in Broadcasting Programme Production Industry], 2004. Available at <http://www.soumu.go.jp/main_content/000030633.pdf> [Only in Japanese].

Shigemura, Hajime. "The Structural Reasons for Japanese Reluctance Toward Overseas Activity and International Exchange in Drama Production – Japan's Unique Broadcasting System and Its Development Process". 19th JAMCO (Japan Media Communication Center) Online International Symposium, 1–28 February 2010. Available at <http://www.jamco.or.jp/en/symposium/19/3/> [in English].

Takahashi, Iwakazu. "Seisan ni kakawaru Trohiki-kankou to Dokkinhou" [Business Practices in Production and Antimonopoly Law]. *Annual Report of Japan Academy of Economic Law*, no. 15 (1994): 17–36 [Only in Japanese]. This article shows the actual conditions of transaction in car manufacturing industry.

22

SMALL ENTERPRISES AND COMPETITION POLICY IN PACIFIC ISLAND COUNTRIES

Andrew F. Simpson and Brent Fisse

Competitive micro, small and medium enterprises (MSMEs) are crucial to private sector development in Pacific islands countries (PICs). MSMEs confront significant challenges, however, including pervasive state engagement in markets, high input costs, and difficulty in accessing legal remedies. Competition policy and law have an important role to play in enhancing business conditions for MSMEs in PICs. This chapter examines the setting in which competition policy and law operates in PICs and considers possible directions for their future development in the Pacific region. Conventional conduct prohibitions and penalties are likely to be necessary but not sufficient. Effective competition policy and law must be geared to the particular circumstances and needs of PICs, including the need to facilitate MSME entry to markets that have hitherto been closed to them. The policy and legal responses that suit the circumstances and needs of MSMEs in PICs may have wider applications in small developed economies or economies that are larger but still developing.

Introduction

The governments of most Pacific islands countries (PICs) have embraced private sector development as central to their strategies for economic development. Competitive markets are perceived as essential to such private sector development. Accordingly, the governments of several PICs are taking steps toward implementing competition policies or reviewing their regulatory institutions (ADB 2014*a*). Economic activity in most PICs is dominated by state-owned enterprises (SOEs) and a handful of multinationals or large privately-owned domestic enterprises. In several PICs, policymakers have been pursuing the corporatization and privatization of SOEs. Typically, there is little competition in the major infrastructure-based industries (telecommunications is an exception) but active competition, at least in urban areas, occurs among smaller scale businesses with lower capital requirements.

Policymakers in PICs, as in other developing economies, are therefore looking to micro, small and medium enterprises (MSMEs) as major drivers of the private sector development that is needed to generate economic growth, create jobs, and alleviate poverty (McIntyre 2001). MSMEs are pivotal to the emergence of competitive markets in PICs but face significant constraints on their ability to compete. While MSMEs in the Pacific bear the substantial weight of development expectations, they are poorly equipped to apprehend the implications of competition laws, obtain independent legal advice, enforce their rights, participate in the policy process, or otherwise advance their legal interests. Competition policies and laws must therefore be tailored and administered in ways that take particular account of the needs and constraints of MSMEs, if they are to have a positive effect on private sector development in small developing PIC economies.

The Pacific Business Environment

The discussion to follow generalizes the characteristics and needs of PICs. However, PICs differ widely and the competition policies and laws that are suitable for each are likely to differ in important respects. The PICs differ culturally (Polynesian, Melanesian, and Micronesian groups are regionally dispersed and overlap); constitutionally (e.g. constitutional monarchy, republics, and independent states); and in terms of their existing laws and institutions. They also differ from one another in their sizes, incomes, and stages of development, as Table 22.1 indicates.

TABLE 22.1
Key Indicators for ADB Pacific Developing Member Countries*

	Land Area (sq. km.)	Population (000s)	GDP	Official Dev. Assistance ($m)**	GNI/Cap. (2011 PPP $)	Adult Literacy (%)	Under-5 Mortality (per 1,000)	Human Dev. Index Rank
Cook Islands‡	237	21 (est.)	306 (2012)	N.A.	14,917	N.A.	7	N.A.
Fiji	18,270	881	3,855	91	7,214	N.A.	22	88
Kiribati	810	102	169	64	2,645	N.A.	60	133
The Marshall Islands	180	53	191	94	4,206	N.A.	38	N.A.
Federated States of Micronesia	700	104	316	143	3,662	N.A.	39	124
Nauru‡	21	10	121 (2012)	N.A.	12,577	N.A.	37	N.A.
Palau	460	21	247	35	12,823	N.A.	21	60
Papua New Guinea	452,860	7,321	15,413	656	2,453	62.4	63	157
Samoa	2,830	190	802	118	4,708	99	18	106
Solomon Islands	27,990	561	1,096	288	1,385	N.A.	31	157
Timor-Leste	14,870	1,133	1,270 (2012)	258	9,674	58.3	57	128
Tonga	720	105	466	80	5,316	99	13	100
Tuvalu	30	10	38	27	5,151	N.A.	30	N.A.
Vanuatu	12,190	253	828	91	2,652	83.2	18	131

Sources: *United Nations Development Program (2013); **World Bank, "Indicators Database" (2015); ‡United Nations, "UN Data" (2015).

Certain issues are common to all these island states, including the need to develop employment for young and growing populations; the need to reduce financial reliance on development assistance and remittances; and government's dominance in the domestic economy (Holden et al. 2004; ADB 2009; World Bank 2014).

Several PICs have taken steps to promote private sector development, notably by means of SOE reform, enhancing access to finance, promoting public-private partnerships and enacting commercial law reforms (ADB 2014*b*). Some PICs are now proposing to adopt or update competition legislation (ADB 2014*a*). Fiji and Papua New Guinea (PNG) were the first PICs to enact competition laws, in 1992 and 2002 respectively. To the extent that other PICs have competition safeguards, those typically are embedded within utilities legislation or consumer protection statutes and, in most PICs, are seldom or never enforced.

Small Enterprises, Competition, and Economic Development

The logic of legislating to protect the competitive process is compelling in economies seeking to increase the size and productivity of their private sector. Porter has emphasized that "a strong antitrust policy [...] is essential to the rate of upgrading in an economy", since active rivalry in domestic markets is associated with successful participation in international markets (Porter 1990, p. 663). Likewise, Stiglitz has observed that: "...strong competition policy is not just a luxury to be enjoyed by rich countries, but a real necessity for those striving to create democratic market economies" (Stiglitz 2001). The case appears strong, though unproven (Aghion and Griffith 2005), for ensuring that effective pro-competitive safeguards are in place to protect nascent competition from being stifled by anti-competitive mergers, abuse of market power, or cartel conduct (Qaqaya and Lipimile 2008; Levenstein and Suslow 2004).

Private sector competition is at a fragile stage of development in most PICs. While data is scarce, MSMEs appear to have a high rate of failure in PICs, as they do in many other developing economies. Further study of critical success/failure factors for MSMEs in PICs would be a valuable aid to policy development in the region. Nevertheless, some fundamental challenges to MSMEs' viability are apparent. They include administrative barriers, high input costs, lack of capital, and mistrust or lack of information among consumers.

Competition policy and law reform in PICs must focus on the removal or reduction of impediments to competition, including those created by the state. Generally, competition laws in developed economies focus on deterring deviations from a competitive norm. In PICs, however, a greater emphasis is needed on the removal of impediments to the emergence of competition. Such impediments include familiar "regulatory barriers" (such as statutory monopolies, licensing regimes, long-term concession arrangements, and over-reaching regulation). Unpredictability, delay and inefficiency in public administration are also significant impediments; they impose costs on firms and inhibit enterprises in progressing from the informal to the formal economy.

Secondly, MSMEs' production costs in PICs are directly affected by high prices for certain inputs (e.g. shipping, airfreight, electricity, fuel, and construction materials) for which supply is highly concentrated and competitive pressure may be slow to develop. An effective competition regime should reduce entry barriers; promote the liberalization of activities that are ancillary to core monopolies; facilitate access to key infrastructure facilities; and apply competitive market standards where rates or terms of supply are regulated.

Thirdly, MSMEs as well as consumers can benefit from improved consumer protection rules and enhanced consumer protection enforcement. In the absence of effective consumer protection, consumers tend to distrust products or product information and thereby reduce consumption, so that vendors sell less than they would otherwise (Muris 2002). For example, broadcasters in one PIC complained to the authors that consumers' distrust of claims made by vendors regarding their goods and services made it difficult for the broadcasters to sell advertising airtime. Consumer protection and competition safeguards should be seen as complementary and mutually reinforcing tools: effective consumer protection laws protect the ability of consumers to make the choices that drive competitive rivalry between suppliers (Nebbia 2012; Cseres 2005).

Locating Competition in Its Institutional, Social, and Cultural Setting

In developed Western economies, competition safeguards generally are premised on assumptions of a well-educated and well-informed business community; a well-resourced enforcement agency; efficient machinery for the administration of justice; and cultural values supportive of rivalry, profit maximization, and maximization of personal utility. These assumptions do not hold true in PICs to anywhere near the same degree. Broadly, the challenges to effective implementation of competition policy and laws in PICs reflect the constraints facing MSMEs and the constraints facing enforcement agencies.

Among the constraints limiting MSMEs' ability to rely on competition laws is the relative inaccessibility to them of legal services and institutions. This is most acute for microenterprises in rural areas. Many of the smallest MSMEs operate in the "informal" economy. In Papua New Guinea, for example, the informal sector consists largely of village-based agriculture, local trade stores, and fishermen. It supports an estimated 85 per cent of the population (OECD 2009, p. 149). In the informal economy compliance with business registration, regulatory and taxation obligations is low. Although informal enterprises are vulnerable to anti-competitive conduct, they are likely to be reluctant to seek a remedy, even if they are aware of their rights. MSMEs have very limited access to competition laws and the agency that enforces them, particularly if the laws are poorly communicated, the supporting rules or guidelines are very technical, or the agency is sparsely represented outside the national capital.

Competition policy and law can be effective only if businesspeople and members of the public are aware of them, understand their purposes, and are able to initiate enforcement action. It may seem trite to suggest that any new competition agency must devote resources to competition "advocacy", but the particular competition advocacy challenges faced in developing countries (Fels and Ng 2013), and the communications and information disadvantages under which MSMEs labour, make efforts by competition agencies in PICs to explain their role and rules to MSMEs especially important.

The ability of consumers, businesspeople, and agency staff to rely on and apply competition and consumer protection laws also depends on those laws being expressed in terms that can be readily understood.

Technically, complex legislation is also likely to make professional advice more costly to obtain for those medium-sized or large enterprises that can afford it, and to delay or obstruct enforcement action by the agency. Competition and consumer protection laws should be expressed in plain language and explained in straightforward guidelines. This is important particularly for consumers and MSMEs, who have little access to professional advisers. In contrast to the highly prescriptive language of some developed economies' competition statutes, the use of principles-based legislation needs to be considered in PICs. Principles-based legislation would rely less on finely detailed rules and more on straightforward statements of the objectives to be attained by the law (Ministry of Consumer Affairs 2010), supplemented by explanatory guidelines and worked examples issued by the competition agency. Explanatory guidelines and worked examples are important, given the need for practical guidance rather than high-level pronouncements. Competition law principles, such as the prohibition against agreements that would be likely to substantially lessen competition in a market, are vacuous unless the meaning of a "substantial" lessening of competition is clarified and illustrated (Leuner 2008).

Finally, it must be recognized that MSME business activity in PICs is socially embedded. Cultural values may even trump such fundamental economic assumptions as the profit motive. Curry (2005, p. 242) has made this point in his study of village businesses in Papua New Guinea:

> The social embeddedness of economic action often leads to market imperatives being subordinated to the needs of the indigenous exchange economy. ... Business enterprises in rural PNG are not focused solely on making profits; the way in which they are established, managed and patronised is an expression of indigenous social and economic life. The act of doing business, whether as customer, manager or investor, reproduces social relationships within the community.

In rural PNG, values connected with kinship obligations, gift exchange, and status enhancement or maintenance may mean that transactions or businesses are valued positively by all participants though they involve a "loss" for at least some of them. The *wantok* system which is embedded in Melanesian tradition involves a social contract between people who speak the same language to assist one another, on a reciprocal basis (Mohanty 2011; Nanau 2011); such kinship obligations have both benefits and costs for entrepreneurs and potentially impact on public administration (de Renzio 2000). How local values affect the form or administration of competition safeguards for MSMEs must be considered on a country-by-country basis, as each PIC is culturally distinct.

Addressing the State as a Commercial Actor

Historically, the state has been the dominant economic actor in PIC economies: the largest employer, the largest buyer of many goods and services, and the largest supplier (directly or through SOEs) of key services and sometimes goods. Opportunities for MSMEs to grow should increase as SOEs in PICs are progressively corporatized and privatized. Governments must address the risk, however, that:

> ... privatizing SOEs into a non-competitive environment may result in economic losses, including deadweight losses associated with monopoly pricing and possibly the further crowding out of the indigenous private sector as private monopolists exploit their economic power (Trebilcock and Prado 2014, p. 171).

Effective competition policy, competition laws, and pro-competitive regulation are necessary to ensure that privatized enterprises and public-private partnerships operate competitively. A competition agency in a PIC has multiple roles. First, it should advocate within government for pro-competitive approaches to serving the public's needs, including the liberalization of markets (Anderson and Jenny 2002). Secondly, it can advise the government on pro-competitive ways of going about projects such as the sale of an SOE. A PIC's competition agency could be given a formal consultative or review role. For example, the agency could be required to prepare a competition impact assessment in respect of new legislation or, at the least, Ministers could be required to have regard to the competitive effects of the decisions they make. Thirdly, the competition agency should either be integrated with, or have a formal relationship to, any sectoral regulators, in order to promote pro-competitive industry regulation.

Empowering Consumers and Small Traders

Consumer protection should operate to reinforce pro-competitive law and regulation. While consumer protection laws and competition laws target different conduct, they are akin in purpose: competition law promotes the availability of choices for consumers and consumer protection law preserves consumers' ability to make informed consumption choices (Nebbia 2012).

By adopting an explicit consumer welfare standard for both competition and consumer protection law, employing consistent language and concepts, and tasking a single agency with enforcement responsibility, it should be possible for PICs to realize useful efficiencies in advocacy and enforcement. Harmonization of consumer protection and competition laws should assist the agency's advocacy efforts and, ultimately, facilitate understanding and support among businesses.

A further possibility for consideration is whether MSMEs constitute a "middle tier" whose ability to compete can be protected by safeguards tailored for their particular needs. Historically, the rights of traders have been protected in common law jurisdictions by legislation on sale of goods, carriage of goods, passing off, and restraint of trade. It may be that MSMEs' interests (and economic development needs) should, in future, be served by a three-tier approach specifically protecting traders' access to inputs and markets, as well as consumers' rights and the competitive process. Efforts in some jurisdictions to extend consumer protections to traders, and to orient competition safeguards towards "fairness" (Cantatore and Marshall 2014; Ayal 2014), exemplify that approach. The pivotal role of MSMEs in PIC development arguably makes the need to develop a harmonized pro-competitive approach more pressing in PICs than in developed economies.

Adaptation of Objectives and Methods

Competition safeguards of the kind familiar in developed economies are likely to be necessary for PICs but not sufficient to protect MSMEs from anti-competitive conduct or uncompetitive factor markets. Laws against anti-competitive mergers, collusion, and misuse of market power, and effective remedies for infringement of those laws, will be important to prevent misconduct by the largest actors in the local economy and by overseas undertakings whose conduct affects markets in the PIC. Such laws will also contribute to the credibility of the regime internationally and assist the responsible agency to participate in international cooperation for training, investigations, and enforcement. Priest argues that "...there is a well-defined set of competition law principles that most accept will enhance competition and, as a consequence, economic welfare for the consumers of any society. These principles are economic, not social or cultural, and will apply across societies" (Priest 2012, p. 85). Apart from debate about how competition law principles should be defined, the laws that are taken to represent "best practice" in large and developed economies are unlikely, by themselves, to be effective to assure a competitive environment for MSMEs. Particular methods and approaches need to be adapted for PICs' purposes from the methods and approaches used in larger developing countries or in smaller developed countries. There is no single solution or ideal formula.

For enforcement agencies, budget constraints limit the number of offices and staff that can be placed in secondary towns and can inhibit recruitment and retention of talented staff (this problem is international, but is particularly severe in PICs). If a PIC has a small pool of qualified people to recruit from and faces significant staff turnover, complexity or uncertainty in its rules will make staff training a slower process. This will affect its ability to perform its mission. With finite resources, an agency may be tempted to focus its efforts on the biggest issues, involving the biggest enterprises, that get media publicity. The competition issues facing MSMEs might attract less attention, and MSMEs (for the reasons outlined above) are likely to be less effective in complaining about particular problems they experience or in seeking solutions.

Constraints of these kinds may be compounded if the particular economy is affected by other factors such as a shortage of legal, economic, and investigative expertise; a high crime rate (Lakhani and Willman 2014); close affiliations between political and business leaders; or corruption. The courts in some PICs are under substantial pressure, judges have little or no experience in competition cases, and few businesses are likely to be able to fund private actions. Competition policy is often politically charged in the early stages of its development. Historically, Cabinet ministers or senior bureaucrats have sat on SOE boards in some PICs. Governments must be convinced of the economic benefits resulting from exposing SOEs to competition, before they will be willing to liberalize their markets. Governments may face pressure from constituents for retention of price controls, rate regulation, tariff controls, and "reserved occupations" lists. Competition enforcement agencies may also be subject to regulatory capture.

Inevitably, the content of competition laws, and of the consumer protection laws that complement them, is critical to their efficacy for MSMEs and their contribution to development. No policy prescription or statute provides a ready-made solution for PICs, although the various model laws and competition toolkits developed by international organizations may assist. Several possible avenues for adaptation of developed world competition law may be considered. First, different emphases, standards, and methods may be required in PICs' substantive competition law. For example, collaboration among competing MSMEs could be expressly permitted in the absence of detrimental effect (e.g. the collaborative venture exception under Section 31(2) of New Zealand's proposed Commerce (Cartels and Other Matters) Amendment Bill 2011), to avoid exposing them to cartel liability or the burden of obtaining authorization. A more robust stance toward price and non-price predatory conduct might be required in developing PICs than that typically taken in developed economies. As another example, developed economies have often found that the exercise of monopsony power contributes to lower prices for consumers, but a different analysis may be required in PICs, where powerful buyers take advantage of MSMEs that lack market power.

Secondly, while the total welfare standard (which looks toward overall economic efficiency) has been influential in competition policy in some jurisdictions (Pitofsky 2008), it would seem appropriate for PICs to pursue an explicit consumer welfare standard. The consumer welfare standard imposes on the agency a lesser analytic burden (since it does not require the agency or court to evaluate any efficiencies that suppliers might realize from conduct that is detrimental to consumers) and is more readily understood by the public and businesspeople (Kirkwood and Lande 2008; Kirkwood 2013).

In developed economies, much emphasis is placed on imposing sanctions that are of a sufficient size to deter breaches of the law. Where small or medium-sized enterprises are involved, a competition authority will generally recognize the need for sanctions that are proportionate, not exterminatory. The fact that many businesses in PICs, and MSMEs in particular, face genuine difficulty in accessing capital should be reflected by legislating for other sanctions apart from fines or pecuniary penalties. For example, the court or relevant tribunal should have a flexible power to make remedial orders, including for compensation, community service, or corrective advertising. The fact that competition and consumer authorities in PICs have limited investigative and prosecutorial resources suggests an important role for administrative sanctions, such as directions by the authority to desist from an unlawful sales practice, correct a misleading advertisement, or resupply a non-compliant service. The fact that few consumers have the resources to enforce their rights against traders suggests the authority should also have the power to bring representative actions. For relatively minor infringements occurring at the level of village trade stores, for example, it might even be appropriate for minor remedies to be ordered by traditional local tribunals (Evans et al. 2010; Allen et al. 2013), though this will depend on the mechanisms available in each country.

Conclusion

In order for MSMEs to drive the continuing economic development of PICs, competition policy and pro-competitive law reform need to promote opportunities for competitive entry and protect the competitive process. Particular challenges arise in small, developing economies for MSMEs. Competition policies and law reforms must respond to those challenges. The problem of determining how to respond to the particular needs of individual countries has been highlighted by Trebilcock and Prado (2014, p. 220):

> The most pressing question for the field of law, institutions and development is how to account for the particularities of different countries, while at the same time sustaining the idea that there are some common elements in this intellectual inquiry that can be used across time, places and contexts. ... This is still an open question from a theoretical, methodological and practical perspective. Thus, the future of the field remains largely unchart[ed] terrain.

Navigating this uncharted terrain may be assisted by insights from experience in large, developing countries as well as in small, developed countries. What has emerged internationally as "best practice" may provide guidance for small, developing countries but is not a blueprint for them. Since transplanted institutions cannot be assumed to work as well in their new setting as they did in their original setting, Trebilcock and Prado (2014, p. 219) rightly caution that "reformers should be mindful of the fact that institution building requires a great deal of adaptation to the particular conditions of each country".

Where private sector development is the long-term objective of PICs whose markets are dominated by state institutions and in which a relatively small private sector consists mostly of MSMEs, it seems essential for competition policy and law to facilitate MSME entry and growth. This is not an argument for "infant industry" protection but rather for competition policy and laws that are particularly alert to MSMEs' vulnerabilities. Competition safeguards should be designed to respond to local challenges of the kinds identified in this chapter, including comprehensibility to MSME owners, practical enforceability, and accommodation of cultural imperatives. Issues that have been lower enforcement priorities in larger economies, such as price discrimination and misuse of monopsony power, may need to be prioritized by competition policymakers in PICs.

In order to make adaptations that suit the particular conditions of a country, it is essential for policymakers and legislators to have access to high-quality information about local conditions relevant to competition, regulatory requirements, cultural factors, and the needs of MSMEs. As noted earlier, studies on matters such as critical success and failure factors for MSMEs would be highly instructive for the further development of competition policy and law in PICs.

Finally, the enactment of competition laws is the beginning, not the end, of the need for technical assistance to a PIC. Having adopted a competition policy or made a commitment to competition law reform, a PIC will require ongoing technical assistance by donors and international competition organizations to implement that policy or law reform. That assistance includes help with establishing the responsible agency, supporting initial training for its staff, undertaking advocacy, building institutional capacity, and supporting the review and improvement of the regime as experience with it grows.

REFERENCES

Aghion, Philippe and Rachel Griffith. *Competition and Growth: Reconciling Theory and Evidence*. Boston: MIT Press, 2005.

Allen, Matthew, Sinclair Dinnen, Daniel Evans, and Rebecca Monson. *Justice Delivered Locally: Systems, Challenges, and Innovations in Solomon Islands*. Washington, D.C.: The World Bank, 2013.

Anderson, Robert and Frédéric Jenny. "Competition Policy as an Underpinning of Development and Trade Liberalization: Its Relationship to Economic Restructuring and Regulatory Reform". Paper presented at Seoul Competition Forum, Korea, 6–8 November 2002.

Asian Development Bank (ADB). *ADB's Approach to Assisting the Pacific (2010–2014)*. Manila: Asian Development Bank, 2009.

————. *Pacific Private Sector Development Initiative: Progress Report 2013*. Manila: Asian Development Bank, 2014a.

————. *Finding Balance 2014: Benchmarking the Performance of State-Owned Enterprises in Island Countries*. Manila: Asian Development Bank, 2014b.

Ayal, Adi. *Fairness in Antitrust: Protecting the Strong from the Weak*. Oxford: Hart Publishing, 2014.

Cantatore, Francina and Brenda Marshall. "Businesses are People Too? Anomalies in Widening the Ambits of 'Consumer' Under Consumer Credit Law". *Australian Business Law Review* 42, no. 2 (2014): 113–23.

Cseres, Katalin J. *Competition Law and Consumer Protection*. The Hague: Kluwer Law International, 2005.

Curry, George N. "Doing 'Business' in Papua New Guinea: The Social Embeddedness of Small Business Enterprises". *Journal of Small Business and Entrepreneurship* 18, no. 2 (2005): 231–46.

de Renzio, Paolo. "Bigmen and Wantoks: Social Capital and Group Behaviour in Papua New Guinea". QEH Working Paper Number 27. Oxford: Oxford Department of International Development, 2000.

Evans, Daniel, Michael Goddard, and Don Paterson. *The Hybrid Courts of Melanesia: A Comparative Analysis of Village Courts of Papua New Guinea, Island Courts of Vanuatu, and Local Courts of Solomon Islands*. Washington, D.C.: The World Bank, 2010.

Fels, Allan and Wendy Ng. "Rethinking Competition Advocacy in Developing Countries". In *Competition Law and Development*, edited by D. Daniel Sokol, Thomas K. Cheng, and Ioannis Lianos. Stanford: Stanford University Press, 2013.

Holden, Paul, Malcolm Bale, and Sarah Holden. *Swimming Against the Tide: An Assessment of the Private Sector in the Pacific*. Manila: Asian Development Bank, 2004.

Kirkwood, John B. "The Essence of Antitrust: Protecting Consumers and Small Suppliers from Anticompetitive Conduct". *Fordham Law Review* 81 (2013): 2425–69.

Kirkwood, John B. and Robert H. Lande. "The Fundamental Goal of Antitrust: Protecting Consumers, Not Increasing Efficiency". *Notre Dame Law Review* 84, no. 1 (2008): 191–244.

Lakhani, Sadaf and Alys M. Willman. *Gates, Hired Guns and Mistrust — Business Unusual: The Cost of Crime and Violence to Businesses in PNG*. Washington, D.C.: The World Bank Group, 2014.

Leuner, Tom. "Time and the Dimensions of Substantiality". *Australian Business Law Review* 36. no. 5 (2008): 327–68.

Levenstein, Margaret and Valerie Y. Suslow. "Contemporary International Cartels and Developing Countries: Economic Effects and Implications for Competition Policy". *Antitrust Law Journal* 71, no. 3 (2004): 801–52.

McIntyre, Robert. *The Role of Small and Medium Enterprises in Transition: Growth and Entrepreneurship*. Research for Action 49. Helsinki: UNU World Institute for Development Economics Research, 2001.

Ministry of Consumer Affairs, New Zealand. *Consumer Law Reform: A Discussion Paper*. Wellington: New Zealand Government, 2010.

Mohanty, Manoranjan. "Informal Social Protection and Social Development in Pacific Island Countries: Role of NGOs and Civil Society". *Asia-Pacific Development Journal* 18, no. 2 (2011): 25–56.

Muris, Timothy J. "The Interface of Competition and Consumer Protection". Paper presented at the Fordham Corporate Law Institute's Twenty-Ninth Annual Conference on International Antitrust Law and Policy, New York City, 31 October 2002.

Nanau, Gordon Leua. "The Wantok System as a Socio-economic and Political Network in Melanesia". *OMNES: The Journal of Multicultural Society* 2, no. 1 (2011): 31–55.

Nebbia, Paolisa. "Competition Law and Consumer Protection Against Unfair Commercial Practices: A More-than-Complementary Relationship?". In *The Global Limits of Competition Law*, edited by Ioannis Lianos and D. Daniel Sokol. Stanford: Stanford University Press, 2012.

Organisation for Economic Cooperation and Development (OECD). *Policy Roundtables: Competition Policy and the Informal Economy*. Paris: OECD, 2009.

Pitofsky, Robert, ed. *How the Chicago School Overshot the Mark: The Effect of Conservative Economic Analysis on U.S. Antitrust*. New York: Oxford University Press, 2008.

Porter, Michael. *The Competitive Advantage of Nations*. New York: The Free Press, 1990.

Priest, George L. "Competition Law in Developing Nations: The Absolutist View". In *The Global Limits of Competition Law*, edited by Ioannis Lianos and D. Daniel Sokol. Stanford: Stanford University Press, 2012.

Qaqaya, Hassan and George Lipimile, eds. *The Effects of Anti-competitive Business Practices on Developing Countries and Their Development Prospects*. New York and Geneva: United Nations Conference on Trade and Development (UNCTAD), 2008.

Stiglitz, Joseph E. "Competing over Competition Policy", 3 August 2001. Available at <http://www.project-syndicate.org/commentary/competing-over-competitionpolicy> (accessed 25 May 2015).

Trebilcock, Michael J. and Mariana Mota Prado. *Advanced Introduction to Law and Development*. Cheltenham: Edward Elgar, 2014.

United Nations. "UN Data". Available at <http://data.un.org/Default.aspx> (accessed 25 May 2015).

United Nations Development Program. "Human Development Reports", 2013. Available at <http://hdr.undp.org/en/data> (accessed 25 May 2015).

World Bank. "Indicators Database". Available at <http://data.worldbank.org/indicator> (accessed 25 May 2015).

———. *Well-being from Work in the Pacific Island Countries*. World Bank East Asia and Pacific Regional Report. Washington, D.C.: World Bank, 2014.

INDEX

www.ingramcontent.com/pod-product-compliance
Lightning Source LLC
Chambersburg PA
CBHW060749220326
41598CB00022B/2379